AutoCAD®/AutoCAD LT® 2018
Fundamentals
Part 1

Student Guide
Metric - 1st Edition

AUTODESK.
Authorized Publisher

CONTINUING EDUCATION AIA

ASCENT - Center for Technical Knowledge®
AutoCAD®/AutoCAD LT® 2018
Fundamentals - Part 1
Metric - 1st Edition

Prepared and produced by:

ASCENT Center for Technical Knowledge
630 Peter Jefferson Parkway, Suite 175
Charlottesville, VA 22911

866-527-2368
www.ASCENTed.com

Lead Contributor: Renu Muthoo

ASCENT - Center for Technical Knowledge is a division of Rand Worldwide, Inc., providing custom developed knowledge products and services for leading engineering software applications. ASCENT is focused on specializing in the creation of education programs that incorporate the best of classroom learning and technology-based training offerings.

We welcome any comments you may have regarding this student guide, or any of our products. To contact us please email: feedback@ASCENTed.com.

Contents Part 1

Contents Part 2

Preface

The *AutoCAD®/AutoCAD LT® 2018: Fundamentals* student guide is designed for those using AutoCAD® or AutoCAD LT® 2018 with a Windows operating system. This student guide is not designed for the AutoCAD for Mac software.

The objective of *AutoCAD/AutoCAD LT 2018: Fundamentals* is to enable students to create a basic 2D drawing in the AutoCAD software.

Part 1 (chapters 1 to 20) covers the essential core topics for working with the AutoCAD software. The teaching strategy is to start with a few basic tools that enable the student to create and edit a simple drawing, and then continue to develop those tools. More advanced tools are introduced throughout the student guide. Not every command or option is covered, because the intent is to show the most *essential* tools and concepts, such as:

- Understanding the AutoCAD workspace and user interface.
- Using basic drawing, editing, and viewing tools.
- Organizing drawing objects on layers.
- Inserting reusable symbols (blocks).
- Preparing a layout to be plotted.
- Adding text, hatching, and dimensions.

Part 2 (chapters 21 to 32) continues with more sophisticated techniques that extend your mastery of the software. For example, here you go beyond the basic skill of inserting a block to learning how to create blocks, and beyond the basic skill of using a template to understand the process of setting up a template. You learn skills such as:

- Using more advanced editing and construction techniques.
- Adding parametric constraints to objects.
- Creating local and global blocks.
- Setting up layers, styles, and templates.
- Using advanced plotting and publishing options.

This student guide refers to both the AutoCAD and AutoCAD LT software as the AutoCAD software. All topics, including features and commands, relate to both the AutoCAD and AutoCAD LT software unless specifically noted otherwise.

Note on Software Setup

This student guide assumes a standard installation of the software using the default preferences during installation. Lectures and practices use the standard software templates and default options for the Content Libraries.

Students and Educators can Access Free Autodesk Software and Resources

Autodesk challenges you to get started with free educational licenses for professional software and creativity apps used by millions of architects, engineers, designers, and hobbyists today. Bring Autodesk software into your classroom, studio, or workshop to learn, teach, and explore real-world design challenges the way professionals do.

Get started today - register at the Autodesk Education Community and download one of the many Autodesk software applications available.

Visit www.autodesk.com/joinedu/

Note: Free products are subject to the terms and conditions of the end-user license and services agreement that accompanies the software. The software is for personal use for education purposes and is not intended for classroom or lab use.

Lead Contributor: Renu Muthoo

Renu uses her instructional design training to develop courseware for AutoCAD and AutoCAD vertical products, Autodesk 3ds Max, Autodesk Showcase and various other Autodesk software products. She has worked with Autodesk products for the past 20 years with a main focus on design visualization software.

Renu holds a bachelor's degree in Computer Engineering and started her career as a Instructional Designer/Author where she co-authored a number of Autodesk 3ds Max and AutoCAD books, some of which were translated into other languages for a wide audience reach. In her next role as a Technical Specialist at a 3D visualization company, Renu used 3ds Max in real-world scenarios on a daily basis. There, she developed customized 3D web planner solutions to create specialized 3D models with photorealistic texturing and lighting to produce high quality renderings.

Renu Muthoo has been the Lead Contributor for *AutoCAD®/AutoCAD LT® Fundamentals* since 2015.

In this Guide

The following images highlight some of the features that can be found in this Student Guide.

Practice Files

FTP link for practice files

Practice Files

The Practice Files page tells you how to download and install the practice files that are provided with this student guide.

Chapter 1

Getting Started

Learning Objectives for the chapter

Chapters

Each chapter begins with a brief introduction and a list of the chapter's Learning Objectives.

Instructional Content

Each chapter is split into a series of sections of instructional content on specific topics. These lectures include the descriptions, step-by-step procedures, figures, hints, and information you need to achieve the chapter's Learning Objectives.

Side notes

Side notes are hints or additional information for the current topic.

Practice Objectives

Practices

Practices enable you to use the software to perform a hands-on review of a topic.

Some practices require you to use prepared practice files, which can be downloaded from the link found on the Practice Files page.

Chapter Review Questions

Chapter review questions, located at the end of each chapter, enable you to review the key concepts and learning objectives of the chapter.

Command Summary

The Command Summary is located at the end of each chapter. It contains a list of the software commands that are used throughout the chapter, and provides information on where the command is found in the software.

Autodesk Certification Exam Appendix

This appendix includes a list of the topics and objectives for the Autodesk Certification exams, and the chapter and section in which the relevant content can be found.

Icons in this Student Guide

The following icons are used to help you quickly and easily find helpful information.

New in 2018	Indicates items that are new in the AutoCAD 2018 software.
Enhanced in 2018	Indicates items that have been enhanced in the AutoCAD 2018 software.

Practice Files

To download the practice files for this student guide, use the following steps:

1. Type the URL shown below into the address bar of your Internet browser. The URL must be typed **exactly as shown**. If you are using an ASCENT ebook, you can click on the link to download the file.

Address bar

http://www.ASCENTed.com/getfile?id=dermaptera

File   Edit   View   Favorites   Tools   Help

2. Press <Enter> to download the .ZIP file that contains the Practice Files.

3. Once the download is complete, unzip the file to a local folder. The unzipped file contains an .EXE file.

4. Double-click on the .EXE file and follow the instructions to automatically install the Practice Files on the C:\ drive of your computer.

   Do not change the location in which the Practice Files folder is installed. Doing so can cause errors when completing the practices in this student guide.

http://www.ASCENTed.com/getfile?id=dermaptera

Stay Informed!

Interested in receiving information about upcoming promotional offers, educational events, invitations to complimentary webcasts, and discounts? If so, please visit:

www.ASCENTed.com/updates/

Help us improve our product by completing the following survey:

www.ASCENTed.com/feedback

You can also contact us at: *feedback@ASCENTed.com*

Getting Started with AutoCAD

In this chapter you learn how to start the AutoCAD® software, become familiar with the basic layout of the AutoCAD screen, how to access commands, use your pointing device, and understand the AutoCAD Cartesian workspace. You also learn how to open an existing drawing, view a drawing by zooming and panning, and save your work in the AutoCAD software.

Learning Objectives in this Chapter

- Complete a basic initial setup of the drawing environment.
- Identify the basic layout and features of the AutoCAD user interface.
- Locate commands and launch them using various command interfaces.
- Locate points in the AutoCAD Cartesian workspace.
- Open, edit, and close existing drawings.
- Move around a drawing using the navigations options.
- Save drawings in various formats and set the automatic save option.

1.1 Starting the Software

You must have Internet Explorer® on your system to load the AutoCAD 2018 software.

The AutoCAD 2018 software runs on most recent versions of the Windows operating system, including Windows 7 Enterprise, Home Premium, Professional, and Ultimate (32 or 64-bit versions), Windows 8.1, 8.1 Pro, and Enterprise (32 or 64-bit versions), and Windows 10 Enterprise and Professional (64-bit version only). The 64-bit versions provide a huge improvement in processing speed.

Launch the software using the Windows desktop icon or the **Start** menu.

When launching the software for the first time, you are prompted to migrate custom settings and files from the earlier releases of the software.

- Double-click on ⬛ (AutoCAD 2018) on the desktop.

- If there is no shortcut on the desktop, click ⬛ (Start) in the Task bar at the bottom of the screen and select **All Programs>Autodesk>AutoCAD 2018>AutoCAD 2018**.

- When the AutoCAD software is launched, an initial Start Window displays.

Start Tab

When you launch the software or if you click in the *Start* tab while working in an active drawing, the initial Start window displays, as shown in Figure 1–1.

- By default, the *Start* tab is always available as the first tab in the *File Tabs* bar as you create and open additional drawings.

- While working in a drawing, you can click the *Start* tab to display the initial Start window.

- You can use <Ctrl>+<Home> to jump from an active drawing to the *Start* tab.

- The Start window contains two content frames: *Learn* and *Create*, as shown in Figure 1–1.

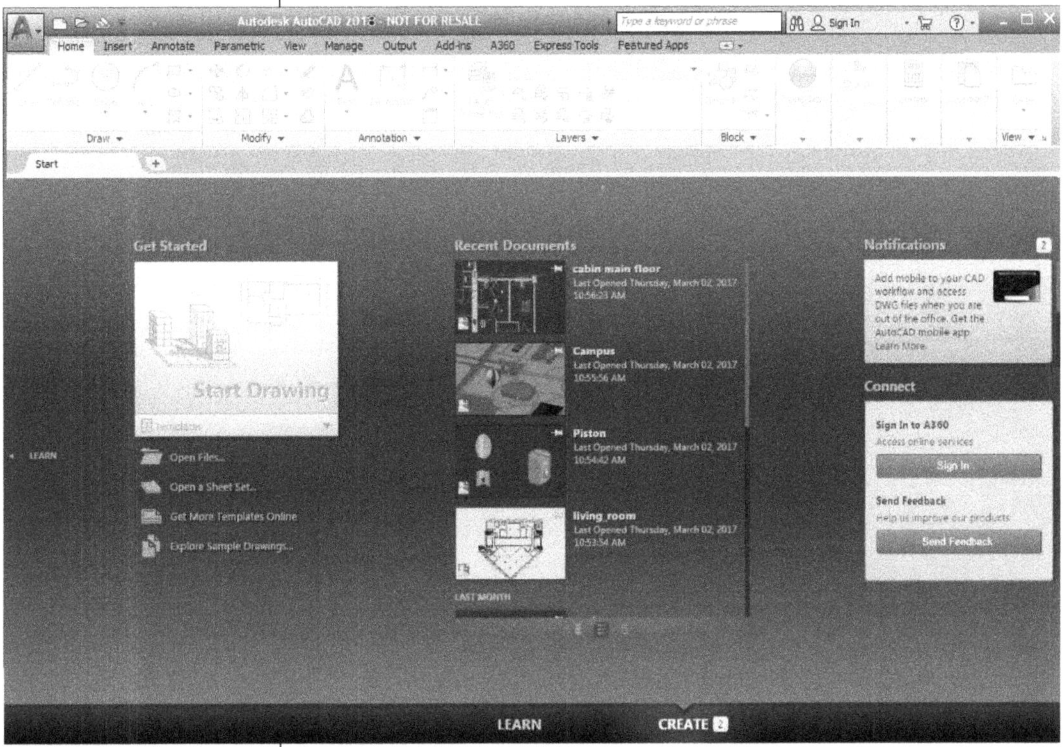

Figure 1–1

Learn

- Contains videos, tips, and online resources to help you learn about new features in the software and how to start using the software.

Create

- Contains tools that enable you to create new drawings or open existing, sample, or recently used files.

- Enables you to connect to Autodesk® A360 to access online services.

- When you click on **Start Drawing**, a new, blank drawing automatically opens. To start another new blank drawing, in the *File Tabs* bar, click (New Drawing). The new drawing is opened and made active.

- Click **Open Files** to open an already saved drawing.

1.2 User Interface

The interface includes the main components that are used to operate the AutoCAD software. By default, the display of the interface uses the Dark color scheme. You can change it to the

Light color scheme by expanding ![A] (Application Menu) and clicking **Options** to open the Options dialog box. In the *Display* tab, in the *Window Elements* area, expand the Color scheme drop-down list and select **Light,** as shown in Figure 1–2. Then, click **OK** for the background color of the interface components to change to light. The light color scheme is used throughout this Student Guide for printing clarity.

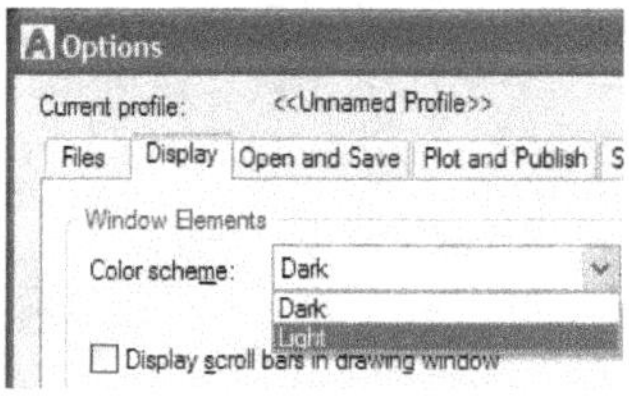

Figure 1–2

The software interface is shown in Figure 1–3. The Drawing Window color has been changed to white for printing clarity.

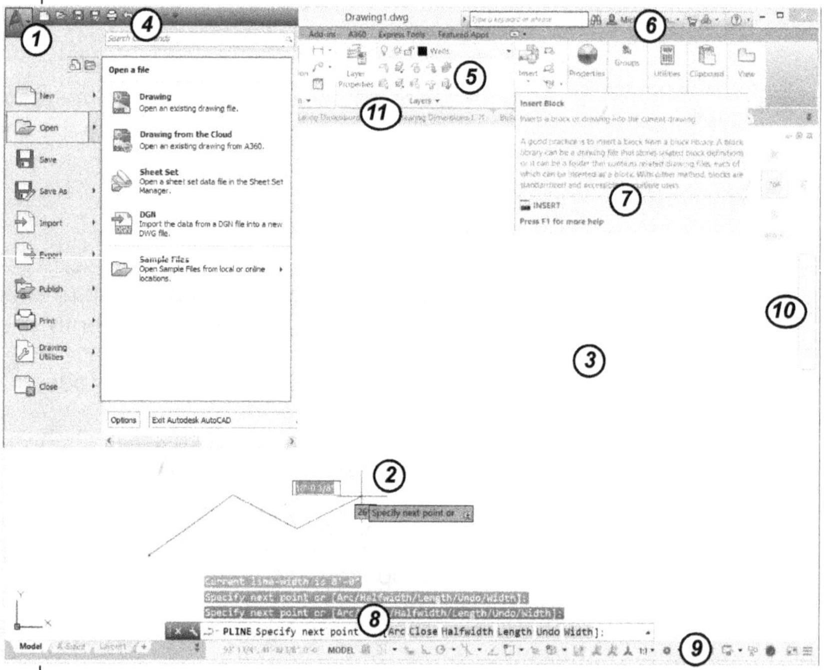

Figure 1–3

1. Application Menu

The *Application Menu* provides access to AutoCAD file commands, settings, and documents. Click ![icon] (Application Menu) to expand the Application Menu and display its contents.

2. Crosshairs and Prompts

The *Crosshairs* indicate the current cursor location. As you draw, prompts display near the cursor to explain how to complete each command. It displays badges that provide additional information when you are working in a command. This can help you to successfully complete the command.

3. Drawing Window

By default, the background of the Drawing Window is dark with a light gray grid. This can be changed in the Options dialog box> Display tab by clicking **Colors**.

The *Drawing Window* is the area of the screen in which the drawing displays. Near the lower left corner of the window a horizontal line labeled **X** and a vertical line labeled **Y** might be displayed. This is called the UCS icon and indicates the current drawing plane. Several drawing windows can be open at the same time. They can be resized, minimized, and maximized.

4. Quick Access Toolbar

The *Quick Access Toolbar* provides access to commonly used commands, such as **New**, **Open**, and **Save**, as shown in Figure 1–4.

Figure 1–4

5. Ribbon

The ribbon contains the AutoCAD tools in a series of tabs and panels, as shown in Figure 1–5. Clicking on a tab displays a series of panels. The panels contain a variety of tools, which are grouped by function.

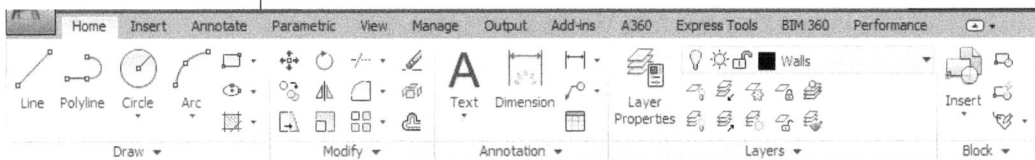

Figure 1–5

Enhanced
in 2018

*In the AutoCAD LT software, the **Autodesk App Store** option is not available.*

6. InfoCenter

The *InfoCenter* (shown in Figure 1–6) provides you with tools that enable you to quickly access the online Help system, stay connected with the online AutoCAD community, and access the Autodesk App Store. You can sign in to your A360 account to access various online services and sync your settings.

Figure 1–6

Clicking [icon] opens the initial help screen, which displays videos about new features and getting started with the software. You can search for a specific help topic by entering a keyword and selecting from the list of available related documents. Commands can be quickly identified in the ribbon, Status Bar, and the Application Menu by clicking **Find** next to the command's icon in the Help window, as shown in Figure 1–7. A red animated arrow displays in the interface identifying the location of the command, as shown in Figure 1–7.

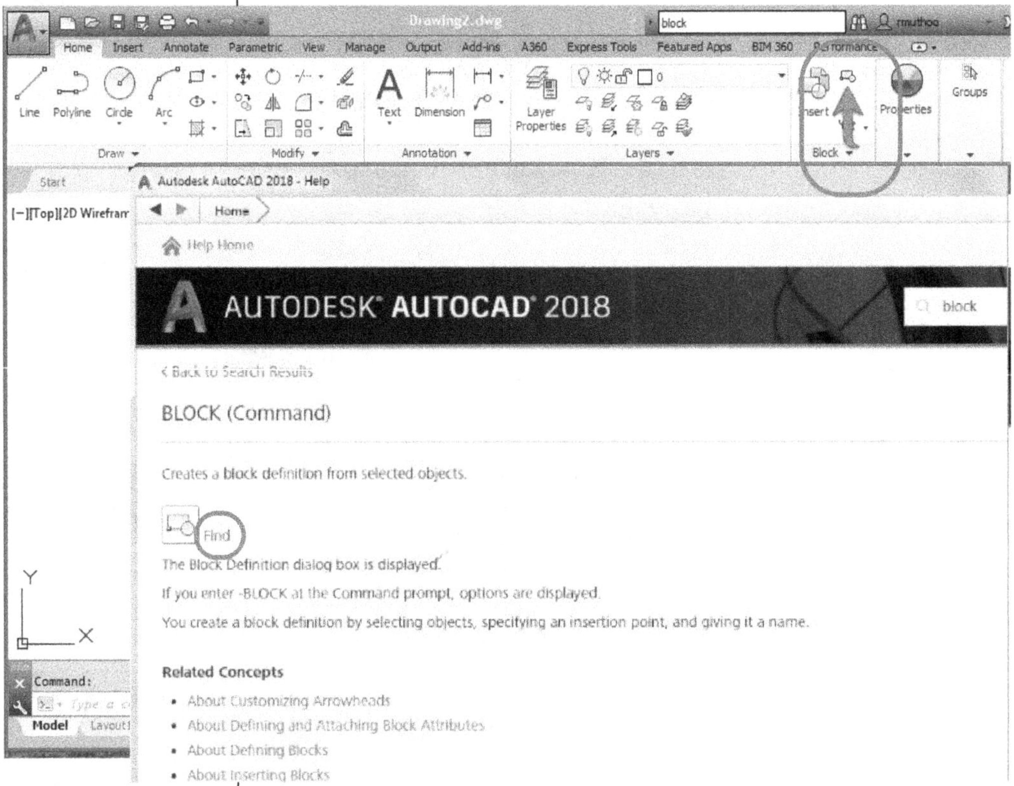

Figure 1–7

7. Tooltips

When you hover the cursor over a tool, a *Tooltip* displays the name of the tool, a short description, and sometimes an extended description, as shown in Figure 1–8. They provide information about tools, commands, and drawing objects. Press <F1> to open the Help window and display the help information related to the currently displayed tooltip.

You can control the display of tooltips using the Options dialog box ((Application Menu)>**Options**), in the *Display* tab> *Window Elements* area. You can also set the delay to display the tooltip and the extended description, as shown in Figure 1–9.

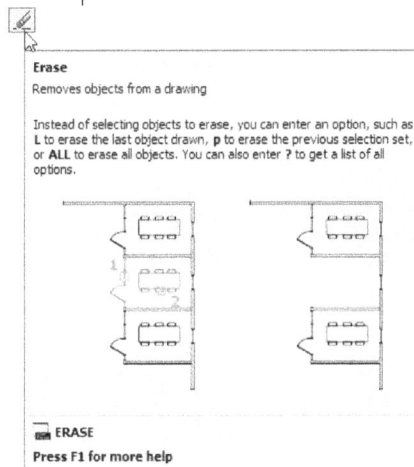

Erase

Removes objects from a drawing

Instead of selecting objects to erase, you can enter an option, such as **L** to erase the last object drawn, **p** to erase the previous selection set, or **ALL** to erase all objects. You can also enter **?** to get a list of all options.

ERASE

Press F1 for more help

Figure 1–8

☑ Show ToolTips

| 1.00 | Number of seconds before display

☑ Show shortcut keys in ToolTips

☑ Show extended ToolTips

| 2 | Number of seconds to delay

☑ Show rollover ToolTips

Figure 1–9

8. Command Line

Command prompts also display in the *Command Line*, which is by default, a text window located at the bottom of the screen, as shown in Figure 1–10. You can dock and undock the Command Line by clicking on the left edge and dragging it around. The command history has a gray background to distinguish it from the active command line.

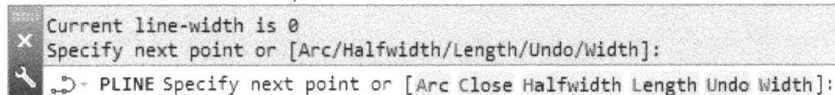

```
Current line-width is 0
Specify next point or [Arc/Halfwidth/Length/Undo/Width]:
PLINE Specify next point or [Arc Close Halfwidth Length Undo Width]:
```

Figure 1–10

9. Status Bar

The *Status Bar* enables you to change many of the AutoCAD software's drafting settings. All of the tools are located in the

≡ (Customization) list and their icons can be displayed or removed from the Status Bar by selecting them in the list. After displaying the tool icons in the Status Bar, you are required to toggle them on to take affect. The icons are highlighted when they are toggled on. If the displayed icons cannot fit in a single row, the Status Bar automatically wraps into two rows to accommodate all of the icons, as shown in Figure 1–11.

*If the Model and Layout tabs are not displayed, set the **LAYOUTTAB** system variable to **1**.*

Along the left side of the Status Bar icons, the *Model* tab and one or more *Layout* tabs display, as shown in Figure 1–11.

Figure 1–11

10. Navigation Bar

The *Navigation Bar* enables you to access the various methods of moving around in the drawing, such as **Zoom** and **Pan**, as shown in Figure 1–12.

If the Navigation Bar is not displayed, in the ribbon, go to the View tab>Viewport Tools panel, and click

(Navigation Bar).

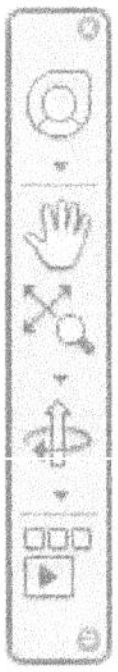

Figure 1–12

11. File Tabs

The drawing's *File* tabs (shown in Figure 1–13) are located near the top of the drawing window. They provide a quick way of switching between open drawings, creating a new ones, or closing the required drawings. The *Start* tab is always the first tab and persists in the *File* tabs bar. Clicking it displays the initial Start window.

Start   Drawing1*   ✕   Dimensioned Plan1-A* ✕   Drawing2*   ✕   +

Figure 1–13

1.3 Working with Commands

Most commands in the AutoCAD software are accessed using the ribbon. For example, to access the **Line** command in the ribbon, in the *Home* tab>Draw panel, click ⁄ (Line), as shown in Figure 1–14. Several of the file commands are available in the Quick Access Toolbar or in the Application Menu. Some commands are available in the Status Bar or through shortcut menus. There are additional access methods, such as Tool Palettes. The names of all of the commands can also be typed in the Command Line or near the cursor in the Drawing Window (Dynamic Input).

Ribbon

The ribbon provides easy access to the tools, which are organized in tabs and panels. The tabs (*Home, Insert*, etc.) contain a series of panels (**Draw, Modify, etc.**) which contain the tools, as shown in Figure 1–14. The tools are organized by function.

By default, the ribbon is docked at the top of the interface, as shown in a partial view in Figure 1–14.

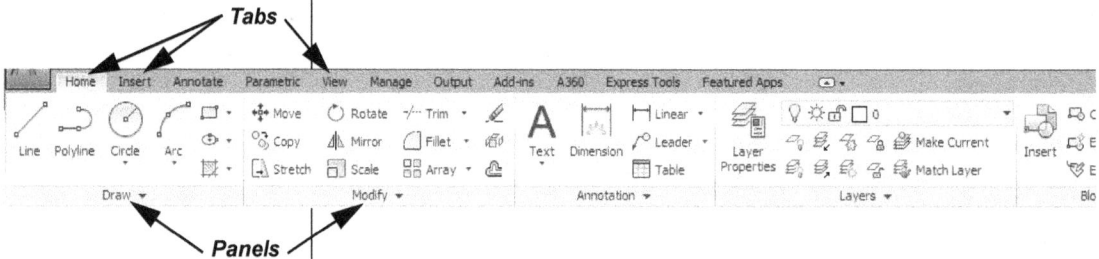

Figure 1–14

Some panels contain additional tools that are not displayed in the main panel. Select the panel title to expand the panel and display the hidden tools. Panels close automatically when you select another panel or when you start a command, unless they are pinned, as shown in Figure 1–15.

Click 📌 (Push Pin) to keep a panel open. The image changes to

🔘 (Push Pin). Click it again to return the panel to its default setting.

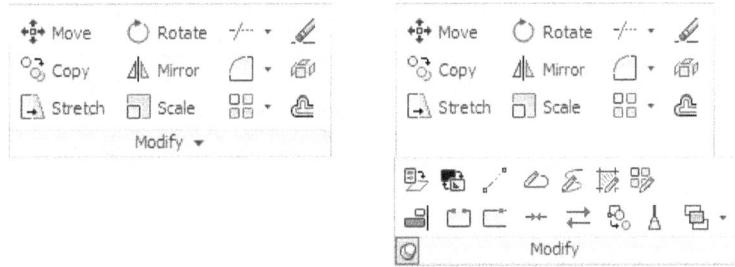

Figure 1–15

- The ribbon can float (as shown in Figure 1–16) and be docked to the side. To float the entire ribbon, right-click in the empty space at the end of the ribbon and select **Undock**.

The ribbon becomes a palette that can be docked to either side and hidden using **Auto-Hide**. If hidden, the ribbon displays when you hover the cursor over its location.

Figure 1–16

- Individual panels can also be floated in the drawing window, as shown in Figure 1–17. To float a panel, drag it by the title and drop it in the drawing window. To return it to the ribbon, drag-and-drop it onto the ribbon. This method can also be used to rearrange the panels available in the ribbon.

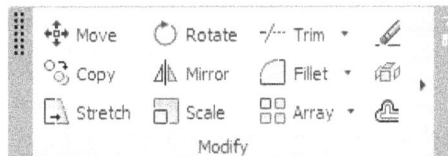

Figure 1–17

- Some tools include a gallery containing thumbnail previews of the available options, as shown in Figure 1–18. The display of these image previews can be controlled by the system variable **GALLERYVIEW** which is set as **1**, by default. To hide the thumbnail preview, the value can be set to **0**.

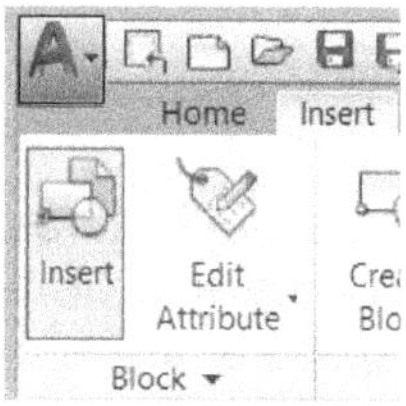

GALLERYVIEW=0

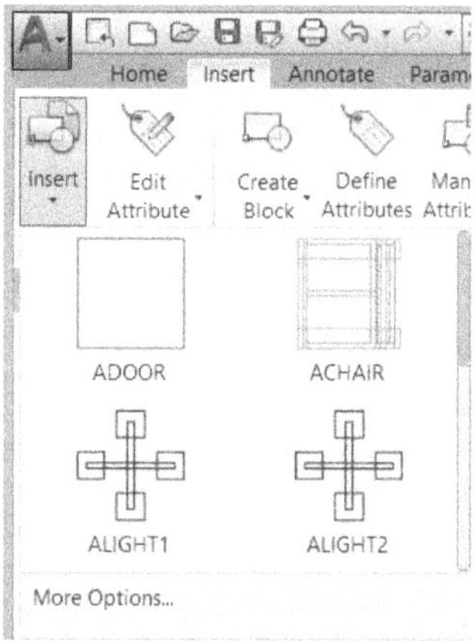

GALLERYVIEW=1

Figure 1–18

Command Line and Dynamic Input Prompt

You can directly enter the name of a command in either the Command Line or in the Dynamic Input prompt. When the **Dynamic Input** option is **On** (by default), and you start typing a command name, a command box displays near the crosshair with the letters you are typing, as shown in Figure 1–19. You can also specifically click and type inside the Command Line. When the **Dynamic Input** option is **Off**, typing a command name automatically starts in the Command Line.

- For both input methods, the **AutoComplete** option automatically completes the entry you are typing when you pause. It also supports mid-string search by displaying all of the commands that contain the word that you typed, as shown in Figure 1–20. You can then scroll through the list and select a command to start it.

Figure 1–19

Figure 1–20

- The order in which commands are listed in the suggestion list adapts as you use the software.

You can also click

 (Customize) to display the Input Settings.

- To set specific options for command input, including the **AutoComplete** feature, right-click on the Command Line, expand **Input Settings**, and select from the various options, such as the ability to search for system variables or to set the delay response time, as shown in Figure 1–21.

Figure 1–21

If you need to stop a command, press <Esc> to cancel it. You might need to press <Esc> more than once.

- As you work in the AutoCAD software, the software prompts you for the information that is required to complete each command. These prompts display in the Dynamic Input prompt and in the Command Line. It is important that you read the command prompts as you work, as shown in Figure 1–22.

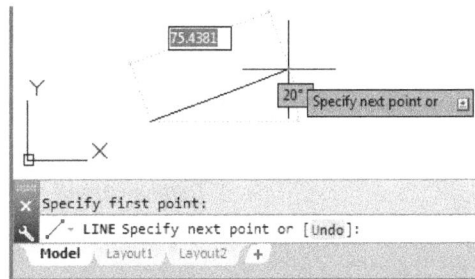

Figure 1–22

- If you press <Enter> when no command is active, it launches the command that you last used. It is a quick and easy way of repeating a command.

- Depending on the Command Line being docked/undocked, pressing <F2> opens an AutoCAD Text Window or an expanded version of the Command Line, which contains a record of each command and prompt that has been used in the current drawing session.

- In the Status Bar, click ≡ (Customization) and select Dynamic Input in the list to display ⁺▦ (Dynamic Input) in the Status Bar, as shown in Figure 1–23. Click to toggle the option on and off. The icons highlight in blue when they are toggled on.

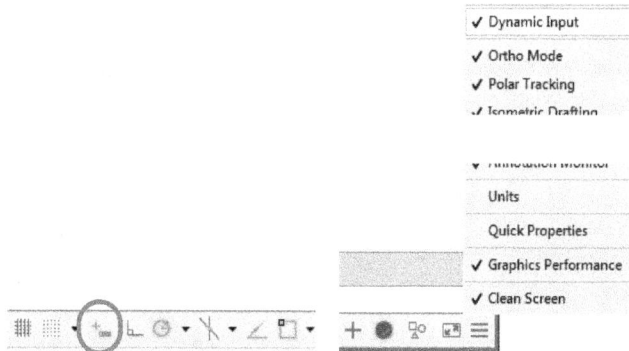

Figure 1–23

Selecting Command Options

If a command has options, you can specify it either in the Command Line, the dynamic input prompt, or the shortcut menu, as shown in Figure 1–24:

Figure 1–24

- In the Dynamic Input prompt, ⊞ indicates that more options are available. Press <Down Arrow> to expand the list and select an option, as shown in Figure 1–24.

- The shortcut menu opens when you right-click. It includes the same selections as dynamic input, and several standard options that display with every command.

- In the Command Line, the command name, its default prompt, and a list of options display. You can select the required option in the Command Line by clicking on it or by typing the option's capitalized letter(s) (displayed in blue) to activate it, as shown in Figure 1–25.

```
Specify start point:
Current line-width is 0'-0"
Specify next point or [Arc/Halfwidth/Length/Undo/Width]:
```

```
× ✎ .⊃ · PLINE Specify next point or [Arc Close Halfwidth Length Undo Width]:    ▲
```

Figure 1–25

Application Menu

The Application Menu (shown in Figure 1–26), contains the file tools. It includes a search field in which you can type command names to locate them in the ribbon, Quick Access Toolbar, or Application menu, and an area in which to browse for recent and open documents.

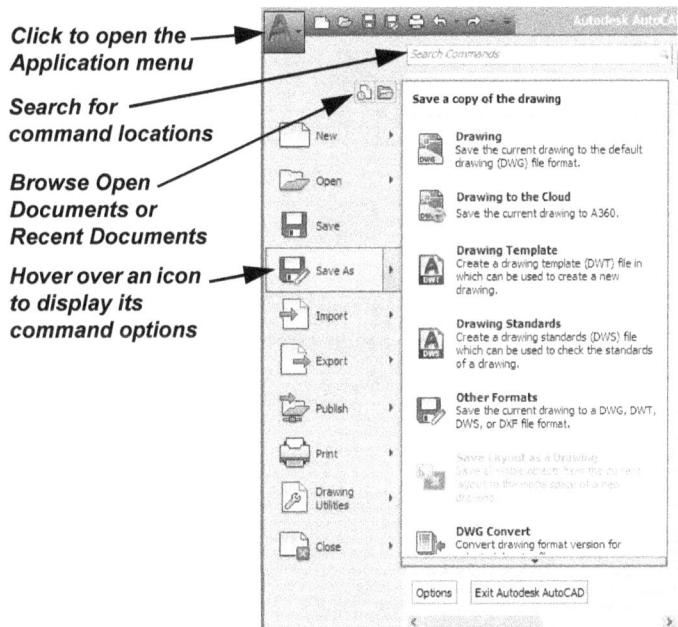

Click to open the Application menu →

Search for command locations →

Browse Open Documents or Recent Documents →

Hover over an icon to display its command options →

Figure 1–26

- Hover the cursor over a primary icon to display its options and select the required option. If you click the primary icon rather than the arrow, the default command starts.

- Click **Options** to open the Options dialog box and modify the default settings to customize how the AutoCAD software performs. For example, to change the color of the drawing window, click **Options**, select the *Display* tab in the Options dialog box, and click **Colors**. In the *Context* area, select **2d model space**, in the *Interface element* area, select **Uniform background**, and in the expanded Color drop-down list, select a color.

- Click **Exit Autodesk AutoCAD** to close the software.

How To: Find Command Access Locations

1. Expand the Application Menu.
2. In the *Search* field, start typing the name of a command. Tools related to the command name you are typing display in the Application Menu, as shown in Figure 1–27.

You do not have to type the full command name. As you start typing, the command options display.

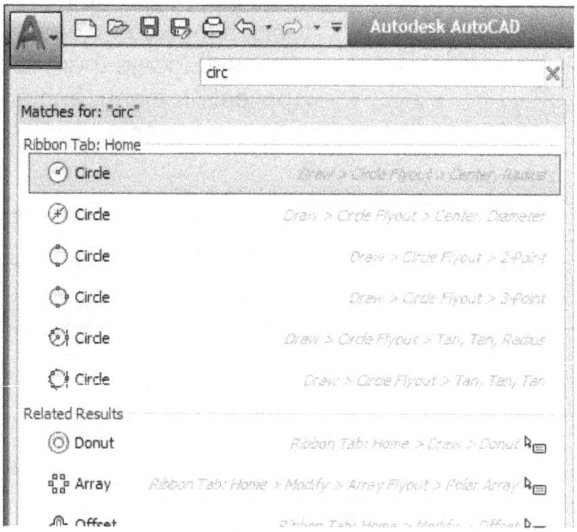

Figure 1–27

3. Select the command that you want to use.

How To: Select Drawings from the Application Menu

1. Expand the Application Menu.

You can also access Recent Documents in the Start tab>Create frame.

2. Ensure that 🔲 (Recent Documents) is selected so that the list of recently opened documents displays, as shown in Figure 1–28.

Figure 1–28

3. The default display option is **By Ordered List**. In the expanded drop-down list you can also select **By Access Date**, **By Size**, or **By Type** to change the display option. You can also change the size of the images, as shown in Figure 1–29.

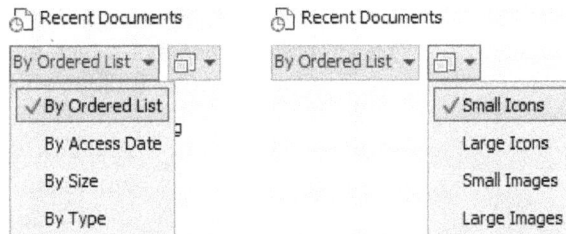

Figure 1–29

4. Click 🗁 (Open Documents) to display a list of open drawings, as shown in Figure 1–30.

Figure 1–30

Quick Access Toolbar

Enhanced
in **2018**

The Quick Access Toolbar provides fast access to the common tools: **New**, **Open**, **Save**, **Save As**, **Plot**, **Undo**, and **Redo**. You can customize it by adding and removing typical commands displayed in the list. Click ⬇ (as shown in Figure 1–31) to expand the list and select from a list of typical commands. The commands with a checkmark are already displayed in the Quick Access Toolbar.

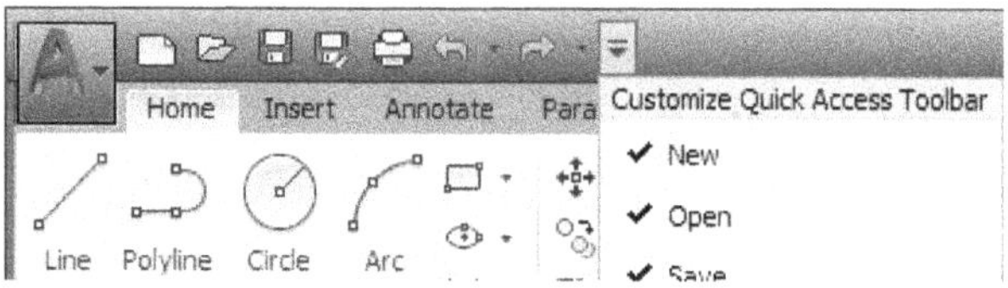

Figure 1–31

- When the *Start* tab is open, only **New**, **Open**, and **Sheet Set Manager** display in the Quick Access Toolbar.

Additional Shortcut Menus

When you right-click, a menu usually displays next to the cursor, called a *shortcut menu*. The menu that displays depends on what you are doing in the AutoCAD software and where you right-click in the AutoCAD interface.

In the Quick Access Toolbar

When you right-click on the Quick Access Toolbar, a list of options displays, which enable you to customize or locate the Quick Access Toolbar, shown in Figure 1–32.

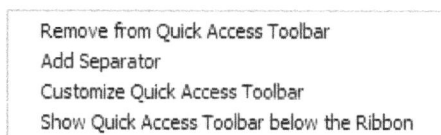

Figure 1–32

In the Ribbon

If you right-click on a tab or in an empty space in the ribbon, you can select which tabs or panels to display. You can also change the visibility and docking status of the ribbon. Right-clicking on a ribbon panel title only displays the tab and the panel options. The options that display in the shortcut menu are determined by where you click in the ribbon, as shown in Figure 1–33.

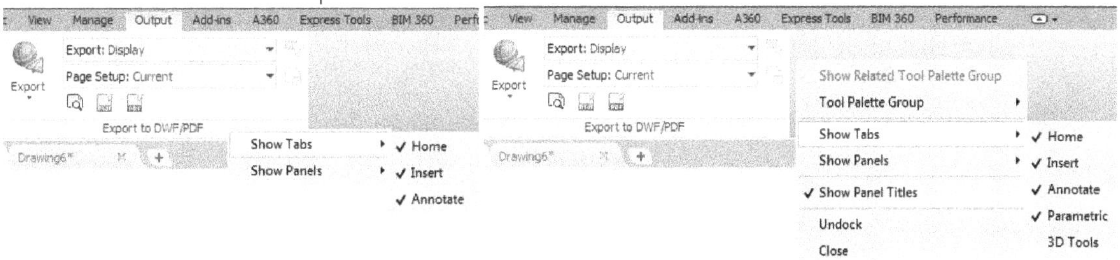

Ribbon shortcut menu by right-clicking on a panel title

Ribbon shortcut menu by right-clicking on the tabs or empty space in the ribbon

Figure 1–33

If you right-click on an icon in a panel, you can select the tabs and panels to be displayed in the ribbon. You can also add the icon to the Quick Access Toolbar, as shown in Figure 1–34.

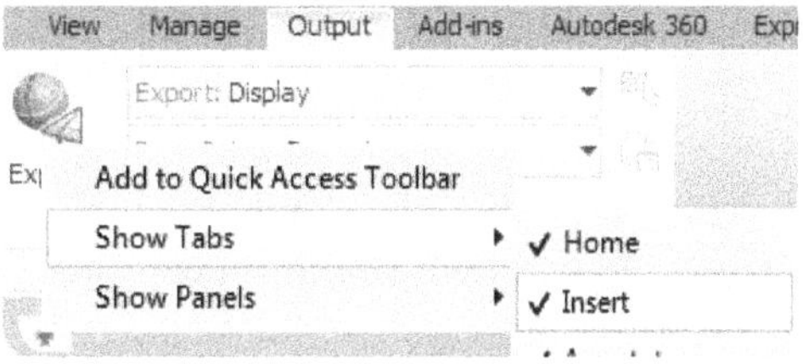

Figure 1–34

In the Command Line

When you right-click on the Command Line, you can select the various **Copy** and **Paste** commands, as shown in Figure 1–35. You can also access the **AutoComplete** options using the **Input Settings** selection. Using the Options dialog box, which can be accessed by selecting **Options...** in the shortcut menu, you can change many of the AutoCAD settings.

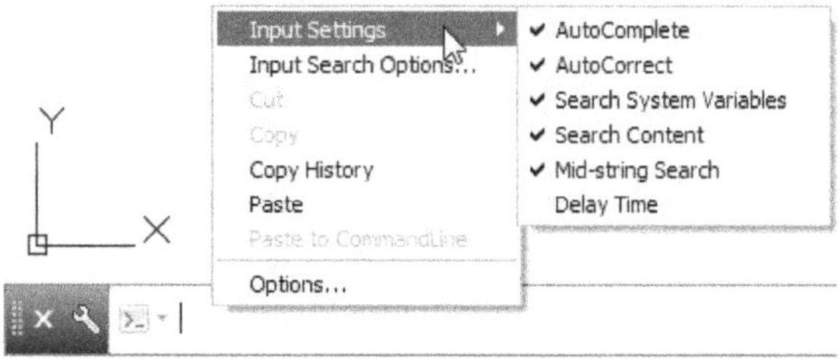

Figure 1–35

In the Drawing Window

If no command is active when you right-click in the drawing window, you have the option of repeating the previous command or recently used commands (**Recent Input**), selecting **Zoom** and **Pan**, and the standard Windows clipboard functions. You can also access several other utilities or open the Options dialog box, as shown in Figure 1–36.

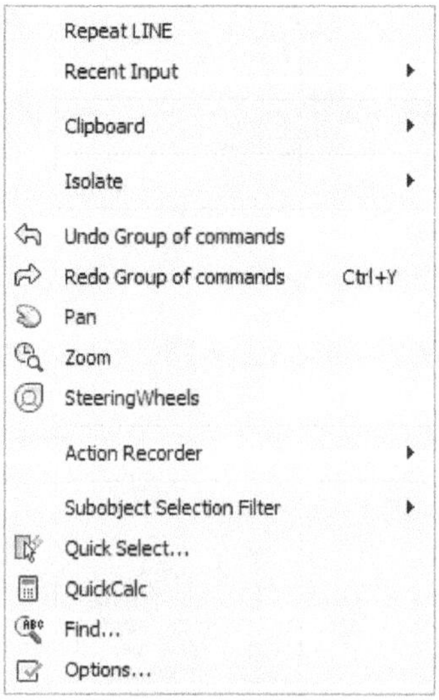

Figure 1–36

1.4 Cartesian Workspace

Locating Points

The AutoCAD software uses Cartesian (X,Y) coordinates to indicate locations in a drawing. Points are located by designating a horizontal (X) and vertical (Y) distance as measured from the origin (0,0), as shown in Figure 1–37. There is also a third coordinate (Z), which is only used in 3D drawings.

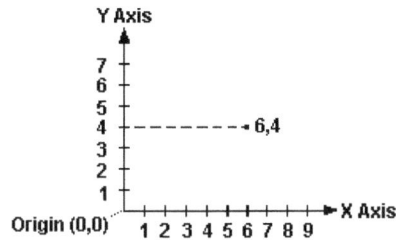

Figure 1–37

The current coordinate location of the cursor can be displayed in the Status Bar, as shown in Figure 1–38. By default, this display is toggled off. If you want to display the coordinates, click

≡ (Customization) in the Status Bar and select **Coordinates**.

Figure 1–38

When you start a drawing command that requires you to select a point, the current coordinates also display near the crosshair in the Dynamic Input prompt (When **Dynamic Input** option is toggled **On**). For example, to draw a line, you must indicate where to begin and end the line. You can specify the point using one of two methods:

- Selecting a point on the screen with the cursor.

- Typing coordinates (when it is requesting point entry) in the form X,Y as shown in Figure 1–39. For example, the point (6,4) would be typed as **6,4**.

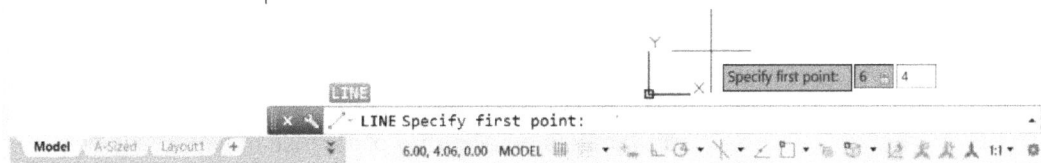

Figure 1–39

Measuring Angles

With the Cartesian coordinate system, you also need to understand how angles work in the AutoCAD software, as shown in Figure 1–40. This becomes important for coordinate entry, rotating objects, and working with arcs.

Figure 1–40

- By default, the AutoCAD software measures angles in a counter-clockwise direction relative to the positive X-axis.

Drawings Created at Full Scale

The AutoCAD Cartesian workspace is essentially unlimited in size. Whatever object you are creating, you typically draw it in the software at full scale, as shown in Figure 1–41. Whether you are drawing a building that is 100 x 200 meters or feet, a city that is 10 square kilometers or miles, or an IC chip that is 0.1" x 0.1", you always draw in the real units of the object. Your drawing area is as big as you need it to be. If needed, the entire solar system could be drawn at full scale in the software.

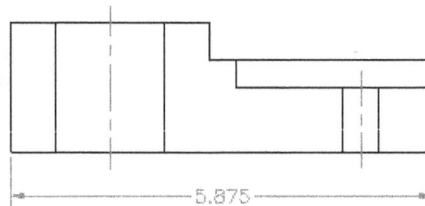

Figure 1–41

- Scaling the drawing only becomes necessary when the drawing is printed.

Hint: Drawing Accuracy

In addition to being potentially enormous, the AutoCAD drawing plane is also remarkably precise. Each point you enter in the software has an accuracy of at least 14 significant digits (e.g., 1.0000000000000).

1.5 Opening an Existing Drawing File

Opening Drawings

The **Open** command enables you to open and edit an existing drawing. This command opens the Select File dialog box that is similar to the standard Windows File dialog box, as shown in Figure 1–42.

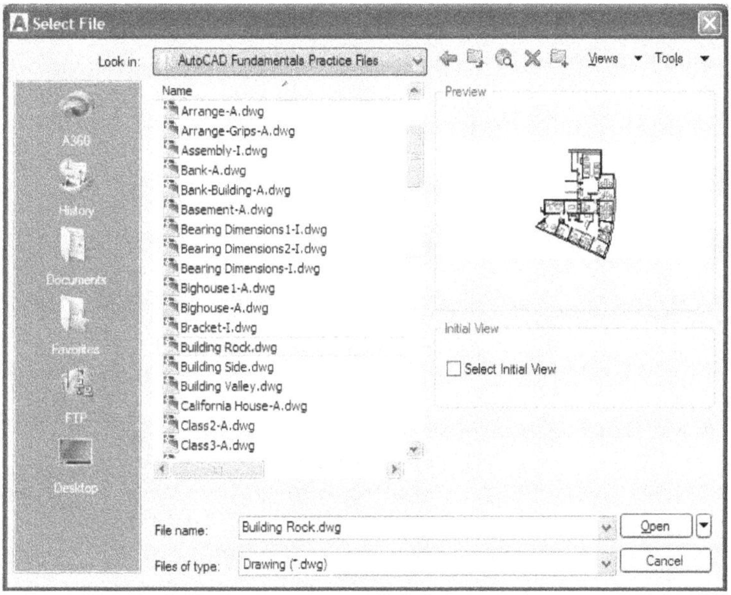

Figure 1–42

You can also access the ***Open*** *command from the Command Line by typing* ***Open***.

- You can access the **Open** command in the Quick Access

  Toolbar or in the Application menu by clicking 📂 (Open). You can also open the command from the Initial Start window (*Start* tab)>Open Files.

- Drawings that have recently been opened can be reopened quickly using Recent Documents in the Application Menu or the initial Start window.

How To: Open a Drawing

1. In the Quick Access Toolbar, click 📂 (Open).
2. In the Select File dialog box, locate the required file folder.
3. Select a drawing from the list. A preview displays on the right side of the dialog box.
4. Click **Open** or double-click on the drawing name.

File Location Options

History: Displays shortcuts to recently opened drawings.

Documents: Goes to the *My Documents* folder.

Favorites: Goes to the *Favorites* folder (*Windows\Favorites*), which stores shortcuts to files or folders. You can add items to the *Favorites* folder by selecting **Tools>Add to Favorites** in the dialog box.

Desktop: Displays the Windows Desktop and enables you to navigate to any folder. Select a file to display a preview.

- (A360) and (FTP) are options for opening drawings from Internet locations.

Navigation and File Options

Back to: Returns to the previous folder.

Up one level: Moves up one level in the directory structure.

Search the Web: Opens the Web Browser window. In this window, you can locate a web site to download files, etc.

Delete: Deletes the selected file(s).

Create new folder: Creates a new folder in the current folder.

Enhanced
in 2018

Views ▼ **Views:** Select the **List**, **Details**, or **Thumbnails** view for files, and toggle the Preview window on or off. If you have selected the details (Date, type, etc.) of the files to be displayed, the sort order of the columns is remembered by the AutoCAD software next time a file is opened.

Tools ▼ **Tools:** Locates files in the AutoCAD search path, adds FTP locations, or adds files or folders to the *Favorites* folder.

- To make your most commonly used folders easier to access, you can select them individually in the Look in: drop-down list and then select **Tools>Add Current Folder to Places** to add them to the File Location drop-down list.

Multiple Drawings

You can have several drawings open at once. You can open them individually and have them open at the same time or open a several files together by using <Ctrl> or <Shift> and selecting them in the Select File dialog box. You can open multiple new drawings by clicking ⊞ (plus) in the *File Tabs* bar.

Note that having several drawings open can slow down the system performance.

- All of the open drawings display as tabs in the *File Tabs* bar. The currently active drawing displays with a white background.

- The drawings that have been changed and not saved, display a * next to their name in the *File Tabs* bar, as shown for **Drawing10*** in Figure 1–43.

Figure 1–43

You can switch between the drawings using any of the following methods:

- Pressing <Ctrl>+<Tab>.

- Selecting the required *File* tab (as shown on the left in Figure 1–44).

- Expanding ⬛ (Application Menu) and selecting a drawing under Open Drawings (as shown on the right in Figure 1–44).

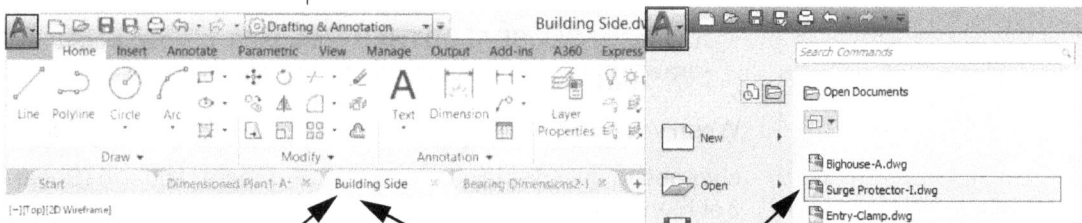

Current drawing

File tabs: Select file tab to switch to that drawing

Application Menu>Open Documents: Select drawing name to switch to that drawing

Figure 1–44

Closing Files

You can close a drawing file without leaving the software using any of the following methods:

- Clicking ▭ (Close) in the Application Menu.

- Clicking ⊠ (Close) in the upper right corner of the drawing window.

- Clicking ⊗ (Close) in the required *File* tab.

The software prompts you to save any changes if you have not yet saved the drawing.

In the Application Menu, ▭ (Close) has two options:

- ▭ (Current Drawing), which closes the current drawing.

- ▭ (All Drawings), which closes all of the drawings together, leaving the *Start* tab open.

The Start tab is always persistent in the File Tabs bar.

You can close all of the drawings using any of the following methods:

- Right-clicking on a tab and selecting **Close All** to close all of the drawings except the *Start* tab.

- Right-clicking on a tab and selecting **Close All Other Drawings** to close all of the drawings except the one where the shortcut menu has been opened from. If not already active, this will also make the drawing the active one.

- Using the **CLOSEALLOTHER** command to close all of the drawings except the current drawing and the *Start* tab.

When you close all of the drawings, the Quick Access Toolbar changes to only display ▭ (New), ▭ (Open), and ▭ (Sheet Set Manager).

Practice 1a | Opening a Drawing

Practice Objective

- Open and close existing drawings, and switch between open drawings.

Estimated time for completion: 5 minutes

In this practice, you will use the Select File dialog box to open two existing files and view them, as shown in Figure 1–45.

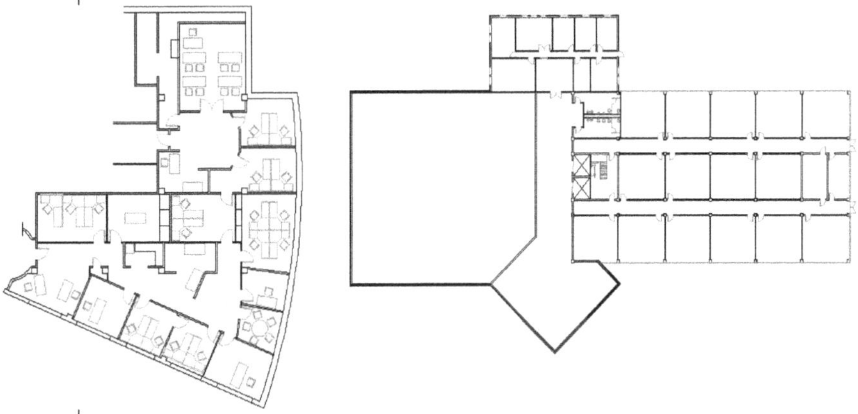

Figure 1–45

You can also click ▷ (Open) in the Application menu.

1. In the Quick Access Toolbar, click ▷ (Open) or if you are in the *Start* tab initial window, select **Open Files** in the *Create* tab.

2. In the Select File dialog box, navigate to and open the practice files folder. In the *Name* area, select **Building Rock-M.dwg** and click **Open**.

3. Start the **Open** command again. In the Select File dialog box, in the *Name* area, select **Building Side-M.dwg** and click **Open**.

4. In the *File Tabs* bar, in addition to the *Start* tab, the names of all opened files display as tabs, as shown in Figure 1–46.

Figure 1–46

---

5. Expand ![A] (Application Menu) and click ![folder] (Open Documents). The two files you have opened are listed as shown in Figure 1–47.

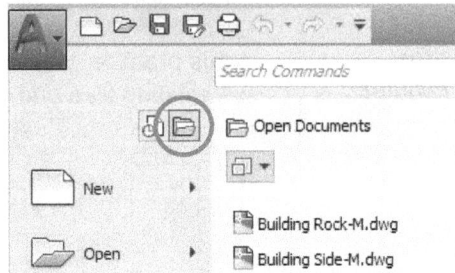

Figure 1–47

6. In the Application Menu, in the Open Documents list, select **Building Rock-M.dwg**. It becomes the active drawing.

7. In the *File Tabs* bar, select **Building Side-M.dwg**. It becomes the active drawing.

8. Press <Ctrl>+<Home>. The *Start* tab is active and the initial Start window displays.

9. In the Start window, in the *Recent Documents* area, select **Building Side-M.dwg** to make it active.

10. In the *File Tabs* bar, right-click in the *Building Side-M* tab and select **Close All**. If prompted to save changes, click **No**. This closes all of the open drawings and the initial Start window displays again.

1.6 Viewing Your Drawing

Because AutoCAD drawings are drawn to full scale, it would be difficult to create them precisely on the computer screen without being able to move in and out around your work.

For example, if you are working on a map of the United States, you need to get closer to clearly display the roads in specific cities. If you are working on a house, you might want to focus on specific areas to be able to place doors precisely, as shown in Figure 1–48.

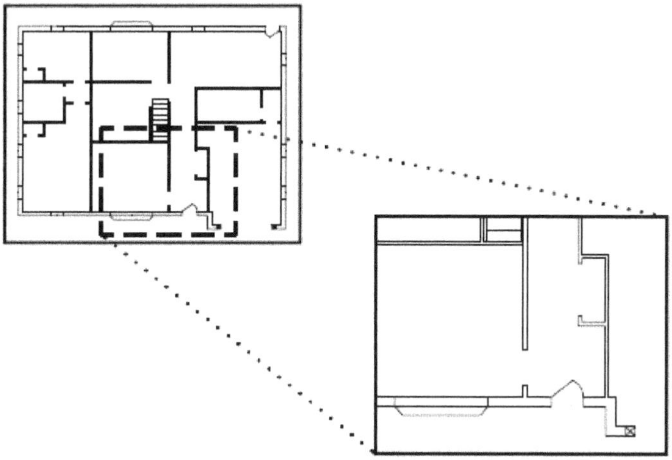

Figure 1–48

The **Zoom** and **Pan** commands enable you to specify which area of the drawing to display on the screen.

Wheel Mouse Zoom and Pan

The easiest way to zoom and pan is to use a wheel mouse.

- Roll the mouse wheel away from you to zoom in and roll the wheel toward you to zoom out. The AutoCAD software zooms in and out around the location of the cursor.

- Hold the wheel and move the cursor to pan. Note that a hand icon displays at the cursor location while panning.

- Double-click on the wheel to fit the entire drawing in the drawing window.

- Press <Ctrl> while you hold the wheel and move the mouse to use another mode of panning, called *joystick pan*.

Navigation Tools

In the AutoCAD LT software, only the 2D Steering Wheel, Pan, and Zoom are available in the Navigation Bar.

Navigation tools are located in the Navigation Bar, as shown in Figure 1–49.

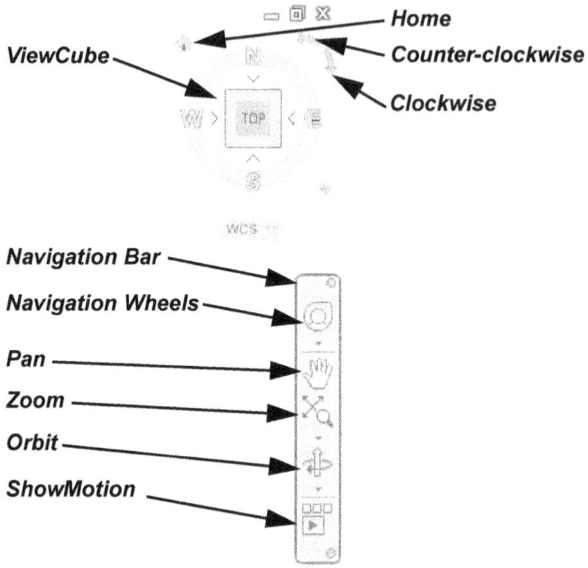

Figure 1–49

The Navigation Bar provides a quick way of accessing the viewing tools. It displays in a very light gray until you hover the cursor over it. ⌁▾⌁ displayed below a tool indicates that it can be expanded and additional options can be selected. In Paper Space, fewer tools display because you can only use 2D viewing commands. The different options are shown in Figure 1–50.

In the AutoCAD LT software, the Navigation Bar displays like the Paper Space version shown in Figure 1–50.

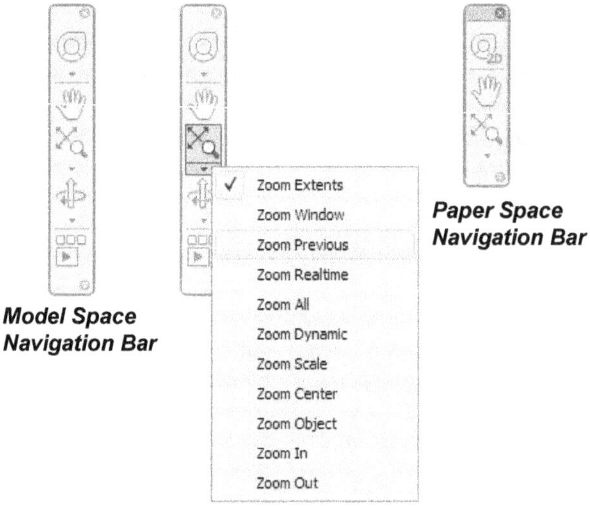

Model Space Navigation Bar

Paper Space Navigation Bar

Zoom Extents
Zoom Window
Zoom Previous
Zoom Realtime
Zoom All
Zoom Dynamic
Zoom Scale
Zoom Center
Zoom Object
Zoom In
Zoom Out

Figure 1–50

In the AutoCAD LT software, the ViewCube is not available.

- Most of the ViewCube options are primarily used in 3D views. However, you can use the Clockwise and Counterclockwise controls to rotate the viewport in the 2D plane, as shown in Figure 1–51.

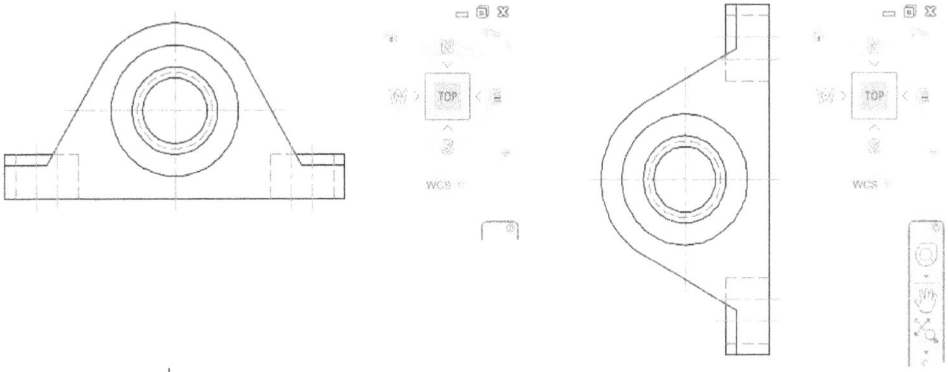

Figure 1–51

In the AutoCAD LT software, only the 2D Navigation Wheel is available.

- Navigation Wheels provide access to groups of commonly used navigation tools. Depending on the wheel selected, you can access a small group of commands, such as **Zoom**, **Rewind**, and **Pan**, or a group with many more options. The Navigation Wheel displays at the cursor, enabling you to quickly select the navigation tools.

*In the AutoCAD LT software, **ShowMotion** is not available.*

- **ShowMotion** is used when creating animations in 3D.

Pan and Zoom Commands

The Navigation Bar and the shortcut menu contain the **Zoom** and **Pan** commands.

The **Realtime** commands are really two parts of one command. **Pan Realtime** enables you to shift the display without changing the current magnification. **Zoom Realtime** enables you to zoom in closer to the drawing or away from the drawing, displaying the results dynamically (in real time) while the command is used.

How To: Pan in Real Time

*You can also right-click in the drawing window and select **Pan**, or type **P** in the Command Line.*

1. In the Navigation Bar, click ✋ (Pan). The crosshair changes to 🖐 (Hand cursor).
2. Position the cursor over the part of the drawing that you want to visually move to a different part of the screen. Hold the left mouse button and drag in the direction you want to go.

3. After you release the mouse button, you can pan again, or press <Esc> or <Enter> to complete the command.

• You can also pan using the scroll bars on the sides of the drawing.

How To: Zoom in Realtime

*You can also right-click in the drawing window and select **Zoom**, or type **Z** in the Command Line.*

1. In the Navigation Bar, expand ⤢⊖ (Zoom) and select **Zoom Realtime**. The crosshair changes to ⊖ (Magnifying glass).
2. Hold the left mouse button and drag the cursor up to zoom in or down to zoom out.
3. After you release the mouse button, you can zoom again, or press <Esc> or <Enter> to complete the command.

• If you select a **Zoom** option in the Navigation Bar, the top level Zoom icon changes to the selected option.

Switching Between Zoom and Pan

In either **Zoom Realtime** or **Pan Realtime**, you can right-click in the drawing window to open a shortcut menu, as shown in Figure 1–52. Select an option and continue with the viewing operation.

Exit
Pan
✓ Zoom
3D Orbit
Zoom Window
Zoom Original
Zoom Extents

Figure 1–52

• **Zoom Window:** Requires you to hold the left mouse button while you drag a window.

• **Zoom Original:** Returns the display to the view that was current before the **Zoom/Pan Realtime** command was started.

• **Zoom Extents:** Fills the screen with all of the objects in the drawing.

Practice 1b

Viewing a Drawing

Estimated time for completion: 5 minutes

Practice Objective

- Display parts of a drawing using the **Zoom** and **Pan** commands.

In this practice, you will use several options in the **Zoom** command and **Pan** to display parts of a large drawing, as shown in Figure 1–53.

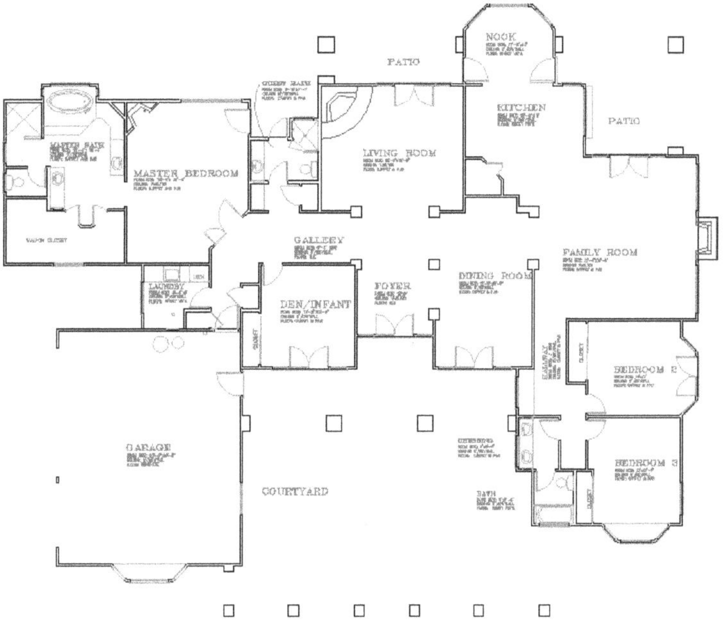

Figure 1–53

1. Open **Bighouse-AM.dwg** from your practice files folder.

2. If you have a mouse wheel, scroll the wheel to zoom and press it to pan. Double-click on the mouse wheel to zoom to the extents of the drawing.

3. In the Navigation Bar, expand (Zoom) and select **Zoom Realtime**. Click, hold, and move the cursor to zoom in and out of the drawing.

4. Right-click and select **Pan**. Click, hold, and move the cursor to pan around the drawing.

5. Right-click and select **Exit**. Double-click on the mouse wheel to zoom to the extents of the drawing.

6. In the Navigation Bar, expand (Zoom) and select **Zoom Window**. Select two corner points for the window to zoom in on the kitchen (in the upper right corner of the house).

7. In the Navigation Bar, click (Pan). Pan from the kitchen to the Master Bedroom (upper left corner).

8. Right-click and select **Zoom Extents**. Right-click again and select **Exit**.

9. In the *File Tabs* bar, click (Close) in the **Bighouse-A** tab to close the drawing. Do not save changes.

1.7 Saving Your Work

Saving your work is vitally important. You should save early and often to avoid losing and redrawing information. To provide added security, you can create automatic saves to a backup file. You can also save your drawings so that they can be used in previous versions of the AutoCAD software that might not be compatible with the one you are using.

- The save commands only save to the current drive. Remember to regularly back up your work to another machine or other data storage.

*You can also quick save from the Command Line by entering **qsave** or by pressing **<Ctrl>+<S>**,*

- When you click 🖬 (Save) in the Quick Access Toolbar or Application Menu, the drawing file you are working on is saved without prompting you for the name or location. This is called a *quick save*.

- If you are working in a new drawing that has not been saved with a specific name, you are prompted for a name and location in the Save Drawing As dialog box.

- Clicking 🖬 (Save As) in the Quick Access Toolbar or Application Menu (or typing **save**) enables you to save the current drawing with another name.

Automatic Saves

Enhanced in 2018

While it is critical for you to save a drawing regularly as you are working on it, the AutoCAD software is also set up to save a drawing to a backup file every 10 minutes. These files can be used to recover work that might not have been saved. They have an SV$ extension.

- By default, the AutoCAD software also creates a backup copy of the file every time you save. It has a .BAK extension.

- Most of the times, automatic saves are performed incrementally. This is much faster than performing full saves, which can take a lot of time.

- You can modify the Automatic Save and backup features in the *Open and Save* tab of the Options dialog box (Application Menu>**Options**). You can also control the interval between saves. By default, the feature is toggled on with an interval of 10 minutes between saves and the **Create backup copy with each save** option is selected, as shown in Figure 1–54.

*In the AutoCAD LT software, the **Full-time CRC validation** option is not available.*

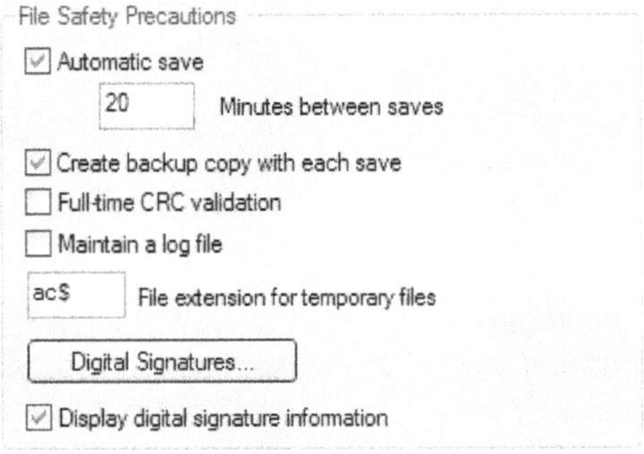

File Safety Precautions

☑ Automatic save

20 Minutes between saves

☑ Create backup copy with each save

☐ Full-time CRC validation

☐ Maintain a log file

ac$ File extension for temporary files

Digital Signatures...

☑ Display digital signature information

Figure 1–54

Saving in Various Formats

Enhanced in **2018**

Using the **Save As** command, you can select an earlier version of the DWG file format so that the file can be opened with earlier versions of the AutoCAD software, as shown in Figure 1–55.

- With the 2018 release, the AutoCAD software uses the **AutoCAD 2018 Drawing** file format to save the drawings. If you want to share a drawing with someone that has the AutoCAD 2017 software or an earlier version of the software, you need to save it in the previously used *AutoCAD 2013* file format.

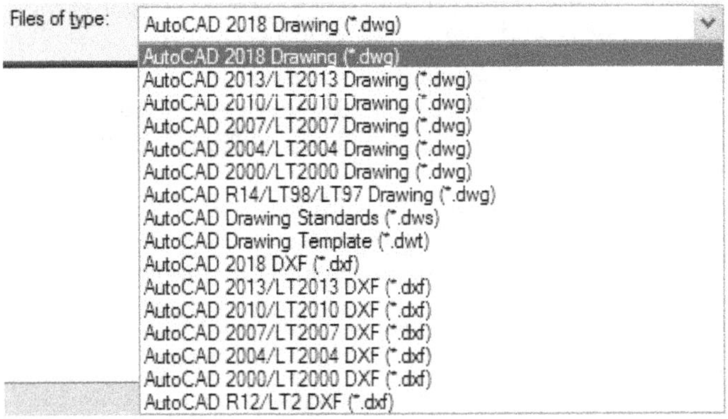

Files of type: AutoCAD 2018 Drawing (*.dwg)

AutoCAD 2018 Drawing (*.dwg)
AutoCAD 2013/LT2013 Drawing (*.dwg)
AutoCAD 2010/LT2010 Drawing (*.dwg)
AutoCAD 2007/LT2007 Drawing (*.dwg)
AutoCAD 2004/LT2004 Drawing (*.dwg)
AutoCAD 2000/LT2000 Drawing (*.dwg)
AutoCAD R14/LT98/LT97 Drawing (*.dwg)
AutoCAD Drawing Standards (*.dws)
AutoCAD Drawing Template (*.dwt)
AutoCAD 2018 DXF (*.dxf)
AutoCAD 2013/LT2013 DXF (*.dxf)
AutoCAD 2010/LT2010 DXF (*.dxf)
AutoCAD 2007/LT2007 DXF (*.dxf)
AutoCAD 2004/LT2004 DXF (*.dxf)
AutoCAD 2000/LT2000 DXF (*.dxf)
AutoCAD R12/LT2 DXF (*.dxf)

Figure 1–55

Practice 1c

Saving a Drawing File

Practice Objectives

- Open and save a drawing.
- Modify the **Automatic save** option.

Estimated time for completion: under 5 minutes

In this practice, you will open a drawing, save it, and modify the **Automatic save** option, as shown in Figure 1–56.

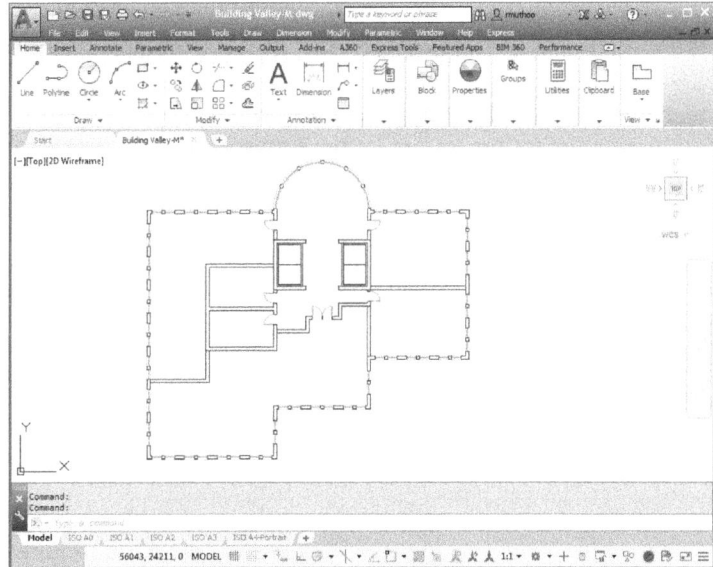

Figure 1–56

1. Open **Building Valley-M.dwg** from your practice files folder.

2. In the Quick Access Toolbar, click (Save). The AutoCAD software performs a quick save.

3. In the Application Menu, click **Options** to open the Options dialog box.

4. In the *Open and Save* tab, change the time for *Automatic save* to **15** minutes.

5. Click **OK** to close the Options dialog box. Note a * beside the **Building Valley** name in the *File Tabs* bar.

6. Save the drawing by clicking (Save) in the Quick Access Toolbar. In the *File Tabs* bar, note that **Building Valley** does not have a * beside it.

7. Close the drawing.

Chapter Review Questions

1. What displays when you click the *Start* tab in the *File Tabs* bar?

   a. The recently opened drawings.

   b. An expanded version of the Command Line.

   c. The Initial Start window.

   d. The Application Menu.

2. How do you cancel a command using the keyboard?

   a. Press <F2>.

   b. Press <Esc>.

   c. Press <Ctrl>.

   d. Press <Delete>.

3. What is the quickest way to repeat a command?

   a. Press <Esc>.

   b. Press <F2>.

   c. Press <Enter>.

   d. Press <Ctrl>.

4. To display a specific ribbon panel, you can right-click on the ribbon and select the required panel in the shortcut menu.

   a. True

   b. False

5. How are points specified in the AutoCAD Cartesian workspace?

   a. X value x Y value

   b. Y value, X value

   c. X value, Y value

   d. X value - Y value

6. How do you know if a file has not been saved after it is modified?

   a. Its tab displays a white background in the *File Tabs* bar.

   b. It displays a * next to its name in the *File Tabs* bar.

   c. Its tab is highlighted in blue in the *File Tabs* bar.

   d. Its tab always displays next to the *Start* tab in the *File Tabs* bar.

7. How can you switch between the open drawings? (Select all that apply.)

   a. By pressing <Ctrl>+<Tab>.

   b. By pressing <Ctrl>+<Shift>.

   c. By right-clicking and selecting **Open** in the shortcut menu.

   d. By selecting the required drawing file tab in the *File Tabs* bar.

8. How do you fit the entire drawing in the drawing window?

   a. Double-click on the right mouse button.

   b. Hold <Ctrl> and scroll the mouse wheel.

   c. Double-click the mouse wheel.

   d. Hold the mouse wheel and move the cursor.

Command Summary

Button	Command	Location
	Close	• **Drawing Window** • **Application Menu** • **Command Prompt:** close
	Close Current Drawing	• **Application Menu** • **Tabs bar shortcut menu**
	Close All Drawings	• **Application Menu** • **Tabs bar shortcut menu**
NA	**Dynamic Input**	• **Status Bar:** expand Customization
Exit Autodesk AutoCAD **Exit AutoCAD**		• **Application Menu**
	Open	• **Quick Access Toolbar** • **Application Menu** • **Command Prompt:** open, <Ctrl>+<O>
	Open Documents	• **Application Menu**
Options	**Options**	• **Application Menu** • **Shortcut Menu:** Options
	Pan	• **Navigation Bar** • **Shortcut Menu:** Pan • **Command Prompt:** pan or P
	Recent Documents	• **Application Menu**
	Save	• **Quick Access Toolbar** • **Application Menu** • **Command Prompt:** qsave, <Ctrl>+<S>
	Save As	• **Quick Access Toolbar** • **Application Menu** • **Command Prompt:** save
	Zoom Realtime	• **Navigation Bar:** Zoom Realtime • **Shortcut Menu:** Zoom • **Command Prompt:** zoom or Z

Basic Drawing and Editing Commands

In this chapter you learn how to draw lines, rectangles, and circles, use Dynamic Input and Polar Tracking, erase objects, and use the Undo and Redo commands.

Learning Objectives in this Chapter

- Draw, edit, or close a line or series of lines.
- Remove objects from a drawing.
- Draw angles, rectangles, circles, and horizontal and vertical lines.
- Reverse the effects of the last command and return the drawing to its state before the last undo.

2.1 Drawing Lines

The most fundamental drawing element is the line. Almost any drawing contains line segments. The **Line** command enables you to add straight-line segments to the drawing as required, as shown in Figure 2–1. Each segment created with the command is a separate object.

Figure 2–1

How To: Draw a Line

*You can also type **L** or **line** in the Command prompt.*

1. In the ribbon, in the *Home* tab>Draw panel, click ⁄ (Line).
2. Select the first point.
3. Select the next point.
4. Continue to select points at the *Specify next point:* prompt to create a series of line segments as required or press <Enter> to complete the command.

Specifying Length and Angle

After you select the first point for the line and move the cursor, the AutoCAD® software displays its length and angle. The length value is highlighted, as shown in Figure 2–2. Enter the required length and press <Tab>, which highlights the angle value. Enter the required angle.

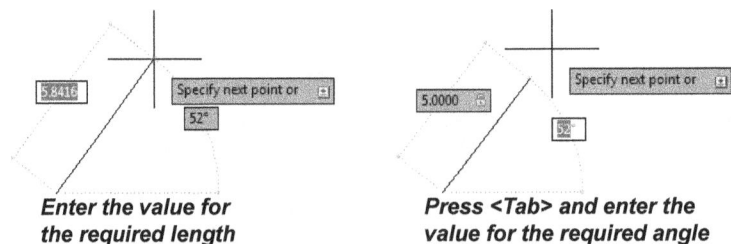

Enter the value for the required length

Press <Tab> and enter the value for the required angle

Figure 2–2

- The angle depends on the direction in which the cursor is moved. For example, 90° can be either straight up or straight down, depending on where the cursor is located. Move the cursor in the approximate direction first.

- Note that 0° is the positive X-direction (straight and to the right).

- In the Status Bar, **Dynamic Input** must be toggled on for the length and angle to be displayed.

Line Command Options

At the *Specify next point:* prompt, press the <Down Arrow> to display the command options at the cursor prompt, as shown in Figure 2–3. Select an option or type the first letter (**C** or **U**) and press <Enter> to exit the command.

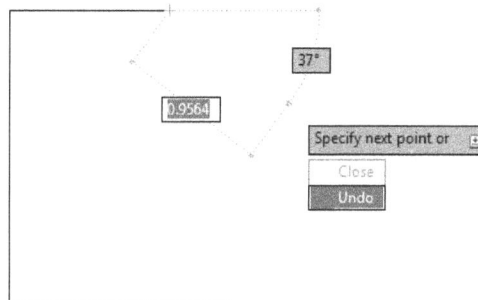

Figure 2–3

Close (C)	After two or more line segments are drawn, this option adds a final line segment between the first and last points entered.
Undo (U)	Removes the last segment drawn.

- You can also right-click at the *Specify next point:* prompt and select **Enter**, **Cancel**, **Close**, or **Undo**.

2.2 Erasing Objects

As with manual drafting, you often need to correct mistakes or make revisions in an AutoCAD drawing. You can erase objects by deleting them or by using the **Erase** command.

The easiest way is to select the objects and then press <Delete>. When you select an object, the object is highlighted and blue squares display, as shown in Figure 2–4. These are called *grips* and are very useful tools for modifying objects.

Figure 2–4

How To: Erase an Object using the Erase command

1. In the *Home* tab>Modify panel, click ✏️ (Erase).
2. The *Select Objects:* prompt displays. Position the cursor so that the small pick box is directly over the object to be erased.

   As soon as it touches an object, the cursor displays as ▫ and turns the object gray, indicating the object before selection, as shown in Figure 2–5.

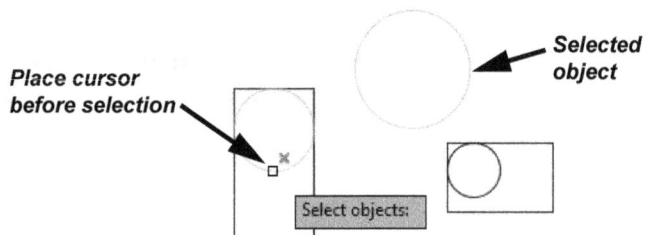

Place cursor before selection

Selected object

Select objects:

Figure 2–5

3. Click on the object to select it.
4. You can continue selecting additional objects to be erased.
5. Press <Enter> or right-click to erase the objects and complete the command.

2.3 Drawing Vertical and Horizontal Lines

Polar Tracking

You can draw lines at specific lengths and angles by typing the numbers, as shown in Figure 2–6. The **Polar Tracking** command is helpful for reducing the amount of typing required as it restricts the movement of the cursor to the already specified (preset) angles.

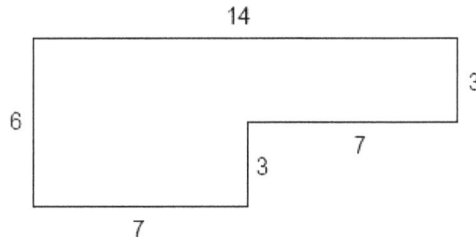

Figure 2–6

- Polar Tracking makes it easy to work with preset angles as you draw. Rather than typing the angle, you move the cursor to find the tracking line (dotted line) and then enter the distance.

- You can set the polar angles as required, but in this section you work with the standard 90° increments.

- To toggle Polar Tracking on and off, click (Polar Tracking) in the Status Bar, as shown in Figure 2–7, or press <F10>.

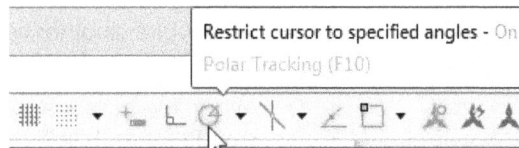

Restrict cursor to specified angles - On

Polar Tracking (F10)

Figure 2–7

How To: Use Polar Tracking to draw Vertical and Horizontal Lines

1. In the Status Bar, click the arrow in ⟲ ▼ (Polar Tracking) to display the angles list. Select **90,180,270,360**, as shown in Figure 2–8.

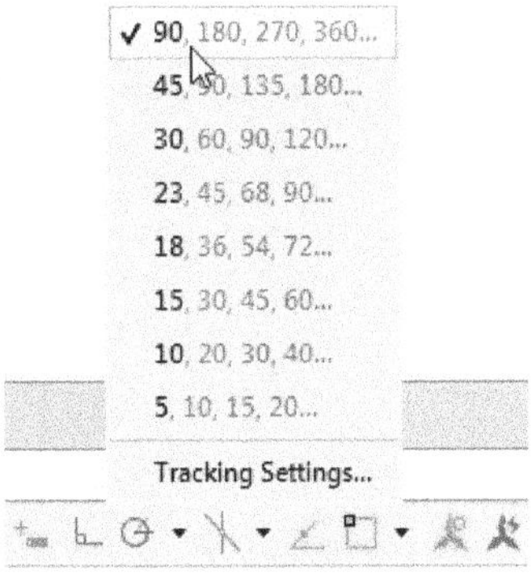

✓ **90**, 180, 270, 360...
45, 90, 135, 180...
30, 60, 90, 120...
23, 45, 68, 90...
18, 36, 54, 72...
15, 30, 45, 60...
10, 20, 30, 40...
5, 10, 15, 20...
Tracking Settings...

Figure 2–8

The tool highlights in blue when it is toggled on.

2. Click ⟲ ▼ (Polar Tracking) or press <F10> to toggle it on, if required.
3. In the *Home* tab>Draw panel, click ∕ (Line) to start the **Line** command.
4. At the *Specify first point:* prompt, select a starting point for the line.
5. At the *Specify next point:* prompt, move the crosshairs in the direction in which you want the line to extend.
6. When the correct Polar Tracking line displays, enter a distance.
7. Press <Enter>. The line is drawn that length in the direction in which you pick.
8. Repeat for another line segment or press <Enter> to end the **Line** command.

- When the cursor approaches one of the polar angles, the dotted Polar Tracking line displays with a tooltip specifying *Polar:*, followed by the distance and angle from the last point (distance<angle), as shown in Figure 2–9.

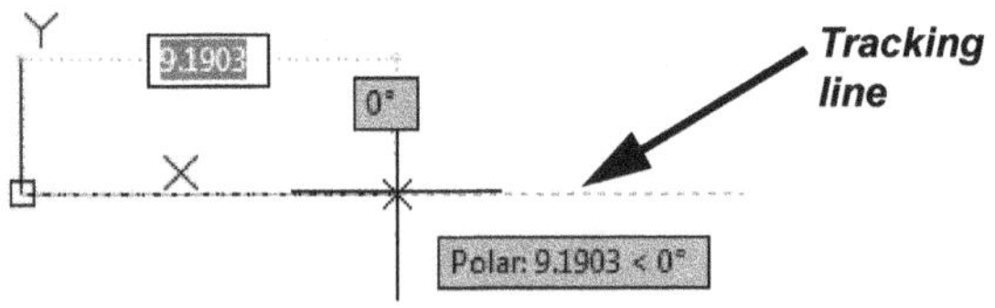

Tracking line

Polar: 9.1903 < 0°

Figure 2–9

- You can use Polar Tracking with or without Dynamic Input.

Ortho Mode

Another way to draw horizontal and vertical straight lines is to use Ortho Mode. It always forces lines to use 90° angles only. To toggle Ortho Mode on or off, click ⌐ (Ortho Mode) in the Status Bar, as shown in Figure 2–10, or press <F8>.

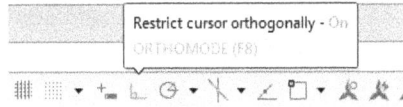

Figure 2–10

- Polar Tracking is the preferred method because it permits other angles to be used and displays the tracking lines.

- ⌐ (Ortho Mode) and ⟲ ▼ (Polar Tracking) cannot be toggled on at the same time.

2.4 Drawing Rectangles

Like lines, rectangles are fundamental building blocks in most drawings, as shown in Figure 2–11. A rectangle can be created from a series of lines or you can create it as a single object using the **Rectangle** command.

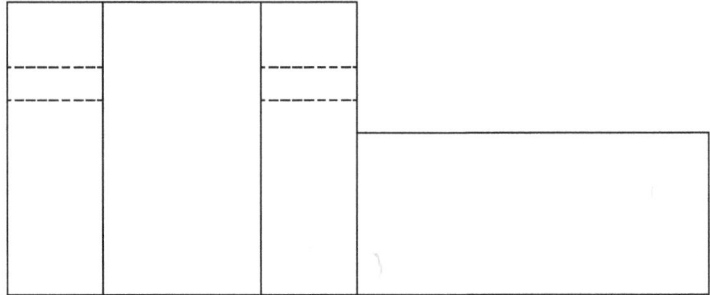

Figure 2–11

How To: Draw a Rectangle

1. In the *Home* tab>Draw panel, click ⬜ (Rectangle).
2. Select the first corner of the rectangle.
3. Select the opposite diagonal corner of the box.

- You can also specify the exact length and width of a rectangle as you create it, using either:

  - **Dynamic Input:** At the *Specify other corner point:* prompt, enter a distance for the X axis (length) and Y axis (width), separated by a comma (e.g., **3,4**). The values (positive or negative) specify the direction in which the rectangle is created. Note that the ⊹ (Dynamic Input) should be toggled **On** in the Status Bar.
  - **Command Line:** At the *Specify other corner point:* prompt, select the **Dimensions** option. At the *Specify length for rectangles* prompt, enter a distance for the length and press <Enter>. At the *Specify width for rectangles* prompt, enter a distance for the width and press <Enter>. A preview of the rectangle displays, which you can reposition using the cursor. Click in the direction in which you want the rectangle.

- The numbers you enter for the length and width are X,Y coordinates that are measured relative to the first corner of the rectangle.

2.5 Drawing Circles

The **Circle** command enables you to place circles in the drawing as stand-alone objects or as parts of a more complex construction, as shown in Figure 2–12.

Figure 2–12

- In the *Home* tab>Draw panel, expand ⊘ (Circle) to open the flyout (shown in Figure 2–12) to access the various options in the **Circle** command.

How To: Draw a Center, Radius Circle

1. In the *Home* tab>Draw panel, in the Circle flyout, click

   ⊘ (Center, Radius).
2. Select the center point of the circle.
3. Specify the radius. The value can be entered or specified by selecting a point on the screen.

- The *Radius* is the distance from the center to the edge of the circle. The *Diameter* is the distance across the circle through the center point, as shown in Figure 2–13.

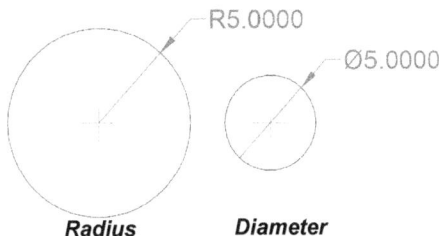

Radius   **Diameter**

Figure 2–13

How To: Draw a Center, Diameter Circle

1. In the *Home* tab>Draw panel, expand the **Circle** flyout and click ⊘ (Center, Diameter).
2. Select the center point of the circle.
3. Specify the diameter. The value can be entered or specified by selecting a point on the screen.

*Type **D** for **Diameter** option if you are using the typed command.*

- If you need to add circles with the same radius or diameter, you can restart the **Circle** command, select the center point, and press <Enter> to use the default value for the radius or diameter. You can also select the value in the Dynamic Input Prompt drop-down list (press <Down Arrow>), as shown in Figure 2–14.

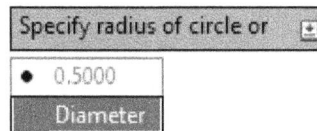

Figure 2–14

- The default value at the prompt is the same value as the last specified distance and is saved as the radius value. For example, if you specified a *Diameter* of **5.0**, the default value of the *Radius* is **2.5** the next time you start the command.

How To: Draw a 2 Point or 3 Point Circle

1. In the *Home* tab>Draw panel, expand the Circle flyout and click ◯ (2-Point) or ◌ (3-Point).
2. Select the two or three points that you want to use to draw the outside of the circle.

How To: Draw a Circle Tangent to Objects

A *tangent* is a point on a circle where another circle or object only touches it at one point, as shown in Figure 2–15. When you use these commands, an icon displays when you hover over a potential tangent point.

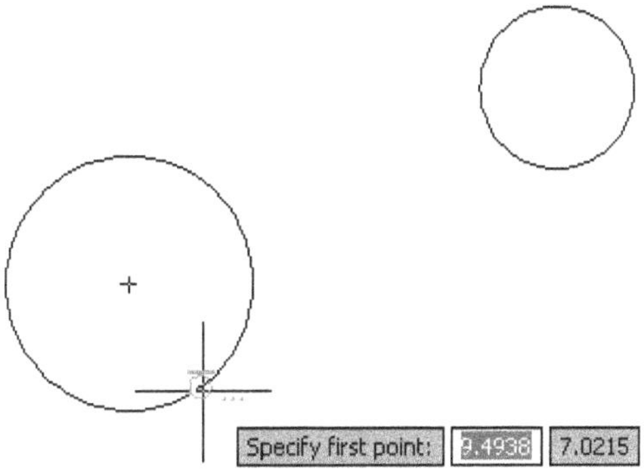

Specify first point: 9.4938 7.0215

Figure 2–15

1. In the *Home* tab>Draw panel, expand the Circle flyout and click (Tan, Tan, Radius).
2. Hover the cursor over an object to which a circle can be tangent and click when the icon displays in the correct location.
3. Hover the cursor over another object to which the circle can be tangent and click to set its location.
4. Enter a radius for the circle or select an additional tangent point for **Tan, Tan, Tan**.

- If the radius is not big enough for the circle to be created in relationship to the tangent points, the circle is not created with a *Circle does not exist:* prompt displayed in the Command Line. This indicates that you need to use a larger radius.

The (Tan, Tan, Tan) option is only available in the Draw panel.

2.6 Undo and Redo Actions

The **Undo** command reverses the effects of the last command. For example, if you draw a circle and then start the **Undo** command, the circle is undone and the drawing displays as it was before you started the **Circle** command. The **Redo** command returns your drawing to the state before the last undo. It is only available immediately after an undo.

- You can access the ⬅ (Undo) and ➡ (Redo) commands in the Quick Access Toolbar or by right-clicking in the drawing window with no command active and selecting **Undo** or **Redo** in the shortcut menu.

- To undo or redo one command, click the respective icon.

- To undo or redo a series of commands, in the Quick Access Toolbar, expand the **Undo** or **Redo** command (as shown for the **Undo** command in Figure 2–16) and select the number of commands that you want to undo.

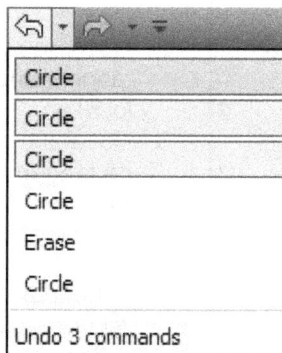

Figure 2–16

Practice 2a

Basic Drawing and Editing Commands

Practice Objectives

- Draw lines using Dynamic Input.
- Delete objects from a drawing using the **Erase** command.
- Draw an object using the **Line** command with Polar Tracking.
- Draw rectangles and circles using various **Circle** command options.

Estimated time for completion: 20 minutes

In this practice, you will use drawing and editing commands. You will draw lines using Dynamic Input and then erase them, as shown on Figure 2–17. In Tasks 3 - 5, you will use Polar Tracking to draw an object. You will also draw rectangles and circles, as shown in Figure 2–18.

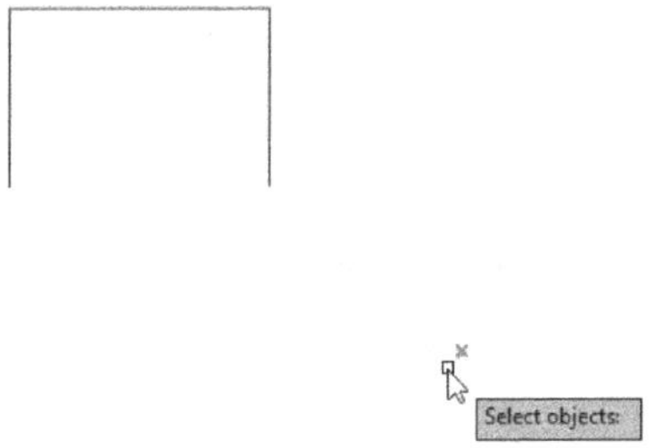

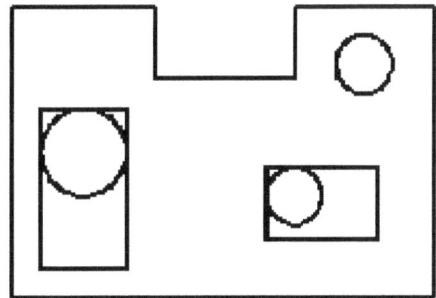

Figure 2–17

Figure 2–18

Task 1 - Draw lines with Dynamic Input.

In this task you will draw lines using Dynamic Input, as shown in Figure 2–19.

The dimensions are for reference only.

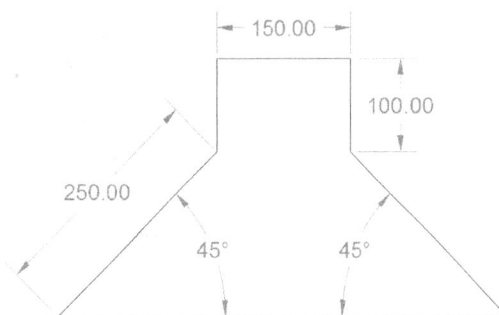

Figure 2–19

1. Open **Object-M.dwg** from your practice files folder. It is an empty drawing.

When the tool is toggled on, it should be highlighted in blue.

2. In the Status Bar, verify that ⁺▬ (Dynamic Input) is toggled on. If grid lines display, you can click ▦ (Grid Mode) in the Status Bar to toggle it off.

3. In the *Home* tab>Draw panel, click ⟋ (Line).

4. At the dynamic input, *Specify first point:* prompt, enter **120,120** (as shown in Figure 2–20) and press <Enter>.

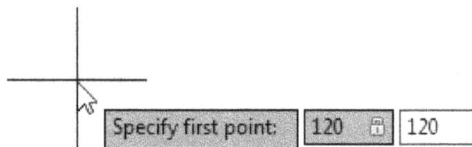

| Specify first point: | 120 | 🔒 | 120 |

Figure 2–20

5. Move the crosshairs up and to the right from the first point, and enter **250** for the distance. Press <Tab>, enter **45** for the angle (as shown in Figure 2–21), and press <Enter>.

250.0000   45

Figure 2–21

6. Move the crosshairs above the last point. Enter **100** for the distance, press <Tab>, enter **90**, and press <Enter> for the angle. This draws the next segment straight up.

7. Move the crosshairs to the right and draw the next segment **150 units** straight to the right (**0°**).

8. Move the crosshairs down and draw the next segment **100 units** straight down (**90°**).

9. Move the crosshairs down and draw the next segment **250 units** at **45°** down and to the right.

10. For the last segment across the bottom of the shape, press <Down Arrow> to display the command options. Select **Close** (as shown in Figure 2–22) to close the figure.

Figure 2–22

Task 2 - Erasing objects.

1. In the *Home* tab>Modify panel, click ✏ (Erase). Hover the cursor over a line segment. It turns light gray. Click on it to confirm selection. Similarly, select several other lines, which turn light gray indicating that they are selected for erasing, as shown in Figure 2–23. Press <Enter>.

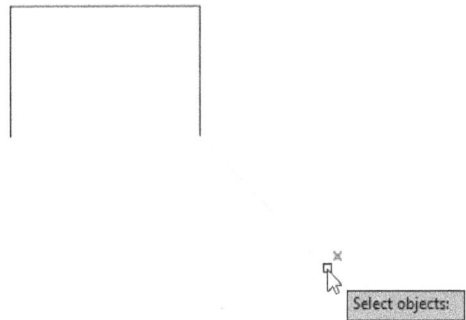

Figure 2–23

2. Without being in a command, select any remaining lines, which are highlighted with grips. Press <Delete>.

Task 3 - Use Polar Tracking.

In this task you will use the **Line** command with Polar Tracking to draw a precise object, as shown in Figure 2–24.

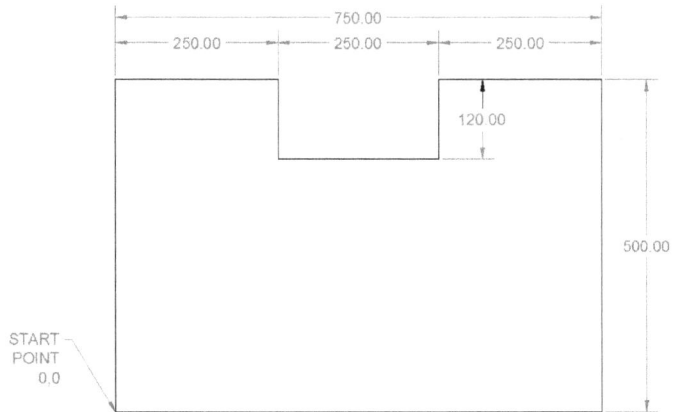

Figure 2–24

1. In the Status Bar, toggle on ⊘ ▼ (Polar Tracking), if it is not already on.

2. Start the **Line** command. At the *Specify first point:* prompt, enter **0,0**, and press <Enter>.

3. Move the crosshairs straight to the right from the start point (you might need to first pan down in the drawing). When the tracking line displays with *Polar: distance < 0* (as shown on the left in Figure 2–25), enter **750**, which automatically overwrites the value in the length edit box (as shown on the right in Figure 2–25). Press <Enter>.

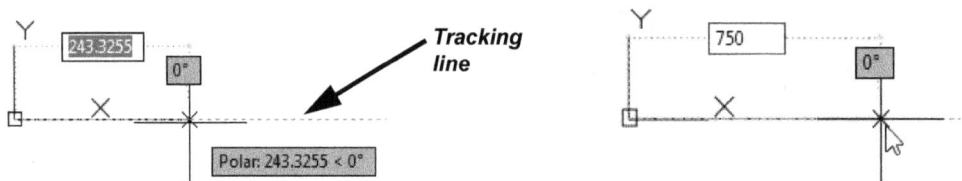

Tracking line

Figure 2–25

4. Move the crosshairs straight up from the new point. When the tracking line displays with *Polar: distance < 90*, enter **500** and press <Enter>.

5. Continue to draw the shape shown in Figure 2–24, moving the crosshairs and typing the distance for each segment.

6. For the last segment, type **C** and press <Enter> to close the figure and exit the **Line** command.

Task 4 - Draw rectangles.

In this task you will draw rectangles and locate them precisely using coordinates and Dynamic Input, as shown in Figure 2–26.

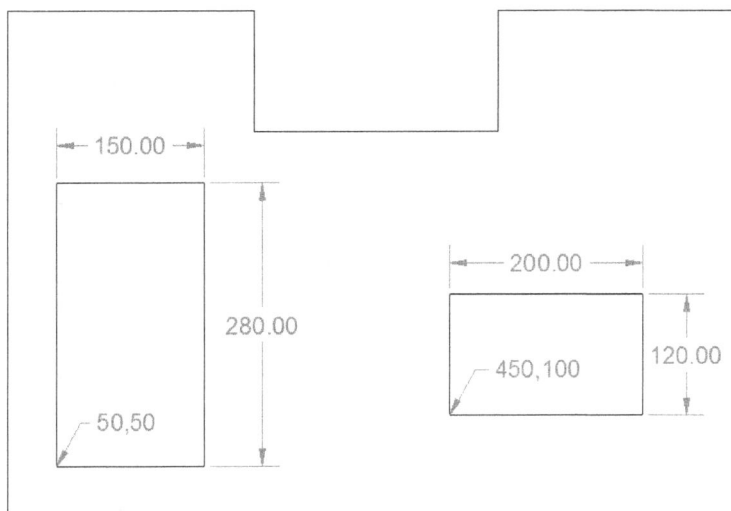

Figure 2–26

In the Status Bar, verify that ⁺▬ (Dynamic Input) is toggled on.

1. In the *Home* tab>Draw panel, click ⬜ (Rectangle).

2. For the first corner point, enter the coordinates **50,50** and press <Enter>.

3. For the other corner, enter **150,280** and press <Enter> to create a **150 x 280** rectangle.

4. Draw a second rectangle **200 x 120** with the first corner at point **450,100** and the dimensions shown in Figure 2–26.

5. Save the drawing.

Task 5 - Draw circles.

In this task you will draw circles using the **Center, Diameter**, **Tan, Tan, Radius**, and **Tan, Tan, Tan** options, as shown in Figure 2–27.

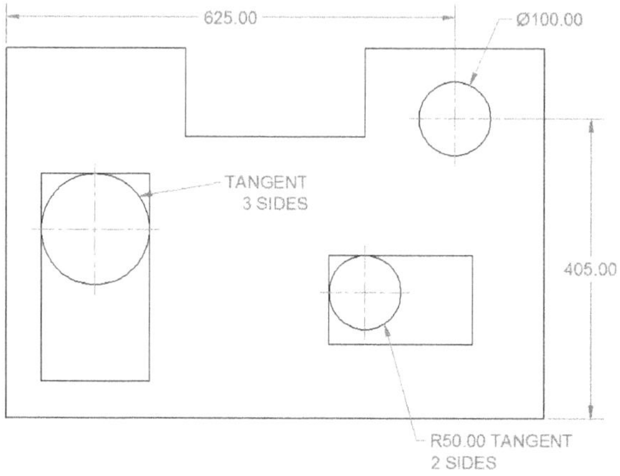

Figure 2–27

1. In the *Home* tab>Draw panel>Circle flyout> click ⊘ (Center, Diameter). To create the circle in the upper right corner, enter **625,405** to place the center point and enter **100** for the diameter.

2. To draw a circle inside the rectangle on the right side, in the

   Circle flyout, click ⊘ (Tan, Tan, Radius). Select the top line of the rectangle as the first deferred tangent point and the left one as the second tangent point. Press <Enter> to accept the default radius of **50**.

3. Draw a circle touching the three sides of the rectangle shown on the left side using the **Tan, Tan, Tan** option.

4. Save and close the drawing.

Chapter Review Questions

1. When using the **Line** command, how do you exit the command once you have finished drawing line segments?

   a. Click the left mouse button.

   b. Double-click.

   c. Press <Enter>.

   d. Type **Done** in the Command Line.

2. When drawing a line using the **Line** command, you can specify its length, but not its angle.

   a. True

   b. False

3. Which of the following statements are true for Polar Tracking and Ortho mode? (Select all that apply.)

   a. With Polar Tracking on, a dotted tracking line displays when the cursor is at a specified angle location.

   b. Ortho Mode enables you to draw lines horizontally and vertically only.

   c. With Ortho Mode on, you can draw lines at specified preset angles.

   d. ⌐ (Ortho Mode) and ⟳ ▾ (Polar Tracking) can be used (toggled on) at the same time.

4. What is the best method to draw a perfectly horizontal line using the **Line** command?

   a. Drag the cursor horizontally until it looks horizontal.

   b. Toggle on Ortho Mode.

   c. Draw a line at any angle and then rotate it until it is horizontal.

   d. Follow the horizontal line of the grid.

5. How do you draw a rectangle using the **Rectangle** command?

   a. Draw individual lines and join them together to form a rectangle.

   b. Click and create three corners of the rectangle with the fourth corner being created automatically.

   c. Click to specify all the four corners of the rectangle.

   d. Click the first corner of the rectangle and then click the diagonally opposite corner.

6. Which one of the following is NOT a method for drawing circles with the **Circle** command?

   a. **Tan, Tan, Radius**

   b. **Center, Radius**

   c. **Tan, Tan, Point**

   d. **2 Points**

Command Summary

Button	Command	Location
	Circle	• **Ribbon:** *Home* tab>Draw panel • **Command Prompt:** circle or C
	Erase	• **Ribbon:** *Home* tab>Modify panel • **Command Prompt:** erase, E, or press <Delete>
	Line	• **Ribbon:** *Home* tab>Draw panel • **Command Prompt:** line or L
	Ortho Mode	• **Status Bar** • **Command Prompt:** ortho or <F8>
	Polar Tracking	• **Status Bar** • **Command Prompt:** <F10>
	Rectangle	• **Ribbon:** *Home* tab>Draw panel • **Command Prompt:** rectangle, rectang, or rec
	Redo	• **Quick Access Toolbar** • **Shortcut Menu:** redo • **Command Prompt:** redo
	Undo	• **Quick Access Toolbar** • **Shortcut Menu:** undo • **Command Prompt:** undo or U

Projects: Creating a Simple Drawing

This chapter contains practice projects that can be used to gain additional hands-on experience with the topics and commands covered so far in this student guide. These practices are intended to be self-guided and do not include step by step information.

Learning Objective in this Chapter

- Create a simple drawing using basic shapes such as lines, circles, and rectangles.

3.1 Create a Simple Drawing

Estimated time for completion: 5 minutes

In this project you will create a simple drawing using the commands **Open**, **Line**, **Circle**, **Rectangle**, **Save**, **Erase**, and **Undo**, as shown in Figure 3–1.

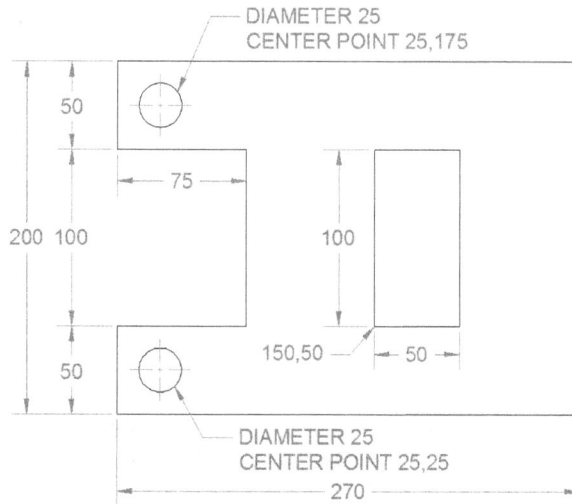

DIAMETER 25
CENTER POINT 25,175

DIAMETER 25
CENTER POINT 25,25

Figure 3–1

1. Open **Simple1-M.dwg** from your practice files folder. It is an empty drawing file.

2. Draw the object shown in Figure 3–1. Start with the lower left corner of the figure at point 0,0. Use exact coordinates to locate the centers of the circles and the first corner of the rectangle. Draw only the object, not the dimensions as they are for reference only.

3. Save and close the drawing.

3.2 Create Simple Shapes

Estimated time for completion: 5 minutes

In this project you will create several simple shapes using the **Line** command, as shown in Figure 3–2.

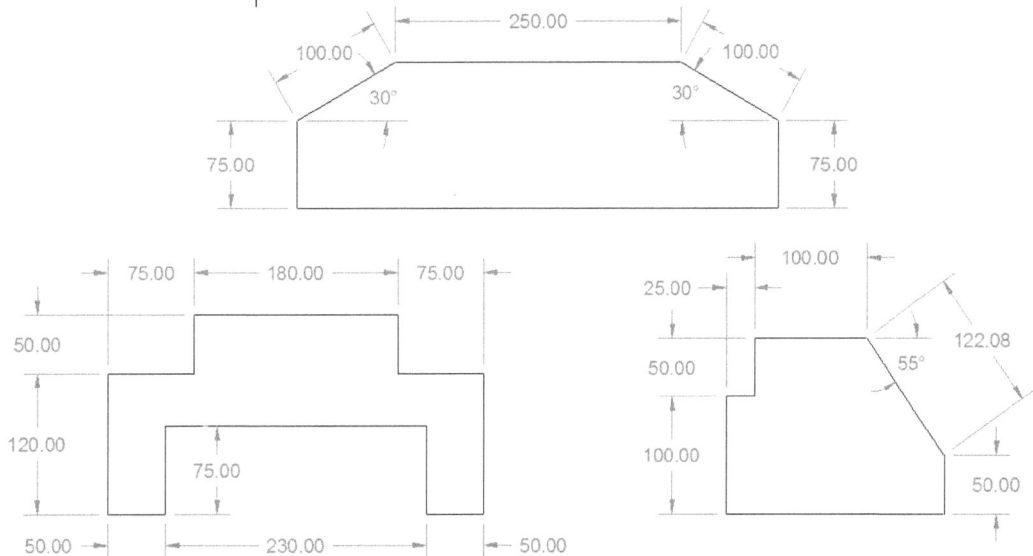

Figure 3–2

1. Open **Simple2-M.dwg** from your practice files folder. It is an empty drawing file.

2. Use the **Line** command to draw the shapes shown in Figure 3–2.

    *   Use the lower left corner of each shape as the starting point and draw the shape clockwise.
    *   Use the **Close** option for the last line segment.
    *   You can select any point on the screen as the starting point, the exact coordinate location does not matter.
    *   If you make a mistake on one segment, use the **Undo** option.

3. Save and close the drawing.

Drawing Precision in AutoCAD

In this chapter you learn how to select exact points on objects using Object Snaps, to use Object Snap overrides, to draw lines at specific angles using Polar Tracking, to specify distances using Polar Snap, to find exact locations using Object Snap Tracking, and to use Snap and Grid (optional).

Learning Objectives in this Chapter

- Snap to specific points on an object and set object snaps to remain toggled on.
- Override running object snaps with a specific object snap to select the correct part of an object.
- Draw vertical and horizontal lines at specific angle increments.
- Locate new points relative to existing ones.
- Restrict the crosshair movement to specific increments.
- Display a grid in the Drawing Window.

4.1 Using Running Object Snaps

When the AutoCAD® software saves information in a drawing file, it saves geometrical descriptions of the objects you have created. For example, a line is saved as two end points and a circle by its center point and radius. Object snaps enable you to take advantage of this geometrical precision by snapping to exact points on objects while you are in a command, as shown in Figure 4–1. You need some object snaps to be on most of the time, which can be set up as *running* object snaps.

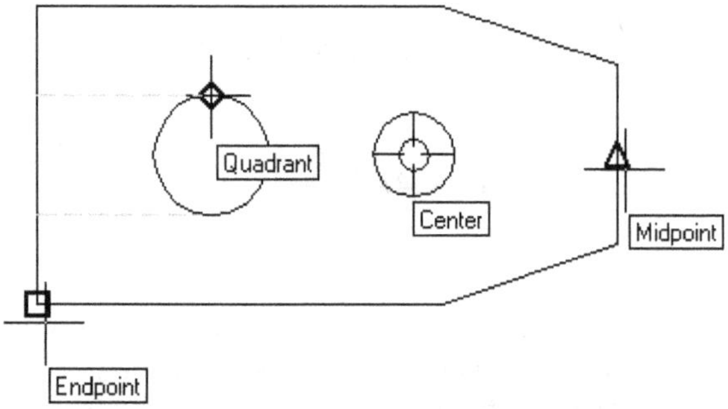

Figure 4–1

How To: Use Running Object Snaps

You can also use <F3> to toggle object snaps on and off.

1. In the Status Bar, toggle on ⬜ ▾ (Object Snap).
2. Start a command, such as **Line** or **Circle**.
3. Hover the cursor over an object. When the cursor is near a snap location, an icon displays that is specific to the object snap option that the cursor finds.
4. Click to select the object snap point.
5. Continue selecting other points, as required.

• When using an Object Snap on an object that might have more than one such point (e.g., **Endpoint** or **Midpoint**), select a point on the object that is close to the required point.

Object Snap Settings

You can set the various running object snap options that are available for use while picking a point. To use them, toggle the Object Snap on in the Status Bar. You can set the running object snaps at the following locations:

- In the □ ▼ (Object Snap) drop-down list in the Status Bar (shown on the left in Figure 4–2).

- In the Drafting Settings dialog box, in the *Object Snap* tab (shown on the right in Figure 4–2). To open the dialog box, expand □ ▼ (Object Snap) in the Status Bar and select **Object Snap Settings...**.

*You can also right-click on □ ▼ (Object Snap) and select **Object Snap Settings...**.*

In the AutoCAD LT® software, the 3D Object Snap tab is not available.

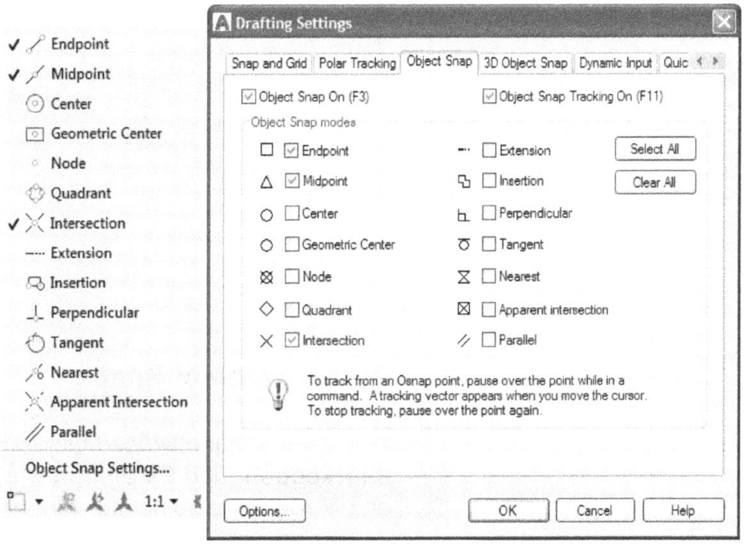

Figure 4–2

- Running object snaps are indicated by a checkmark.

- You can add or remove the Object snap options when you are in the middle of a command.

- The symbol for each Object snap mode displays in the drawing window when you hover the cursor over the snap location. After a short delay, a small tooltip also displays the name of the snap.

- Object snap settings are saved in the system (not in individual drawings) and remain set until changed.

- When you toggle ⬚ ▾ (Object Snap) on or off in the Status Bar, it does not change the settings.

- Clicking **Options** in the Drafting Settings dialog box opens the Options dialog box in the *Drafting* tab. Here, you can change the color of the Autosnap marker and modify other settings, as shown in Figure 4–3.

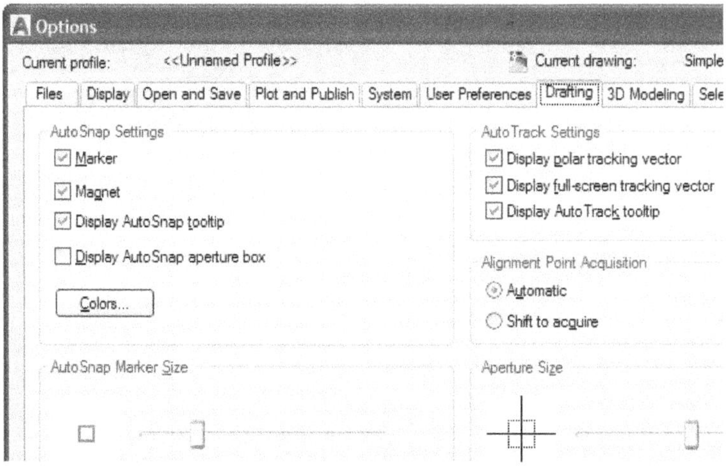

Figure 4–3

Primary Object Snaps

The most frequently used Object Snaps are **Endpoint**, **Center**, **Intersection**, and **Extension** where as **Quadrant**, **Midpoint**, and **Node** are also helpful in certain situations.

✎ ☐ ☑ Endpoint	Snaps to the end point of a line or arc.
✎ △ ☑ Midpoint	Snaps to the midpoint of a line or arc.
◎ ○ ☑ Center	Snaps to the center point of a circle or arc. You can hover the cursor over the edge of the circle or arc to get the center point, if **Quadrant** is not toggled on.
○ ⊠ ☐ Node	Snaps to a permanent reference point.
◈ ◇ ☐ Quadrant	Snaps to the quadrant point of a circle or arc (often described as clock positions (i.e., 12, 3, 6, and 9 o'clock).

✕ ✕ ☑ Intersection	Snaps to the intersection of two objects. **Intersection** can be used in two ways: click directly on the intersection, or select the first object for the intersection and then the second. Intersections that do not actually exist, but would if the two lines were extended, can be selected in this manner.
---- ▪▪ ☑ Extension	Snaps to a point on the continuation of an object.

How To: Use the Extension Object Snap

The **Extension** Object Snap works differently than the rest of the primary Object Snaps. Instead of selecting a point, it enables you to specify a start point at a distance from another point. In the example shown in Figure 4–4, the **Extension** Object Snap is used to start a new wall at a distance from another wall.

Figure 4–4

1. In the Status Bar, toggle on ☐ ▾ (Object Snap) and verify that the **Extension** object snap is selected.
2. Start a command, such as **Line** or **Circle**.
3. Hover the cursor over an object in the drawing. One of the standard Object Snap icons displays. Instead of selecting a point, move the cursor away. A small plus symbol (glyph) displays at the snap location.
4. When the cursor reaches a point along the line of the object, a dashed line displays from the end of the object to the crosshairs. In addition, a snap tip displays indicating the distance from the object and its angle. Enter the distance that you want to be from the original point.

Geometric Center Object Snap

The **Geometric Center** object snap tool finds the geometric center (centroid) of a closed polyline, as shown in Figure 4–5. It finds the geometric center of any closed irregular shape.

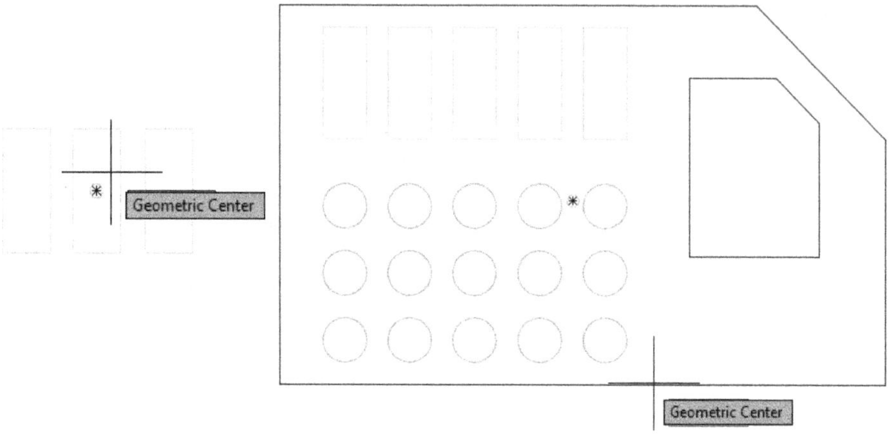

Figure 4–5

Practice 4a

Using Object Snaps

Practice Objective

Estimated time for completion: 5 minutes

- Draw a fence and rooflines using Object Snaps.

In this practice, you will set Object Snaps and use them to draw a fence line and rooflines, as shown in Figure 4–6.

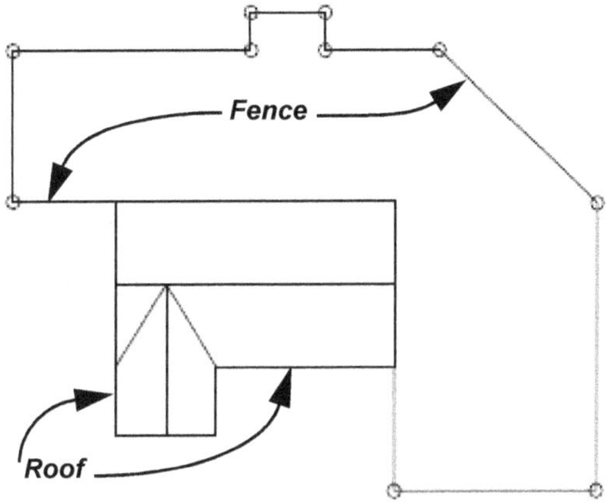

Figure 4–6

Task 1 - Draw the fence.

1. Open **Fence-AM.dwg** from your practice files folder.

2. In the Status Bar, expand ⬜ ▼ (Object Snap) to display the object snaps list. Set the Object Snap modes to **Endpoint**, **Midpoint**, **Center**, and **Extension**. Toggle Object Snap on.

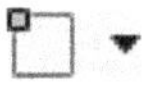

3. Start the **Line** command to draw a fence as shown in Figure 4–6. Start by snapping and clicking to the endpoint of the upper left corner of the house. Moving clockwise, snap and click to the center of each of the fence posts (i.e., the small circles provided in the drawing). End the fence by snapping and clicking to the endpoint of the bottom right corner of the house.

Task 2 - Draw the roof lines.

1. In the Status Bar, expand ▢ ▼ (Object Snap) and select **Intersection**.

2. In the Status Bar, toggle on ⟳ ▼ (Polar Tracking), if required. Start the **Line** command again and draw line (1) from the midpoint on the right side of the house straight left to the point where it intersects the left side, as shown in Figure 4–7. This indicates the main roof ridge.

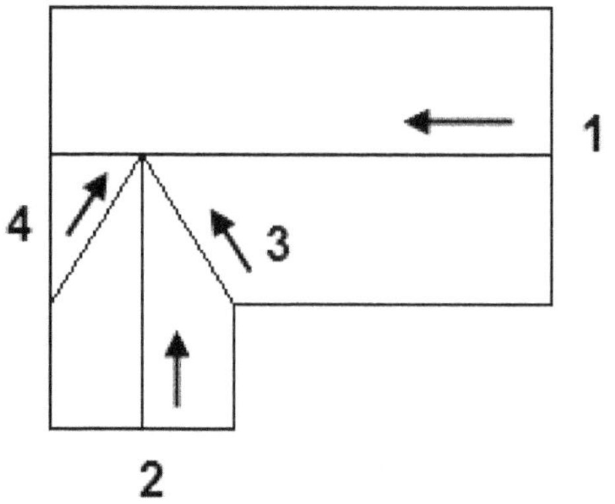

Figure 4–7

3. Draw line (2) from the midpoint of the front wing of the house straight up to the intersection of the ridge you just drew. This creates the ridge of the wing.

4. Draw line (3) from the top right corner enpoint of the wing to the intersection of the two ridge lines.

5. For line (4), after starting the **Line** command, hover the cursor over the bottom left corner of the house and then pull it up without selecting the point. The **Extension** Object snap tooltip displays near the cursor indicating that it is enabled. Enter a distance of **2500**. Press <Enter>. The line starts at this point. End it at the intersection of the two ridge lines.

6. Save and close the drawing.

4.2 Using Object Snap Overrides

You can use ☐ ▼ (Object Snap) for the points to which you normally snap. Other snaps, such as **Tangent** or **Perpendicular**, are required less often. Instead of selecting and then clearing those Object snaps using the ☐ ▼ (Object Snap) list, you can apply them as one-time *object snap overrides*. Object Snaps applied as overrides are only active for the next point you select. You can access overrides through shortcut menus when you are in a command, as shown in Figure 4–8.

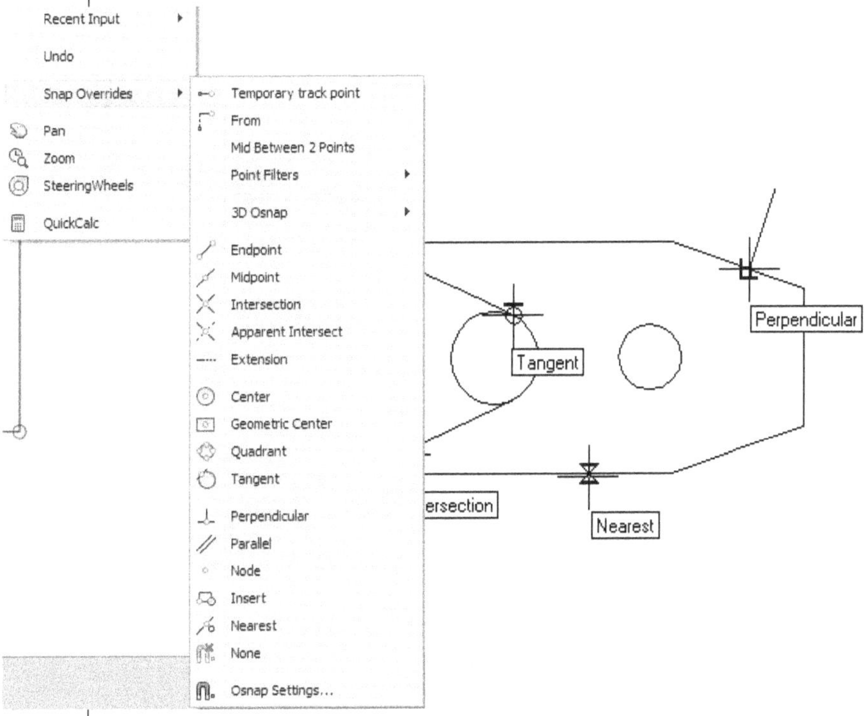

Figure 4–8

- You must start a command before using an Object Snap override. You can then set the Object Snap override in the shortcut menu by selecting **Snap Overrides**, or by holding <Shift> while right-clicking.

How To: Use an Object Snap Override

1. Start a command where point input is required, such as **Line** or **Circle**.
2. Before selecting the point, select an Object Snap override.
3. Move the crosshairs near the location of the object to which you want to snap. An icon for the running object snap displays at the snap location.
4. Click to select the point.

- If you select the wrong Object Snap, do not press <Esc> or use the **Undo** command (doing so would cancel the command). Instead, select the correct Object Snap override twice. The first time cancels the previous snap and the second sets the new snap.

Typical Object Snap Overrides

○ Tangent	Snaps to a point on a circle or arc that forms a line tangent to the object.
⊥ Perpendicular	Snaps to a point that creates a perpendicular line from one object to another.
// Parallel	Snaps to a point that creates a line parallel to the selected object.
⮂ Insert	Snaps to the insertion point of text, a block, or an external reference.
⁄o Nearest	Snaps to the point on an object that is visually closest to the crosshairs.
None	Toggles off object snaps for the next point selected.

How To: Use the Parallel Object Snap

Parallel can only be used to draw linear objects. At least one point must be selected before **Parallel** can be used. The new line is drawn parallel to the selected object, as shown in Figure 4–9.

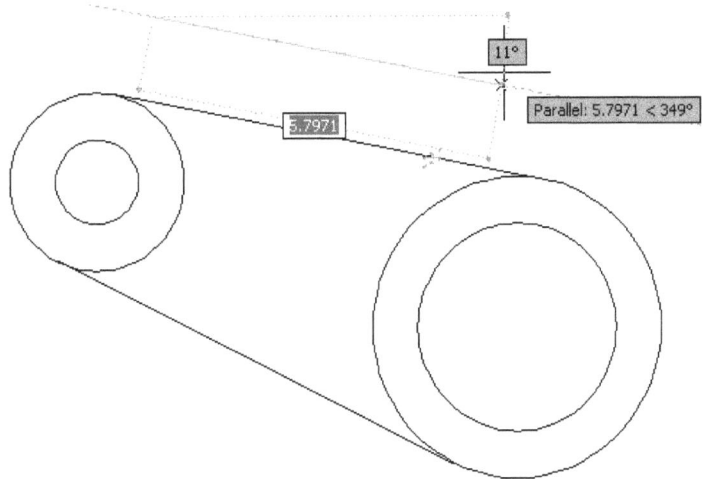

Figure 4–9

1. Start the **Line** command.
2. Select a starting point in the drawing.
3. Select the Parallel Object Snap override.
4. Hover the cursor over the object to which the new line should be parallel. First, the **Parallel** icon displays and when you move the cursor away a small plus symbol displays on the object.
5. Move the crosshairs away from the object. When you reach a point that makes the new line parallel to the selected object, a dashed line displays indicating the parallel direction. In addition, a parallel marker and snap tip display. Enter the distance or select the point that you want to use.

Practice 4b | Object Snap Overrides

Practice Objective

- Draw objects at precise locations with respect to already present objects in a drawing.

Estimated time for completion: 5 minutes

In this practice, you will use a variety of running object snaps and overrides in conjunction with the **Line** and **Circle** commands to complete a drawing, as shown in Figure 4–10.

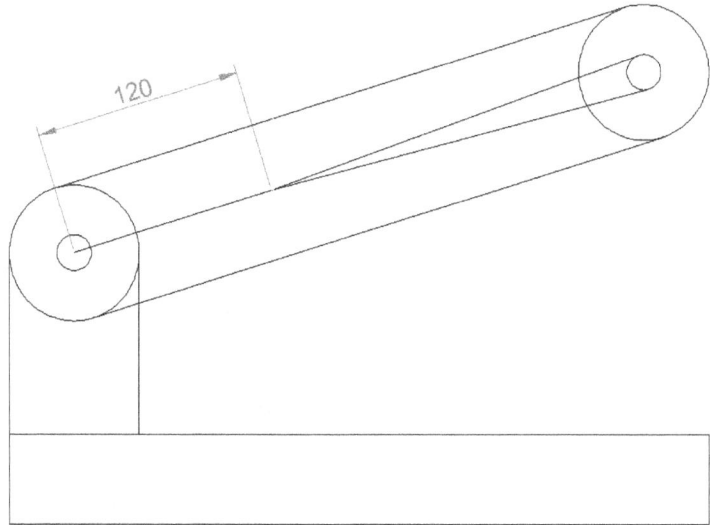

Figure 4–10

1. Open **Arm-M.dwg** from your practice files folder.

2. Set the object snaps to **Endpoint**, **Midpoint**, and **Center** and toggle ⬜ ▼ (Object Snap) on, if required.

Click anywhere on the circumference of the circle to snap to its center point.

3. With Circle> ⊘ (Center Radius), draw circles with a radius of **10** at the center of the two existing circles.

The object snap overrides must be specified each time you use one.

4. Draw lines connecting the large circles tangent to each circle. Start the **Line** command and at *Specify point*, use <Shift>+ right-click to open the shortcut menu. Select **Tangent** override. Click anywhere along the upper edge of the bigger lower left large circle, as shown in Figure 4–11.

Figure 4–11

5. Use <Shift>+ right-click again and select the **Tangent** override. Click along the upper edge of the bigger upper right large circle. Press <Enter> to exit the **Line** command. A line is drawn along the top tangent points of the two large circles.

6. Similarly, draw another line along the bottom tangent points of the two large circles.

7. Start the **Line** command and use <Shift>+ right-click to select the **Quadrant** override. Click along the 9 o'clock quadrant of the lower large circle. Click along the upper left end point of the rectangle to draw the line. (The **Endpoint** object snap is already selected.)

8. Draw a line from the 3 o'clock quadrant of the lower large circle perpendicular to the top of the rectangle.

9. Draw a line that starts at the center of the small circle on the left, parallel (use the **Parallel** override) to one of the diagonal lines and **120 units** long. From that point, continue the line tangent to the small circle on the right.

10. Draw one more line from the end point of the parallel line tangent to the other side of the small circle on the right side.

11. Save and close the drawing.

4.3 Polar Tracking at Angles

You can use Polar Tracking to draw horizontal lines, vertical lines, and lines at specific increment angles. ↻ ▼ (Polar Tracking) can be toggled on or off in the Status Bar. Right-click on ↻ ▼ (Polar Tracking) to select from the list of standard angles (as shown in Figure 4–12) to set the increment angles. You can also set the increment angle while working in a command.

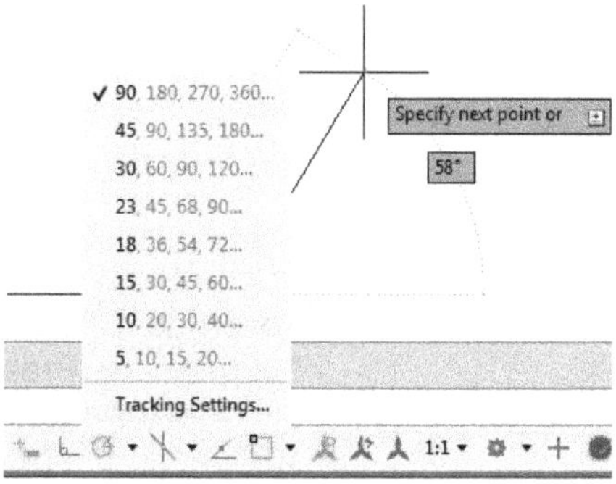

Figure 4–12

Polar Tracking Settings

You can also right-click on ↻ ▼ (Polar Tracking) and select Tracking Settings...

For more Polar Tracking options, expand ↻ ▼ (Polar Tracking) and select **Tracking Settings...** to open the Drafting Settings dialog box, as shown in Figure 4–13. In this dialog box you can specify additional angles and modify other settings.

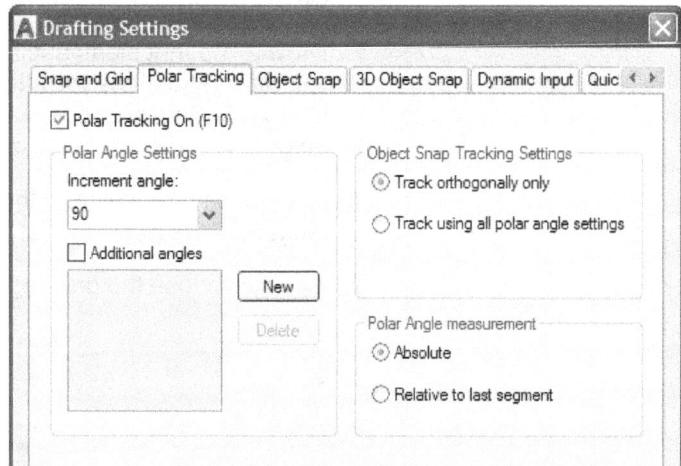

Figure 4–13

Increment angle: [dropdown]	Select an angle in the Increment angle list. All these angles are listed in the Polar Tracking list, which is available in the Status Bar.
☑ Additional angles 35	Select this option to use angles other than the one specified in the Increment angle list. You can only snap to this angle (not to its multiples) and to multiples from the Increment angle list. The angle gets added to the Polar Tracking list.
New	Click to add an additional angle. You can add up to ten additional polar tracking alignment angles.
Delete	Deletes selected additional angles.

- When the **Absolute** option is selected, Polar Tracking is relative to the current X- and Y-axes. For example, if the *Increment Angle* is set to **90** and you draw a diagonal line at 40 degrees for the first segment, the subsequent line is still drawn in increments of 90 degrees relative to the X- and Y-axes (to the right, left, up, or down), as shown on the left in Figure 4–14.

- When the **Relative to last segment** option is selected, Polar Tracking is relative to the last segment drawn or to a segment to which you snap using OSNAP. This means that you can draw the subsequent line in 90 degree increments from the diagonal line drawn, as shown on the right in Figure 4–14.

Figure 4–14

- In the Polar Tracking settings, you can select **Track orthogonally only** (i.e., horizontally and vertically) or **Track using all polar angle settings**.

Practice 4c | # Polar Tracking

Practice Objective

- Draw an outline of a part using Polar Tracking and by setting the Polar Tracking options.

Estimated time for completion: 5 minutes

In this practice, you will adjust the Polar Tracking settings and then use **Polar Tracking** to draw the outline of the part, as shown in Figure 4–15.

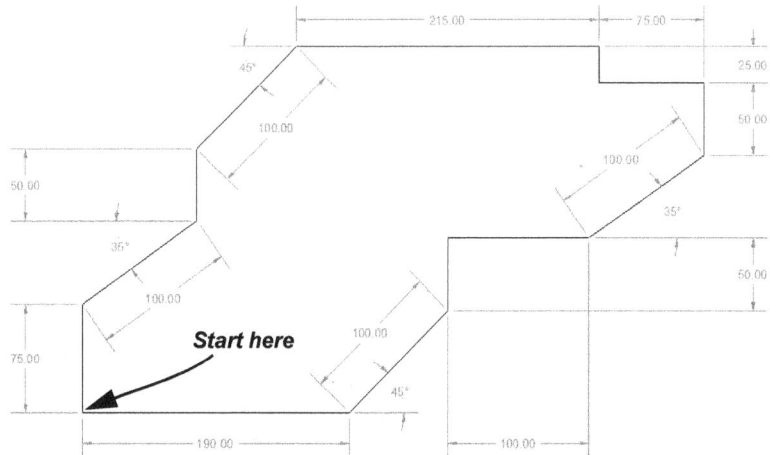

Figure 4–15

1. Open **Pattern-M.dwg** from your practice files folder. It is an empty drawing file.

2. In the Status Bar, expand ⟲ ▼ (Polar Tracking) and select **Tracking Settings...**.

3. In the Drafting Settings dialog box, select **Additional angles** and click **New.** In the edit box that is highlighted, enter **35** to add an additional angle. Click **OK**.

4. In the Status Bar, expand ⟲ ▼ (Polar Tracking) and select **45,90,135,180...**. Ensure that **Polar Tracking** is toggled **On**.

5. Start the **Line** command and select a point in the lower left corner of the screen (shown as "Start here" in Figure 4–15). Move the cursor straight to the right so that the tracking line at 0 degrees displays. Enter **190** and press <Enter>.

6. Move the cursor up and to the right until the 45 degree tracking line displays. Enter **100** and press <Enter>.

The opposite (or complementary) angle for 45 degrees is 135 degrees.

7. Continue to draw the outline (as shown in Figure 4–15) finding the appropriate tracking angle and typing the distance for each segment.

8. For the last angled segment, the 35 degree tracking does not work (because it is the opposite or complementary angle of 145 degrees, which is not set). Enter a distance of **100** (do not press <Enter>) and then use <Tab> to enter the angle as **145**.

9. Save and close the drawing.

4.4 Object Snap Tracking

Object Snap Tracking enables you to locate new points in relation to one or two existing points, as shown in Figure 4–16. Using Object Snaps and Object Snap Tracking together can speed up your work.

Object Snaps must be toggled on to use Object Snap Tracking.

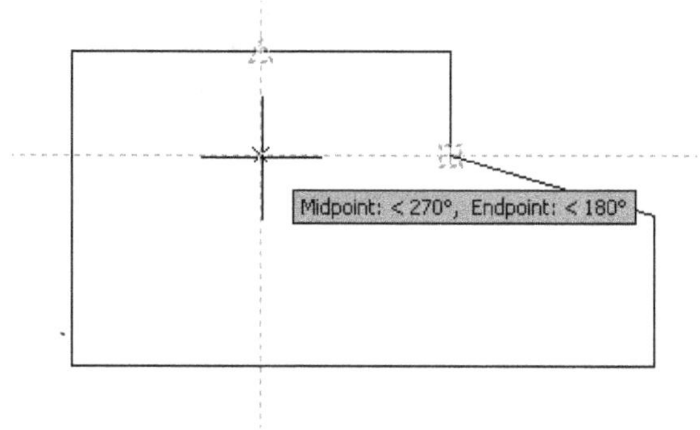

Figure 4–16

- Tracking builds a new point based on coordinates taken from two other points. The new X-coordinate is from one point and the new Y-coordinate from another point.

- When a point is selected for Object Snap Tracking, a small plus displays at the point. The point is said to be *acquired*. A dotted line displays from that point to indicate tracking.

- To clear an acquired point, move the cursor over the point again. Ensure that the small plus disappears.

- You can use Object Snap Tracking with Polar Tracking toggled on or off. However, in some cases Polar Tracking can interfere with the effects of Object Snap Tracking.

How To: Use Object Snap Tracking With One Point

You can also use <F11> to toggle object snap tracking on and off.

1. In the Status Bar, toggle on both ⬚ ▾ (Object Snap) and ◺ (Object Snap Tracking) and set the Object Snap options that you want to use.
2. Start a command, such as **Line**.

3. Hover the cursor over the point from which you want to track (do not click on it). A small plus marks the point, as shown in Figure 4–17.

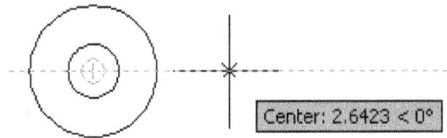

Figure 4–17

4. Move the cursor away from the point. A dotted line and tooltip display when the cursor locks into a tracking angle.
5. Enter the distance that you want to use and press <Enter>.

How To: Use Object Snap Tracking With Two Points

1. In the Status Bar, toggle on both ⬚ ▼ (Object Snap) and ⟋ (Object Snap Tracking) and set the Object Snap options that you want to use.
2. Start a command, such as **Line**.
3. Hover the cursor over the points from which you want to track (do not click on them). Small plusses mark each point.
4. Two dotted lines display, each passing through an acquired point. Move the cursor to the point at which the lines intersect. A description of each dotted line displays in the tooltip, as shown in Figure 4–18.

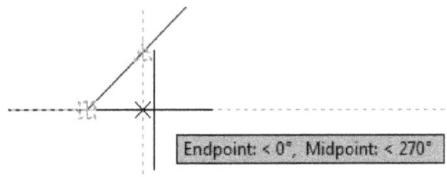

Figure 4–18

5. Select the point at the intersection of the tracking lines.

Practice 4d | Object Snap Tracking I

Estimated time for completion: 5 minutes

Practice Objective

- Create a top view of a part by using Object Snap Tracking.

In this practice, you will create a top view of a part by tracking the locations from the existing front and side views, as shown in Figure 4–19. Construction lines have been provided from the side view, and the other construction lines do not need to be drawn.

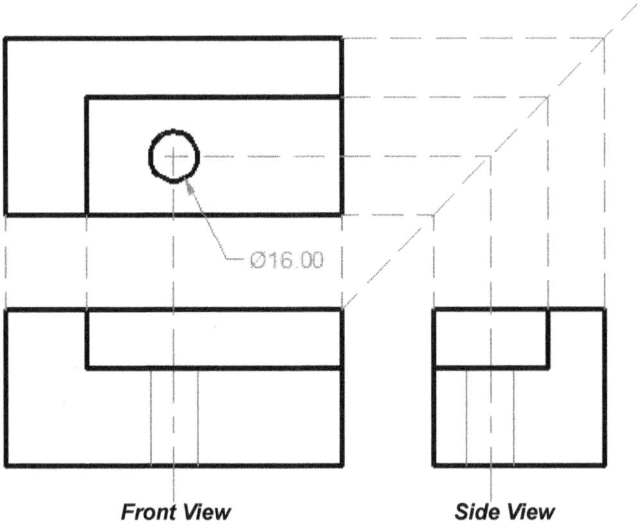

Front View   *Side View*

Figure 4–19

1. Open **Missing View-M.dwg** from your practice files folder.

2. Set the current Object Snaps as **Endpoint**, **Midpoint**, **Center**, **Quadrant**, and **Intersection**.

3. Toggle on ⬚ ▾ (Object Snap) and ∠ (Object Snap Tracking), if required.

4. Start the **Line** command. At the *Specify first point:* prompt, hover the cursor over the top left corner of the front view, which displays the **Endpoint** object snap icon. Then, without clicking, move the cursor. Note that a small green plus mark displays at the top left corner of the front view. Hover the cursor over the top end point of the shortest construction line coming from the side view.

5. Move the cursor to where the two tracking lines intersect at a point, as shown in Figure 4–20. Select that point as the first point for the line.

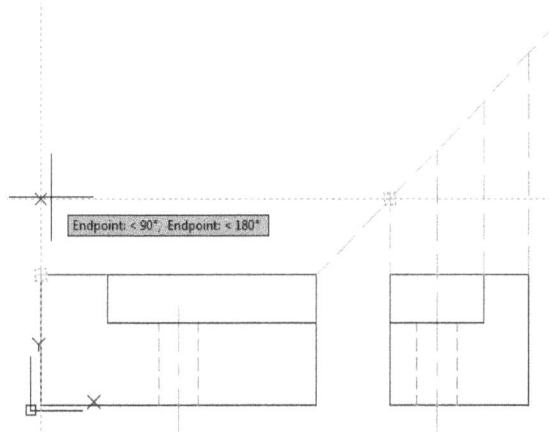

Endpoint: < 90°, Endpoint: < 180°

Figure 4–20

6. Continue to draw the rectangular outline of the top view, tracking from the appropriate points.

7. Draw the two interior lines on the top view (as shown in Figure 4–19) using tracking points.

8. Draw a circle (diameter=**16**) whose center point is established by tracking points.

9. Save and close the drawing.

Practice 4e

Object Snap Tracking II

Estimated time for completion: 10 minutes

Practice Objective

- Draw lines in a schematic diagram using Object Snap Tracking.

In this practice, you will use Object Snap Tracking to draw lines in a schematic diagram.

1. Open **Process-M.dwg** from your practice files folder.

2. Set the Object Snaps to **Midpoint** and **Quadrant**. Ensure that ⬜ ▼ (Object Snap) and ◿ (Object Snap Tracking) are toggled on.

3. Use Object Snap Tracking to add lines between the Bleed Storage and Pump.

   - Zoom in on the two parts.
   - Start the **Line** command.
   - Select the midpoint on the bottom line of the Bleed Storage as the first point. Doing so also acquires the midpoint as a tracking point.
   - Hover the cursor over the left quadrant osnap of the Pump and then move the cursor away from that point (do not click). A small cross displays at the point.
   - Move the cursor to the left of the Pump. A snap tip and dotted tracking lines display from the Bleed Storage and Pump. When both tracking lines display (as shown on the left in Figure 4–21) click to place the second point of the line.
   - For the next point, select the left quadrant of the Pump, as shown on the right in Figure 4–21.

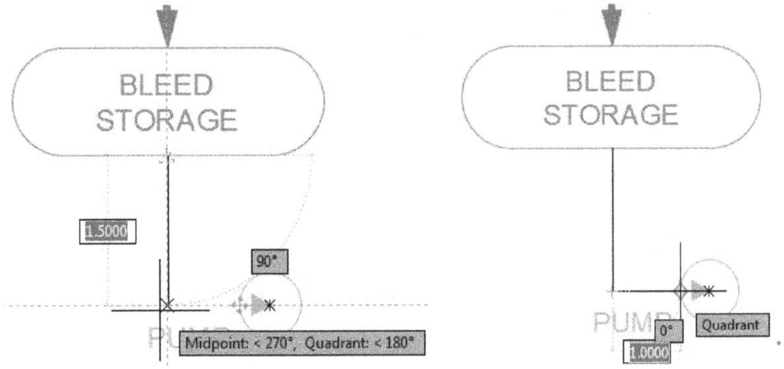

Figure 4–21

4. Draw additional lines between the components, as shown in Figure 4–22.

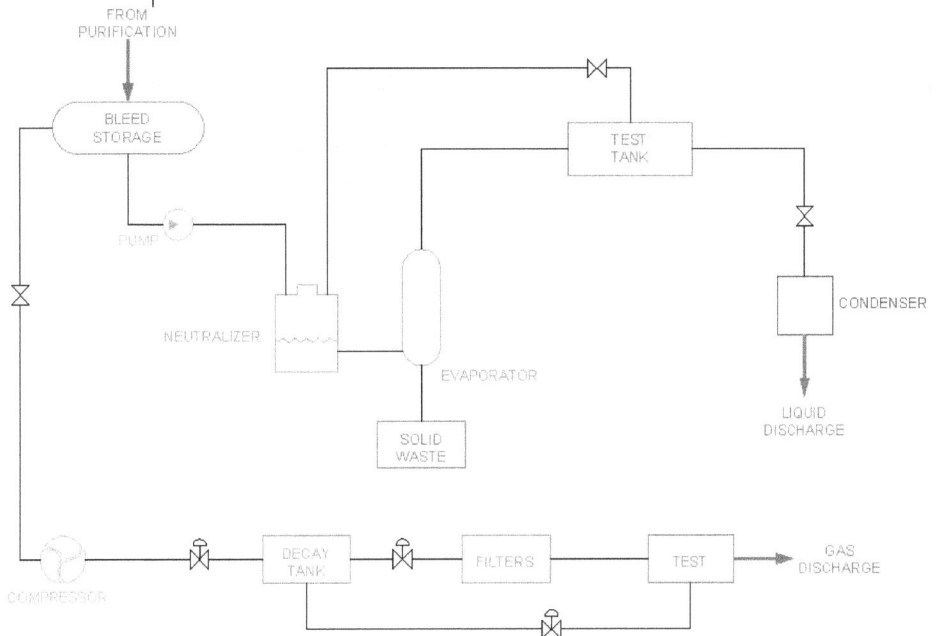

Figure 4–22

5. Save and close the drawing.

4.5 (Optional) Drawing with Snap and Grid

The AutoCAD Snap Mode and Grid Display are useful in schematic drawings, in which the objects are not drawn using real-world sizes or distances but are often lined up and evenly spaced, as shown in Figure 4–23.

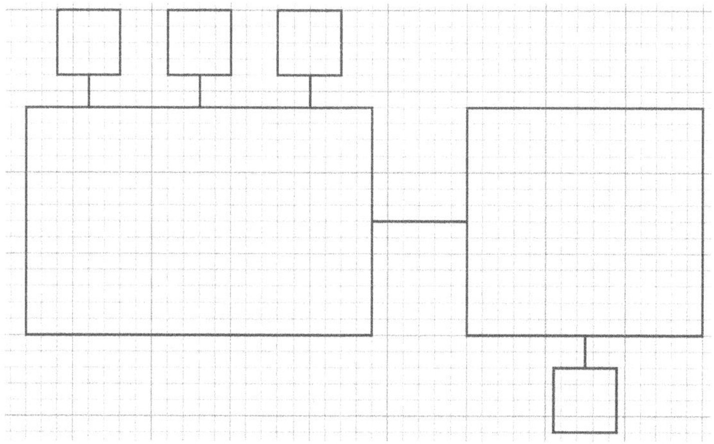

Figure 4–23

Snap Mode restricts the movement of the crosshairs to specific increments, such as 1 unit or 0.5 units. When **Snap Mode** is toggled on, objects you draw are forced to use an invisible snap grid based on the set *Snap spacing*. Click ⣿ ▼ (Snap Mode) in the Status Bar or press <F9> to toggle it on or off, as shown in Figure 4–24.

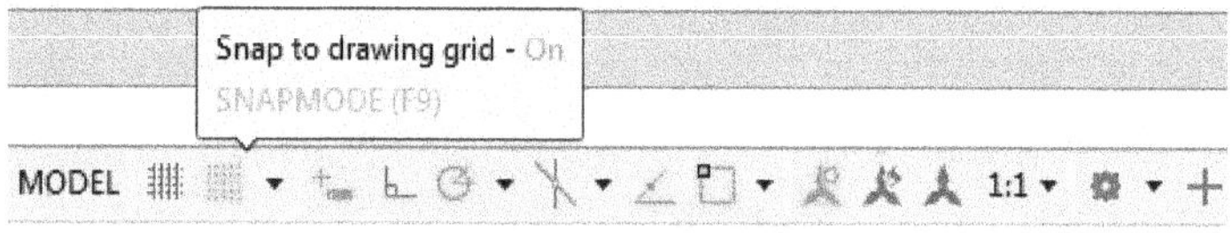

Snap to drawing grid - On
SNAPMODE (F9)

MODEL

Figure 4–24

The **Grid Display** is a series of lines in the drawing window, which act as a visual reference. In appearance it is similar to engineering graph paper. The *Grid spacing* can be the same as or different to the Snap spacing. The command does not affect the movement of the crosshairs and does not print. Click

▓ (Grid Display) in the Status Bar or press <F7> to toggle it on or off, as shown in Figure 4–25.

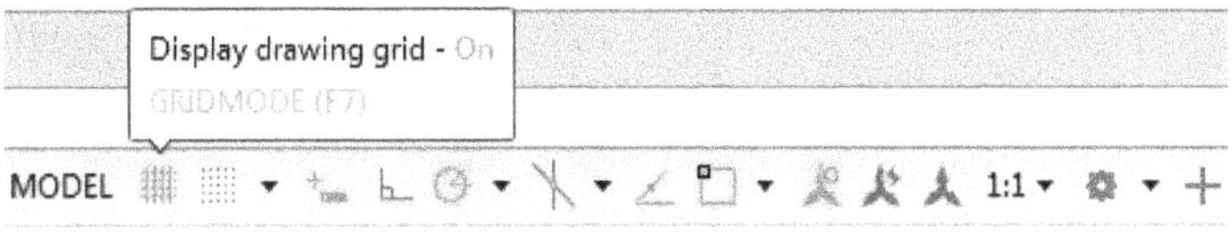

Figure 4–25

Snap and Grid Settings

You can set the various snap and grid options in the Drafting Settings dialog box, in the *Snap and Grid* tab, as shown in Figure 4–26. Expand ▒ ▼ (Snap Mode) and select **Snap Settings** to open the Drafting Settings dialog box.

*   To set the Snap or Grid spacing in a drawing, set the X- and Y-spacing for the Snap and/or Grid (these are usually the same).

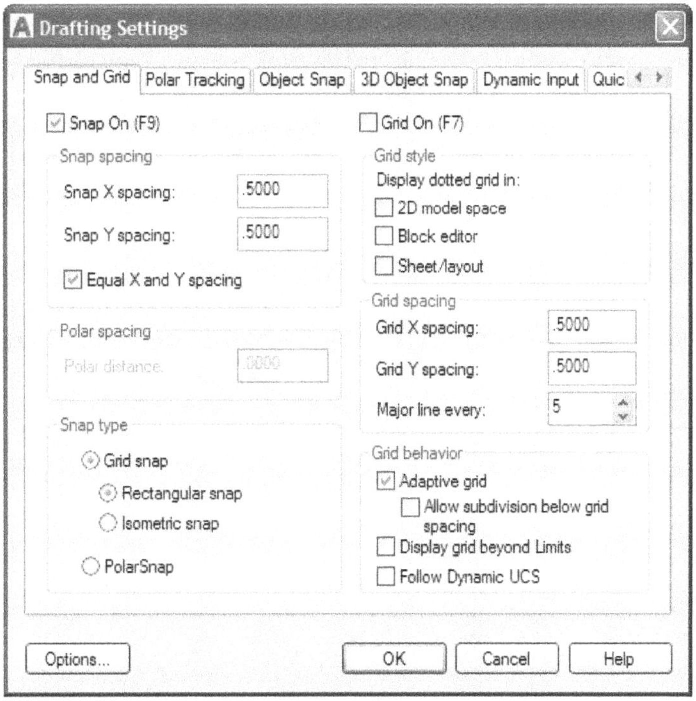

*In the AutoCAD LT software, the **Follow Dynamic UCS** option is not available.*

Figure 4–26

The Snap type options can be easily set from the ⊞ ▼ *(Snap Mode) drop-down list.*

- The normal *Snap type* is **Grid snap>Rectangular snap**, which is a rectangular array similar to the grid. If the *Snap type* is set to **Polar Snap** instead, the snap increments are measured along the Polar tracking lines (this only works when Polar Tracking is on). In this case, you set the Polar spacing for the required increment.

- When the *Snap type* is set to **Isometric snap**, the grid and cursor become angled. This makes it much easier to draw a 2D isometric part, as shown in Figure 4–27.

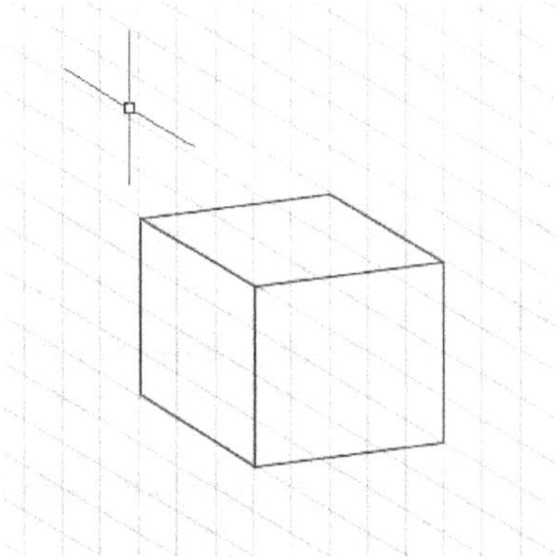

Figure 4–27

- The *Grid style* options enable you to display the grid as a series of dots rather than lines and have it display differently for specific functions, such as the Block editor.

- You can use *Grid behavior* to further control how the grid is used. These tools are especially useful when you start working in 3D.

*The **Legacy** option is only available as a Command Line option of the **Snap** command.*

- You can use the **Legacy** option, which forces the cursor to always snap to the snap grid. If the **Legacy** option is toggled off, you cannot snap to the snap grid unless you are in an active command. Type **Snap** in the Command Line and select **Legacy**. Select **Yes** to toggle on the option.

Isometric Drawing Environment

When the Isometric Drafting is toggled on, the icon displays the cursor lines in red and green.

When the *Snap type* is set to **Isometric snap**, the rotation of the grid can be controlled using the **Isometric Drafting** tool in the Status Bar.

- Click ⟨ ▾ (Isometric Drafting) in the Status Bar to toggle the Isometric Drawing environment on or off.

- Expand ⟨ ▾ (Isometric Drafting) and click on one of the following options to select the environment in which you want to draw.

  - ⟨ (Isoplane Left)

  - ✕ (Isoplane Top)

  - ⟨ (Isoplane Right)

  The cursor and grid display is oriented to suit the selected option, as shown for **Isoplane Top** in Figure 4–28.

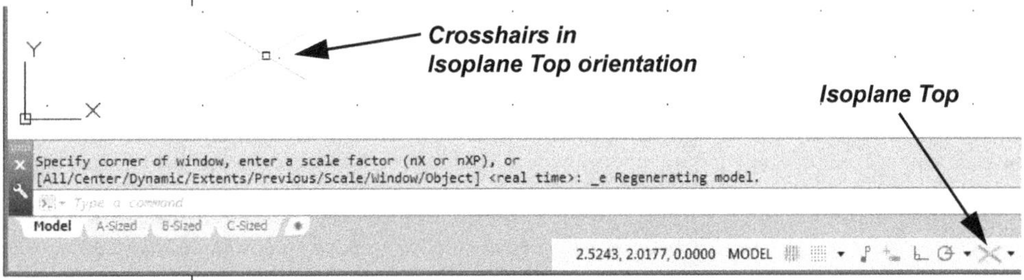

Crosshairs in Isoplane Top orientation

Isoplane Top

Specify corner of window, enter a scale factor (nX or nXP), or
[All/Center/Dynamic/Extents/Previous/Scale/Window/Object] <real time>: _e Regenerating model.

Model   A-Sized   B-Sized   C-Sized

2.5243, 2.0177, 0.0000   MODEL

Figure 4–28

Practice 4f

Estimated time for completion: 10 minutes

Placing Objects on a Drawing

Practice Objective

- Place objects in a drawing precisely.

In this practice, you will draw objects using Snap and Grid to help place them precisely, as shown in Figure 4–29.

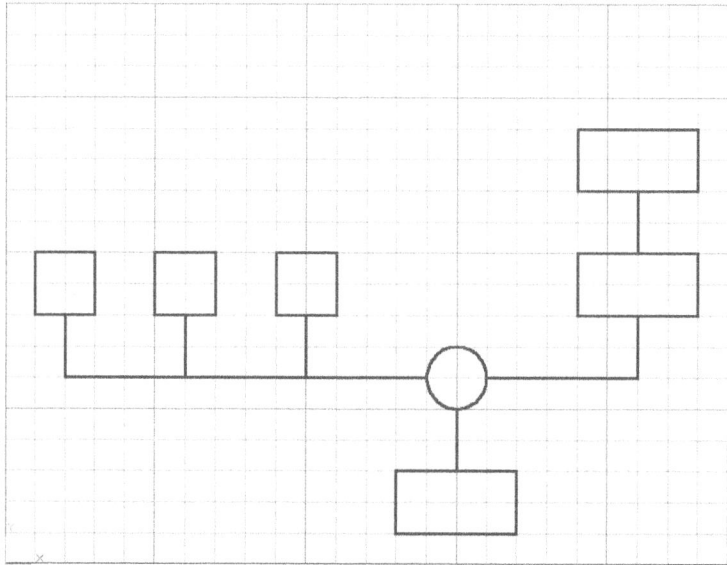

Figure 4–29

1. Open **Schematic-M.dwg** from your practice files folder. It is an empty drawing.

2. In the Status Bar, toggle on ⬚ ▾ (Snap Mode) and ⯐ (Grid Mode). Expand ⬚ ▾ (Snap Mode) and select **Snap Settings**. Set the *Snap* and *Grid spacing* (both X and Y Spacing) to **1.0** and click **OK**.

3. Toggle off ▢ ▾ (Object Snap).

4. Draw the objects shown Figure 4–29, starting with the circle (**radius=1**). The rectangles should be **2 x 2** and **4 x 2**. The exact distance between objects does not matter, only that they line up evenly.

5. Save and close the drawing.

Chapter Review Questions

1. When you set Object Snap options in the Drafting Settings dialog box, the object snaps are:

   a. Tracking points for Object Snap Tracking.

   b. Overrides to preset object snaps.

   c. The same as the object snaps in the shortcut menu.

   d. Available when you need to pick a point.

2. What types of objects does the **Center** object snap work with?

   a. Circles and lines.

   b. Circles, arcs, and rectangles.

   c. Circles, arcs, and lines.

   d. Circles and arcs.

3. Which tool enables you to position an object at the exact center of a rectangle that was created using the **Rectang** command?

   a. Center Object Snap

   b. Geometric Center Object Snap

   c. Midpoint Object Snap

   d. Intersection Object Snap

4. When can you use an Object Snap override from the shortcut menu?

   a. When Snap Mode is toggled on in the Status Bar.

   b. When Object Snap Mode is toggled on in the Status Bar.

   c. When you start a command and the software prompts you for a point.

   d. Any time.

5. If you set the Polar Tracking increment angles to 18, 36, 54,... you can track to the multiples of 18 degrees in addition to horizontal and vertical lines.

   a. True

   b. False

6. Which settings in the Status Bar should be toggled on to use the Object Snap Tracking?

    a. Object Snap Tracking and Polar Tracking.

    b. Object Snap Tracking and Object Snap.

    c. Object Snap Tracking and Snap.

    d. Only Object Snap Tracking.

7. What happens when you type **Snap** in the Command Line, select **Legacy**, and then select **Yes** to toggle it on?

    a. It forces the cursor to always snap to the snap grid, even if you are not in an active command.

    b. It displays the grid as a series of dots rather than lines.

    c. The snap increments are measured along the Polar tacking lines and works when Polar Tracking is on.

    d. The grid and cursor become angled and makes it easier to draw a 2D isometric part.

Command Summary

Button	Command	Location
	Grid Mode	• **Status Bar** • **Command Prompt:** (*toggle on/off*) <F7>
	Object Snap	• **Status Bar** • **Command Prompt:** (*toggle on/off*) <F3>
N/A	**Object Snap Overrides**	• **Shortcut Menu:** *(when in a command)* Snap Overrides or <Shift> + right-click • **Command Prompt:** *(when in a command) first three letters of the object snap name*
	Object Snap Tracking	• **Status Bar** • **Command Prompt:** (*toggle on/off*) <F11>
	Polar Tracking	• **Status Bar** • **Command Prompt:** (*toggle on/off*) <F10>
	Snap Mode	• **Status Bar** • **Command Prompt:** (*toggle on/off*) <F9>

Making Changes in Your Drawing

In this chapter you learn how to select objects for editing, how to move, copy, rotate, scale, and mirror objects, and how to edit with grips.

Learning Objectives in this Chapter

- Select, move, scale, and rotate objects using various commands.
- Make copies of selected objects.
- Create reversed or symmetrical copies of objects around a mirror line.
- Modify the location, number, and size of objects using grips options.

5.1 Selecting Objects for Editing

When you start most editing commands, the crosshairs display as a small selection box along with the Select objects prompt, as shown in Figure 5–1.

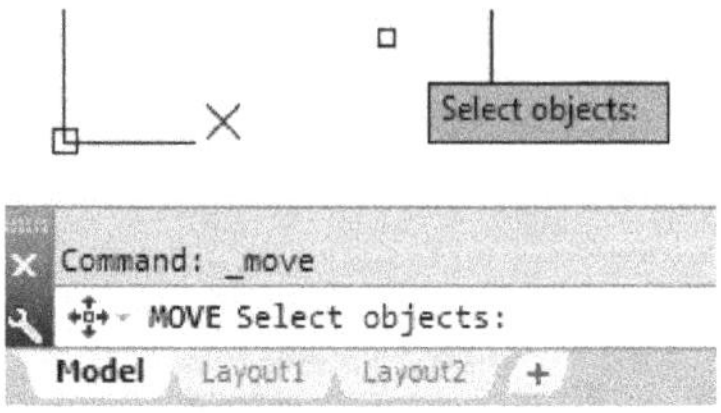

Figure 5–1

How To: Select Objects

1. After starting an editing command, hover the small selection box over an object. The object is highlighted in a thicker line weight.
2. Click to select the object, which highlights in blue, as shown in Figure 5–2.

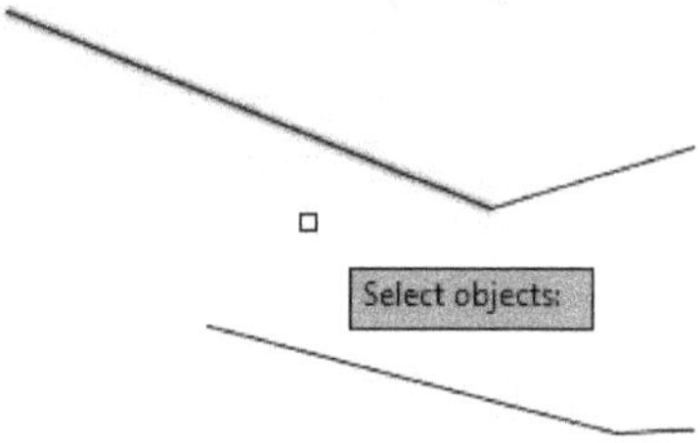

Figure 5–2

3. The cursor continues to display as the small selection box. You can click on another object to add to the selection.
4. Continue selecting objects if you want to add more objects to the selection.
5. When all of the objects have been selected, press <Enter> or right-click to exit the *Select objects:* prompt and continue with the command.

Implied Selection

You can select individual objects or draw a box, line, or lasso around multiple objects to select them together. When using any of the selection methods, the objects to be selected are highlighted in a thicker line weight before the selection is completed. Once the objects have been selected, they are highlighted in blue and a thicker line weight.

*You can also start a Window or Crossing selection by typing **W** or **C** at the Select objects: prompt. With this method, it does not matter how you select the points to define the selection box.*

- **Window selection:** If you click to select the first point and then move the cursor to the right, a blue area with a solid border displays, as shown on the left in Figure 5–3. Any objects that are completely inside the boundary are selected.

- **Crossing selection:** If you click to select the first point and then move the cursor to the left, a green area with a dashed border displays, as shown on the right in Figure 5–3. Any objects inside or crossing the boundary are selected.

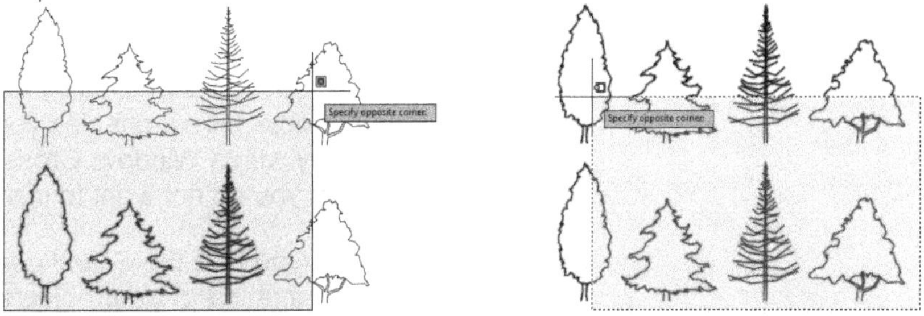

Window (blue)   *Crossing (green)*

Figure 5–3

- **Lasso selection:** If you click and hold the mouse button to select the first point and then drag the cursor to the left or right, a lasso shape displays. If you drag to the right, the selection area displays in blue with a solid outline, as shown on the left in Figure 5–4. Objects are selected as they would be when using a Window selection. If you drag to the left, the selection area displays in green with a dashed border, as shown on the right in Figure 5–4. Objects are selected as they would be when using the Crossing selection. You can use the Lasso selection to create non-rectangular shapes. You can also press <Spacebar> to toggle between the Window, Crossing, and Fence selection modes when using the Lasso selection.

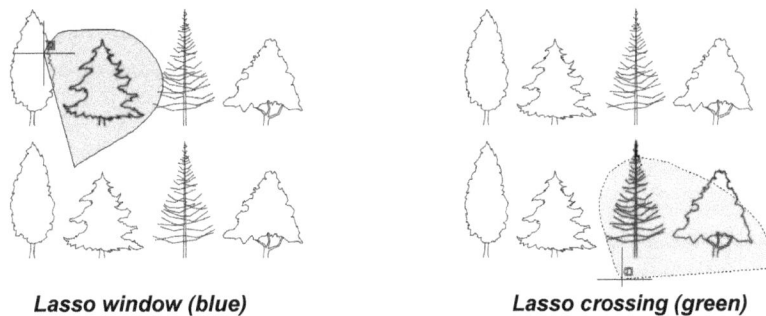

Lasso window (blue)   *Lasso crossing (green)*

Figure 5–4

- **Fence selection:** You can also type **F** at the *Select objects:* prompt to start a Fence style object selection in which you pick a first point, and then continue to select additional points as if creating line segments. When you have finished creating the fence, press <Enter> to make the selection. Any object that the fence crosses is also selected.

- You can also start a Window or Crossing Polygon selection by typing **WP** or **CP** at the *Select objects:* prompt. With this method, you pick a first point, and then various other points to define an irregularly shaped area.

- You can clear a selected object by pressing <Shift> and selecting the object. This enables you to select a group of objects quickly with a Window, Crossing, or Lasso, and then clear any that you do not want to include in the selection set.

- You can also type **R** at the *Select objects:* prompt and use any selection method to clear objects from the selection set. Then type **A** at the *Select objects:* prompt to return to adding objects to the selection set.

- A variety of selection methods can be combined in a single command to build the selection set.

Selecting Objects Before the Command

The standard AutoCAD procedure is to start a command and then select the objects. However, you can select the objects before you start the command.

- If you have already selected objects and then you start a command, you are not prompted to *Select objects:* but the already selected objects are automatically used by the command.

- When you select objects before starting the command, the objects highlight in blue, with a thicker line weight, and contain blue squares called *grips*, as shown in Figure 5–5.

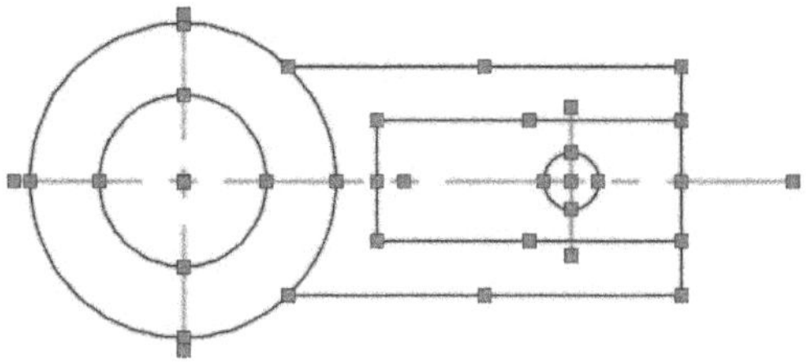

Figure 5–5

Practice 5a

Selecting Objects

Practice Objective

Estimated time for completion: 5 minutes

* Select objects using the various selection methods.

In this practice, you will use the Crossing, Window, and Lasso methods to select objects shown in Figure 5–6, for use with an editing command.

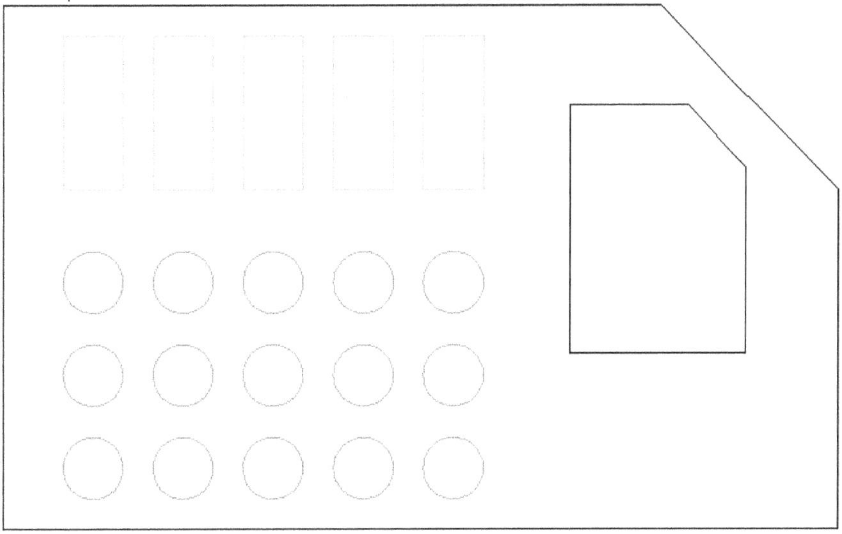

Figure 5–6

1. Open **Select-M.dwg** from your practice files folder.

2. Start an editing command, such as **Move,** by clicking

   ⊕ (Move) in *Home* tab>Modify panel.

3. At the *Select objects:* prompt, click in an empty area near the right side of the top row of circles and then move the cursor left to create a crossing window (green), as shown on the left in Figure 5–7. Note that the objects that touch the crossing boundary are highlighted and will be included in the selection.

4. Click to complete the selection. Note that the selected objects display in blue with a thicker line weight, as shown on the right in Figure 5–7.

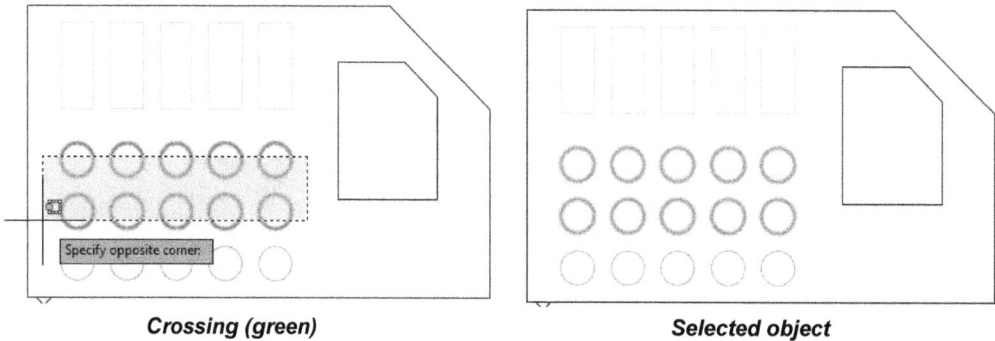

Crossing (green)   *Selected object*

Figure 5–7

5. Press <Esc> to abort the command and leave the circles intact.

6. Start the **Move** command again. At the *Select objects:* prompt, click in an empty area near the left side of the top edge of the shape and then move the cursor diagonally right to create a selection window (blue), as shown in Figure 5–8. Note that the objects that touch the window boundary are not highlighted and only the objects completely inside the window boundary are selected, as shown in Figure 5–9.

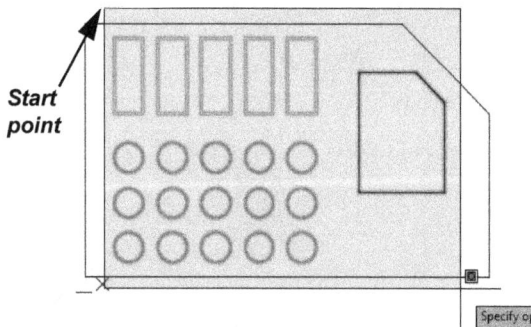

Window (blue)

Figure 5–8

Objects selected

Figure 5–9

7. Hold <Shift> and create a window around the top row of rectangles to remove them from the selection.

8. Click on the middle rectangle to add it to the selection set.

9. Press <Esc> to abort the command and leave the geometry intact.

10. Close the drawing. Do not save changes.

5.2 Moving Objects

The **Move** command enables you to relocate a selected object or group of objects from one place in the drawing to another.

How To: Move an Object

1. In *Home* tab>Modify panel, click ⊹ (Move).
2. Select the objects that you want to move.
3. Press <Enter> or right-click to end the object selection.
4. Specify the base point, which is the *handle* by which you hold the objects.
5. Move the cursor. ◈ displays at the cursor and the selected objects get attached to the cursor. A temporary rubber-band (dashed) line extends from the original location to the new location of the objects, as shown in Figure 5–10. A paler (light gray) version of the selected object(s) displays at its original location.

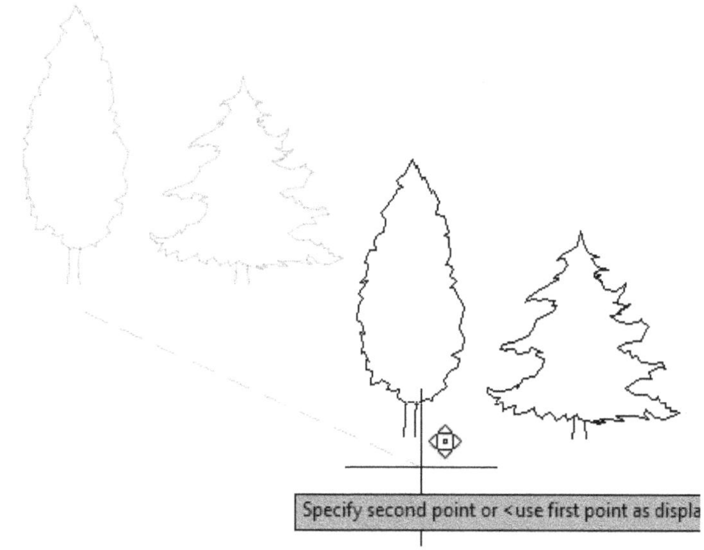

Specify second point or <use first point as displa

Figure 5–10

6. Specify a second point at which to place the objects. The original objects are moved to the new location.

- You can select the objects first and then start the **Move** command.

- You can also select the objects first (highlighted in blue with a thicker line weight and contains *grips)* and then click and drag them to a new location. Ensure that you do not select one of the grips. This method does not permit you to move precisely.

- You can also select the objects first, press and hold <Ctrl>, and use the appropriate arrow key to **Nudge** the selected objects a few pixels in the specified direction.

Hint: Drawing Aids for Moving Objects

Several drawing aids can help you to move objects precisely including Object Snaps, Coordinate Entry, and Object Snap Tracking.

- **Object Snaps:** Start the **Move** command and select an object to move. Use Object Snaps to select a base point on the object, such as an end point. Then use Object Snaps to select the new location for the object, such as the center of a circle.

- **Coordinate Entry:** Start the **Move** command and select an object to move. Enter coordinates for the base point and press <Enter> when prompted for the second point. The coordinates determine the distances and directions in which the object is moved. For example, entering **2,5** for the base point moves the object 2 units in the X-direction and 5 units in the Y-direction.

- **Object Snap Tracking:** Start the **Move** command and select an object to move. With Osnap Tracking toggled on, hover the cursor over objects where the selected object is going to be placed and select two tracking points. Place the selected object at the intersection of the tracking points.

You can also combine these methods to move an object. For example, you can use Object Snaps to select the base point and then enter coordinates for the second point.

5.3 Copying Objects

The **Copy** command is used to make additional copies of selected objects. The prompts for this command are similar to those used for **Move**.

How To: Copy an Object

1. In the *Home* tab>Modify panel, click ⊙ (Copy).
2. Select the objects that you want to copy.
3. Press <Enter> or right-click to end the object selection.
4. Select the base point.
5. Move the cursor to copy the objects to a new location.

   ⊙ displays at the cursor and the selected object(s) get attached to it. A temporary rubber-band (dashed) line extends from the original location to the new location of the objects, as shown in Figure 5–11. A highlighted version of the selected object(s) displays at the original location.

Specify second point or

| Select second point | Original and copied objects |

Figure 5–11

6. Continue selecting points to create more copies, or press <Enter> or <Esc> to finish.

- Copied objects have the same color, linetype, and layer properties as the original. This rule also applies to other commands that make duplicates of objects.

- The **Undo** option enables you to undo the placing of a copy while remaining in the command.

- You can select the objects first and then start the **Copy** command.

- Similar to the **Move** command, you can use Object Snaps, Coordinate Entry, and Object Snap Tracking to select points for the **Copy** command.

- You can also select the objects first, select a point on an object that does not touch a grip, drag the objects to a new location, and press <Ctrl> to make a copy. Do not press <Ctrl> until after you have started dragging, as it has a different purpose when you are selecting objects in 3D.

Hint: Editing Commands in the Shortcut Menu

If you select objects when a command is not active and then right-click, the shortcut menu displays some basic editing commands, as shown in Figure 5–12. This is another way of starting these commands.

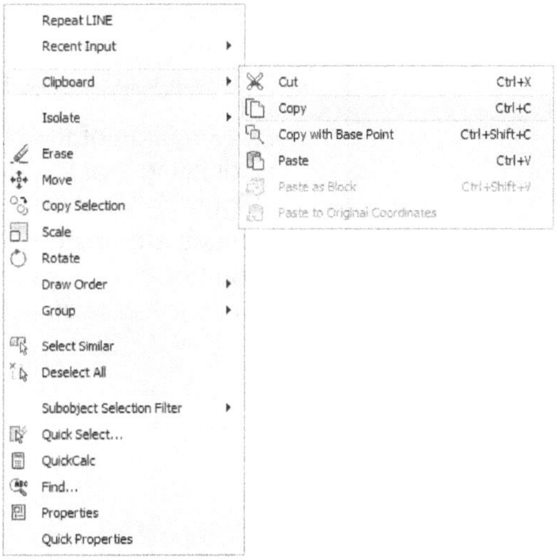

Figure 5–12

You can also **Cut**, **Copy**, and **Paste** to the Clipboard from the shortcut menu by expanding the **Clipboard** option. The objects you select can then be pasted into other AutoCAD drawings and programs, such as spreadsheets and documents.

The **Clipboard>Copy** command in the shortcut menu is actually **Copy to Clipboard**. The **Copy Selection** command is the same as the standard AutoCAD **Copy** command.

Enhanced
in **2018**

Hint: Rubber-band line color

By default, the rubber-band line that you get after selecting and moving the cursor in the **Move** and **Copy** commands, is a light orange color. You can control its color in the *Interface element* list in the Drawing Window Colors dialog box, which can be opened from Options dialog box>*Display* tab>**Colors**.

5.4 Rotating Objects

Design changes sometimes require modifying the placement angle of an object. The **Rotate** command rotates selected objects around a defined pivot point.

How To: Rotate an Object

1. In the *Home* tab>Modify panel, click ⟳ (Rotate).
2. Select the objects to rotate.
3. Press <Enter> to end the object selection.
4. Select the base point around which the objects are going to rotate.
5. Move the cursor to rotate the objects. A dashed line indicates the location of the base point. 🔄 displays at the cursor, indicating that the **Rotate** command is active, as shown in Figure 5–13. It also indicates the direction in which typed values are going to be rotated, in this case, counter-clockwise (default). The original objects fade to gray while the new objects maintain their original properties.

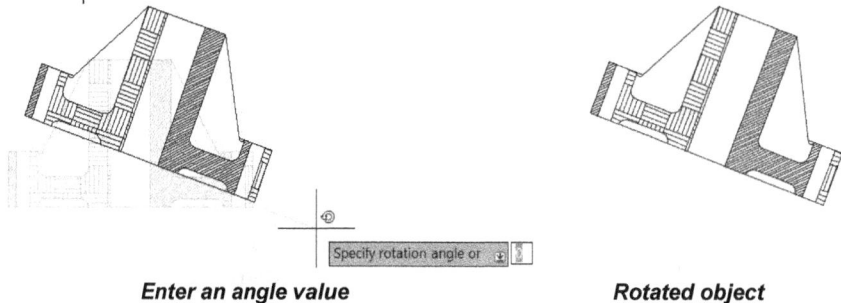

Specify rotation angle or

Enter an angle value   **Rotated object**

Figure 5–13

6. Enter a *Rotation Angle* or select a point to specify the rotation.

• A negative rotation angle enables you to turn the object clockwise.

- Polar Tracking can be used to constrain the rotation to a precise angle.

- At Specify rotation angle prompt, you can access the **Copy** option, which leaves the original object in place and rotates a copy of it.

- You can select the objects first and then start the **Rotate** command.

- You can change the default rotation direction used by the **Rotate** command by selecting or clearing the **Clockwise** option in the Drawing Units dialog box, as shown in Figure 5–14. (Application Menu> **Drawing Utilities>Units**)

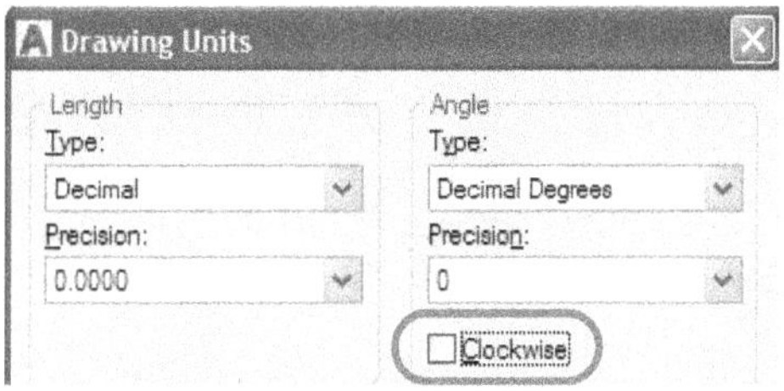

Figure 5–14

5.5 Scaling Objects

The **Scale** command enlarges or reduces the size of selected objects around a defined reference point.

How To: Scale an Object

1. In *Home* tab>Modify panel, click ☐ (Scale).
2. Select the objects to scale.
3. Press <Enter> or right-click to end the object selection.
4. Select the base point to be used for scaling.

5. Move the cursor to scale the objects. ⬓ displays at the cursor, indicating that the **Scale** command is active, as shown in Figure 5–15. The original objects fade to gray while the new objects maintain their original properties.

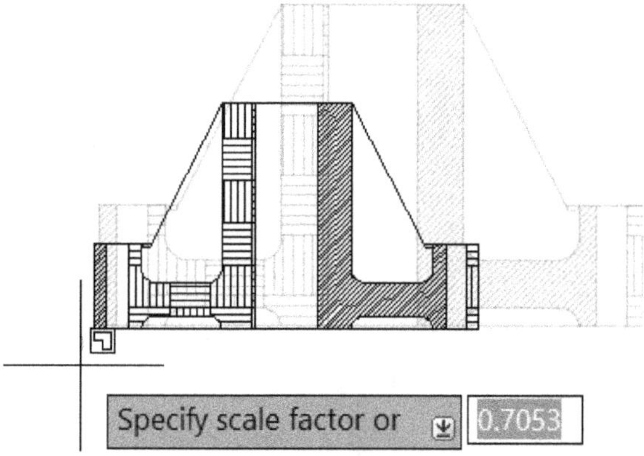

Specify scale factor or   0.7053

Figure 5–15

6. Enter a value for the scale factor.

- The **scale factor** enables you to set the required level of enlargement or reduction in size. Scale factors smaller than 1 decrease the size and scale factors larger than 1 increase the size.

- The **Copy** option in the **Scale** command leaves the original object unscaled and creates a scaled copy.

5.6 Mirroring Objects

The **Mirror** command creates reversed or symmetrical copies of objects across a user-specified mirror line.

How To: Mirror an Object

1. In the *Home* tab>Modify panel, click ⊿⊿ (Mirror).
2. Select the object(s) you want to mirror.
3. Press <Enter> to end the selection set.
4. Select the first point of the mirror line. The mirror line is the axis of symmetry or hinge about which the object(s) are mirrored.
5. Move the cursor to mirror the objects. A preview displays the mirror line and the potential location of the new mirrored object, as shown in Figure 5–16.

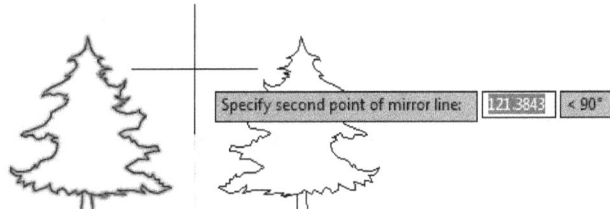

Specify second point of mirror line: 1.21.3843 < 90°

Figure 5–16

6. Select the second point of the mirror line.
7. At the *Erase source objects?* prompt, select **No** (default) to keep the original objects or **Yes** to delete them.

• Polar Tracking is useful for controlling the angle of the mirror line.

Practice 5b | Modifying Objects

Practice Objective

Estimated time for completion: 25 minutes

- Modify the location, quantity, and size of objects.

In this practice, you will use the **Move**, **Copy**, **Rotate**, **Scale**, and **Mirror** commands to place furniture in a floorplan, as shown in Figure 5–17. Some of the objects in the drawing are locked in place so that you do not move them by mistake.

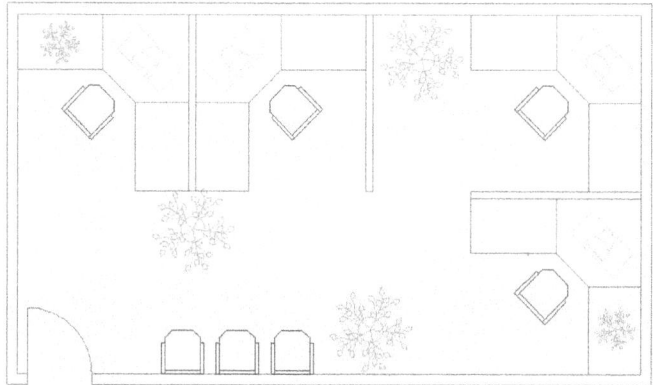

Figure 5–17

Task 1 - Move an object.

In this task you will use the **Move** command to place furniture in a floorplan, as shown in Figure 5–18.

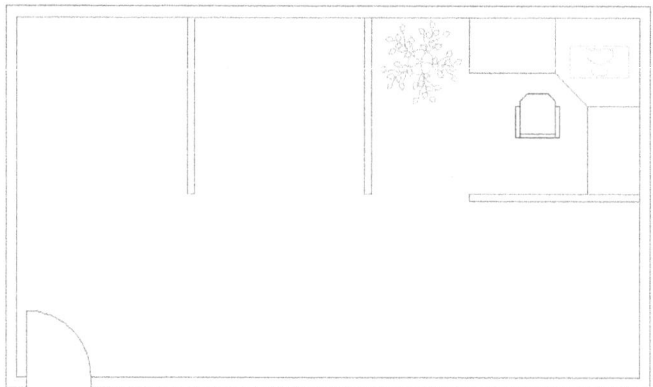

Figure 5–18

1. Open **Arrange-AM.dwg** from your practice files folder.

2. In the Status Bar, toggle off ⟳ ▼ (Polar Tracking) and ∠ (Object Snap Tracking). Toggle on ▢ ▼ (Object Snap) and verify that **Endpoint** is selected.

3. In the *Home* tab>Modify panel, click ⊹ (Move).

4. Select the desk and press <Enter> to end the object selection.

5. For the base point, snap to the end point at the back corner (upper right) of the desk.

6. Hover the cursor and snap it (without clicking) to the inside corner of the top right cubicle, as shown in Figure 5–19. The original objects fade to gray while the new objects maintain their original properties.

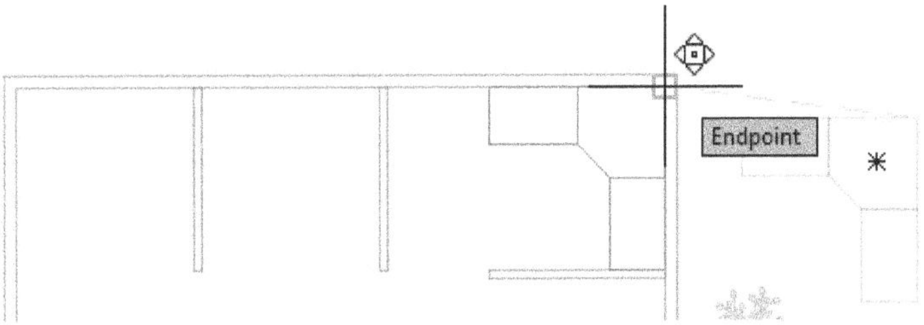

Figure 5–19

7. Click at that point to confirm the move.

8. Toggle off ▢ ▼ (Object Snap).

9. Move the chair to place it in front of the desk (use approximate location) and move the PC onto the desk, as shown in Figure 5–18. Do not rotate them now.

10. Move the plant to the open space next to the desk, as shown in Figure 5–18.

Task 2 - Copy an object.

In this task you will use the **Copy** command to copy several chairs and plants in the floorplan, as shown in Figure 5–20.

Figure 5–20

1. In the *Home* tab>Modify panel, click ⊙ (Copy).

2. Select the plant and press <Enter> to end the object selection.

3. For the base point, click near the center of the plant.

4. Move the cursor near the bottom of the left most inner wall, as shown in Figure 5–21. Note that a copy of the plant is attached with the cursor. A dashed line connects with the cursor indicating the new location with the original object highlighted, as shown in Figure 5–21. Once you locate the required location for the copy (bottom of the leftmost inner wall), click to place the plant.

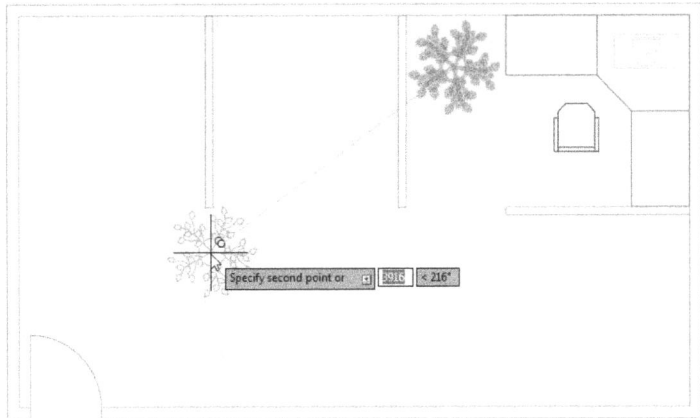

Figure 5–21

5. With the plant and the dashed line still attached to the cursor, move the cursor again and click to place another copy along the bottom wall, as shown in Figure 5–20. Press <Enter> to exit the command.

6. Copy the chair to the locations shown in Figure 5–20. (**Tip:** To position the chairs flush along the wall, use the **Midpoint** or **Endpoint** object snap to select the base point at the back of the chair. Then, select the **Nearest** object snap override (<Shift>+ right-click) to select points along the wall.)

Task 3 - Rotate an object.

In this task, you will rotate the chair and PC and then copy the entire set of furniture to other locations, as shown in Figure 5–22.

Figure 5–22

1. In the Status Bar, expand ⊙ ▼ (Polar Tracking) and select **45,90,135,180...**, if required. Toggle on ⊙ ▼ (Polar Tracking) and toggle off ☐ ▼ (Object Snap).

2. In the *Home* tab>Modify panel, click ○ (Rotate) and select the chair near the desk. Press <Enter> and select the base point near the middle of the chair. Pull the cursor away from the chair until you see the 315 degree angle (multiple of 45) and the seat is facing the desk, as shown in Figure 5–23. Note that the original objects fade to gray while the new objects maintain their original properties. Click to accept the angle.

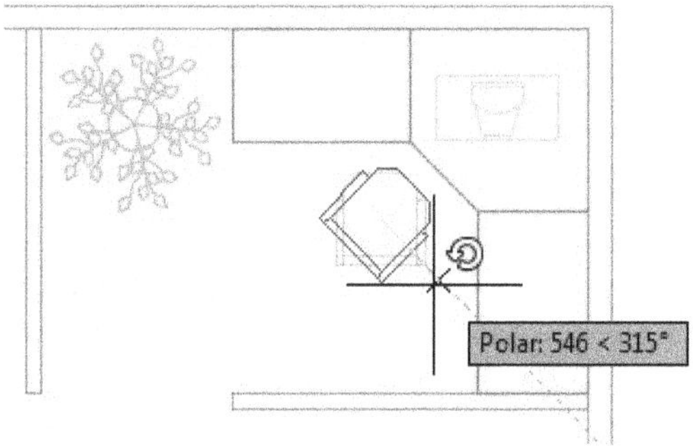

Figure 5–23

3. Repeat the process to rotate the PC using 135 degree angle such that the monitor is facing the chair, as shown in Figure 5–22.

4. Move the chair as required, to place it correctly in front of the desk. Do the same for the PC to center it on the desk.

Select the object and use <Ctrl> and the required arrow key to nudge the objects in place.

5. Toggle on ☐ ▼ (Object Snap) and verify that it is set to **Endpoint**.

6. Start the **Copy** command. Select the chair, desk, and PC, and then press <Enter>. For the base point, select the back corner (top right) of the desk. Copy the objects to the other three cubicles, as shown in Figure 5–22.

7. Save the drawing.

Task 4 - Scale an object.

In this task you will copy and scale some of the plants, as shown in Figure 5–24.

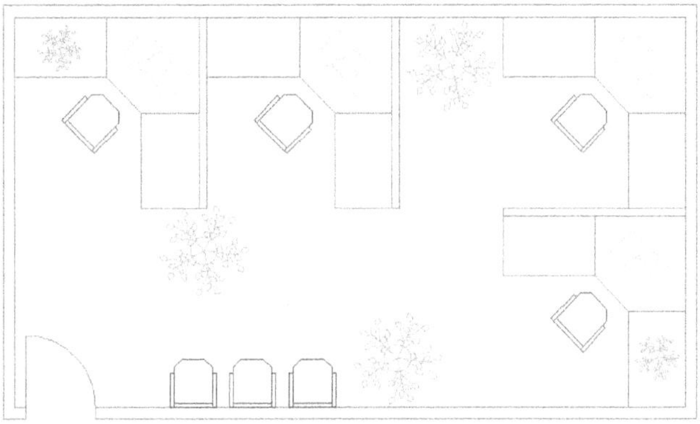

Figure 5–24

1. Copy one of the plants to the desk in the upper left cubicle.

2. In the *Home* tab>Modify panel, click ⬚ (Scale). Select the plant, press <Enter>, and select the center of the plant as the base point. Enter **0.5** for the scale factor and press <Enter> to make it half of the original plant.

3. Copy the scaled plant to the desk in the lower right cubicle.

Task 5 - Mirror objects.

In this task you will use the **Mirror** command to mirror the contents of a cubicle, as shown in Figure 5–25.

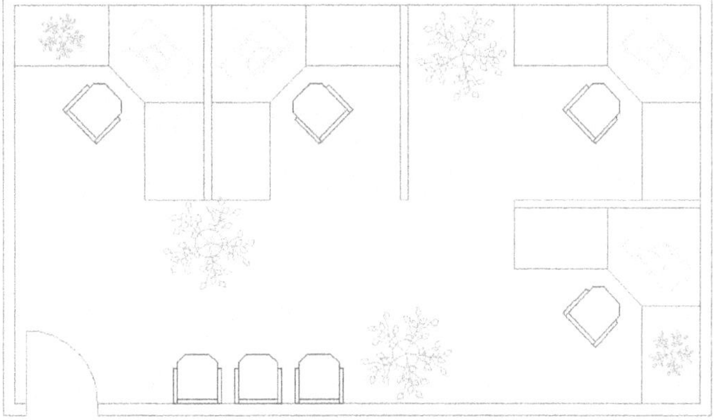

Figure 5–25

1. In the *Home* tab>Modify panel, click △∥△ (Mirror).

2. At the *Select objects:* prompt, select the desk, PC, and chair in the middle cubicle, and press <Enter>.

3. At the *Specify first point of mirror line:* prompt, select the end point of the line that separates the corner desk section from the straight desk section at the top of the cubicle, as shown on the left in Figure 5–26.

4. At the *Specify second point of mirror line:* prompt, select a bottom end point, as shown on the right in Figure 5–26. At the *Erase source objects?* select **Yes** from the drop-down list. The contents of the middle cubicle are mirrored and the original objects are deleted.

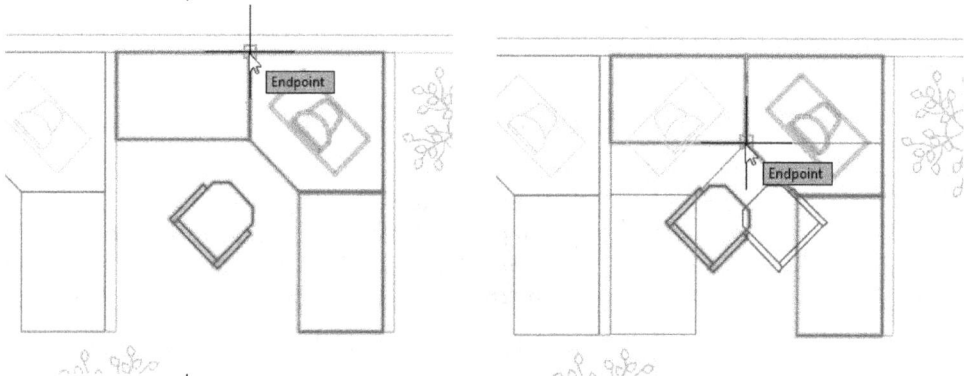

Figure 5–26

5. Save and close the drawing.

5.7 Editing with Grips

You can modify objects by using their grips without using an editing command. The AutoCAD software stores information about objects as geometric formulas. Therefore, lines are defined by their end points, circles by their center and radius, etc. The software can easily compute additional points, such as the midpoint of a line or quadrants of a circle, and enable you to modify them, as shown in Figure 5–27.

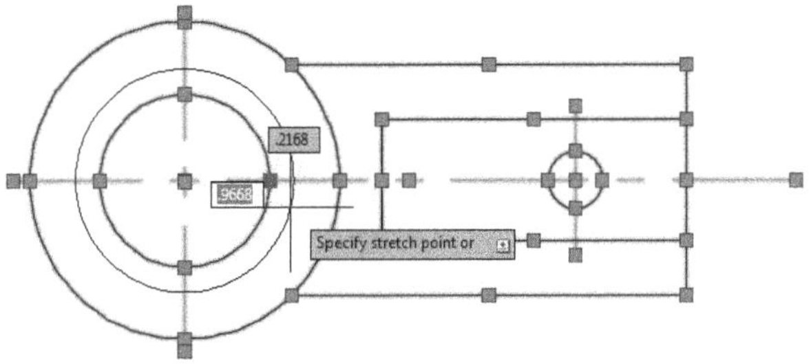

Figure 5–27

- By default, grips display as blue boxes on an object when it is selected without starting a command.

- If you hover the cursor over a grip but do not select it, the color changes to pink.

Working with Hot Grips

When you click directly on a grip, it changes to a selected or *hot grip* (red by default), as shown in Figure 5–28.

- Depending on the grip you make hot, the default mode is automatically enabled. For example, the quadrant grip of a circle stretches it, but the center grip moves the circle, as shown in Figure 5–28.

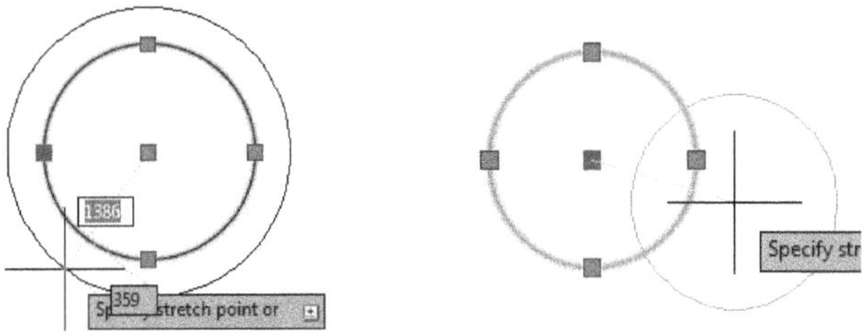

Hot grip selected on quadrant   *Hot grip selected in center and used as Move*

Figure 5–28

- If you hover the cursor over certain multi-functional grips, additional options display, as shown in Figure 5–29. The options for the endpoint grips of line segments and arcs include **Stretch** and **Lengthen**, and for the middle grip of arcs include **Stretch** and **Radius**.

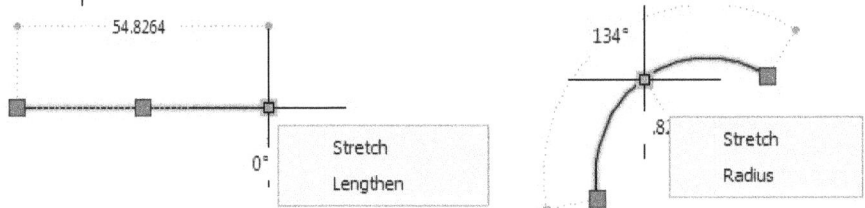

Figure 5–29

- To select a different option after you make a grip hot, you can right-click to display the various editing commands in the shortcut menu, as shown in Figure 5–30.

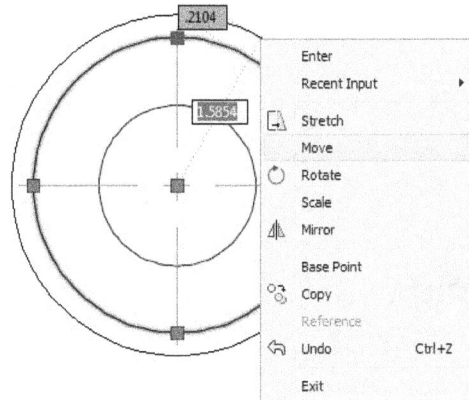

Figure 5–30

You can also press \<Spacebar\> to cycle through the available commands.

- Once a grip and an editing command have been selected, various advanced options (for the selected command) display by pressing \<Down Arrow\>, as shown in Figure 5–31.

Figure 5–31

- To clear objects and their grips, press <Esc>.

- When using grips, their default mode and multi-functional mode only apply to the object with the hot grip. However, **Move**, **Mirror**, **Scale**, and **Rotate** affect all of the selected objects.

- You can hold <Shift> to activate multiple modes of grips.

- When using grips on a block, **Stretch** has the same effect as **Move**. This is because you cannot stretch a standard block object.

- You can change the display of grips (size and color) and other settings in the *Selection* tab in the Options dialog box (Application Menu>**Options**).

Grips with Dynamic Dimensions

Grips enable you to quickly check the dimensions of an object. For example, when you hover the cursor over the end point grip of a line, dynamic dimensions display the line's length and angle and the quadrant grip on a circle displays the circle's radius, as shown in Figure 5–32.

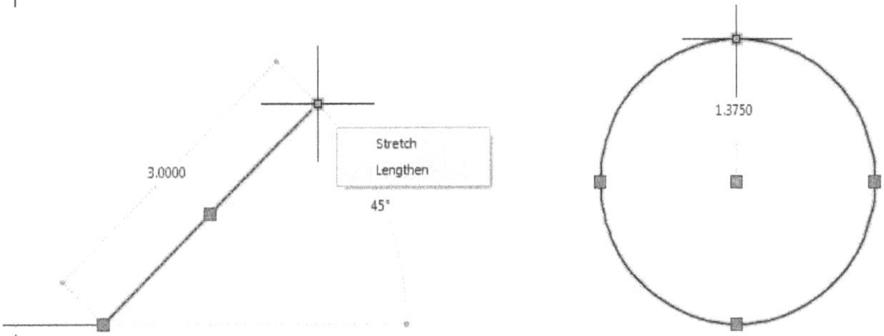

Figure 5–32

- ⁺ (Dynamic Input) must be toggled on for the dimensions to be displayed.

- When you select the stretch grip of an object, you can edit the dimension instead of dragging the hot grip.

How To: Stretch a Line by 5 Units Using Grips

1. Select the line to display the grips.
2. Select the endpoint grip of the line.
3. Move the cursor to the right, as shown in Figure 5–33.

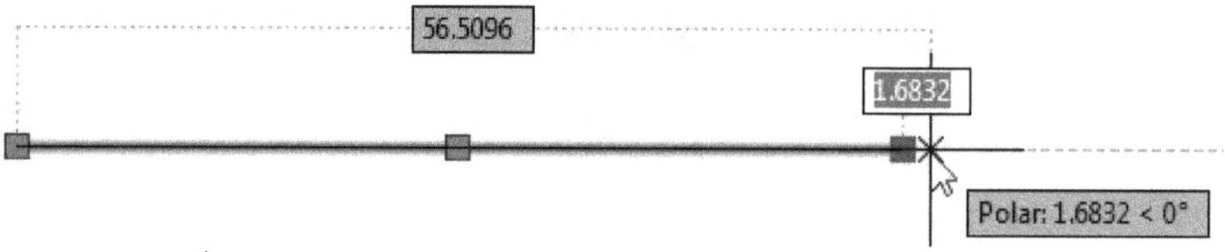

Figure 5–33

4. Enter **5** (as shown in Figure 5–34), and press <Enter> to change the length. The line length increases by 5 units and the angle does not change.

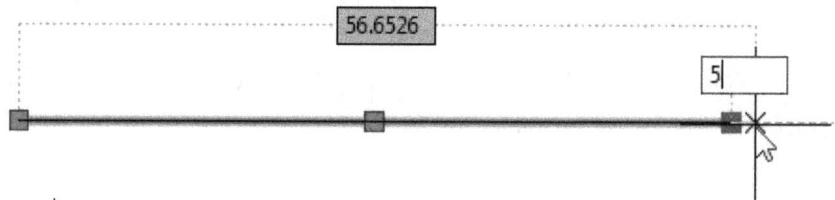

Figure 5–34

- If you press <Tab> when the change in length is highlighted, you can enter a new total length instead. Press <Tab> again to change the angle.

Practice 5c

Editing with Grips I

Practice Objective

Estimated time for completion: 10 minutes

• Modify objects using grips.

In this practice, you will use grips to move, copy, rotate, mirror, and scale objects on the façade of a building. You will also use <Shift> to copy and specify a new base point, as shown in Figure 5–35.

Figure 5–35

1. Open **Facade-AM.dwg** from your practice files folder.

2. Set the object snaps to **Endpoint**, **Midpoint**, and **Intersection**, and toggle ▢ ▼ (Object Snap) on. Toggle ↻ ▼ (Polar Tracking) off. Toggle on ⁺▭ (Dynamic Input) if it is not already on.

3. With no command active, select the double door. Select the grip to make it hot (red by default). Move the door to the midpoint of the bottom line on the building. Press <Esc> to clear the object.

4. Repeat Step 3 with the arched window and place the grip at the midpoint of the top of the door.

5. Select the square window and select the grip. Right-click and select **Copy**. Select the intersections of the blue center lines to place windows at each intersection (9 in total). Press <Esc> twice to finish.

6. Erase the light blue center lines.

7. Select the four angled lines of the roof. Select the grip at the right end of one of the lines. Right-click and select **Mirror**, then right-click again and select **Copy** to keep the original objects. Select the midpoint of the roofline as the second point for the mirror line. Press <Esc> twice to finish.

8. Select the center top window in the top row and select the grip. Right-click and select **Base Point**. For the base point, select the intersection of the mullions at the center of the window.

9. Right-click again and select **Rotate**. For the rotation angle, enter **45** and press <Enter>.

10. Select the window grip again and change the base point to the center of the mullions. Right-click and select **Scale**. For the scale factor, enter **0.7** and press <Enter>. Press <Esc> to finish.

11. Select the arched window above the door and select the grip. Right-click and select **Scale**. For the scale factor, enter **0.65** and press <Enter>. Press <Esc> to finish.

12. Select the bottom line along the base of the building. Hover the cursor over the grip at either end point to display the dimension. What is the length of the line?

13. Select the top roofline on the left side of the building, and hover the cursor over the end point at the top. What is the length and angle of the line?

14. Save and close the drawing.

Practice 5d

Editing with Grips II

Practice Objective

* Modify objects using grips.

Estimated time for completion: 10 minutes

In this practice, you will use grips to move, copy, rotate, and scale objects as shown in Figure 5–36.

Figure 5–36

1. Open **Arrange-Grips-AM.dwg** from your practice files folder.

2. Use grips to move, copy, rotate, and scale objects (as shown in Figure 5–37) so that they are placed as shown in Figure 5–36.

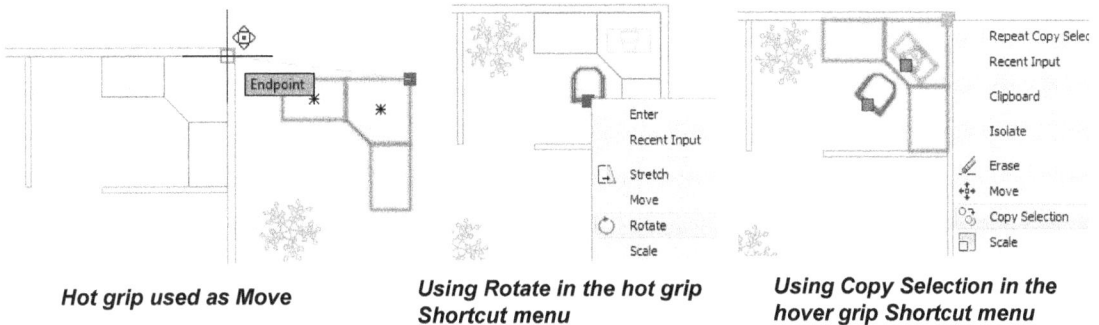

Hot grip used as Move

Using Rotate in the hot grip Shortcut menu

Using Copy Selection in the hover grip Shortcut menu

Figure 5–37

Chapter Review Questions

1. What is the difference between a Window and a Crossing selection box?

   a. Window selects everything inside and Crossing selects everything touching the selection box.

   b. Window selects everything inside or touching the selection box and Crossing selects everything inside the selection box.

   c. Window selects everything inside and Crossing selects everything inside or touching the selection box.

   d. Window selects everything touching the selection box and Crossing selects everything inside the selection box.

2. How can you clear a selected object?

   a. Pick the object again.

   b. Hold <Shift> and pick the object.

   c. Right-click on the object and select **Clear**.

   d. Hold <Ctrl> and pick the object.

3. What happens to objects when you select them before starting any command?

   a. They highlight in black with a thicker line weight.

   b. They highlight in blue with a thicker line weight and contain red squares.

   c. They highlight in blue with a thicker line weight and contain blue squares.

   d. They stay the same.

4. The **Move**, **Copy**, **Rotate**, and **Scale** commands use a base point, which is always the center or a midpoint of an object.

   a. True

   b. False

5. What happens to the selected objects in the active **Rotate** command?

    a. The original objects fade to gray and the new objects maintain their original properties.

    b. The original objects maintain their original properties and the new objects fade to gray.

    c. The original objects are highlighted with a thicker line weight and the new objects fade to gray.

    d. The original objects maintain their original properties and the new objects are highlighted with a thicker line weight.

6. Which Scale Factor should you use to make an object half of its current size?

    a. -2.0

    b. 0.5

    c. 0.2

    d. -0.5

7. When selecting objects for a command, such as **Move** or **Copy**, how do you end the object selection?

    a. Press <Alt>.

    b. Press <Esc>.

    c. Press <Ctrl>.

    d. Press <Enter>.

8. What is the default mode of the hot grips of a circle?

    a. A quadrant hot grip stretches the circle whereas the center hot grip moves the circle.

    b. A quadrant hot grip moves the circle whereas the center hot grip stretches the circle.

    c. Both the quadrant hot grip and the center hot grip stretch/scale the circle.

    d. Both the quadrant hot grip and the center hot grip move the circle.

Command Summary

Button	Command	Location
	Copy	• **Ribbon:** *Home* tab>Modify panel • **Command Prompt:** copy or CO
	Mirror	• **Ribbon:** *Home* tab>Modify panel • **Command Prompt:** mirror or MI
	Move	• **Ribbon:** *Home* tab>Modify panel • **Command Prompt:** move or M
	Rotate	• **Ribbon:** *Home* tab>Modify panel • **Command Prompt:** rotate or RO
	Scale	• **Ribbon:** *Home* tab>Modify panel • **Command Prompt:** scale or SC

Projects: Making Your Drawings More Precise

This chapter contains practice projects that can be used to gain additional hands-on experience with the topics and commands covered so far in this student guide. These practices are intended to be self-guided and do not include step by step information.

Learning Objectives in this Chapter

- *Schematic:* Create an electronic schematic using the drawing tools, with object snaps and movement commands to help you to precisely place objects and symbols.

- *Architectural:* Create a plot of land using the drawing tools, with Polar Tracking, object snaps, and movement commands to help you to precisely place objects and buildings.

- *Mechanical:* Create mechanical parts and drawing components using the drawing tools, with Polar Tracking, object snaps, and movement commands to help you to precisely place features in the model.

6.1 Schematic Project: Electronics Diagram

Estimated time for completion: 10 minutes

In this project you will move, copy, and rotate electronic symbols to the appropriate places on a diagram, as shown in Figure 6–1. Use Object Snaps to position the objects precisely.

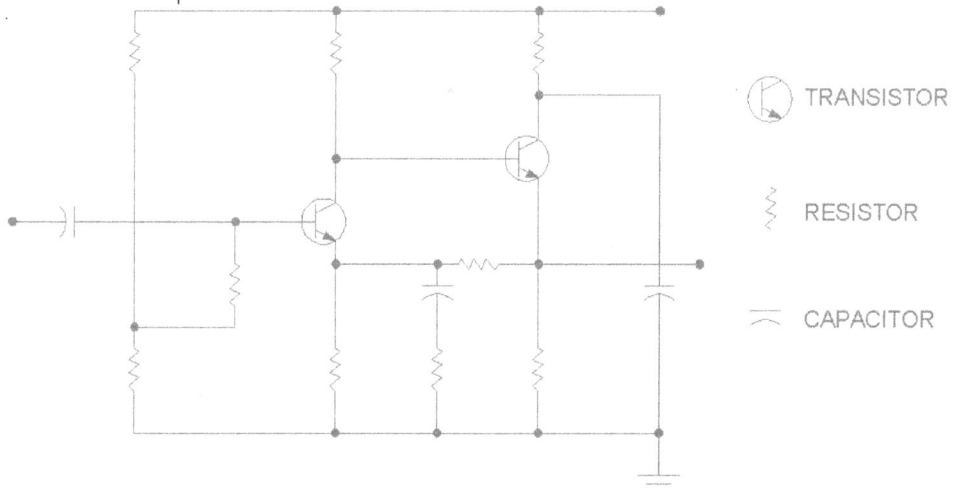

Figure 6–1

1. Open **Diagram-M.dwg** from your practice files folder.

2. Set the Object Snap settings to **Midpoint** and **Endpoint** and verify that ⬚ ▼ (Object Snap) is toggled on.

3. Copy the symbols from the key to the appropriate places on the diagram. Ensure that you snap to the exact base points to help position the objects precisely. For example, the base point for the transistor should be the midpoint of its vertical line. Some objects need to be rotated.

4. Save and close the drawing.

6.2 Architectural Project: Landscape

Estimated time for completion: 20 minutes

In this project you will draw a house and garage, as shown in Figure 6–2, and landscape the yard by arranging trees and shrubs. Commands that you will use include: **Line**, **Move**, **Copy**, **Scale**, and **Rotate**. Use Polar Tracking and Object Snap Tracking to help draw the buildings precisely.

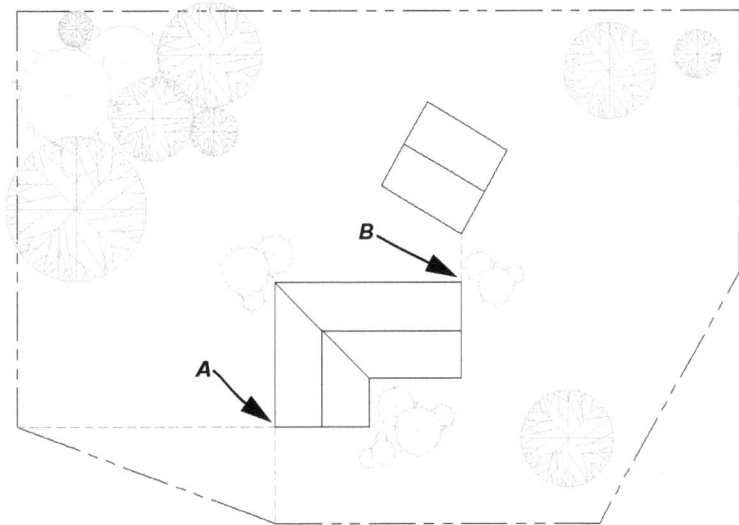

Figure 6–2

1. Open **Land-CM.dwg** from your practice files folder. The dashed boundary is a plot of land. The green objects are shrubs and trees.

2. Set the Object Snap modes to **Endpoint** and **Midpoint**, and toggle on ☐ ▼ (Object Snap), ∠ (Object Snap Tracking), and ↺ ▼ (Polar Tracking).

3. Use the dimensions shown in Figure 6–3 to draw the house. Use Object Snap Tracking to establish point A as shown in Figure 6–2.

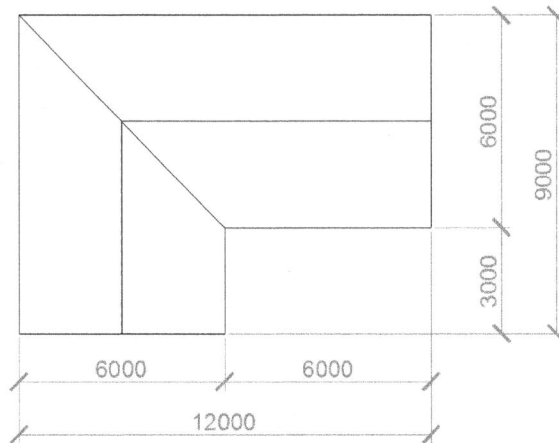

Figure 6–3

4. To draw the garage, expand ⟳ ▼ (Polar Tracking) and set a **30** degree angle for the Polar Tracking increment angle. Use the **Line** command with Object Snap Tracking to position the first point **3000 units** above the corner of the house at point B. Then use Polar Tracking to draw the **6000 x 6000** garage at the angle shown in Figure 6–4.

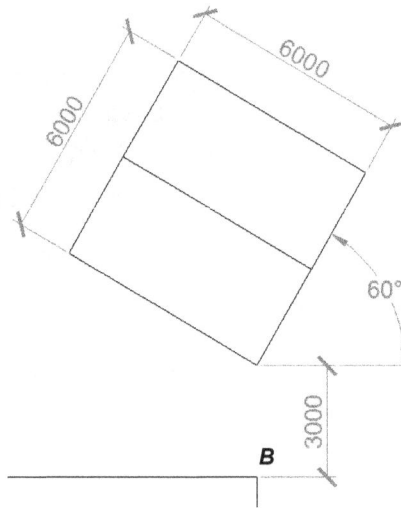

Figure 6–4

5. Place shrubs and trees in the yard, as shown in Figure 6–2. Scale, rotate, copy, and move them as required.

6.3 Mechanical Project: Using Polar and Tracking

Estimated time for completion: 10 minutes

In this project you will draw a mechanical part using **Line** and **Circle**, as shown in Figure 6–5. You will use Polar Tracking and Object Snap Tracking to draw them precisely. Draw only the object, not the dimensions.

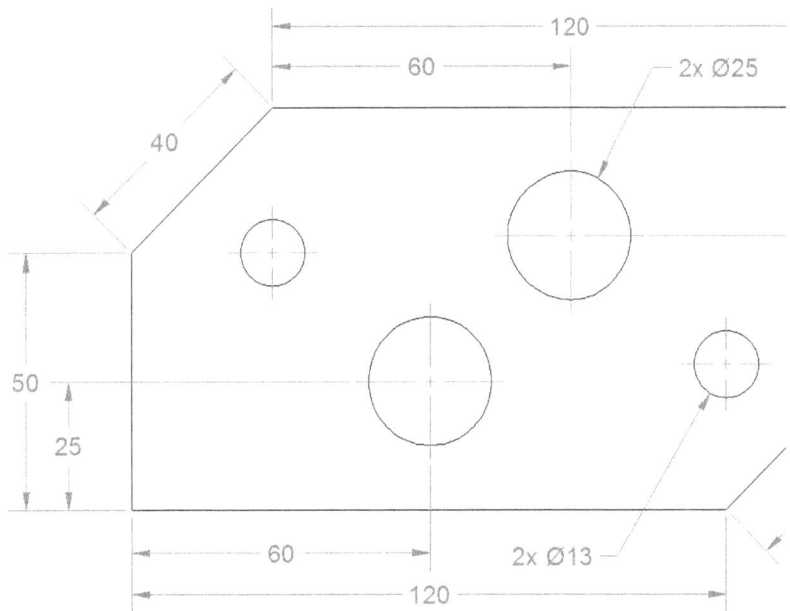

Figure 6–5

1. Open **Plate-M.dwg** from your practice files folder. It is an empty drawing.

2. Draw the object shown in Figure 6–5. Set the *Polar Tracking* angle to **45** degrees to draw the lines. Use Object Snap Tracking to position the circles at the midpoints or endpoints of the nearby lines. The diameters of the circles are **13** and **25**.

6.4 Mechanical Project: Surge Protector

Estimated time for completion: 10 minutes

In this project you will arrange objects in a drawing using the **Move**, **Copy**, **Rotate**, and **Scale** commands, as shown in Figure 6–6.

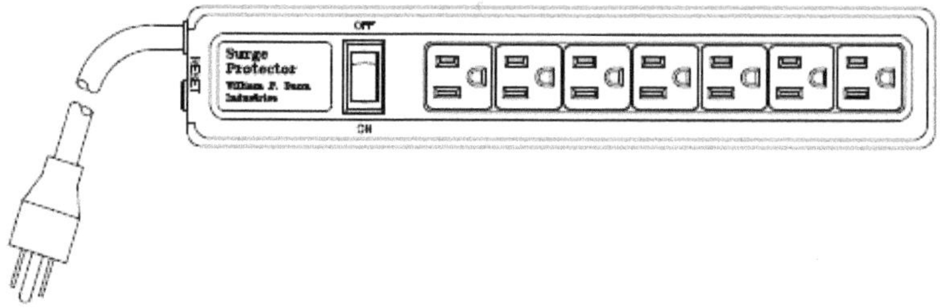

Figure 6–6

1. Open **Surge Protector-M.dwg** from your practice files folder.

2. Arrange the drawing as shown in Figure 6–6. Make copies of the objects as required. Position the outlets precisely using Object Snaps. Use the **Scale** command to make the text larger.

Estimated time for completion: 10 minutes

6.5 Mechanical Project: Satellite

In this project you will assemble drawing components using the **Copy**, **Move**, and **Rotate** commands, as shown in Figure 6–7.

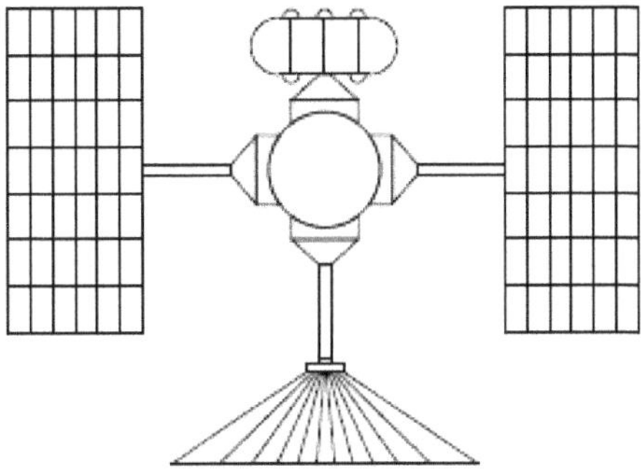

Figure 6–7

1. Open **Satellite-M.dwg** from your practice files folder.

2. Arrange the components as shown in Figure 6–7. Copy and rotate the objects as required. Use Object Snaps to place the components together precisely. (Tip: Set ▢ ▼ (Object Snap) to **Quadrant** and **Midpoint** to speed up the assembly process.)

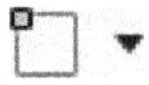

Organizing Your Drawing with Layers

In this chapter you learn how to create a new drawing with a template, make a layer current, draw on specific layers, control the state of a layer, and change the layer of an object.

Learning Objectives in this Chapter

- Create new drawings using templates.
- Organize a drawing into logical categories using layers.
- Control which parts of a drawing are displayed or plotted.
- Draw objects with specific saved properties.
- Modify object layers and layer states.

7.1 Creating New Drawings With Templates

What is a Template?

When you start a new drawing, you are actually creating a copy of an existing *template* file. A template is a drawing that contains all of the objects and settings required in new drawings. Some of the settings stored in a template file include units, limits, layers, layouts with a border and titleblock, text styles, and dimension styles.

- In addition to the predefined templates that are supplied with the AutoCAD® software, you can also create your own custom templates.

Starting New Drawings

Two commands are available for starting new drawings: **QNew** and **New**.

- Clicking ⊞ (New Drawing) in the *File Tabs* bar or clicking **Start Drawing** in the initial Start screen starts the **Qnew** command, which automatically opens a new drawing based on a default template.

- If you want to select a different template, click ⬜ (New) in the Quick Access Toolbar or in the Application Menu to open the Select template dialog box, as shown in Figure 7–1.

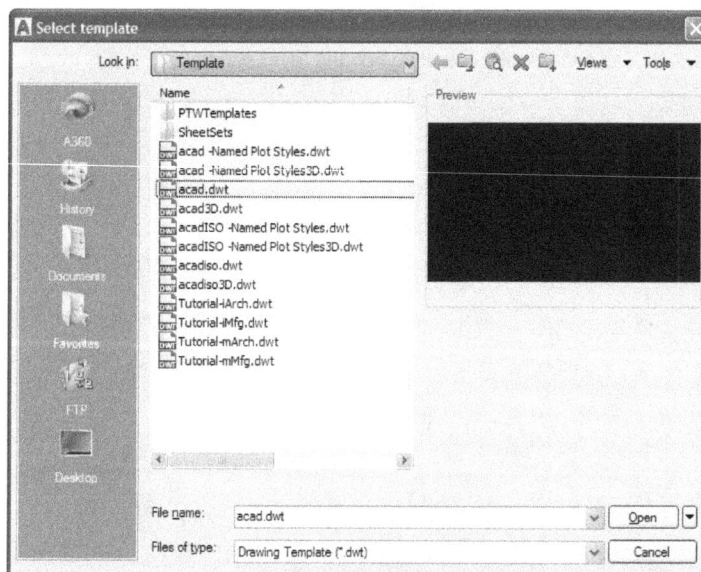

Figure 7–1

- AutoCAD template files have the extension DWT. Drawing files have the extension DWG.

Hint: Setting the Default Template for QNEW

If you have a template that you use frequently, you can set it as the default for **Qnew** in the Options dialog box. In the Application Menu, click **Options**. In the *Files* tab, select **Template Settings>Default Template File Name for QNEW**, as shown in Figure 7–2.

Template Settings
    Drawing Template File Location
    Sheet Set Template File Location
    Default Template File Name for QNEW
      → c:\<username>\acad.dwt
    Default Template for Sheet Creation and Page Setup Overrides

Figure 7–2

Working With Different Types of Units

In the template file, you typically set the type of units to use in the drawing, as shown in Figure 7–3. For example, if you set the template file to feet and inches or decimal units, the same units are used in the drawing.

Architectural	3'-4 1/4"
Decimal	3.25
Engineering	3' 4.25"
Fractional	3 1/4"
Scientific	3.25I +01

Figure 7–3

- Decimal units can represent feet, inches, meters, kilometers, miles, or any other type of units you want to use.

- The AutoCAD software usually accepts either a decimal or a fraction as input (it accepts 1/2 or 0.5). If you use fractions, separate the whole number from the fraction with a hyphen (1-1/2). If you do not use the hyphen, the software interprets the space as an <Enter>.

- When typing decimals, leading zeros are not required (.5 is the same as 0.5), and trailing zeros do not affect the AutoCAD precision (0.5 is as precise as 0.50000).

Practice 7a

Using a Template to Start a Drawing

Practice Objective

*   Start drawings using different templates.

Estimated time for completion: 10 minutes

In this practice, you will start drawings using different template files that were created for this student guide.

Note: If the templates specified here are not listed in the dialog box, browse to the practice folder to find them.

Mechanical

1. In the Application Menu, click **New**. Start a new drawing based on **Mech-Millimeters.dwt**, which is located in your practice files folder.

If the coordinates are not displayed, expand

≡ *(Customization) in the Status Bar and select Coordinates.*

2. Move the crosshairs in the drawing window and note the coordinate display in the Status Bar, as shown in Figure 7–4. The drawing is in Decimal units with a precision of four decimal places.

86.4870, 17.3512, 0.0000 MODEL

Figure 7–4

The dimensions are for your reference only.

3. Create the sketch shown in Figure 7–5. **Tip:** You can toggle **ORTHOMODE** on to draw perfectly horizontal and vertical lines.

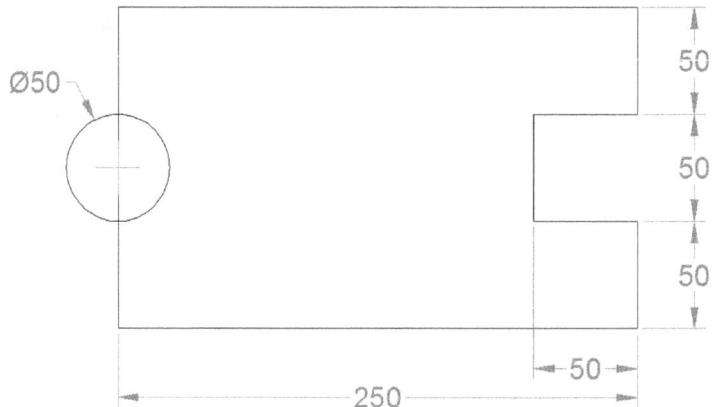

Ø50

50

50

50

50

250

Figure 7–5

4. In the Application Menu, click **Save As** and name the drawing **Mech1.dwg**.

Architectural

1. In the Application Menu, click **New**.

2. Start a new drawing based on **AEC-Millimeters.dwt**, which is located in your practice files folder.

3. Move the crosshairs in the drawing window and note the coordinate display in the Status Bar. This drawing is in Decimal units with a precision of 0.

4. Create the sketch shown in Figure 7–6.

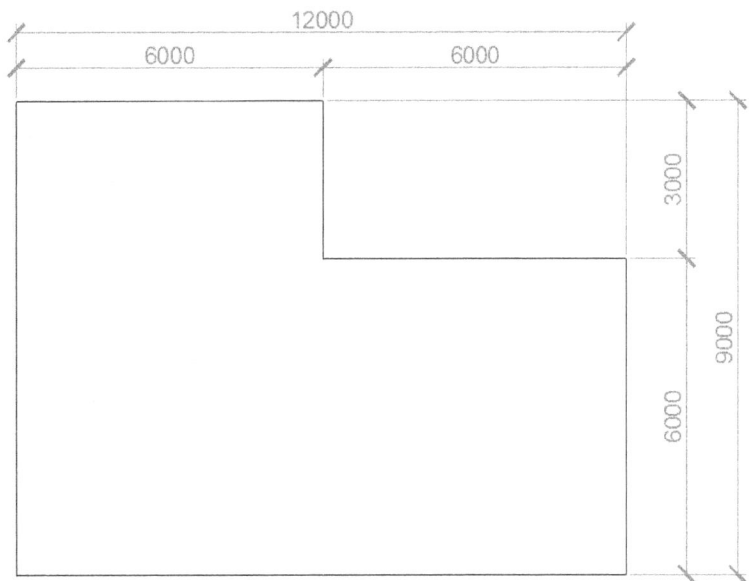

Figure 7–6

5. Save the drawing as **Plan1.dwg**.

6. Close both of the drawings.

7.2 What are Layers?

The AutoCAD software enables you to create an infinite number of layers in a drawing to organize the objects. Similar to overlays or transparencies, layers assist with editing, presentation, and system performance.

Layers organize a drawing into logical categories. For example, in mechanical drafting, views, hidden lines, sections, symbols, notes, and dimensions might be placed on separate layers. In an architectural drawing, there would be layers for walls, furniture, plumbing features, etc., as shown in Figure 7–7.

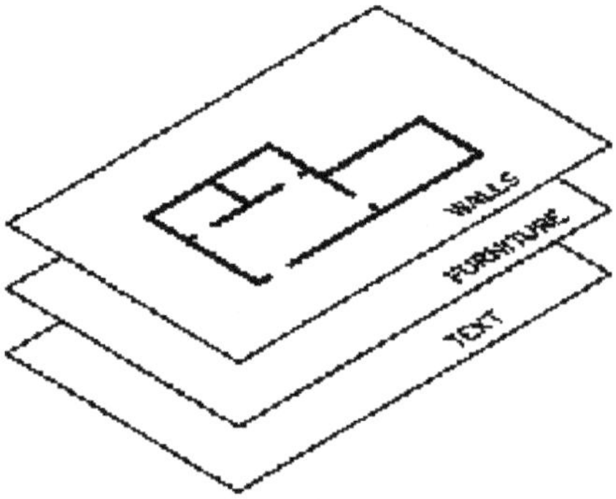

Figure 7–7

*   The *current layer* is the layer on which newly drawn objects, such as lines, circles, and text, are placed.

*   A color, linetype, and lineweight are assigned to each layer. When a layer is made current, you are automatically drawing in its assigned color, linetype, and lineweight.

*   By toggling layers *on* or *off*, you can control which part of the drawing displays or plotted.

*   The layer **0** is present in every drawing and cannot be removed or renamed. It is normally not used like the other layers and has special properties for blocks.

Setting the Current Layer

The current layer displays in the Layer Control in the *Home* tab>Layers panel, as shown on the left in Figure 7–8. Selecting the current layer name displays the drop-down list containing all of the existing layers in the current drawing, as shown on the right in Figure 7–8.

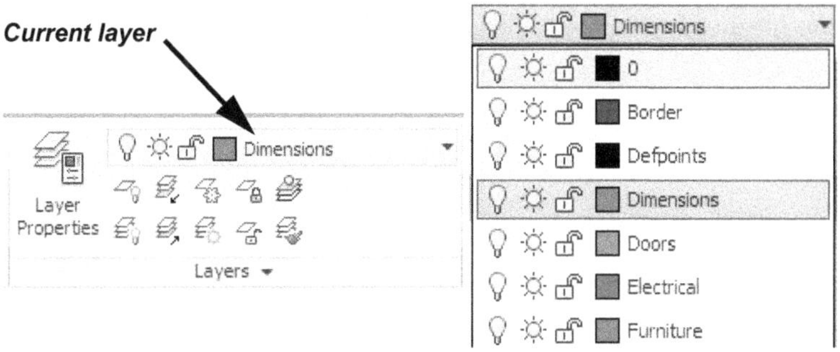

Figure 7–8

- To make a layer active, select its name in the Layer Control drop-down list.

- Another way to make a layer active is to select an object in the drawing and then in the *Home* tab>Layers panel, click ⬚ (Make Current). This makes the selected objects' layer active. You can also click ⬚ (Make Current) first and then select an object.

Using ⬚ (Make Current) indicates the active layer name in the Command Line as well.

- For easy access to various Layer tools, you can display the Layer Control bar in the Quick Access Toolbar, as shown in Figure 7–9. By default, the Layer Control does not display in the Quick Access Toolbar, but you can display it by selecting **Layer** in the ⬇ (Quick Access menu).

Enhanced
in 2018

Figure 7–9

Hint: Properties Panel

You can change the layer and *color, linetype, lineweight, plot style*, and *transparency* of individual objects. In the *Home* tab, the Properties panel enables you to set these characteristics for objects (as shown in Figure 7–10), just as the Layer Control enables you to set the layer.

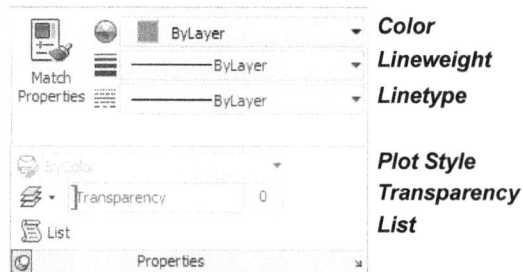

Figure 7–10

Normally, these properties are set to **ByLayer**, indicating that the objects do not have a specific color, linetype, lineweight, plot style, and transparency of their own. Instead, the layer that the objects are on defines their properties.

Although you can assign colors, linetypes, lineweights, plot style, and transparency to individual objects, it is usually best to let the object take its properties from its layer. This method ensures greater consistency and control over properties. You can easily change the color, lineweight, linetype, plot style, and transparency of all of the objects on a specific layer by changing the properties of the layer.

7.3 Layer States

The state of the layer determines how the objects on it are displayed and selected.

- The following three aspects of a layer's state can be changed in the Layer Control by selecting the appropriate symbol, as shown on the left in Figure 7–11.

- You can also use an object in the drawing to change its layer state by using the appropriate icon in the Layers panel, as shown on the right in Figure 7–11.

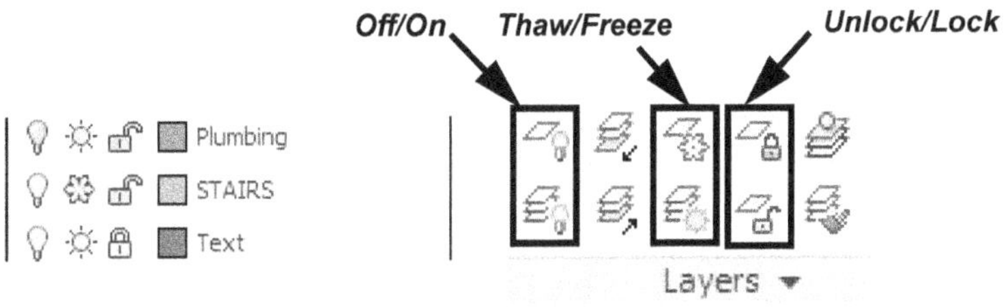

Figure 7–11

♀♀ On/Off

A layer can be toggled on (displayed) or toggled off (hidden). Toggling a layer off is like temporarily removing it from the drawing. Layers that are toggled off are not displayed and are not plotted.

- The current layer can be toggled off, but the software warns you with an alert box. If the current layer is toggled off, you can draw but cannot see what you are drawing.

☼❄ Thaw/Freeze

Layers that are not needed or displayed for a long time should be frozen. Freezing a layer is similar to toggling it off, except that the layer does not require calculation time when regeneration occurs.

- You cannot freeze the current layer and a frozen layer cannot be made current.

- If you thaw a layer, you might need to perform a regeneration operation to display the layer.

🔒🔓 Lock/ Unlock

Objects on layers that are locked can be viewed but not edited. When you hover the cursor over them, a small lock icon displays. By default, locked layers are also slightly grayed out.

- Locking a layer is useful when you do not want to accidentally edit the objects in the layer.

Returning a Layer to its Previous State

You sometimes need to change the state of layers to edit a drawing and then change them back to their previous state. After you have changed the current layer or state of layers, in the

Home tab>expanded Layers panel, use 🗒 (Layer Previous) to return to the previous layer settings.

Practice 7b

Working with Layers and Layer States

Practice Objectives

Estimated time for completion: 10 minutes

- Draw an object on specific layers.
- Change the state of a layer using Layer Control.

In this practice, you will draw an object on specific layers and then change the state of the layers.

Task 1 - Draw on and change layers.

In this task you will draw an object on specific layers, as shown in Figure 7–12.

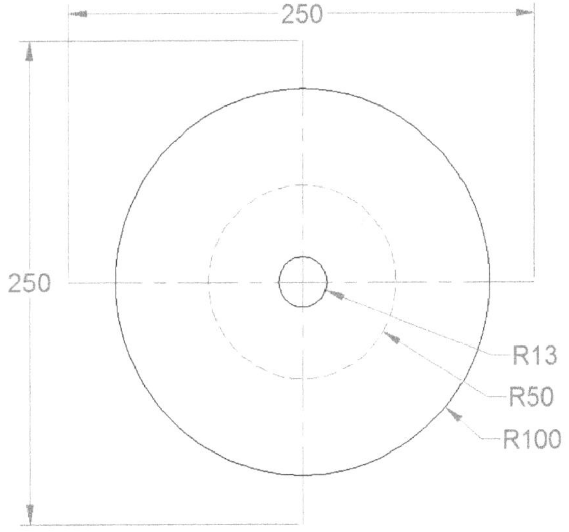

Figure 7–12

1. In the Application Menu, click **New**. Start a new drawing based on **Mech-Millimeters.dwt**, which is located in your practice files folder.

2. In the *Home* tab>Layers panel, expand the Layer Control and select **Center** to set it as the current layer.

You can also toggle on Layer Control in the Quick Access Toolbar and use the Layer tools there.

3. Draw a horizontal line, **250 units** long near the center of the screen. The line should be gold with a centerline style.

4. Draw a vertical line, **250 units** long separate from the line you just drew. Move it so that its midpoint is on the midpoint of the other line.

5. Change the current layer to **Object** by selecting it in the Layer Control.

6. Draw a circle with a radius of **100** with its center point at the intersection of the gold lines. The circle should be white on a black background (or black if the background is white).

7. Change the current layer to **Hidden**.

8. Draw another circle with a radius of **50** at the same center point as the first circle. It should be blue/green with a hidden line style.

9. In the *Home* tab>Layers panel, click 🖼 (Make Current) and select the large black circle. The current layer changes to **Object**.

10. Draw another circle with a **13** radius at the same center point. It should be white (or black) and continuous.

11. Save the drawing as **Wheel.dwg**.

Task 2 - Change the layer state.

In this task, you will change the state of layers.

1. Make layer **0** the current layer.

2. Use the Layer Control to toggle off the layer **Center**, as shown in Figure 7–13. The center lines should disappear.

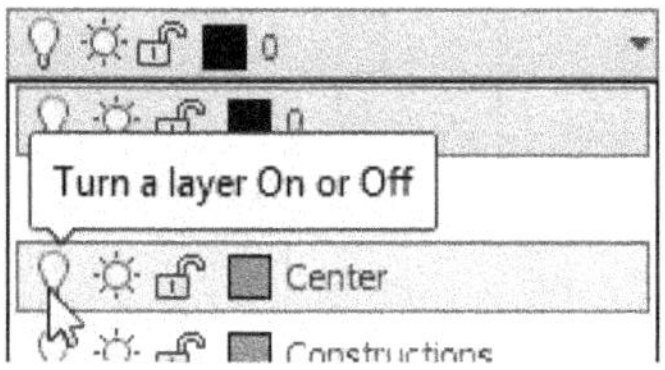

Figure 7–13

3. Use the Layer Control to freeze the layer **Hidden**, as shown in Figure 7–14. The blue/green circle should disappear.

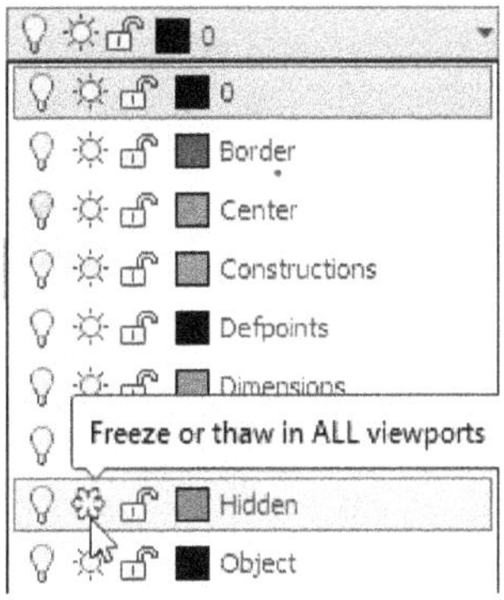

Figure 7–14

4. Use the Layer Control to lock the layer **Object**. The circles on that layer stay displayed, but are slightly grayed out.

5. Try to erase the largest circle and then try to move it. You cannot edit the circle because it is on the locked layer **Object**.

6. Use the Layer Control to unlock the layer **Object**.

7. Erase the largest circle. Use **Undo** to bring it back.

8. Save and close the drawing.

7.4 Changing an Object's Layer

You can move objects from one layer to another so that they show differently in the drawing, as shown in Figure 7–15.

Figure 7–15

Change with Layer Control

You can change the layer of a selected object(s) using the Layer Control.

How To: Change Object Layers with the Layer Control

1. Select an object before you start a command. The Layer Control displays the layer of the object.
2. Expand the Layer Control, and hover the cursor on another layer. Note that the selected object previews with the new layer, as shown in Figure 7–16.

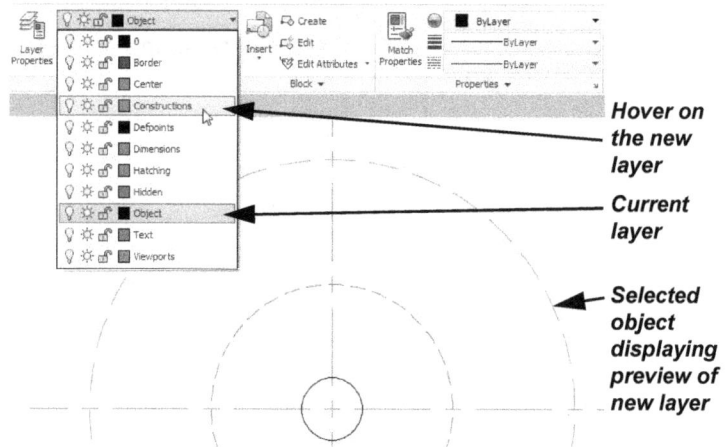

Hover on the new layer

Current layer

Selected object displaying preview of new layer

Figure 7–16

3. Select the layer to change it.

4. Press <Esc> to clear the selected object.

- You can select multiple objects to change their layers. If the selected objects are on different layers, a layer name does not display in the Layer Control. You can still hover to preview and then select a layer to move all of the objects to that layer.

Match Layer

Another way to change the layer of an object is to use the **Match Layer** command. This command can be used when you have other objects on that layer in your drawing.

How To: Match Layers

1. In the *Home* tab>Layers panel, click ⬕ (Match Layer).
2. Select the objects that you want to change.
3. Press <Enter> to finish the selection set.
4. Select an object on the destination layer.
5. Instead of selecting an object on the destination layer, you can press the <Down Arrow> which lists the **Name** option. Selecting **Name** opens the Change to Layer dialog box, in which you can select a layer name from a list, as shown in Figure 7–17.

Use this option if you do not know which object layer to select. Otherwise, it is faster to select the objects and then select the layer in the Layer Control.

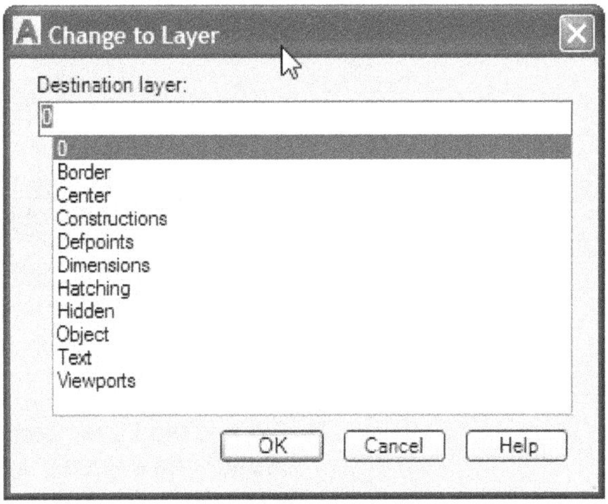

Figure 7–17

Practice 7c

Estimated time for completion: 5 minutes

Changing an Object's Layer

Practice Objective

- Move objects to different layers.

In this practice, you will use the Layer Control and the **Match Layer** command to move objects to different layers, as shown in Figure 7–18.

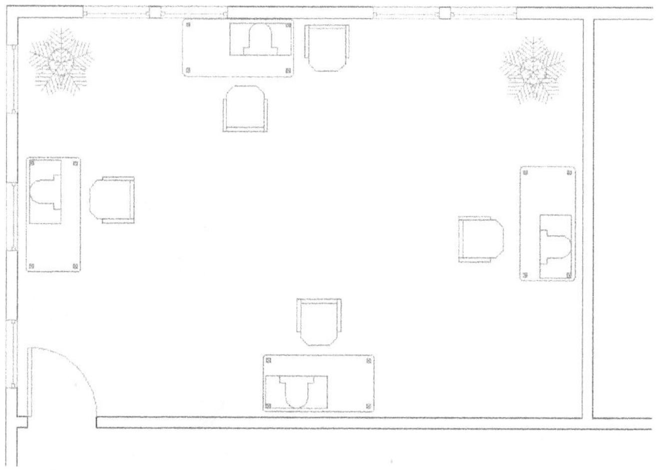

Figure 7–18

1. Open **Suite-AM.dwg** from your practice files folder. Currently, all of the objects are on layer **0**.

2. With no command active, select any one line of the wall (blue grips display on the line and it highlights in blue with a thicker lineweight). The layer of that line (layer **0**) displays in the Layer Control.

3. Expand the Layer Control and hover the cursor over the layer **Walls**. The selected wall changes to blue color (the color of layer Wall). Click to change the layer to **Walls**. Press <Esc> to clear the line.

4. Select one of the desks and repeat Step 3 to change its layer to the layer **Furniture**.

5. In the *Home* tab>Layers panel, click (Match Layer). Select the other desks in the room as the objects to be changed, and then press <Enter> or right-click. Select the desk that you changed in Step 4 as the object on the destination layer. All of the desks change layers to match the destination desk.

6. Use (Match Layer) to change the remaining walls to the layer **Walls** using the changed wall as the destination layer.

7. With no command active, select the two plants. Use the Layer Control to change their layer to **Misc**.

8. Change the remaining objects (chairs, PCs, door, and windows) to the appropriate layers. Use layer **Furniture** for chairs and layer **Electrical** for PCs.

9. Save and close the drawing.

Chapter Review Questions

1. Objects on layers that are frozen stay displayed in the drawing but cannot be edited.

   a. True

   b. False

2. How do you move an existing object to a different layer?

   a. Recreate the object on the correct layer.

   b. Use the **Move** command.

   c. Change the current layer, select the object, and press <Enter>.

   d. Select the object and pick the required layer in the Layer Control.

3. If you have finished drawing the walls in a floor plan drawing and want to display the objects, but do not want them to be erased or moved, what should you do?

   a. Lock the layer.

   b. Make a different layer current.

   c. Toggle the layer off.

   d. Freeze the layer.

4. After creating an object, how do you locate it on the same layer as another object in the drawing?

   a. Use **Match Layer**.

   b. Change the current layer.

   c. Use **Make Current (Layer)**.

   d. Redraw it on the correct layer.

5. When objects do not display on a specific layer and do not regenerated with the drawing, the layer is:

   a. Thawed

   b. Current

   c. Frozen

   d. Locked

6. A drawing file designed to be the basis of new drawing is called a:

   a. Setup File

   b. Prototype

   c. Template

   d. Seed File

Command Summary

Button	Command	Location
	Layer Control	• **Ribbon:** *Home* tab>Layers panel
	Layer Previous	• **Ribbon:** *Home* tab>Layers panel • **Command Prompt:** layerp
	Make Current (Layer)	• **Ribbon:** *Home* tab>Layers panel • **Command Prompt:** laymcur
	Match Layer	• **Ribbon:** *Home* tab>Layers panel • **Command Prompt:** laymch
	New/Qnew	• **Quick Access Toolbar:** New • **Application Menu:** New • **Command Prompt:** qnew or new

Chapter 8

Advanced Object Types

In this chapter you learn how to draw and edit arcs, polylines, polygons, and ellipses.

Learning Objectives in this Chapter

- Draw arcs, polylines, and ellipses using various commands.
- Create complex single objects consisting of lines and arcs.
- Modify polylines to add or remove vertices, change widths, or convert lines to arcs and vice-versa.
- Convert different objects into polylines.
- Create closed objects with three or more equal sides.
- Draw an ellipse by specifying the end points of the major and minor axes.

8.1 Drawing Arcs

The **Arc** command is used to add curved segments to a drawing, as shown in Figure 8–1. The information or geometry you have originally determines the option you use.

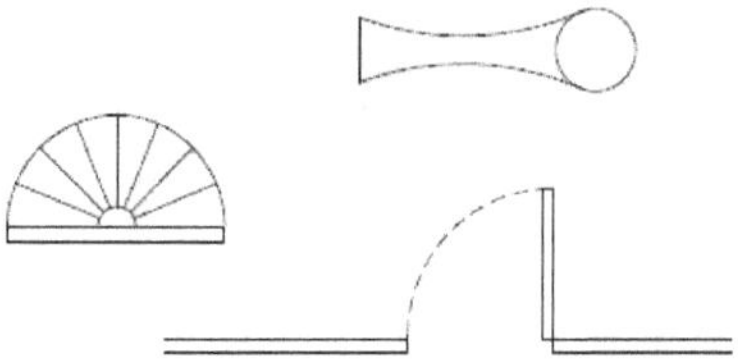

Figure 8–1

Arc Command Options

The **Arc** command has many options that enable you to create arcs. In the *Home* tab>Draw panel, expand (Arc) to access the different arc construction options available in the software, as shown on the left in Figure 8–2. The geometric definitions used for drawing arcs is shown on the right in Figure 8–2.

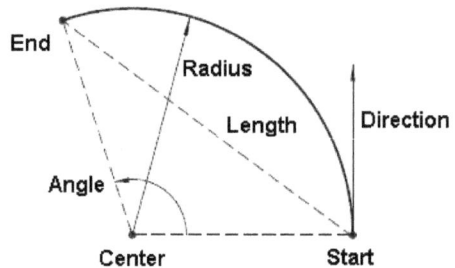

Figure 8–2

Start	Starting point of an arc.
Center	Center (or focal) point of an arc.
End	Ending point of an arc.
Radius	Radius of an arc.
Angle	Included angle turned by an arc.
Direction	Starting direction of an arc.
Chord (Length)	Chord length of an arc. (Distance between arc start and end points.)

Notes on Arcs

- Most arcs in the AutoCAD software are drawn in a counter-clockwise direction from the starting point. You can hold <Ctrl> to reverse the direction when constructing an Arc.

- Pressing <Enter> at the *Specify start point:* prompt starts drawing the arc from the end point of the last line or arc segment drawn. (This feature is only available when the *Specify start point:* prompt is the first prompt for the type of arc being created.)

- You can also type, use the shortcut menu, or use the <Down Arrow> menu to access the arc options.

Practice 8a

Drawing an Arc

Practice Objective

- Draw arcs using various options.

Estimated time for completion: 10 minutes

In this practice, you will draw door swings in a floorplan using the **Arc** command, as shown in Figure 8–3.

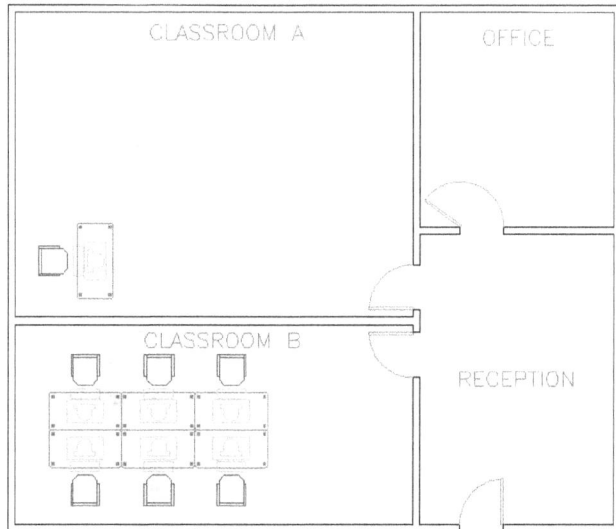

Figure 8–3

1. Open **Class-AM.dwg** from your practice files folder.

2. In the Layer Control, set the current layer to **Doors**.

3. Verify that the **Endpoint** Object Snap is on.

4. Zoom in on the office door.

5. In the *Home* tab>Draw panel, expand (Arc) and click (Start, Center, End).

6. At the *Specify start point of arc:* prompt, select the upper right corner of the doorway wall, as shown in Figure 8–4.

7. At the *Specify center point of arc:* prompt, select the point where the door and wall meet, as shown in Figure 8–4.

8. At the *Specify end point of arc:* prompt, select the upper left corner of the door, as shown in Figure 8–4. The arc that indicates the door swing is created, as shown in Figure 8–4.

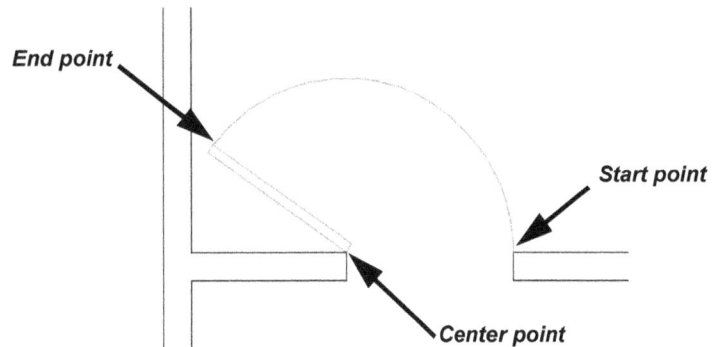

End point

Start point

Center point

Figure 8–4

9. Pan over to Classroom A's door.

10. In the *Home* tab>Draw panel, expand (Arc) and click (Start, Center, Angle).

11. At the *Specify start point of arc:* prompt, select the upper left corner of Classroom A's doorway wall.

12. At the *Specify center point of arc:* prompt, select the point where the door and wall meet.

13. For the angle, enter **90** and press <Enter>.

14. Pan over to Classroom B's door.

15. In the *Home* tab>Draw panel, expand (Arc) and click (Start, Center, Angle).

16. For the start point, select the lower left corner of Classroom B's doorway wall. For the center point, select the point where the door and wall meet, and for the angle, enter -**90**. Press <Enter> to create the door swing and complete the command.

17. Pan over to the last door (Reception). Add the arc for the door swing using a **Start, Center, End**. **Tip:** To create the door arc in clockwise direction, press and hold <Ctrl> before selecting the end point of the arc.

18. Save and close the drawing.

8.2 Drawing Polylines

Polylines are complex objects consisting of lines and arcs. Each segment in a polyline sequence is considered to be part of a single object. In addition, polylines can be assigned a width that can vary for each segment.

Polylines are ideal for drawing complex single objects, such as walls, transmission lines, ductwork, and schematic traces or area outlines, as shown in Figure 8–5.

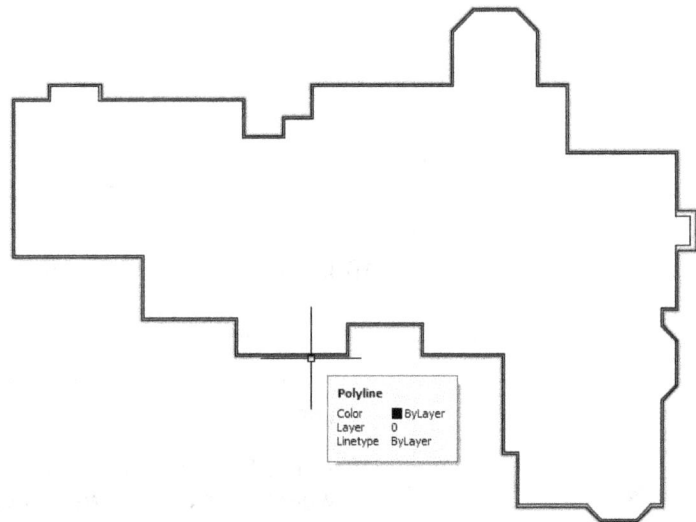

Figure 8–5

- Polylines can be used anywhere a regular line or arc can be used.

- When creating one continuous object, you cannot leave and restart the **Polyline** command.

- A polyline can be either open or closed. An open polyline can only have one start point and one end point.

How To: Draw a Polyline with Width and Arcs

1. In the *Home* tab>Draw panel, click ⌐⌐ (Polyline).
2. Select a start point. A cross displays, indicating that it is the start point. This is useful when creating complex polylines. The cross disappears when the polyline creation is completed.

3. (Optional) Select the **Width** option in the <Down Arrow> menu (as shown on the left in Figure 8–6), or type **W** and press <Enter>.

4. Enter a starting width or select two points to define the width.

5. Enter an ending width. If you want it to be the same as the starting width, you can press <Enter> to accept the default.

6. Select the next point(s).

7. (Optional) When you want to create an arc segment, do not end the **Polyline** command. Instead, select the **Arc** option in the <Down Arrow> menu or type **A** and press <Enter>.

8. Follow the prompts to create the required type of arc. The prompts are similar to those in the **Arc** command. When drawing an arc, you can press <Ctrl> to draw in the opposite direction.

9. To switch back to line segments, type **L** and press <Enter> or select the **Line** option from the <Down Arrow> menu, or the shortcut menu, as shown on the right in Figure 8–6.

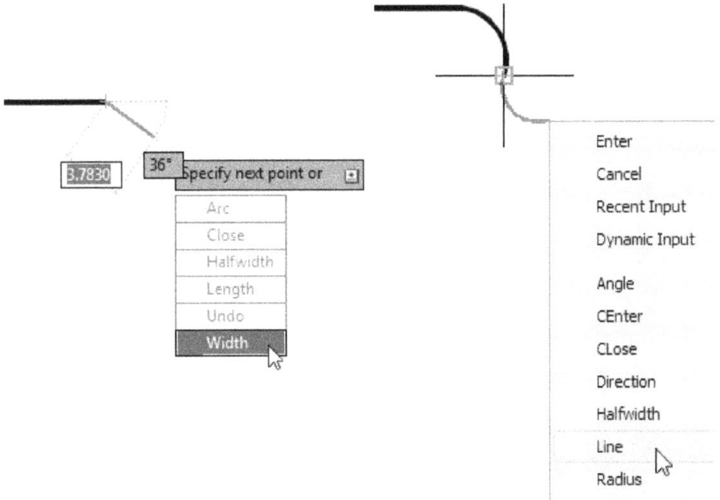

In the Polyline arc, use <Down Arrow> to display the Arc options.

Figure 8–6

10. If you want to create a closed polyline, use the **Close** option (CL). It attaches the last segment back to the start point.

• You can use the **Undo** option to remove the last segment drawn without ending the command.

• Other options include **Halfwidth**, which specifies the distance from the center of a wide polyline to one of its edges, and **Length**, which draws a segment of the specified length at the same angle as the previous segment.

8.3 Editing Polylines

You can edit polylines by moving a vertex, changing its width, joining polylines or lines and arcs together, and converting polylines into individual segments. You can also add and remove vertices from existing polylines and convert arcs to lines and vice-versa.

How To: Change the Width of an Existing Polyline

1. In the *Home* tab>expanded Modify panel, click ✏ (Edit Polyline).
2. At the *Select polyline:* prompt, select the polyline. An options menu displays, as shown in Figure 8–7.

You can also double-click on a polyline to display the options menu.

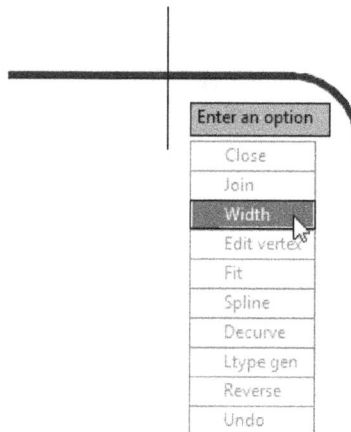

| Enter an option |
| Close |
| Join |
| **Width** |
| Edit vertex |
| Fit |
| Spline |
| Decurve |
| Ltype gen |
| Reverse |
| Undo |

Figure 8–7

3. Select the **Width** option.
4. At the *Specify new width for all segments:* prompt, enter the new width and press <Enter>.
5. Press <Enter> to end the command.

How To: Modify Vertices in Polylines using Edit Polyline

1. In the *Home* tab>expanded Modify panel, click ✏ (Edit Polyline).
2. Select the polyline that you want to edit. You can also double-click on a polyline to display the options menu.
3. Select the **Edit vertex** option.
4. An icon displays on the polyline, indicating the vertex that is currently being edited. To select a different vertex, select the **Next** option until the one you want to edit displays.

5. Select one of the following options to modify the current vertex:

Break	Breaks the polyline at the selected vertex, separating it from the rest of the polyline. If you break a polyline in more than one place, the separated objects remain polylines.
Insert	Inserts a new vertex at the selected point on the polyline. You can place the new vertex anywhere on the polyline.
Move	Moves a vertex to a new position on the polyline. You can move the current vertex to a new location, anywhere on the polyline.
Straighten	Deletes segments and vertices between two selected vertices, and replaces them with a single straight line segment.
Tangent	Attaches a tangent direction to the selected vertex to be used for curve fitting later.
Width	Modifies the width of the selected line or arc between two adjacent vertices.

6. Use the **Next** and **Previous** options to continue modifying vertices. Select **eXit** to return to the **Edit Polyline** command options, or press <Esc> to end the command.

Modifying Polyline Vertices using Grips

If you select a polyline when you are not in a command, the vertex grips and midpoint grips display. You can modify them by adding or deleting vertices, stretching them, and converting them from a line to an arc and vice-versa. You can access these options by hovering the cursor over a multifunctional vertex grip and selecting an option in the list, as shown in Figure 8–8.

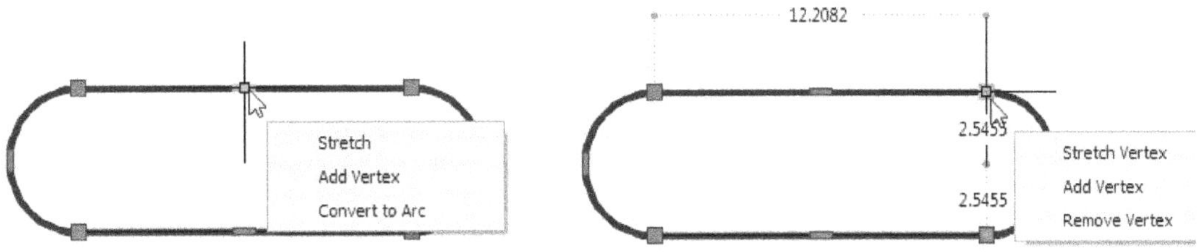

Figure 8–8

How To: Use Vertices to Convert a Line to an Arc

1. When not in a command, select a polyline to display its vertices.
2. On the object, hover on a vertex that you want to change. For example, if you want to change a line into an arc, hover on the midpoint vertex on the line.
3. Select **Convert to Arc**.
4. Drag the arc to the required size or enter the required dimension.
5. Continue selecting vertices and modifying them or press <Esc> to end the command.

Converting Lines and Arcs to Polylines

In some cases, creating lines and arcs and then turning them into a polyline is easier than using the **Polyline** command from the start. While separate lines and arcs work in most cases, having them work together as a polyline can be useful. For instance, selecting one object to move is easier than selecting all of the pieces from which it has been created, as shown in Figure 8–9.

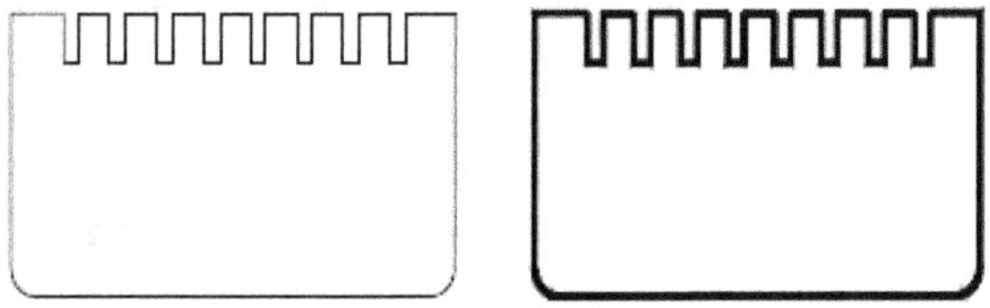

Figure 8–9

How To: Convert Lines and Arcs into a Single Polyline

1. In the *Home* tab>expanded Modify panel, click ✐ (Edit Polyline).
2. At the *Select polyline or:* prompt, select a line or arc.
3. At the *Do you want to turn it into one?:* prompt, press <Enter> to select the Y option.
4. Select **Join** in the options menu that displays.
5. Select the other objects that you want to join to the polyline, which get highlighted.
6. Press <Enter> once to end the *Select objects:* prompt.
7. Press <Enter> again to end the command.

- The **Multiple** option (at the *Select Polyline:* prompt) enables you to edit several polylines at once, or to convert multiple line segments into polylines at the same time.

- To be joined, each line segment or arc must be attached to the end point of the next.

- For open polylines, **Edit Polyline** displays the **Close** option; for closed polylines, it displays the **Open** option.

Hint: Joining Objects

━┼━ (Join) (in the *Home* tab>expanded Modify panel) joins broken polylines, lines, arcs, elliptical arcs, and splines, as shown in Figure 8–10. Polylines that can be joined can overlap, gap, or touch end points. If you select two lines, they need to be touching each other end to end.

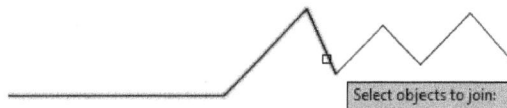

Select objects to join:

Figure 8–10

You can join objects of different types (e.g., lines, polylines, and splines). The final joined object becomes the most complex of the selected objects. Therefore, if you select a line and a polyline, the final joined object is a polyline.

- With arcs, the **Close** option can be used to close arcs (e.g., to form circles).

- The source object determines the properties (e.g., layer, color, etc.) of the new object.

Turning Polylines into Lines and Arcs

When a polyline has been created, you might want to break it into all of its separate component parts, so that you can remove individual segments or make other changes.

- In the *Home* tab>Modify panel, click 🗐 (Explode) to convert a polyline into individual arcs and lines.

- Exploding a wide polyline causes it to lose its width information.

- The **Explode** command works on other object types that are made from polylines, such as rectangles or polygons. It also works on blocks.

Hint: Splines

The **Edit Polyline** command has a **Spline** option that converts a polyline into an approximation of a smooth curve, called a *spline curve*, as shown in Figure 8–11. (The **Fit** option is similar but the curve is not as smooth.)

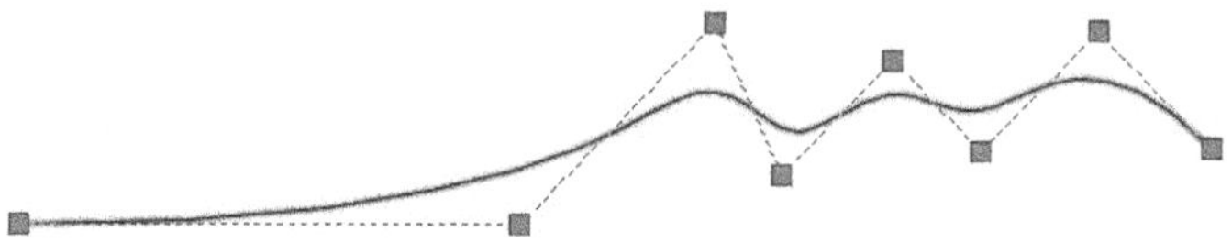

Figure 8–11

You can also use $\overset{\curvearrowright}{\;}$ (Spline Fit) or $\overset{\curvearrowright}{\;}$ (Spline CV) in the *Home* tab>expanded Draw panel for creating true spline curves. These are mathematically more exact and easier to control than splined polylines. After a spline has been created, its shape can be further refined using $\oslash$ (Edit Spline) in the *Home* tab>expanded Modify panel.

Splines are important in special drawing applications that use curves extensively (such as contour maps), or that require exact control of complex curves (such as the shape of a hull in shipbuilding, or the aerodynamic surfaces of airplanes and cars.)

Practice 8b

Drawing and Editing Polylines

Practice Objectives

- Draw polylines and convert a polyline into separate lines and arcs.
- Convert lines and arcs into a polyline.
- Change the width of a polyline.

Estimated time for completion: 15 minutes

In this practice, you will draw polylines. You will edit several polylines and change their width so that they will be used as symbols in a flowchart.

Task 1 - Draw polylines for a flowchart.

In this task you will create several polylines as symbols to be used in a flowchart, as shown in Figure 8–12.

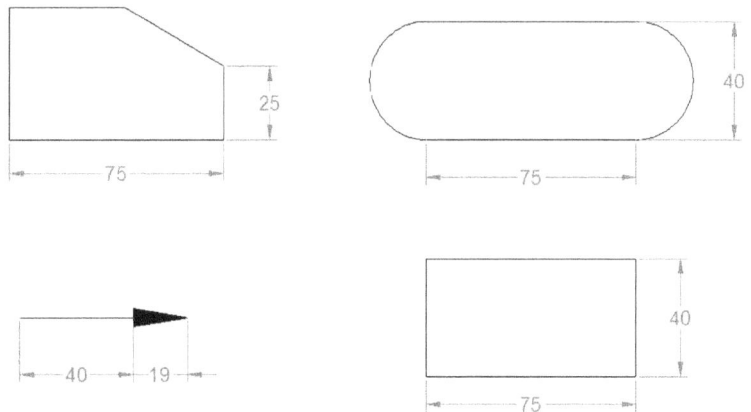

Figure 8–12

1. Start a new drawing based on **Mech-Millimeters.dwt**, which is located in your practice files folder, and save it as **Flowchart.dwg**.

2. Verify that 🔲 ▾ (Object Snap) and ∠ (Object Snap Tracking) are both toggled on. The Object Snaps should be set to **Endpoint, Midpoint**, and **Extension**.

3. Expand ⟳ ▾ (Polar Tracking) and select **30,60,90,120...**. Ensure that it is toggled on.

4. In the *Home* tab> Draw panel, click ⌐◡ (Polyline) and draw the top left symbol, as shown in Figure 8–12.

    •   Specify the start point anywhere.

    •   Move the cursor right, enter **75**, and press <Enter>.

    •   Move the cursor straight up, enter **25**, and press <Enter>.

    •   Move the cursor at an angle of **150** degrees, enter **40**, and press <Enter>.

    •   Make the next point straight to the left, but track it to make it directly above (even with) the start point.

    •   Type **C** and press <Enter> to close the figure and finish the command.

5. Start the **Polyline** command again and draw the top right symbol, as shown in Figure 8–12.

    •   Specify the start point anywhere.

    •   Move the cursor right, enter **75**, and press <Enter>.

    •   Type **A** and press <Enter> to switch to the **Arc** option.

    •   Move the cursor straight up, enter **40**, and press <Enter>.

    •   Type **L** and press <Enter> to switch to the **Line** option.

    •   Move the cursor left, enter **75**, and press <Enter>.

    •   Switch to the **Arc** option and type **CL** to close the figure and finish the command.

A rectangle is also a polyline.

6. The bottom right symbol shown in Figure 8–12 can be drawn using the **Rectangle** command or **Polyline** command.

7. Start the **Polyline** command and draw the arrow, as shown in Figure 8–12.

    •   Specify the start point anywhere.

    •   Move the cursor right, enter **40**, and press <Enter>.

    •   Type **W** and press <Enter> to switch to the **Width** option.

    •   For the starting width, enter **6** and press <Enter>.

    •   For the ending width, enter **0** and press <Enter>.

    •   Move the cursor straight to the right, enter **19**, and press <Enter>.

    •   Press <Enter> to finish the command.

8. Arrange the objects to create the simple flowchart shown in Figure 8–13. Move, copy, and rotate the objects as required.

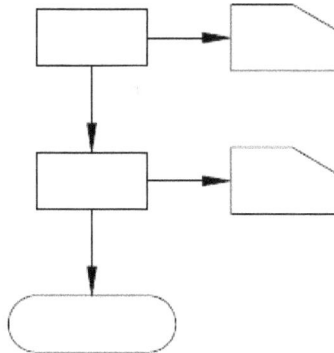

Figure 8–13

9. Save the drawing.

Task 2 - Edit polylines.

In this task you will explode a polyline, and then use the **Edit Polyline** command to join arcs and lines into a polyline and change the width, as shown in Figure 8–14.

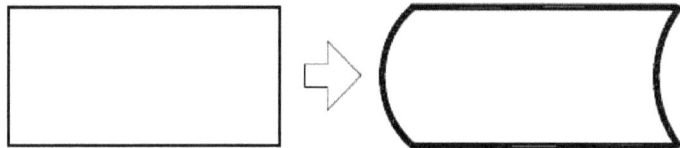

Figure 8–14

1. Make a copy of the rectangle.

2. Select the copied rectangle and explode it (in the *Home* tab>Modify panel, click (Explode)). Erase the vertical lines. You can select the lines individually because the object is no longer a polyline.

3. Draw a 3-point arc at each end of the two lines remaining from the rectangle that you exploded in Step 2. Use the **Endpoint** object snap to connect the arcs to the lines. (**Tip:** Draw it at one end and then copy it to the other end).

4. In the *Home* tab>expanded Modify panel, click (Edit Polyline) and select one of the lines. At the *Do you want to turn it into one?:* prompt, press <Enter> to select **Yes**.

---

5. In the options menu, select **Join**.

6. At the *Select objects:* prompt, select the other line and the arcs and press <Enter>.

7. Select the **Width** option. Set the *width* to **1** and press <Enter>. Press <Enter> again to exit the command.

8. Use the **Move** command to move the shape. It is now all one object.

9. Verify that you are not in a command and select the polyline.

10. Hover the cursor over one of the midpoint grip vertices on one of the arcs and select **Convert to Line**.

11. Repeat the previous step for the other arc. The shape is now a rectangle.

12. Save and close the drawing.

8.4 Drawing Polygons

The **Polygon** command generates closed geometric figures with three or more equal sides, such as triangles, hexagons, and diamonds, as shown in Figure 8–15.

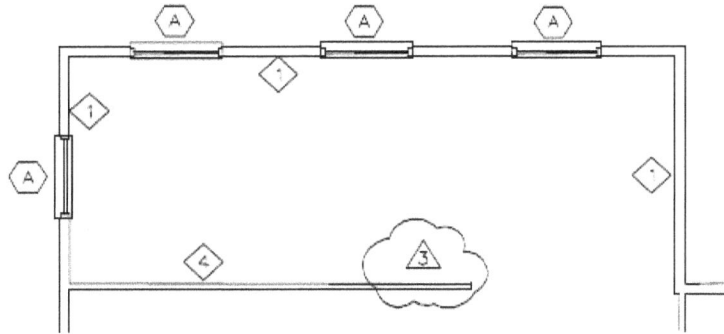

Figure 8–15

- The AutoCAD software builds these objects from polylines. Therefore, all of the sides form one unified object.

- Since polygons are made from polylines, you can use the **Edit Polyline** command to assign a width, explode them to create separate segments, or edit the vertices.

How To: Draw an Inscribed or Circumscribed Polygon

1. In the *Home* tab>Draw panel, expand the Rectangle drop-down list and click ⬠ (Polygon).
2. Enter the number of sides for the polygon, and press <Enter>.
3. Locate the center point anywhere in the drawing window.

4. Select **Inscribed in circle** or **Circumscribed about circle**, as shown in Figure 8–16.

- An *inscribed* polygon is defined by the distance from the specified center to one of its vertices (inscribed in the imaginary circle).

- A *circumscribed* polygon is defined by the distance from the specified center to one of the edges (circumscribed about the imaginary circle).

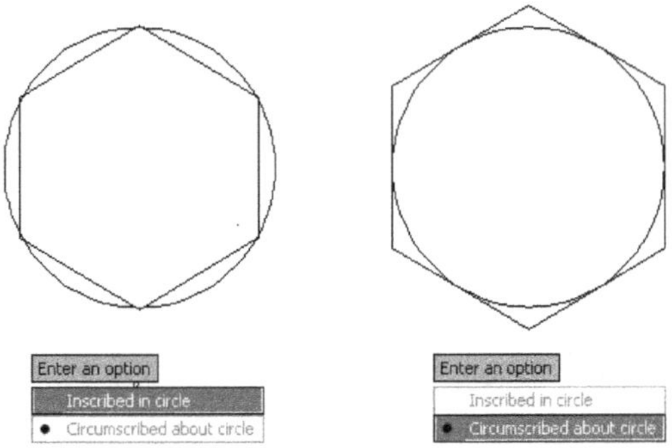

Figure 8–16

5. Enter the radius of the circle.

How To: Draw a Polygon by Edge

1. In the *Home* tab>Draw panel, expand the Rectangle drop-down list and click  (Polygon).
2. Enter the number of sides for the polygon, and press <Enter>.
3. At the *Specify center of polygon:*, type **E** for the **Edge** option.
4. At the *Specify first endpoint of edge:*, select a point to locate an endpoint of one of the sides of the polygon.
5. At the *Specify second endpoint of edge:* prompt, select a point to locate the other endpoint of the side of the polygon. This input defines the length of all of the sides (edges) and the angle at which the polygon is rotated, as shown in Figure 8–17.

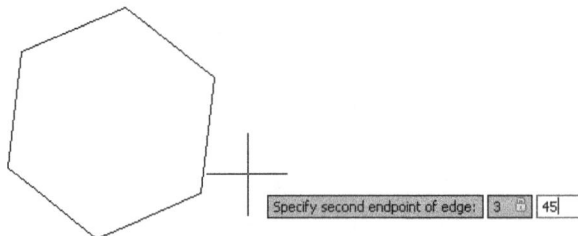

Figure 8–17

Practice 8c

Drawing Polygons

Practice Objective

Estimated time for completion: 5 minutes

- Create polygons.

In this practice, you will create symbols using the **Polygon** and **Rectangle** commands, as shown in Figure 8–18.

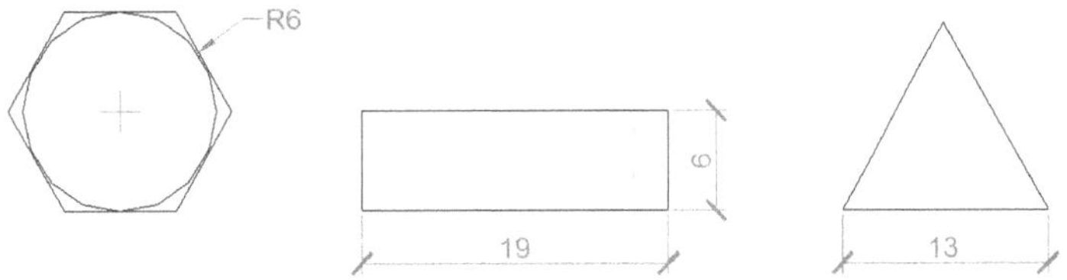

Window Tag   **Room Number**   **Revision Triangle**

Figure 8–18

1. Start a new drawing based on **AEC-Millimeters.dwt**, which is located in your practice files folder, and save it as **Symbols.dwg**.

Draw only the objects, not the text or dimensions.

2. Draw the symbols shown in Figure 8–18. For the Window Tag, start the **Polygon** command (In the *Home* tab>Draw panel, expand the Rectangle drop-down list and click

   (Polygon)). For the number of sides, enter **6** and press <Enter>. Select anywhere in the drawing window as its center. Select **Circumscribed about circle** and enter **6** as the radius. Press <Enter> to complete the command. To zoom in closely, use **Zoom Extents**. (Note: You do not have to draw the circle inside of the polygon. It is for reference only.)

3. Draw the Room Number using the **Rectangle** command and the Revision Triangle using 3 sided **Polygon** command.

4. Save and close the drawing.

8.5 Drawing Ellipses

The **Ellipse** command creates full ellipses or elliptical arcs. An ellipse is defined by two axes. You specify one axis first by selecting its two end points, or by selecting the center of the ellipse and one end point. The first axis can be either the major (longer) or minor (shorter) axis, as shown in Figure 8–19. You then specify the second axis.

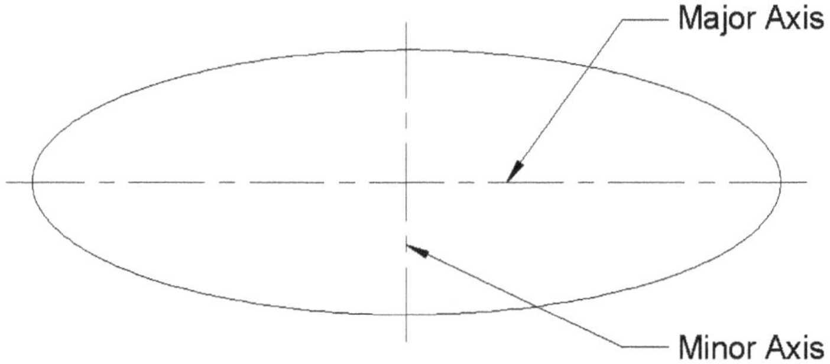

Figure 8–19

How To: Draw a Basic Ellipse

1. In the *Home* tab>Draw panel, expand the Ellipse drop-down list and click ⬭ (Ellipse-Axis,End).
2. Specify the first axis end point of the ellipse and then the second axis end point. This describes the length of the ellipse.
3. Specify the distance to the other axis. This describes the width of the ellipse.

- To create an elliptical arc, you define a full ellipse first, and then specify which portion of it is going to be included in the arc. In the *Home* tab>Draw panel, expand the Ellipse drop-down list and click ⬭ (Elliptical Arc) to start the **Ellipse** command with the **Arc** option.

- ⬭ (Ellipse - Center) starts the **Ellipse** command with the **Center** option.

Additional Command Options

Rotation	Enables you to define the major to minor axis ratio by rotating a circle around the first axis.

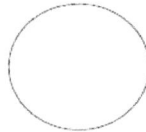

ROTATION = 30   ROTATION = 45   ROTATION = 60

Center	Enables you to define the first axis by selecting the center of the ellipse and one end point of the axis.
Arc	Prompts you to create a full ellipse using any of the methods above, and then specify which portion to include in the arc.

Arc Options

Start Angle/ End Angle	Enables you to select or enter the starting and ending angles for the arc.
Included	Enables you to select or enter a value to define the included angle beginning at the start angle.
Parameter	Prompts for the same input as **Start Angle**. However, the software uses a parametric vector equation to calculate the elliptical arc.

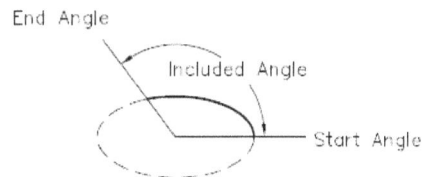

End Angle

Included Angle

Start Angle

Practice 8d

Drawing Ellipses

Practice Objective

Estimated time for completion: 5 minutes

- Create an ellipse and an elliptical angle.

In this practice, you will use the **Ellipse** command to create a 2D drawing of a cylinder, as shown in Figure 8–20.

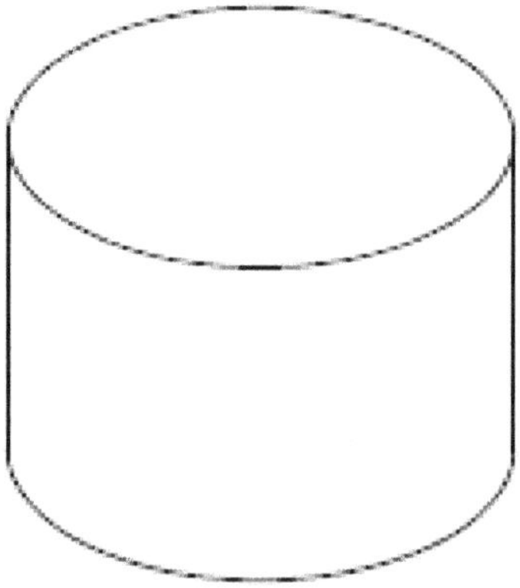

Figure 8–20

1. Start a new drawing based on **Mech-Millimeters.dwt**, which is located in your practice files folder, and save it as **Drum.dwg**.

2. Draw a vertical line **75** units long.

3. Copy that line **120** units to the right to create a parallel line.

4. In the *Home* tab>Draw panel>Ellipse drop-down list, click (Axis,End).

5. For the first axis end point, select the upper end point of the left line.

6. For the other axis end point, select the upper end point of the right line.

7. At the *Specify distance to other axis:* prompt, type **R** for Rotation, press <Enter>, and enter **60**.

8. In the *Home* tab>Draw panel>Ellipse drop-down list, click (Elliptical Arc).

9. Select the lower end points of the lines as the axis end points.

10. At the *Specify distance to other axis:* prompt, type **R** for Rotation, press <Enter>, and enter **60**.

11. At the *Specify start angle:* prompt, select the lower end point of the left line.

12. At the *Specify end angle:* prompt, select the lower end point of the right line.

13. Save and close the drawing.

Chapter Review Questions

1. Which of the following is a valid method for constructing an arc in the AutoCAD software?

   a. **3 Points**

   b. **2 Points**

   c. **4 Points**

   d. **Center, Diameter**

2. Which of the following is NOT true for a polyline?

   a. The segments are all considered to be one object.

   b. It cannot include arcs.

   c. It can have varying widths in each segment.

   d. They can be open or closed.

3. Which command breaks a polyline into individual line and arc segments?

   a. **Break**

   b. **Explode**

   c. **Edit Polyline**

   d. **Snap**

4. Which command enables you to convert regular lines into a polyline?

   a. **Union**

   b. **Edit Polyline**

   c. **Join**

   d. **Make Polyline**

5. Polygons are built from polylines and can be modified using the **Edit Polyline** command.

   a. True

   b. False

6. How many axes are required to define and create an ellipse?

   a. 1

   b. 2

   c. 3

   d. 4

7. A series of continuous line and/or arc segments that act as one unified object is a:

   a. Rectangle

   b. Construction Line

   c. Polyline

   d. Block

Command Summary

Button	Command	Location
	Arc	• **Ribbon:** *Home* tab>Draw panel • **Command Prompt:** arc or A
	Edit Polyline	• **Ribbon:** *Home* tab>expanded Modify panel • **Command Prompt:** pedit or PE
	Edit Spline	• **Ribbon:** *Home* tab>expanded Modify panel • **Command Prompt:** splinedit
	Ellipse (Center)	• **Ribbon:** *Home* tab>Draw panel • **Command Prompt:** ellipse or EL
	Ellipse (Axis, End)	• **Ribbon:** *Home* tab>Draw panel • **Command Prompt:** ellipse or EL
	Ellipse (Elliptical Arc)	• **Ribbon:** *Home* tab>Draw panel • **Command Prompt:** ellipse or EL
	Explode	• **Ribbon:** *Home* tab>Modify panel • **Command Prompt:** explode or X
	Polygon	• **Ribbon:** *Home* tab>Draw panel (*under the Rectangle drop-down list*) • **Command Prompt:** polygon or POL
	Polyline	• **Ribbon:** *Home* tab>Draw panel • **Command Prompt:** pline or PL
	Join	• **Ribbon:** *Home* tab>expanded Modify panel • **Command Prompt:** join
	Spline Fit	• **Ribbon:** *Home* tab>expanded Draw panel • **Command Prompt:** spline
	Spline CV	• **Ribbon:** *Home* tab>expanded Draw panel • **Command Prompt:** spline

Analyzing Model and Object Properties

In this chapter you learn how to get information about objects and to measure exact distances and areas.

Learning Objectives in this Chapter

- Display and modify the basic properties of single or multiple objects.
- Measure distances, radii, diameters, angles, areas, and volumes in a drawing.

9.1 Working with Object Properties

Every object in the AutoCAD® software has properties, such as layer, color, and linetype, and geometric information (e.g., the end points of a line, center points of a circle or arc, etc.). Many properties can be changed using Quick Properties, the Properties palette, or **Match Properties**. You can also use properties to help you select objects when using **Quick Select**.

- Hover the cursor over an object to display a tooltip containing basic information about the object, as shown in Figure 9–1.

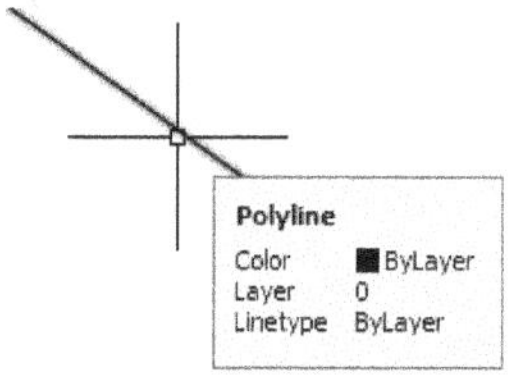

Figure 9–1

Quick Properties

When you select an object when not in a command and display its grips, the basic information about that object displays in the Quick Properties panel, as shown in Figure 9–2. These vary depending on the type of object selected.

Figure 9–2

Press <Esc> to clear a selected object.

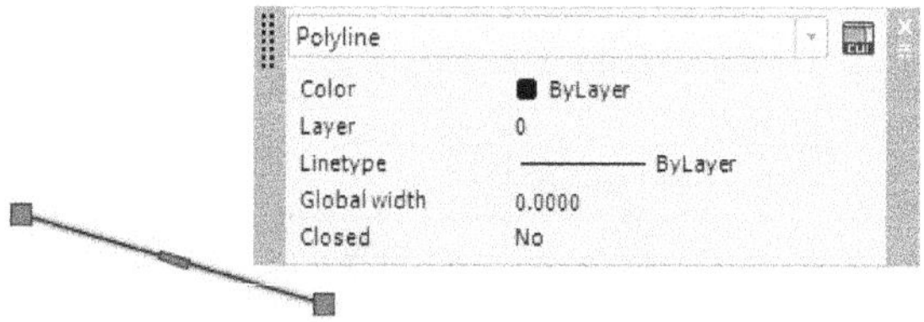

- The Quick Properties panel displays along with a selected object (in grip mode) when ▦ (Quick Properties) is toggled **On** in the Status Bar.

To display ▦ (Quick Properties) in the Status Bar, expand ▤ (Customization) and select Quick Properties.

- When ▦ (Quick Properties) is toggled **Off, y**ou can display the Quick Properties for individual objects by selecting them (in grip mode), right-clicking, and selecting **Quick Properties** in the shortcut menu.

- You can preview and change some properties in the Quick Properties panel. Click on a property and select a different option from the drop-down list, as shown in Figure 9–3.

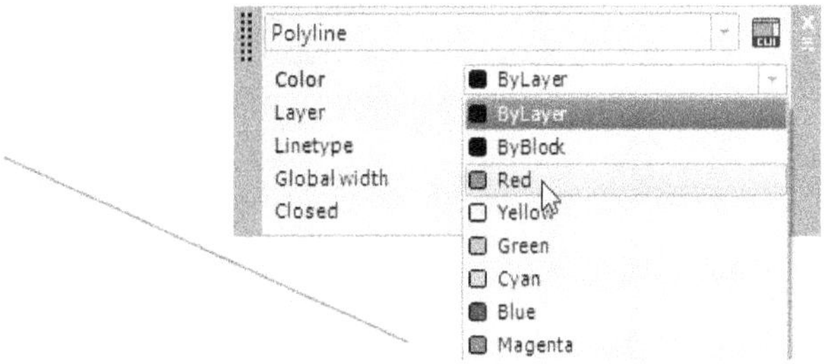

Figure 9–3

- You can also display a list of the basic properties for an object

  using ▤ (List) in the *Home tab*>expanded Properties panel. The AutoCAD Text window opens, displaying some of the properties of the selected object. You cannot change any properties using the **List** command.

Properties Palette

The primary way to get detailed information about the objects in your drawing is to use the Properties palette, as shown in Figure 9–4. It reports all of the properties of the object and enables you to change many of them.

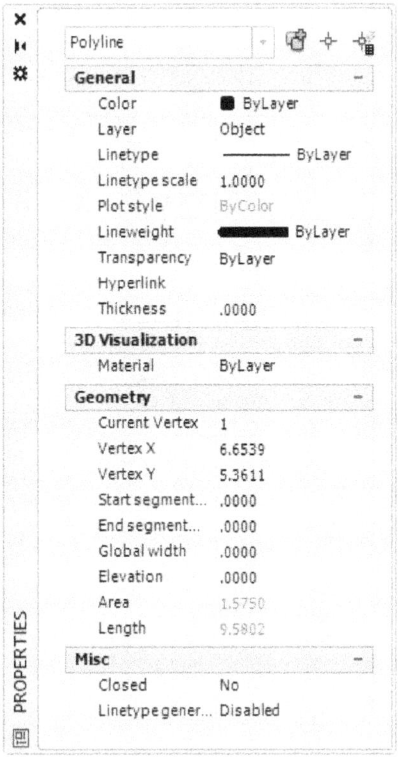

Figure 9–4

- You can toggle the Properties palette on or off using any of the following methods:
  - In the *View* tab>Palettes panel, click ▣ (Properties).
  - Press <Ctrl>+<1>.
  - In the *Home* tab>Properties panel, click ⌐ .
  - In grip mode, right-click on an object and select **Properties** in the shortcut menu.

- You can have the Properties palette open even when an object is not selected. Once you select any object, its properties display in the open Properties palette.

- As with other palettes, you can dock the Properties palette to any side of the screen. Click, hold, and drag using its title bar and move it to either side of the screen. Once it shows the docking outline, leave the cursor as it automatically docks it in place. You can also hide the palette by clicking the ◄ icon located in the Properties title bar, as shown in Figure 9–5. Once hidden, it displays as a bar along the docked side and you can temporarily unhide it by hovering the cursor over the bar. You can also unhide it permanently by clicking ► in the title bar. Use **X** to close the palette.

PROPERTIES	◄ ✕

Figure 9–5

How To: Modify Objects Using Properties

1. Open the Properties palette if it is not already open and select an object. The properties of the object display in the palette, as shown in Figure 9–6.

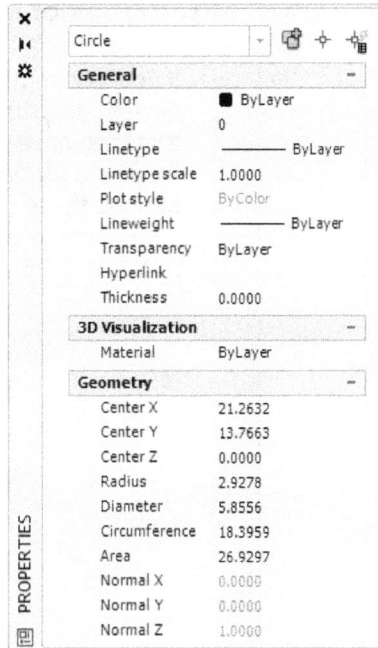

Figure 9–6

2. Change the properties as required by selecting the value you want to change and then typing or selecting a new value.

   • As you move the cursor over the options in the drop-down lists, the object in the Drawing window changes to provide a preview of the highlighted option.

3. To clear the object, move the cursor into the drawing window and press <Esc>.

• Some properties display a list of options, such as the *Layer* property shown on the left in Figure 9–7.

• Other options are numerical, as shown on the right in Figure 9–7. You can enter a number, click 🖩 to open the QuickCalc calculator dialog box, or click 🕏 to modify the location of a point on the screen.

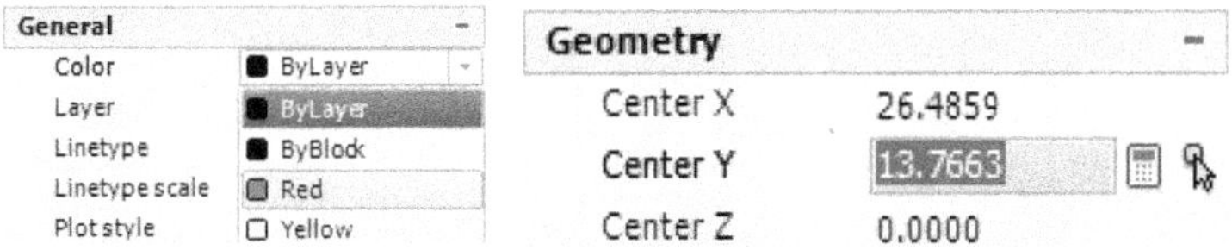

Figure 9–7

• Information in grayed-out cells cannot be changed.

Properties of Multiple Objects

- If you select more than one object of the same type (e.g., two circles), the AutoCAD software lists the types of properties that they have in common. If their values are different they are listed as ***VARIES***, as shown in Figure 9–8. You can change these properties for all of the selected objects at the same time (e.g., select several circles and change their radius to 2.25).

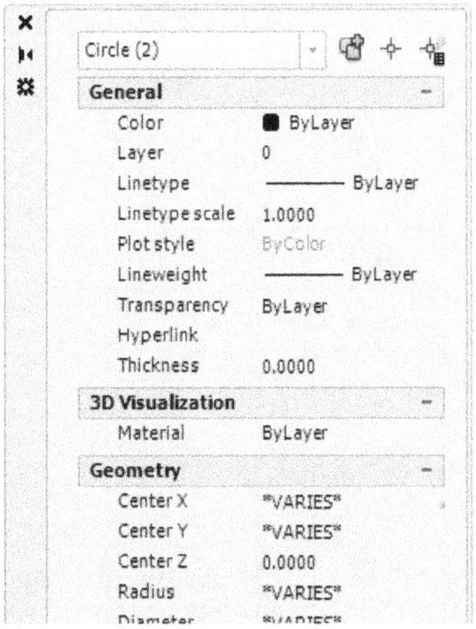

Figure 9–8

- If you select different types of objects (e.g., a circle and a line), the AutoCAD software displays the only types of properties that they have in common. If their values are different, they are listed as ***VARIES***. You can change the common properties of all of the selected objects at the same time. You can also switch between different types of objects using the drop-down list, as shown in Figure 9–9.

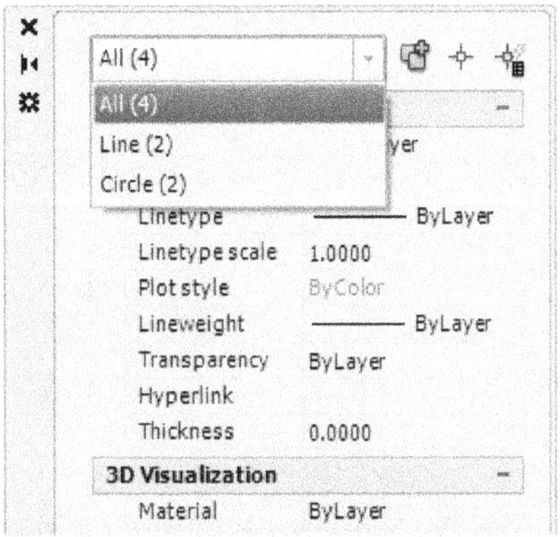

Figure 9–9

Matching Properties

To make objects in your drawing have the same properties as another object, use the **Match Properties** command. It enables you to select one object as a *model* and then copy its properties to any other object you select.

How To: Copy an Object's Properties

1. In the Home tab>Properties panel, click ![icon] (Match Properties).
2. At the *Select source object:* prompt, select the object you want to use as a model. The cursor changes into a small square box with a paint brush.
3. As you move the cursor over the object that you are going to select, the object changes and displays a preview of the new properties. Select the objects to which you want the properties to be copied.
4. Press <Enter> to end the command.

- **Match Properties** works across drawings. Specify the source object in one drawing, and in the drawing tab bar click on another drawing to switch to it and select the destination objects. If the layer does not exist in the destination drawing, it is created. When you hover over the object in the second drawing, the object highlights but does not display a preview of the new properties.

- **Match Properties** enables you to match all or some of an object's properties. To control which properties are matched, use the **Settings** option (available in the shortcut menu or Command Line) when you have started the command and selected the source object. By default, all of the properties are selected, as shown in Figure 9–10.

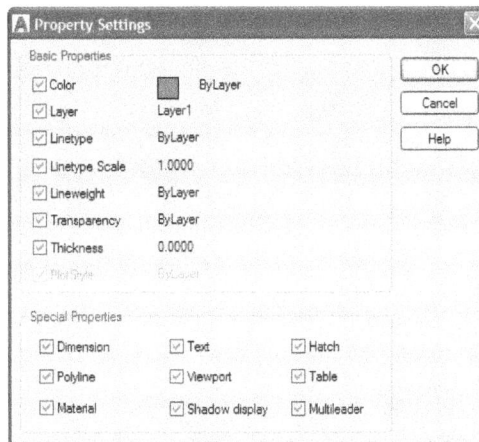

Figure 9–10

Quick Select

Quick Select can be used to select objects using their properties. It opens a dialog box in which you can specify a selection set by object type and/or properties (such as all of the circles with a radius of 0.25), as shown in Figure 9–11.

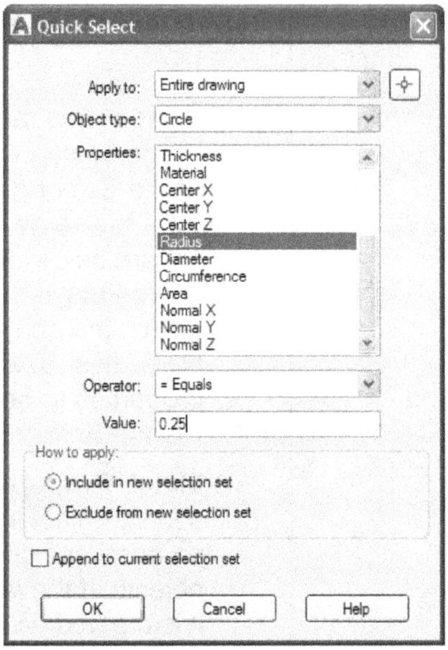

Figure 9–11

How To: Select Objects Using Quick Select

To select all of the objects in your drawing, in the Home tab>Utilities panel, click ✛ (Select All).

1. In the *Home* tab>Utilities panel or in the Properties palette, click (Quick Select).
2. In the Quick Select dialog box, in *Apply to*, use **Entire drawing** or click (Select objects) to create a selection set.
3. Select the required *Object type*. **Multiple** selects all of the object types. Only object types that are currently in the selection set display in the drop-down list.
4. In *Properties:*, select the property that you want to filter. This varies according to the selected object type.
5. Select an *Operator:*, as shown in Figure 9–12. The available operators vary depending on the selected property type.

*To select all of the objects of a specific type, regardless of their properties, use **Select All** for the Operator. For example, you can use this method to find all of the circle objects.*

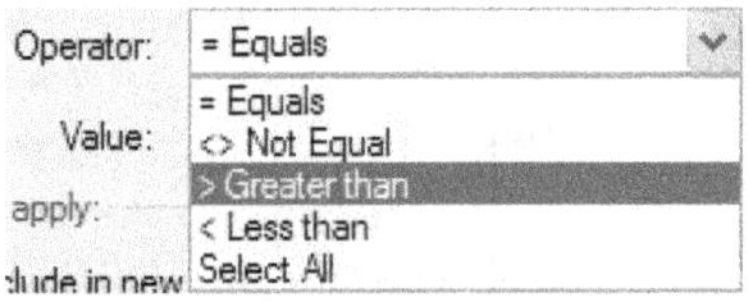

Figure 9–12

6. Specify the value that you want to find for the selected property. The available values vary depending on the selected property type. For example, values for the property **Layer** include all of the layers defined in the drawing. For the Radius value (of a circle), you need to enter a number.

7. Select an option for how the filter is going to be applied:

   - **Include in new selection set:** Places all of the objects that meet the criteria in a new selection set.

   - **Exclude from new selection set:** Places all of the objects that DO NOT meet the criteria in a new selection set.

8. If you want to build a selection set from several filters, select the **Append to current selection set** option, which adds the results to the current selection, rather than creating a new selection set.

9. Click **OK** to close the Quick Select dialog box. Objects that match the criteria are selected.

10. Use an editing command on the selected objects (such as **Erase** or **Properties**) to modify them.

Practice 9a

Working with Object Properties (Mechanical)

Practice Objective

* Obtain information about objects.

Estimated time for completion: 5 minutes

In this practice, you will get information about some objects (as shown in Figure 9–13) and then make changes to them, using the Quick Properties panel and the Properties palette.

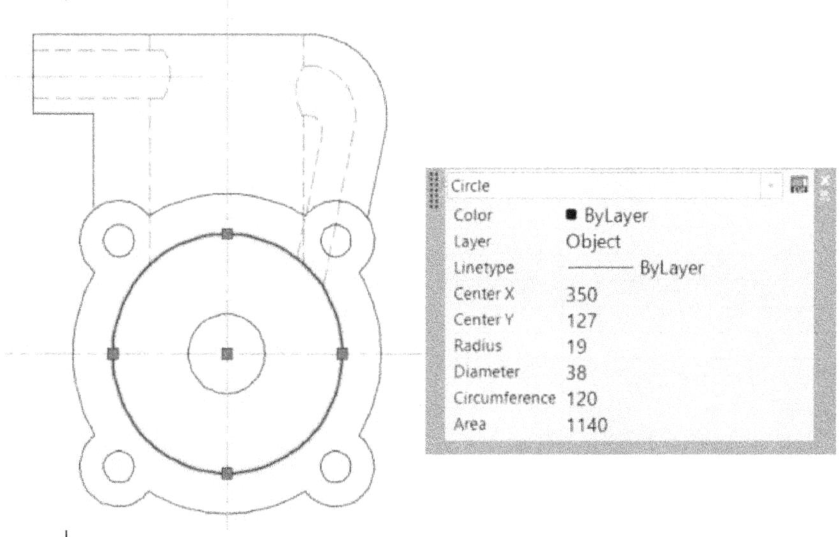

Circle	
Color	■ ByLayer
Layer	Object
Linetype	———— ByLayer
Center X	350
Center Y	127
Radius	19
Diameter	38
Circumference	120
Area	1140

Figure 9–13

1. Open **Crank-M.dwg** from your practice files folder.

2. In the Status Bar, toggle on ▦ (Quick Properties).

3. Select the large full circle to display the Quick Properties panel, as shown in Figure 9–13. Press <Esc> to clear the selection.

4. Select the gray horizontal center line at the top left of the object. In its Quick Properties, note that it contains the *Layer* **CONSTRUCTION**. Click anywhere in the *CONSTRUCTION* row to open its edit box. Expand the Layer drop-down list. Hover the cursor over the layer Center and note how the gray line previews as orange, as shown in Figure 9–14. Select **Center** to change the layer.

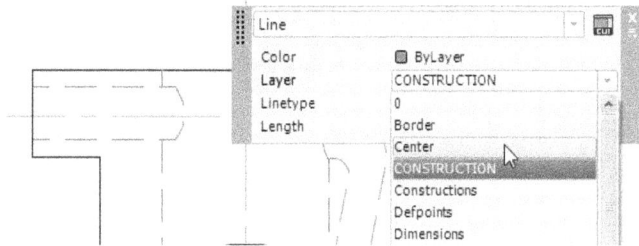

Figure 9–14

5. Clear your selection and toggle ▦ (Quick Properties) off in the Status Bar.

6. In the *Home* tab>Utilities panel, click ✛▤ (Quick Select).

7. In the Quick Select dialog box, set the *Object type* to **Circle**, *Properties* to **Diameter**, and *Operator* to **= Equals**. In the, *Value* edit box, enter **5** and click **OK**. The objects with the above properties (four small circles with the diameter 5) are selected and highlighted in the drawing.

8. Click ⌐ in the *Home* tab> Properties panel to open the Properties palette. To dock the palette to one side of the screen, click, hold, and drag using its title bar and move it to either side of the screen. Once it shows the docking outline, leave the cursor as it automatically docks it in place.

9. In the *Geometry* area, change the diameter to **7**, as shown in Figure 9–15. As soon as you press <Enter>, note that the selected circles become bigger.

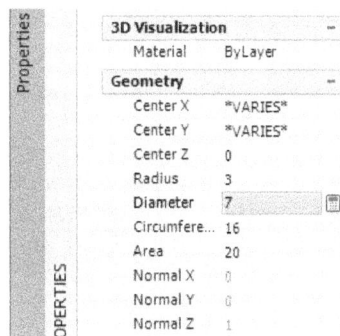

Figure 9–15

10. Clear the selection.

11. Hover the cursor on the Properties title bar and click **X** to close the Properties palette.

12. Save and close the drawing.

Practice 9b

Working with Object Properties (Architectural)

Practice Objective

Estimated time for completion: 10 minutes

- Locate objects based on their properties and change their values.

In this practice, you will use the Properties palette and Quick Select to find objects based on their layer, and then move them to the correct layer. You will also find text based on its height and change it to the correct height, as shown in Figure 9–16.

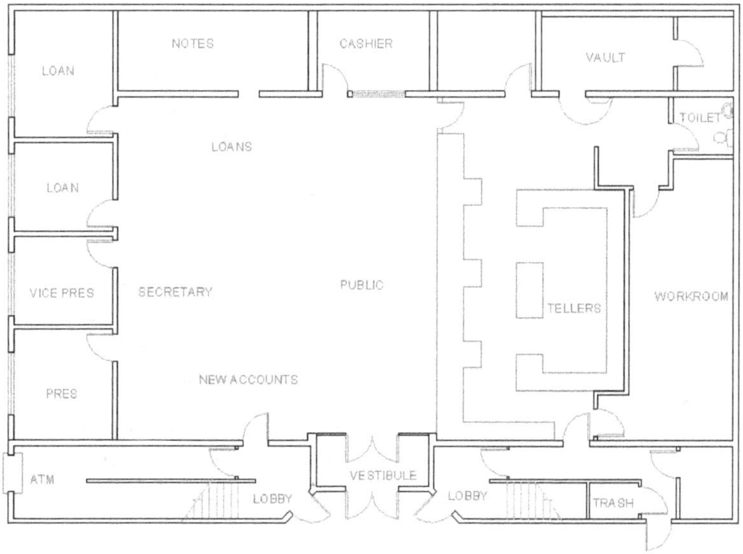

Figure 9–16

1. Open **Bank-Building-AM.dwg** from your practice files folder.

2. In the *Home* tab>Layers panel, expand the Layer Control and scroll through the names. The Layer Control contains the layers **WALL** and **Walls**. You need to place all of the walls on the layer **Walls**.

Click ⬚ in the Home tab>Properties panel or use <Ctrl>+<1> to open the Properties palette.

3. Open the Properties palette, if it is not already open. Dock it to one side and hide it by clicking the ◄ icon located in the Properties title bar.

4. In the *Home* tab>Utilities panel, click 🔲 (Quick Select). To select everything on the layer **WALL**, in the Quick Select dialog box, set the *Object type* to **Multiple**, *Properties* to **Layer**, *Operator* to **= Equals**, and *Value* to **WALL**, as shown in Figure 9–17. Click **OK**. The selected objects are highlighted in the drawing.

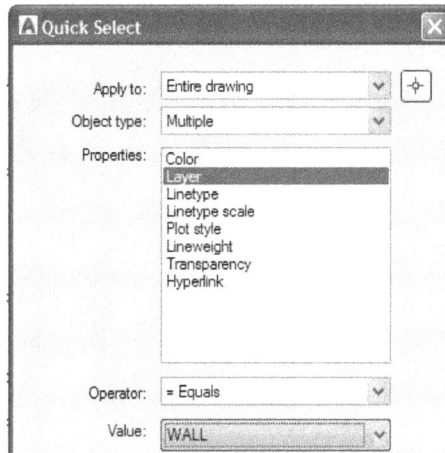

Figure 9–17

5. Hover the cursor over its title bar to unhide the Properties palette. In the *General* area, in the *Layer edit box,* change the *WALL* to layer **Walls** and press <Esc> to clear the objects.

6. In the *Home* tab>Utilities panel, click 🔲 (Quick Select), and in the dialog box, set the *Object type* to **Text** and the *Operator* to **Select All**. Click **OK**. All of the text in the drawing is highlighted. What layer is the text on? In the Properties palette, change the text to layer **Text** and press <Esc> to clear the objects.

7. Use 🔲 (Quick Select) and the Properties palette to select all of the text that is less than **250** in height and change its *Height* to **300**.

8. Close the Properties palette.

9. Save and close the drawing.

9.2 Measuring Objects

In drawings, you need to obtain the exact measurements of the objects that you create. For example, you might need to check the diameter of a machine cylinder, the distance from the property line to the corner of a parking lot, or the area of a room in a house as shown in Figure 9–18.

If you enter the information accurately, you retrieve accurate information.

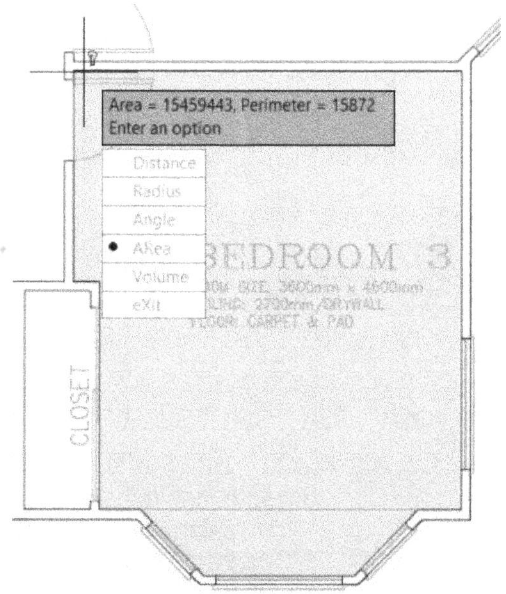

Figure 9–18

- Object snaps enables you to select points when measuring distances and areas to get exact and accurate measurements.

Using the Measure Tools

The **Measure** command enables you to measure distances, radii, diameters, angles, areas, or volumes. In the *Home* tab>Utilities panel, expand ▭ (Measure) and select an option as shown in Figure 9–19.

*The **Measure** tool that you select automatically replaces the default measure tool until another one is selected or you end your current AutoCAD session.*

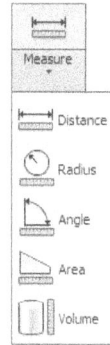

Figure 9–19

Measuring Distances

One of the most basic measurements you need to make is the distance between points.

How To: Measure a Distance

1. In the *Home* tab>Utilities panel, expand ⊨⊣ (Measure) and click ⊨⊣ (Distance). The cursor displays ⚲.

Use Endpoint object snap to select the points.

*Typing **DIST** in the Command Prompt also starts a distance measurement command, which enables you to measure the distance between two selected points.*

2. Select the first point and then the second point between which you want to measure the distance. The distance displays as shown in Figure 9–20.

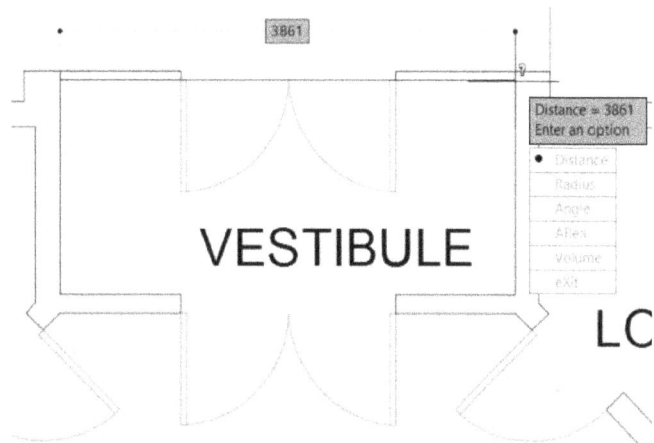

Figure 9–20

3. Press <Enter> to measure another distance or select a different option as shown in Figure 9–20.
4. Select the **eXit** option or press <Esc> to end the command.

How To: Get a Running Total of Distances

1. In the *Home* tab>Utilities panel, expand ⊨⊨ (Measure) and click ⊨⊨ (Distance). The cursor displays 💡.
2. Select the first point to measure.
3. Select the **Multiple Points** option (<Down Arrow> and select Multiple points or type **M**).
4. Select the other points that you want to measure.
5. Press <Enter> to end the command and display the total.

Hint: ID Point

📐 (ID Point), located in the *Home* tab>expanded Utilities panel, provides the X-, Y-, and Z-axis coordinates of any selected point. Use object snaps to select a precise point.

Measuring Radius and Diameter

To find the radius and diameter data for circles or arcs you can expand ⊨⊨ (Measure) and click ◷ (Radius). Select the circle or arc to measure. A tooltip displays the information in the drawing area as shown in Figure 9–21.

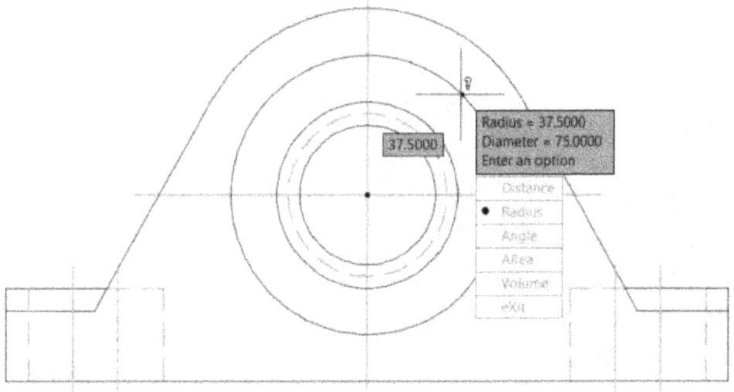

Figure 9–21

Measuring Angles

(Angle) in the **Measure** command can be used to display the angle between two lines, the opening angle of an arc, or any angle defined by a vertex and to other locations.

How To: Measure the Angle between Two Lines

1. In the *Home* tab>Utilities panel, expand (Measure) and click (Angle). The cursor displays .
2. Select one line.
3. Select a second line. The angle displays as shown in Figure 9–22.

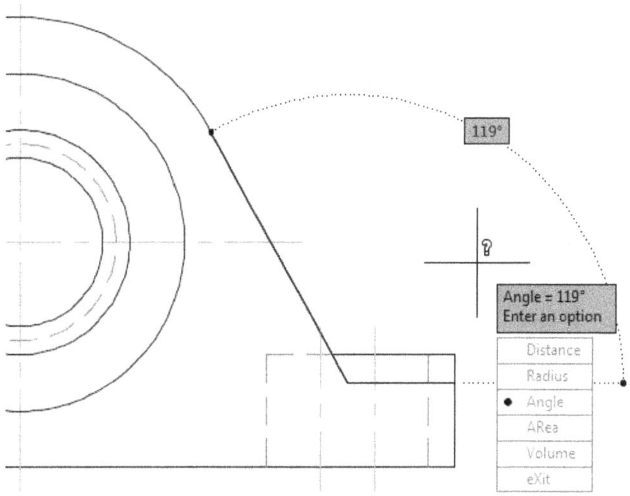

Figure 9–22

- To display the opening angle of an arc, click on the arc.

How To: Measure a Angle using a Vertex

1. In the *Home* tab>Utilities panel, expand (Measure) and click (Angle).
2. At the *Select arc, circle, line or <Specify vertex>:* prompt, press <Enter> to specify a vertex.

3. Select a point (1) for the vertex, as shown in Figure 9–23.
4. Select a point (2) for the first angle end point.
5. Select a point (3) for the second angle end point.

*If you click on a circle, it also enters the **Vertex** option. The first click on a circle also determines the first point of the angle. Selecting a second point on the circle or outside the circle completes the angle measurement.*

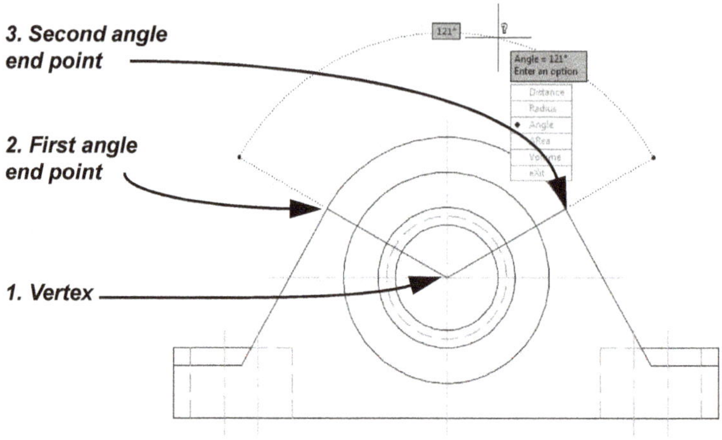

3. Second angle end point

2. First angle end point

1. Vertex

Figure 9–23

Measuring Areas

To measure the area of an object you can either pick points or select closed objects, such as polylines or circles to define areas. You can also add and subtract areas that you want to include.

How To: Measure an Area by Picking Points

1. In the *Home* tab>Utilities panel, expand ⬚ (Measure) and
   click ⬚ (Area). The cursor displays ⬚.
2. Select points around the area that you want to measure, as shown in Figure 9–24. A green fill indicates the selected area.

Use Object Snaps to select the exact points to measure.

*When you pick points you can switch between lines and arcs using the same options as the **Polyline** command.*

Figure 9–24

3. When you are finished, press <Enter> to display the total. The area and perimeter display.

How To: Measure the Area by Selecting a Closed Object

1. In the *Home* tab>Utilities panel, expand ⊨⊨⊨ (Measure) and click ◺ (Area). The cursor displays ⚐.
2. At the *Specify first corner:* prompt, type **O** and press <Enter> to select the **Object** option.
3. Select an object, such as a polyline, circle, or rectangle. The area and perimeter display as shown in Figure 9–25.

*The temporary fill automatically disappears when the **Measure** command is finished.*

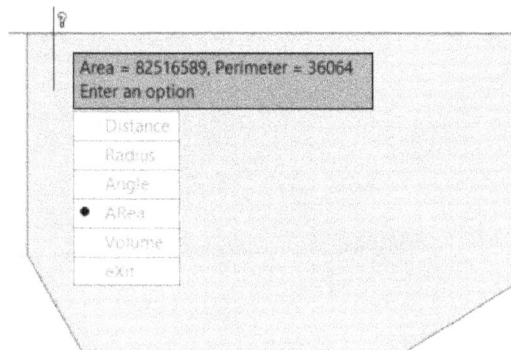

Figure 9–25

How To: Add and Subtract Areas

1. In the *Home* tab>Utilities panel, expand ⊨⊨ (Measure) and click ◻ (Area). The cursor displays ?.
2. Select the **Add area** option first (<Down Arrow> and select **Add area**). You are placed in ADD mode and can select items to add by selecting points or using the **Object** option.
3. Press <Enter> to end ADD mode.
4. Select the **Subtract area** option (<Down Arrow> and select **Subtract area**).
5. Select the areas to subtract by selecting points or using the **Object** option. When you are in SUBTRACT mode, the selected areas display with a brown fill, as shown in Figure 9–26.

*◻▯ (Volume) calculates the volume of 3D objects using a method that is similar to the **Area** option. If you are working with 2D objects, set the boundaries as you do with area. You are then prompted to define a height to complete the calculation.*

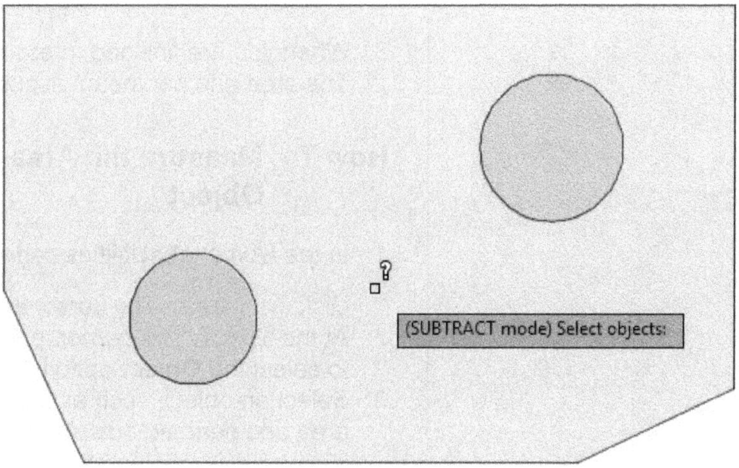

(SUBTRACT mode) Select objects:

Figure 9–26

6. Press <Enter> to end Subtract mode. The area and parameter information display.
7. Select **eXit** or press <Esc> to end the command.

Practice 9c

Measuring Objects (Architectural)

Practice Objective

Estimated time for completion: 5 minutes

- Check areas and distances in a floorplan.

In this practice, you will check areas and distances in a floorplan using the various Measure tools, as shown in Figure 9–27.

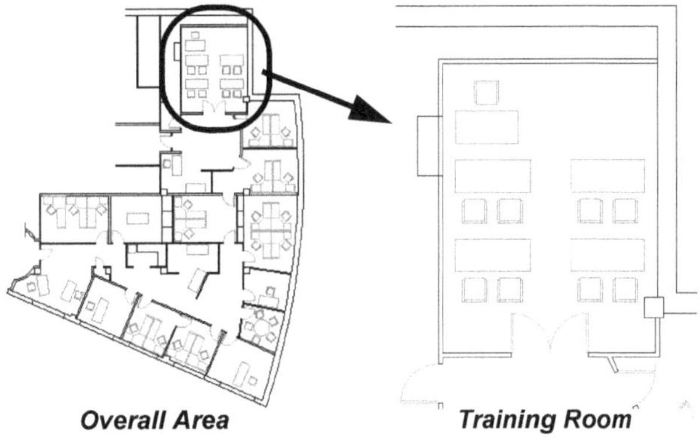

Overall Area   *Training Room*

Figure 9–27

1. Open **Office Plan-AM.dwg** from your practice files folder.

2. Zoom in on the training room at the back of the building (top of the floor plan). In the *Home* tab>Utilities panel, expand

   (Measure) and click (Area) to determine the area of the room in square meters (use the **Endpoint** osnap to pick the four corners of the training room and ignore the column and door opening). **Note:** Depending on your unit settings, the software might display the area in square millimeters. Convert them into square meters. The area in square meters is:

   a. 33.8

   b. 3.38

   c. 34.1

   d. 40.2

3. In the training room, the size of the column in millimeters is (Use **Measure>Distance** command):

   a. 500 x 500

   b. 452 x 452

   c. 420 x 420

   d. 600 x 600

4. Thaw the layer **Area**. It contains a magenta polyline that outlines a section of the building. Using the **Measure>Area** command with the **Object** option, what is the area rounded to the nearest square meter?

   a. 369.8

   b. 300.8

   c. 372.8

   d. 366.8

5. Close the drawing. Do not save changes.

Practice 9d

Estimated time for completion: 5 minutes

Measuring Objects (Mechanical)

Practice Objective

- Find the area of objects.

In this practice, you will find the areas of objects in a drawing (shown in Figure 9–28) using the Measure tools.

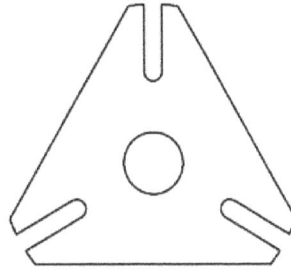

Figure 9–28

1. Open **Triangular-Plate-M.dwg** from your practice files folder.

2. Hover the cursor over various parts of the outline. Note that it consists of separate lines and arcs.

3. Use the **Edit Polyline** command with the **Join** option to turn the outside of the object into a single polyline.

4. Select the new polyline and review the information in Properties palette. To display the exact location of each vertex, click on the arrow buttons (as shown in Figure 9–29), to scroll through the vertices.

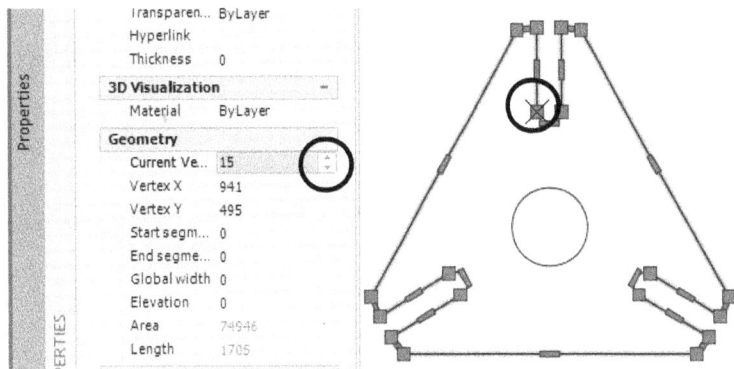

Figure 9–29

5. Use the **Measure>Area** command with the **Object** option to find the area of the outside shape.

   a. 72837

   b. 74946

   c. 75624

   d. 65306

6. Use the **Measure>Area** command to find the area of the shape with the hole removed. First use the **Add** and **Object** options, and then select the outline to find the total area. Press <Enter> to exit the Add mode. Then use the **Subtract** and **Object** options and select the circle (as shown in Figure 9–30). The total area of the shape minus the hole is:

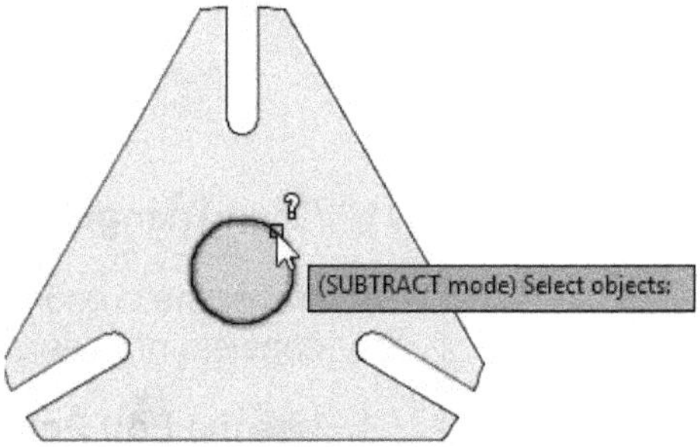

Figure 9–30

   a. 69943

   b. 65824

   c. 67941

   d. 70254

7. Close the drawing. Do not save changes.

Chapter Review Questions

1. Which command reports the length of a line?

   a. **ID Point**

   b. **Measure>Length**

   c. **Quick Select**

   d. **Properties**

2. Which tool should you use when measuring distances and areas to get exact measurements?

   a. Object Snap

   b. Object Snap Tracking

   c. Grid

   d. Polar Tracking

3. How do you specify the area to measure with the **Measure>Area** command?

   a. Pick points to define the boundary of the area.

   b. Pick a single point on the boundary of the area.

   c. Double-click inside a closed area.

   d. Pick any point inside a closed area.

4. One of the differences between List and the Properties palette is that with **List** you can only view the information, while with the Properties palette you can edit some of the information to modify the object.

   a. True

   b. False

5. Which of the following cannot be measured using the **Measure>Angle** command?

   a. The angle between two lines.

   b. The opening angle of an arc.

   c. The distance between the centers of two circles.

   d. Any angle defined by a vertex or other locations.

6. When you select multiple objects, the Properties palette only displays which of the following?

   a. Their colors and layers.

   b. Their lineweights and linetypes.

   c. The properties that they have in common.

   d. Their X and Y values.

Command Summary

Button	Command	Location
	ID Point	• **Ribbon:** *Home* tab>expanded Utilities panel • **Command Prompt:** ID
	List	• **Ribbon:** *Home* tab>Properties panel • **Command Prompt:** list
	Match Properties	• **Ribbon:** *Home* tab>Clipboard panel • **Command Prompt:** matchprop or MA
	Measure> Angle	• **Ribbon:** *Home* tab>Utilities panel, expand Measure • **Command Prompt:** measuregeom (*select Angle option*)
	Measure> Area	• **Ribbon:** *Home* tab>Utilities panel, expand Measure • **Command Prompt:** measuregeom (*select Area option*)
	Measure> Distance	• **Ribbon:** *Home* tab>Utilities panel • **Command Prompt:** measuregeom (*select Distance option*)
	Measure> Radius	• **Ribbon:** *Home* tab>Utilities panel, expand Measure • **Command Prompt:** measuregeom (*select Radius option*)
	Properties	• **Ribbon:** *Home* tab>expanded Properties panel • **Ribbon:** *View* tab>Palettes panel • **Shortcut Menu:** (*on a selected object*)> Properties • **Command Prompt:** properties, PR, or <Ctrl>+<1>
	Quick Properties	• **Double-click:** (*on certain types of objects*) • **Status Bar:** expanded Customization
	Quick Select	• **Ribbon:** *Home* tab>Utilities panel • **Shortcut Menu:** Quick Select • **Command Prompt:** qselect • **Properties Panel:** top
	Select All	• **Ribbon:** *Home* tab>Utilities panel

Projects: Drawing Organization and Information

This chapter contains practice projects that can be used to gain additional hands-on experience with the topics and commands covered so far in this student guide. These practices are intended to be self-guided and do not include step by step information.

Learning Objectives in this Chapter

- *Architectural:* Create a building outline with interior walls using lines and polylines.
- *Mechanical:* Create a mechanical part with layers using polylines and objects.
- *Civil:* Create a property outline with layers using polylines.

10.1 Architectural Project

Estimated time for completion: 20 minutes

In this project you will draw an outline of a building using a polyline and add lines for interior walls, as shown in Figure 10–1. When you have finished the drawing, use the **Properties** and **Measure** commands to answer the questions in Task 2.

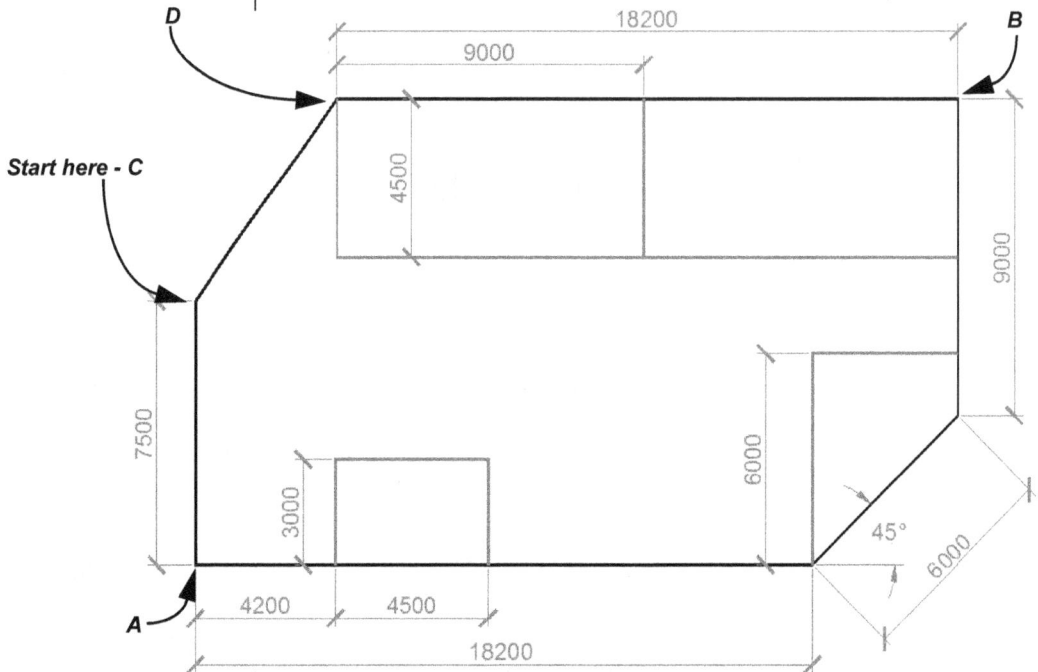

Figure 10–1

Task 1 - Draw the building outline.

1. Start a new drawing based on **AEC-Millimeters.dwt**, which is located in your practice files folder. Save it as **Office1.dwg**.

2. Set the layer to **Walls**.

3. Use the **Polyline** command to draw the outside wall starting at point **C** at **3000,3000**, drawing counter-clockwise, as shown in Figure 10–1.

4. Set the layer to **Partitions**.

5. Draw the inside walls using the **Line** command and use Object Snaps and Polar Tracking to place the walls correctly.

Task 2 - Measure objects in the drawing.

1. What is the direct distance between points **A** and **B**?

   a. 25886

   b. 26058

   c. 25668

   d. 26688

2. Set the current layer to **0** and toggle off the layer **Partitions**. What is the area (to the nearest square meter) of the outer Walls outline?

   a. 260

   b. 288

   c. 276

   a. 270

3. Select the outer Walls polyline and open the Properties palette. Scroll through the Vertex numbers to point **B**. The current vertex displays an **X** at the point. What are the exact X,Y coordinates of point **B**?

   a. 25243,18437

   b. 25243,17743

   c. 25443,8743

   d. 22243,15743

4. Explode the polyline. Select the line **CD** and open the Properties palette. What is the angle of the line?

   a. 125

   b. 234

   c. 260

   d. 167

10.2 Mechanical Project

Estimated time for completion: 20 minutes

In this project you will draw the outline of a mechanical part using a polyline, and then add other objects on a different layer, as shown in Figure 10–2. Once you have finished the drawing, answer the questions in Task 2 using the Properties palette and **Measure**.

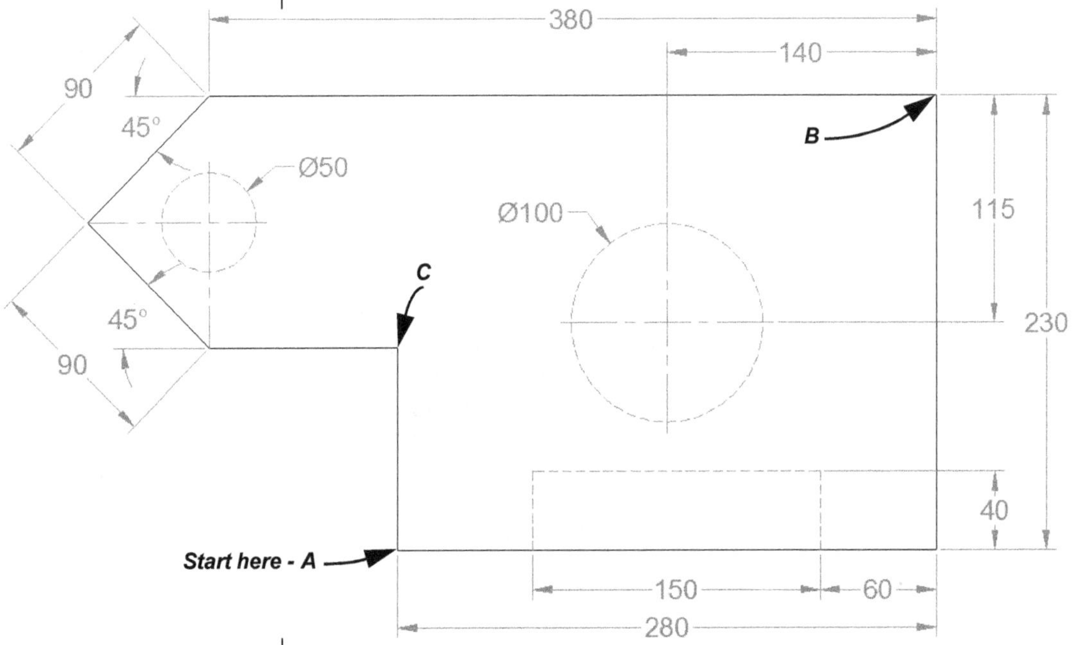

Figure 10–2

Task 1 - Draw the mechanical part.

1. Start a new drawing based on **Mech-Millimeters.dwt**, which is located in your practice files folder. Save it with the name **Part1.dwg**.

2. Set the current layer to **Object**.

3. Use the **Polyline** command to draw the outside of the object, starting with **point A** at **250,50** and drawing counter-clockwise, as shown in Figure 10–2.

4. Set the current layer to **Hidden**.

5. Draw the objects shown with hidden lines in Figure 10–2.

Task 2 - Measure objects in the drawing.

1. What is the direct distance between points A and B?

   a. 425.2578

   b. 362.3534

   c. 250.1208

   d. 524.9342

2. Select the **Ø100** circle. Open the Properties palette. What are the precise X,Y coordinates of its center point?

   a. 250,550

   b. 150,160

   c. 390,165

   d. 140,260

3. Toggle off the layer **Hidden**. What is the area of the outline object?

   a. 72530.1565

   b. 52628.2112

   c. 92623.1331

   d. 81177.9221

4. Select the outside polyline and open the Properties palette. Scroll through the Vertex numbers to point **C**. The current vertex displays with an **X** at the point. What are the exact X,Y coordinates of point **C**?

   a. 250,152.7208

   b. 200,100.5115

   c. 280,160.7509

   d. 350,250.0015

10.3 Civil Project

Estimated time for completion: 30 minutes

In this project you will draw the outline of a building and a property line using polylines and different layers, as shown in Figure 10–3. Once you have finished the drawing, answer the questions in Task 2 using the Properties palette and **Measure** command.

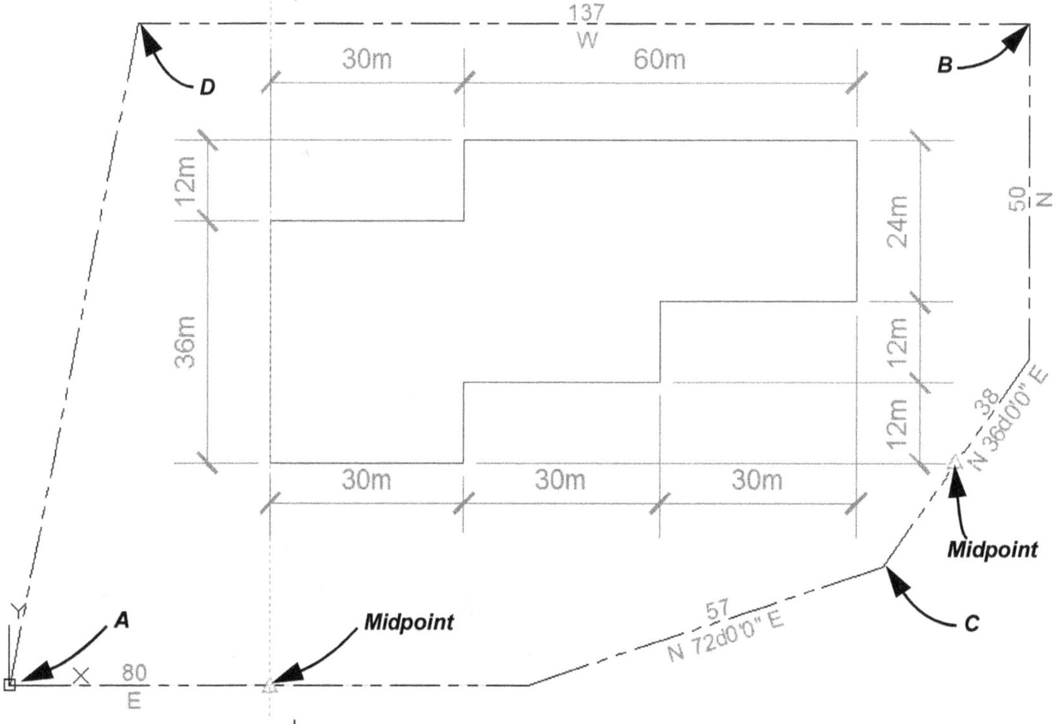

Figure 10–3

Task 1 - Draw the property line and building outline.

1. Start a new drawing based on **Civil-Meters.dwt**, which is located in your practice files folder. Save it with the name **Plat1.dwg**.

2. Set the current layer to **Property Line**.

3. Set the *Polar increment angle* to 18 degrees (18 degrees matches the Cartesian coordinate angle for N 72d0'0" E and 54 degrees for N 36d0'0" E).

4. Draw the outer boundary shown in Figure 10–3, starting with **point A** at **0,0**, and going counter-clockwise. (**Hint:** Use the **Polyline** command.).

5. Set the current layer to **Building**.

6. Draw the building outline, as shown in Figure 10–3. Use Polar Tracking with the **Midpoint** object snap for the start point.

Task 2 - Measure objects in the drawing.

1. What is the direct distance between points **A** and **B** rounded to the nearest meter?

   a. 235

   b. 205

   c. 185

   d. 165

2. Turn the property lines into a polyline if it has not already been drawn as a polyline. Select the polyline and open the Properties palette. Scroll through the Vertex numbers to point **C**. The current vertex displays with an **X** at the point. What are the X,Y coordinates of point **C** (rounded to the nearest meter)?

   a. 234,17

   b. 190,18

   c. 134,18

   d. 150,17

3. Toggle off the layer **Building**. What is the perimeter of the outline (layer Property Line) rounded to the nearest meter?

   a. 462

   b. 583

   c. 612

   d. 553

4. Explode the property line and select the line **DA**. What is the angle of the line?

   a. 186

   b. 355

   c. 259

   d. 248

Chapter 11

Advanced Editing Commands

In this chapter you learn how to trim, extend, stretch, fillet, and chamfer objects.

Learning Objectives in this Chapter

- Remove part of an object that extends past a user-defined cutting edge.
- Create rounded corners and beveled edges on an object.
- Move or extend parts of objects.
- Create objects parallel or concentric to other objects.
- Create a rectangular pattern of duplicate objects in rows and columns.
- Create a radial pattern of duplicate objects.
- Create a pattern of duplicate objects along a path.

11.1 Trimming and Extending Objects

Trim and **Extend** commands can be used to modify already existing objects to ensure that they have the correct size and length, as shown in Figure 11–1.

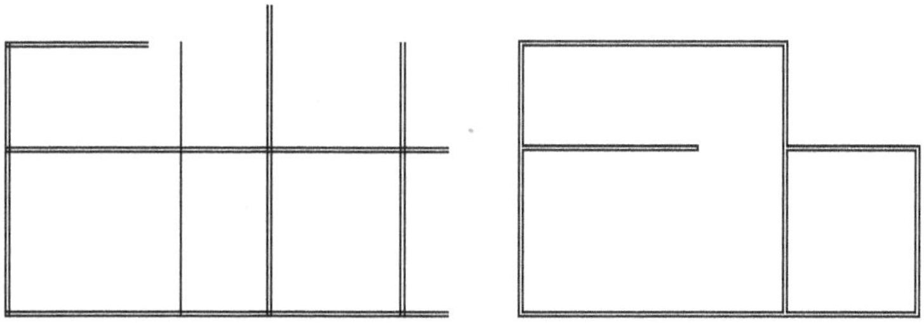

Figure 11–1

Trimming Objects

The **Trim** command erases any part of an object that extends past a user-defined cutting edge. It simplifies many drawing tasks. For example, an easy way to create an arc is to draw and then trim a circle.

How To: Trim Objects

1. In the *Home* tab>Modify panel, click ⫟ (Trim).
2. Select the cutting edges (they highlight in blue with a thicker line weight) or press <Enter> to select all of the edges (these edges do not highlight).
3. If you selected specific edges, press <Enter> to end the selection of cutting edges.

4. Hover the cursor over the part of the object that you want to trim. The portion is faded in a light gray line weight, providing a preview of the part that is going to be removed, as shown in Figure 11–2.

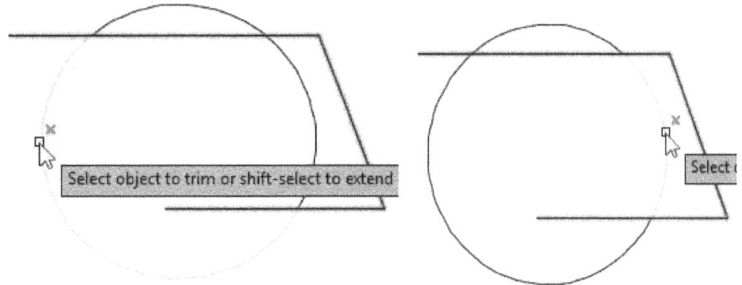

You can also use the **Trim** *command to extend an object. At the Select object to trim or Shift-select to extend prompt, you can hold <Shift> and select to extend an object.*

Select object to trim or shift-select to extend

Figure 11–2

5. Select the part to be removed.
6. Press <Enter> to complete the command.

- If you select something by mistake, you can use the **Undo** option in the command (<Down Arrow> menu) to restore the

  last object trimmed. You can also click (Undo) in the Quick Access Toolbar for the **Trim** and **Extend** commands. However, doing so causes you to lose all of the trimming you have done to that point.

Hint: Selecting Objects to Trim or Extend

Any method of object selection can be used to select the cutting or boundary edge(s). Objects to be trimmed or extended can be selected using the point-and-pick, Crossing, or Fence methods of object selection.

When you select the **Crossing** option, you are prompted to select two opposite corners, as shown in Figure 11–3. Everything touching or in the box is previewed (faded light gray) and is then trimmed or extended when you select the second corner. You remain in the command so that you can select more objects as required.

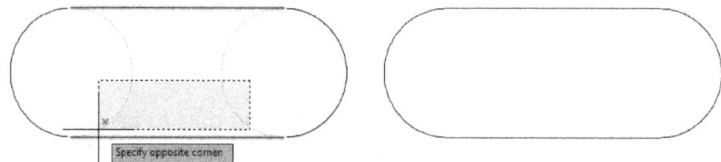

Figure 11–3

When you select the **Fence** option, you are prompted to select fence points. Everything touching these line segments is selected to be trimmed and displays a preview (faded light gray), as shown in Figure 11–4. Press <Enter> to trim the object. You remain in the command so that you can select more objects as required.

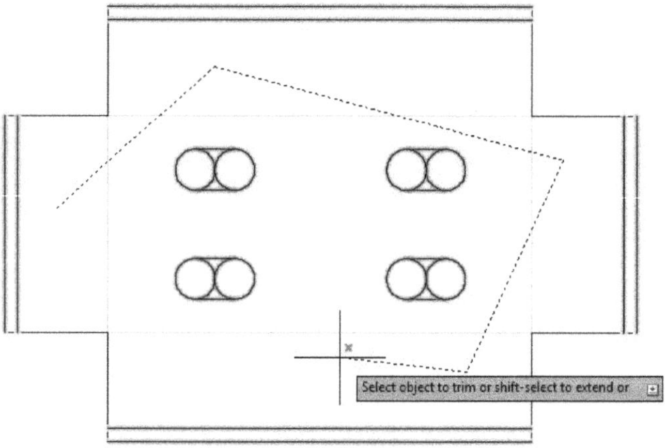

Figure 11–4

Hint: Trimming Objects without Cutting Edges

The **Break** command can be used to cut an object without any overlapping edges. Two different options of the command are available in the *Home* tab>expanded Modify panel:

- ⬜ **(Break):** Removes a portion of an object between two user-defined points, leaving a gap. This has the same effect as trimming between two cutting edges.

- ⬜ **(Break at Point):** Breaks an object at one point so that it becomes two pieces, but does not have a gap. This option is useful if you need to change a portion of a line into a different linetype.

Extending Objects

*You can also use the **Extend** command to trim an object, At the Select object to extend or Shift-select to trim prompt, you can hold <Shift> and select to trim an object.*

Using the **Extend** command, any object that does not reach a boundary edge is lengthened until it meets the boundary, as shown in Figure 11–5.

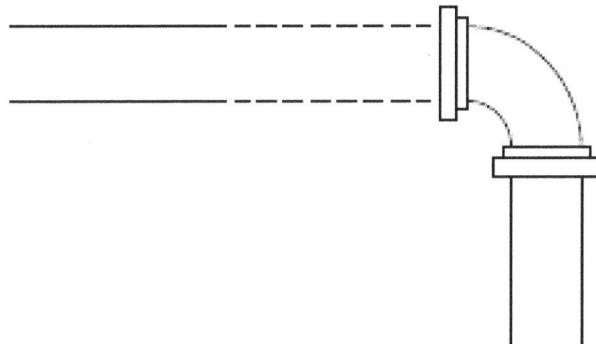

Figure 11–5

How To: Extend Objects

1. In the *Home* tab>Modify panel, click ⌐/ (Extend).
2. Select the boundary edges (they highlight in blue with a thicker line weight) or press <Enter> to select all of the edges (these edges do not highlight). If you selected specific edges, press <Enter> to end the selection of boundary edges.
3. Hover the cursor over the object that you want to extend (closer to the boundary edge), and a preview of the part that is going to be added displays.
4. Select to extend the object.
5. Press <Enter> to complete the command.

You can also draw a crossing or fence across multiple objects. Press <Enter> to select the object.

Practice 11a

Extending and Trimming Objects

Practice Objective

- Remove and extend objects.

In this practice, you will extend and trim lines to complete a drawing, as shown in Figure 11–6.

Estimated time for completion: 10 minutes

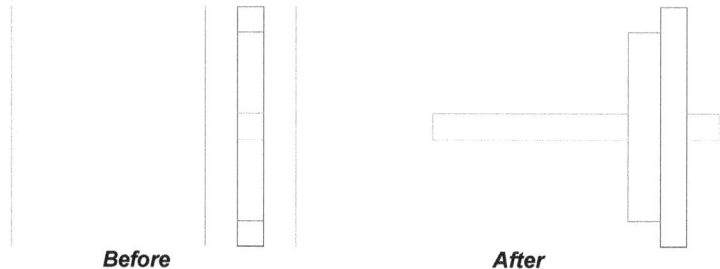

Before   *After*

Figure 11–6

1. Open **Shaft-M.dwg** from your practice files folder.

2. In the *Home* tab>Modify panel, click ⁻⁻/ (Extend).

3. Select the two vertical red lines as the boundary edges, and press <Enter>. Note that they are highlighted in blue and a thicker line weight.

4. Select the pair of short horizontal red lines to extend them to the vertical red lines. You will need to select each short red line twice, closer to either end, to extend it on both sides. Press <Enter> to complete the command.

5. Start the **Extend** command again. Select the vertical blue line as the boundary edge. Extend the pair of short horizontal blue lines to the vertical blue line.

6. In the *Home* tab>Modify panel, click ⁻/⁻⁻ (Trim). Select the two horizontal red lines as the boundary objects and press <Enter>. Select the top and bottom portions of both vertical red lines and press <Enter>.

7. Start the **Trim** command again to clean up the object, as shown on the right in Figure 11–6.

8. Save and close the drawing.

Practice 11b

Trimming Objects on a Drawing

Practice Objective

- Remove parts of objects.

Estimated time for completion: 5 minutes

In this practice, you will use the **Trim** command to remove parts of lines and to trim circles to create slots, as shown in Figure 11–7.

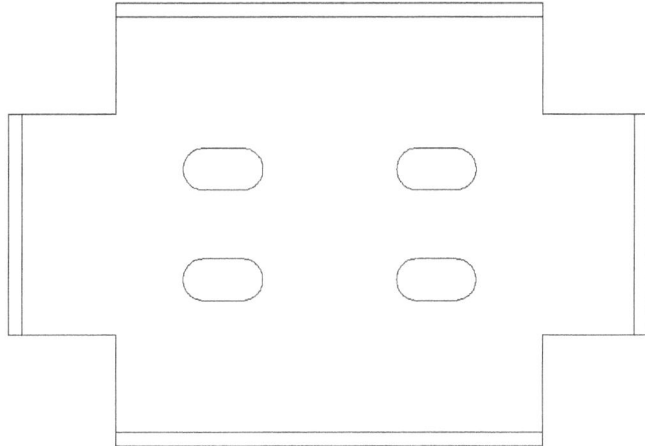

Figure 11–7

1. Open **Bracket-M.dwg** from your practice files folder.

2. Start the **Trim** command. At the *Select objects or <select all>:* prompt, select the two long horizontal and two long vertical lines in the middle of the drawing. Press <Enter>.

Select the four lines to trim individually, without using a fence or crossing window.

3. At the *Select object to trim:* prompt, select the four lines again, in the middle of each line. Press <Enter> to complete the command.

4. Zoom in closer to the four sets of circles and lines.

5. Start the **Trim** command again. At the *Select objects or <select all>:* prompt, press <Enter> to select all of the objects.

Note that it might work differently than how it is shown in the Figure. Depending on which portions got trimmed, click and remove the inner parts to have the hollow shapes.

6. At the *Select object to trim:* prompt, select near the center part of the circles, as shown in Figure 11–8. You might have to select the middle portion twice until a gap is created. Select the arcs in both circles, on the sides where they touch, as shown in Figure 11–8.

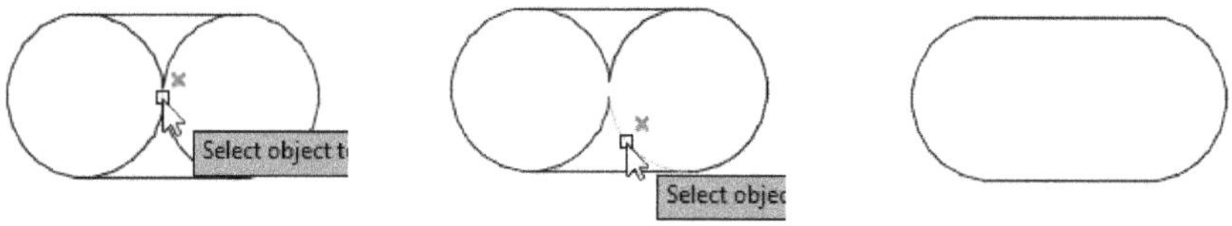

| Before | Gap created and select arcs | After |

Figure 11–8

7. Without leaving the command, select and trim the same parts in the other three circle pairs.

8. Press <Enter> to exit the command.

9. Save and close the drawing.

Practice 11c | Break at Point

Practice Objective

- Break lines into segments and change the linetype of the new segments.

Estimated time for completion: 5 minutes

In this practice, you will use the **Break at Point** command to break lines into separate segments and then change the linetype of the new segments using Quick Properties, as shown in Figure 11–9.

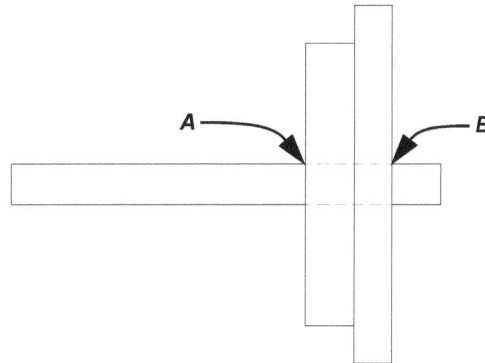

Figure 11–9

1. Open **Shaft2-M.dwg** from your practice files folder.

2. Select the two long horizontal lines. Note that they are single line segments. Press <Esc> to clear the lines.

3. In the Object snap menu, select **Intersection** and toggle ⬜ ▼ (Object Snap) on.

4. In the *Home* tab>extended Modify panel, click ⬜ (Break at Point).

5. At the *Select object:* prompt, select the top long horizontal line.

6. For the first break point, select the Intersection labeled **A** as shown in Figure 11–9.

7. Start the **Break at Point** command again. At the *Select object:* prompt, select the portion of the same horizontal line, between points **A** and **B**.

8. For the first break point, select the Intersection labeled **B** as shown in Figure 11–9.

Verify that ▦ (Quick Properties) is toggled on in the Status Bar.

9. Select the horizontal line between points A and B. It is now a separate segment. In the Quick Properties panel, click in the *Layer* row and expand the drop-down list. Select **Construction** to change the layer, as shown in Figure 11–10. Clear the selection.

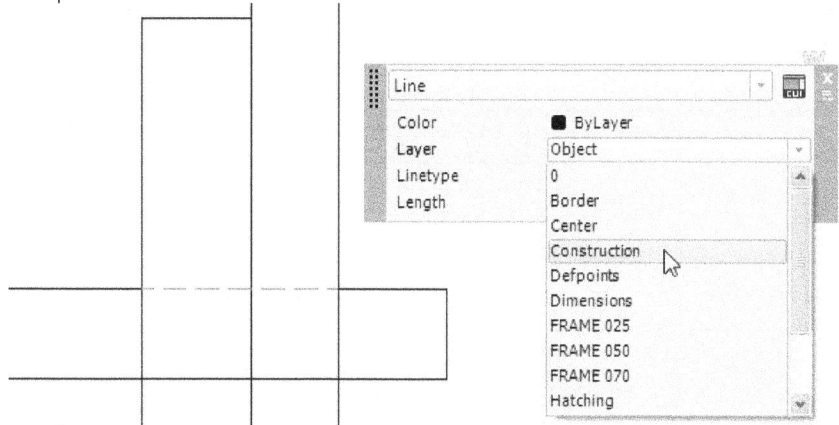

Figure 11–10

10. Repeat the procedure on the lower horizontal line.

11. Save and close the drawing.

11.2 Stretching Objects

The **Stretch** command enables objects and/or parts of objects to be moved and/or extended, leaving other objects and parts of objects stationary.

How To: Stretch Objects

1. In the *Home* tab>Modify panel, click ⌐⊾ (Stretch).
2. Use a *Crossing* selection to select the objects to stretch. The objects are highlighted in blue.
3. Press <Enter> to finish the selection set.
4. Select the base point (the *handle* by which you hold the objects).
5. Move the cursor in the direction in which you want to stretch the object. A preview displays of the original objects now faded to gray, while the new objects have maintained their original properties, as shown in Figure 11–11.

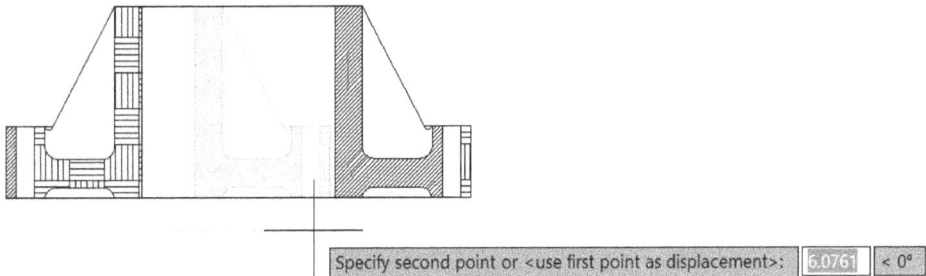

Specify second point or <use first point as displacement>: 6.0761 < 0°

Figure 11–11

6. Select the second point (which in conjunction with the base point defines the distance and direction to which you are stretching) or enter a distance and press <Enter>.

Notes on Stretching Objects

- Objects to be stretched must be selected using the **Crossing** or **Crossing Polygon** selection methods. A Crossing Polygon enables you to draw an irregularly shaped polygon by selecting each of the polygon's vertices (it displays in green), as shown in Figure 11–12. Anything inside or touching the polygon is selected.

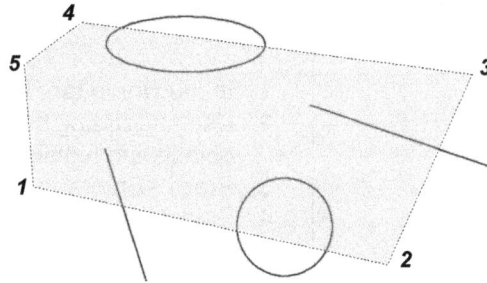

Figure 11–12

Circles, ellipses, and blocks do not stretch because they do not have end points.

- The stretching of objects is based on their end points or their insertion point.

  - Objects *outside* the crossing window are unchanged.
  - Objects *crossing* the crossing window are stretched or contracted accordingly.
  - Objects *inside* the crossing window are moved.

- While **Scale** reduces or enlarges an entire object proportionately in all directions, **Stretch** only changes it in one direction.

Practice 11d

Stretching Objects

Estimated time for completion: 5 minutes

Practice Objective

- Increase the width of objects by stretching them.

In this practice, you will use the **Stretch** command to increase the width of the entire building and then increase the width of the office and reception area, as shown in Figure 11–13.

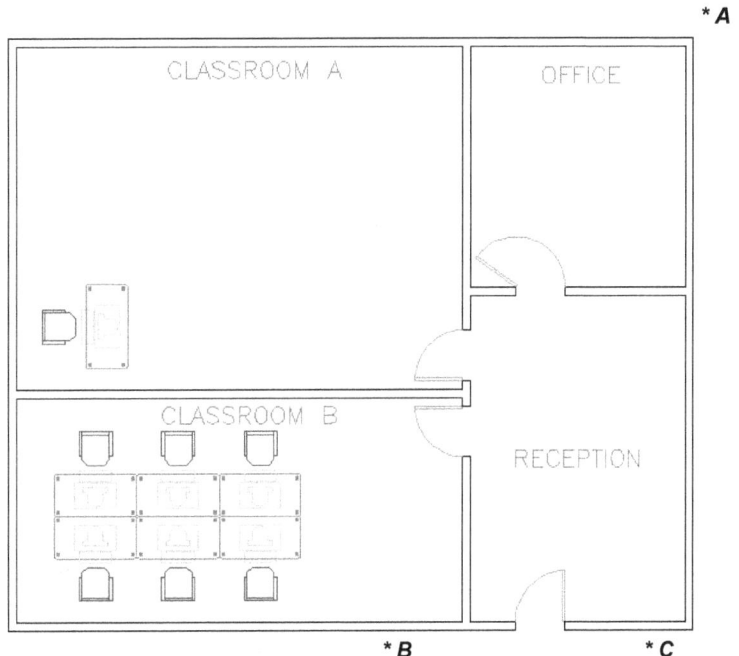

Figure 11–13

1. Open **Class2-AM.dwg** from your practice files folder.

2. Toggle ⌐ (Orthomode) on to restrict the cursor orthogonally.

3. In the *Home* tab>Modify panel, click ⬓ (Stretch). At the *Select objects:* prompt, use a Crossing selection with corners starting at point **A** and dragging it to point **B**, as shown in Figure 11–13. Press <Enter>.

4. At the *Specify base point:* prompt, select a point near the upper right corner of the office. At the *Specify second point:* prompt, pull the cursor to the right, enter **2400**, as shown in Figure 11–14. Press <Enter> and note that only the horizontal Classroom walls are stretched

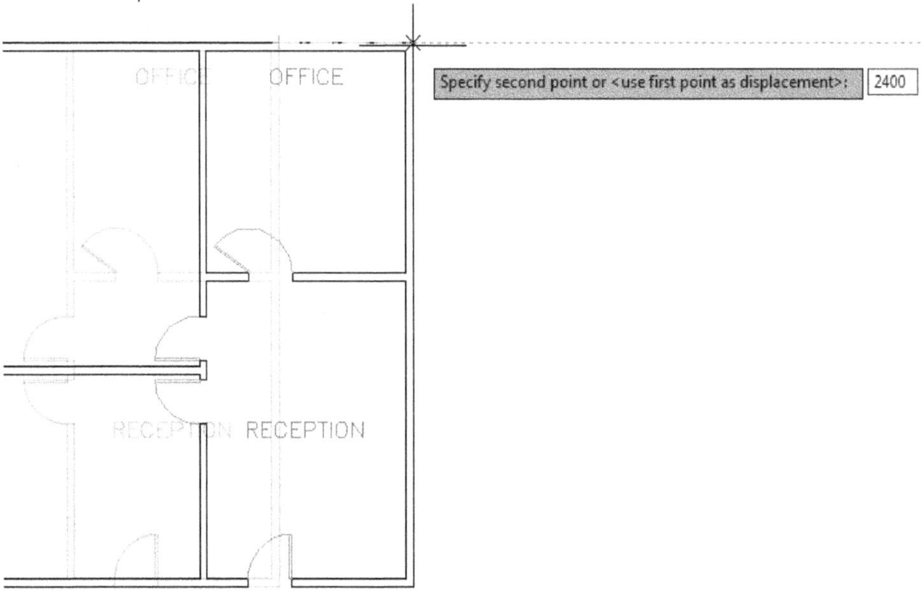

Specify second point or <use first point as displacement>: 2400

Figure 11–14

5. Start the **Stretch** command again. At the *Select objects:* prompt, use a *Crossing* selection with corners at points **A** and **C**, as shown in Figure 11–13. Press <Enter>.

6. At the *Specify base point:* prompt, select a point near the upper right corner of the office. At the *Specify second point:* prompt, pull the cursor to the right, enter **1200**, and press <Enter>.

7. Save and close the drawing.

11.3 Creating Fillets and Chamfers

Fillets and chamfers are used to create rounded corners and beveled edges respectively, as shown in Figure 11–15.

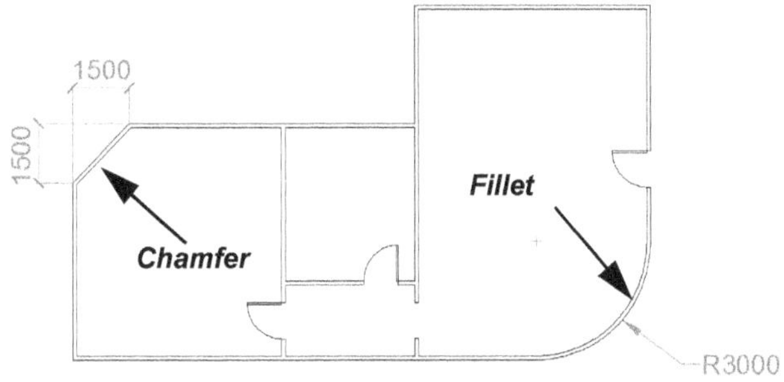

Figure 11–15

Filleting Objects

The **Fillet** command modifies the intersection of two objects and can be used to create inside and outside rounded corners, as shown in Figure 11–16. It can also be helpful in cleaning up a drawing by forcing lines to meet at an exact intersection.

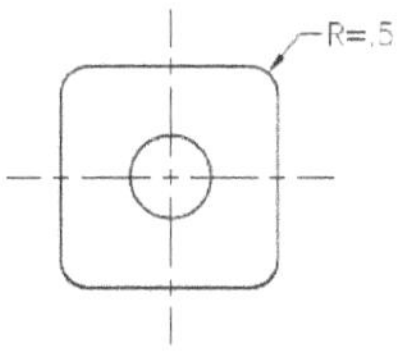

Figure 11–16

*The **Radius** option enables you to specify the fillet radius. This value should be selected and set before you pick the objects to fillet.*

How To: Fillet Objects

1. In the *Home* tab>Modify panel, click ⬜ (**Fillet**).
2. Select the **Radius** option (<Down Arrow> menu), enter the new radius, and press <Enter>.
3. If you are filleting several sets of objects, select the **Multiple** option (<Down Arrow> menu).
4. Select the first line that you want to fillet.

5. Hover the cursor over the second line that you want to fillet. A preview displays the fillet being highlighted in blue and the original object faded in light gray, as shown in Figure 11–17.

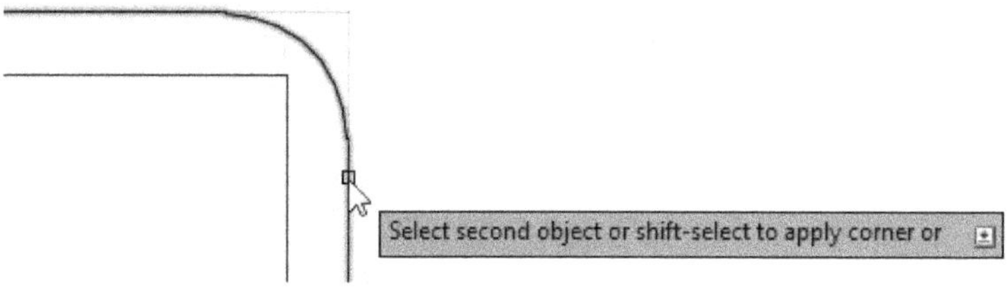

Select second object or shift-select to apply corner or

Figure 11–17

6. Select the second line to confirm the fillet.
7. If you have selected the **Multiple** option, you can continue selecting two lines to fillet until you press <Enter> to complete the command.

• A fillet with the **Radius** option set to **0** can be used to make lines meet at a square corner. You can also hold <Shift> as you select the two lines without having to change the radius.

• You can fillet two parallel lines. In this case, the radius is automatically calculated so that the arc is tangent to both lines.

• The **Undo** option undoes the last fillet without exiting the command.

• The **Polyline** option fillets all of the vertices of a selected polyline. You can still fillet one vertex by selecting segments to fillet.

• The **Trim/NoTrim** option determines whether selected lines are trimmed after the arc is added.

• You can fillet both the lines and arcs in a polyline.

Chamfering Objects

The **Chamfer** command angles or bevels the intersection of two lines to create an angled corner, as shown in Figure 11–18.

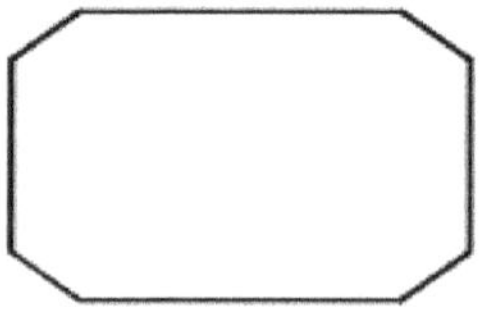

Figure 11–18

How To: Chamfer Objects

1. In the *Home* tab>Modify panel, click ◳ (Chamfer).
2. Select the **Distance** option and enter two distances.
3. If you are chamfering several sets of objects, select the **Multiple** option.
4. Select the first line that you want to chamfer, which is highlighted in blue.
5. Hover the cursor over the second line that you want to chamfer. A preview displays the chamfer being highlighted in blue and the chamfered portion being faded in light gray, as shown in Figure 11–19.

The first chamfer distance is used on the first line that you select and the second chamfer distance is used on the second line that you select. Distances are measured from the intersection of the two lines.

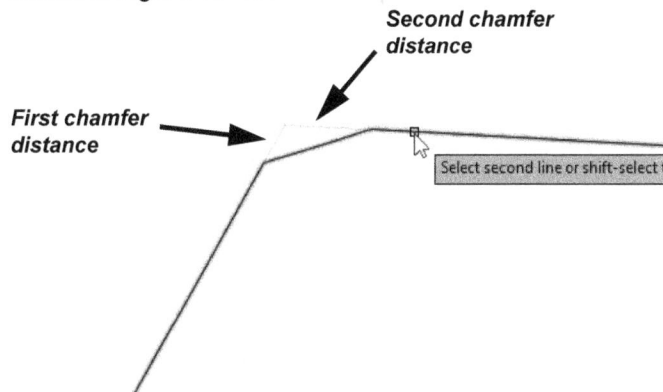

Figure 11–19

6. Select the second line.
7. If you selected the **Multiple** option, you can continue selecting two lines to chamfer until you press <Enter> to complete the command.

- Another way to specify the chamfer is to set the **Angle** option, which sets the chamfer length of the first line you select and then the angle between the original line and the chamfered edge.

- The distance and angle information are stored separately. Therefore, you can use the **Method** option to change between the two options in the same command. The last method you selected is used when a new command is started.

- The **Undo**, **Trim/NoTrim**, and **Polyline** options work the same way as when using the **Fillet** command.

Practice 11e | Filleting Objects

Practice Objective

Estimated time for completion: 5 minutes

- Create rounded corners and fillet parallel lines.

In this practice, you will use the **Fillet** command to round the outer corners of a part with two different radius sizes, as shown in Figure 11–20. You will also fillet parallel lines to create slots.

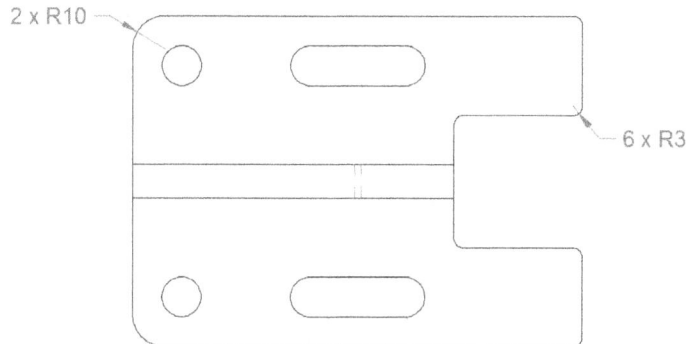

Figure 11–20

1. Open **Visebase-M.dwg** from your practice files folder.

2. In the *Home* tab>Modify panel, click ⬜ (**Fillet**).Set the **Radius** option (<Down Arrow> menu or enter **R**). Set *Radius* to **10**.

3. Select the two upper lines that create the upper left corner to fillet that corner.

You are not required to re-enter the radius. It has been set in Step 2.

4. Repeat the command to fillet the lower left corner with the same radius. Select the lines without entering the **Radius** option.

5. Start the **Fillet** command again. Select the **Radius** option and enter the radius as **3**. Select the **Multiple** option to make the command repeating. Fillet the six corners on the right side of the object. Press <Enter> to complete the command.

6. Start the **Fillet** command again. Select the two horizontal lines in the rectangle near the top of the part, selecting near the left end of the lines. Repeat for the right end of the lines. Erase the short vertical lines to clear out the slot.

7. Repeat Step 6 for the other rectangle.

8. Save and close the drawing.

Practice 11f

Chamfering Objects

Practice Objective

- Create different sizes of angled edges.

Estimated time for completion: 5 minutes

In this practice, you will use the **Chamfer** command with several different distances to create the angled edges on a part, as shown in Figure 11–21.

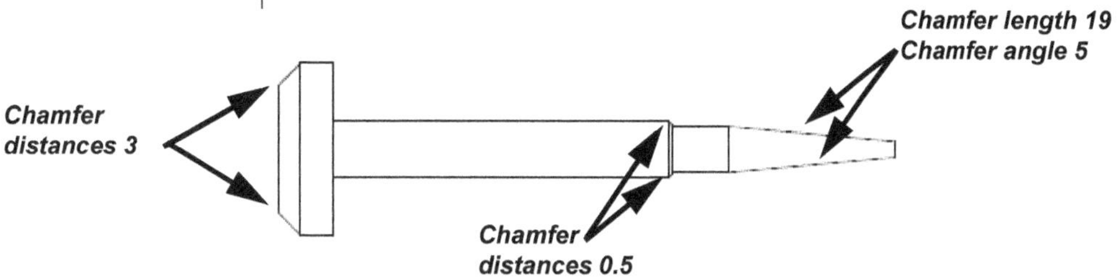

Chamfer length 19
Chamfer angle 5

Chamfer distances 3

Chamfer distances 0.5

Figure 11–21

1. Open **Punch-M.dwg** from your practice files folder.

*Select **Distance** in the <Down Arrow> menu or enter **D**.*

2. In the *Home* tab>Modify panel, click ⬜ (Chamfer). Select the **Distance** option. Set both *Chamfer distances* to **3**.

3. Select the two lines in the top left corner of the part to apply the chamfer.

4. Repeat the command to chamfer the bottom left corner using the same distances.

5. Start the **Chamfer** command and select the **Distance** option. Set both *Chamfer distances* to **0.5**. Select the **Multiple** option to make the command repeating. Chamfer both corners where the shaft changes size.

6. Start the **Chamfer** command and select the **Angle** option. Set the *Chamfer length* on first line to **19**. Set the *chamfer angle* to **5**. Apply the chamfer to the right end of the part, selecting the top horizontal line first, and then the short vertical line. Repeat for the bottom corner of the right end.

7. Add vertical lines to indicate the edges of the three chamfers, as shown in Figure 11–21.

8. Save and close the drawing.

11.4 Offsetting Objects

The AutoCAD software enables you to create parallel shapes with a single editing command called **Offset,** as shown in Figure 11–22.

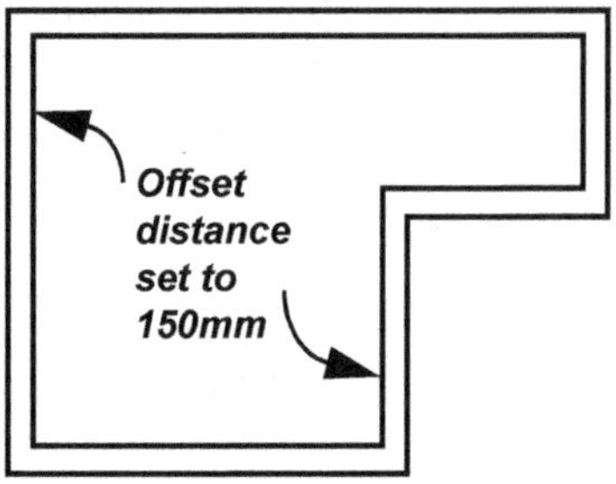

Offset distance set to 150mm

Figure 11–22

- The **Offset** command works with lines, circles, arcs, and polylines.

- You can specify a distance between the original object and the offset copy, or select a point through which the copy is going to pass.

How To: Offset Objects Using a Distance

1. In the *Home* tab>Modify panel, click 🔳 (Offset).
2. Enter the offset distance and press <Enter>.
3. Select the object to offset.
4. Hover the cursor on either side of the object to display a preview of the offset copy.

- You can change the offset distance before selecting the side to place the offset copy.

5. Select a point on either side of the object to place the offset copy on that side.
6. Select another object to offset by the same distance, or press <Enter> to complete the command.

- If you want to offset one object multiple times, select the **Multiple** option before you select the side you want to offset. The new objects are placed at the same distance from the last object that was offset.

- The **Through** option enables you to select a point through which the offset object must pass. You can drag the cursor on either side of the object to display a preview of the offset copy before placing the offset.

- The **Erase** and **Layer** options are settings that remain active until you change them. By default, objects from which you offset are not erased, and the layer of the new object matches the layer of the source object rather than the current layer.

- If you offset a polyline, all of the sides are offset equally, as shown in Figure 11–23. To only offset one side of a polyline, you need to explode it first.

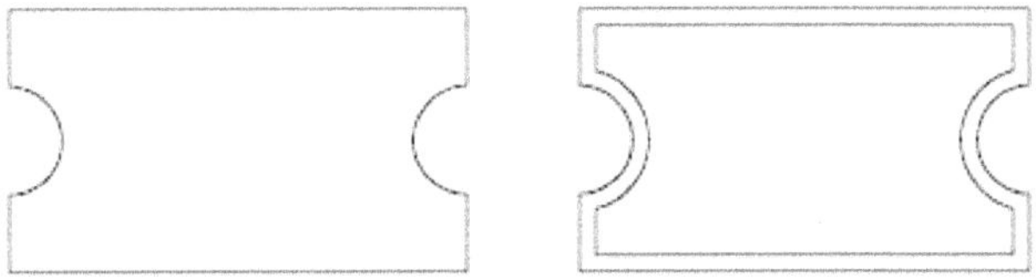

Figure 11–23

Practice 11g

Offsetting Objects

Practice Objective

- Offset polylines, lines, and arcs.

Estimated time for completion: 10 minutes

In this practice, you will use the **Offset** command on polylines, lines, and arcs to create walls and steps, as shown in Figure 11–24.

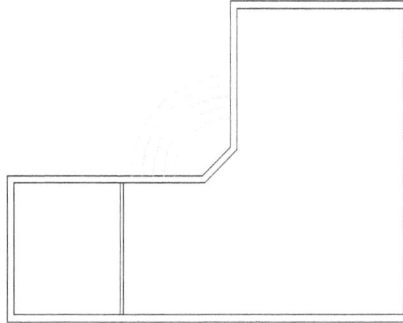

Figure 11–24

1. Open **Offset-AM.dwg** from your practice files folder.

2. In the *Home* tab>Modify panel, click ⬜ (Offset). Enter the *offset distance* as **300** and press <Enter>. Select the large polyline as the object to offset. Drag the cursor inside the polyline to display the preview of the offset copy.

3. Select a point inside the polyline to create the offset copy on the inside. Press <Enter> to complete the command.

4. Start the **Offset** command. Enter the *offset distance* as **450** and press <Enter>. Select the yellow arc as the object to offset. Drag the cursor outside (above) the arc to display the preview and select a point outside (above) the arc to create the offset copy.

5. Note that you are still in the **Offset** command and at the *Select object to offset:* prompt, select the arc you just created. At the *Specify point on side to offset:* prompt, press <Down Arrow> and select the **Multiple** option to make the command repeating. Select three points outside (above) the arcs to have a total of five arcs. Press <Enter> twice to complete the command.

6. Use the **Explode** command to turn the inner polyline you created into multiple single line objects.

7. Start the **Offset** command again, and set the *offset distance* to **4500**. Select the inside vertical line on the left bottom as the object to offset. Move the cursor to right of the line to preview the offset line (as shown on the left in Figure 11–25). Select a point to place the offset line.

Since you had previously selected the **Multiple** *option, the setting remains active.*

8. Note that you are still in the **Offset** command. At the *Select object to offset:* prompt, select the line you just created. Note that an offset line is previewed at **4500**. In the offset distance edit box, enter **150**, (as shown on the right in Figure 11–25) to change the offset distance. Press <Enter> to place the offset line to make an interior wall. Press <Enter> again to exit the command.

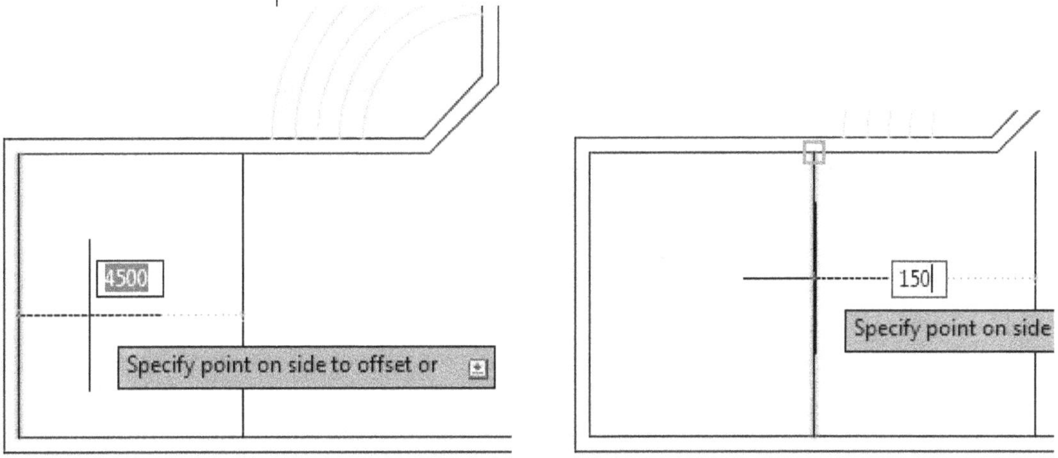

Figure 11–25

9. Save and close the drawing.

11.5 Creating Arrays of Objects

The **Array** commands generate copies of selected objects at fixed intervals of rows and columns, around a center point, or along a path, as shown in Figure 11–26. For example, a rectangular array can be used to create light fixtures in a ceiling grid. Holes around a circular gasket or radial wings of a building are examples of a polar array. A path array can be used for lights along a walkway or the edge of an irregular shaped pool.

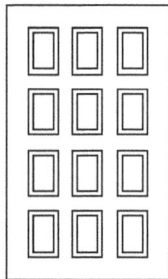

Rectangular Array   *Polar Array*   *Path Array*

Figure 11–26

Rectangular Array

A rectangular array consists of a pattern of objects that are divided into rows and columns.

* While creating rectangular arrays, you can use the **Angle** option to control the orientation angle of the array.

How To: Create a Rectangular Array

1. In the *Home* tab>Modify panel, expand the Array drop-down list and click ⊞ (Rectangular Array).
2. At the *Select objects:* prompt, select the object(s) that you want to array and press <Enter>.

You can use windows or crossing selection to select objects.

3. A preview of the array displays a default number of objects in rows and columns, as shown in Figure 11–27. It also displays grips that enable you to modify the array.

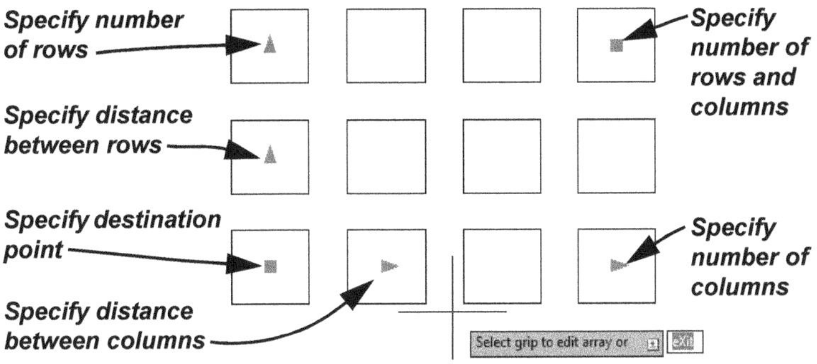

Figure 11–27

4. To specify the number of items to be in the array, use one of the following methods:

   • Use the *Specify number of rows*, *Specify number of columns*, and *Specify number of rows and columns* grips to change the number of columns and rows.

   • At the *Select grip to edit array or:* prompt, type **COU** and press <Enter> to use the **Count** option. You are prompted to enter a value for the number of columns, and then for the number of rows. Press <Enter> after you enter each value.

5. Specify the spacing between the arrayed items, using one of the following methods:

   • Use the *row* spacing and *column spacing* grips to change the number of columns and rows.

   • At the *Select grip to edit array or:* prompt, type **S** and press <Enter> to use the **Spacing** option. You are then prompted to enter a value for the distance between the columns and then for the rows. Press <Enter> after you enter each value.

6. If required, you can modify the location of the array by selecting the *Specify destination point* grip and then picking a destination point in the drawing window.

7. Press <Enter> to complete the command.

Polar Array

A polar array consists of a pattern of objects that are copied about a central radius.

- When creating polar arrays you can use the **ROWs** option to add additional offset rows around the center point, and the **ROTate items** option to set the arrayed items to be rotated in their orientation (or not) as they are placed around the center point.

How To: Create a Polar Array

1. In the *Home* tab>Modify panel, expand the Array drop-down list and click ⊡ (Polar Array).
2. At the *Select objects:* prompt, select the object(s) that you want to array. Press <Enter> to end the selection of objects.
3. At the *Specify center point of array:* prompt, select a point on the screen to be the center of the polar array.
4. A preview of the array displays a default number of objects in a radial pattern, as shown in Figure 11–28. Additionally, it displays grips and an *Array Creation* contextual tab in the ribbon that enable you to modify the array.

| Home | Insert | Annotate | Parametric | View | Manage | Output | Add-ins | A360 | Express Tools | Featured Apps | BIM 360 | Performance | Array Creation |

	Items:	6		Rows:	1		Levels:	1				
Polar	Between:	60		Between:	1.1250		Between:	1.0000			Associative Base Point Rotate Items Direction	Close Array
	Fill:	360		Total:	1.1250		Total:	1.0000				
Type		Items			Rows ▾			Levels			Properties	Close

Figure 11–28

5. Specify the number of items in the Items panel.
6. Depending on the number of items and the *Fill* angle, the *Between* angle value changes to fit the specified number.
   - Using the **Fill** option, enter the angle that you want the arrayed items to fill.
7. If required, you can modify the rotation of the items and the direction of the array using the **Rotation Items** and **Direction** buttons is the contextual tab.
8. Press <Enter> to complete the command.

Path Array

A path array consists of a pattern of objects that are copied along a straight, curved, or irregular linear path.

- When using the path array, you might want to place the arrayed object in its final orientation and position. You need to place it near the start end point of the path for simplicity. Otherwise, you need to use the **Orientation** option to indicate how the object is to be oriented and positioned along the path.

- You can use the **Method** option, with its **Divide** option to evenly space the objects along the path.

How To: Create a Path Array

1. In the *Home* tab>Modify panel, expand the Array drop-down list and click ⌓ (Path Array).
2. At the *Select objects:* prompt, select the object(s) that you want to array. Press <Enter> to end the selection of objects.
3. At the *Select path curve:* prompt, select the object that you want to use as the path.
4. A preview of the array displays a default number of objects copied along a path, as shown in Figure 11–29. It also displays grips that enable you to modify the array.

Figure 11–29

5. Specify the number of items in the array by selecting the square grip (as shown in Figure 11–29), typing a value, and pressing <Enter>.
6. Specify the distance between the items along the path by selecting the arrow grip (as shown in Figure 11–29), typing a value, and pressing <Enter>. You can also select the grip and drag the cursor to change the value.
7. Press <Enter> to complete the command.

Hint: Array Contextual Tabs

Once the required objects have been selected to be arrayed in any array style, you can use the *Array Creation* contextual tab in the ribbon to set the number of items, rows, columns, levels, or other properties.

Practice 11h

Rectangular Array

Practice Objective

* Make copies of objects at fixed intervals of rows and columns.

Estimated time for completion: 5 minutes

In this practice, you will use a **Rectangular Array** to make copies of a workstation in a classroom, as shown in Figure 11–30.

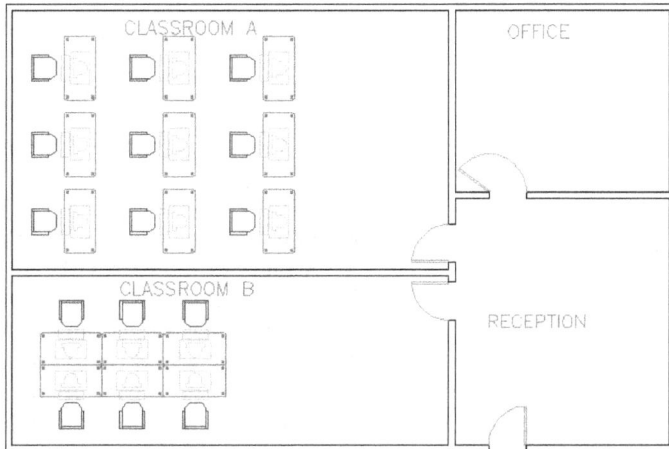

Figure 11–30

1. Open **Class3-AM.dwg** from your practice files folder.

2. In the *Home* tab>Modify panel, expand the Array drop-down list and select (Rectangular Array).

You can use the window or crossing selection to select the three objects.

3. At the *Select objects:* prompt, select the desk, chair, and computer in Classroom A and press <Enter>.

The top right square grip specifies the number of rows and columns.

4. At the *Select grip to edit array*, select the top-right corner grip (square grip) and enter **3**, as shown in Figure 11–31. Press <Enter>.

Select this grip and enter 3

Figure 11–31

The middle left arrow grip specifies the row spacing.

5. Select the middle grip along the left side (upward facing arrow grip) and verify that **ROW SPACING** displays at the cursor prompt. Enter **1800**, as shown on the left in Figure 11–32. Press <Enter>.

The middle bottom arrow grip specifies the column spacing.

6. Select the middle grip along the bottom (right facing arrow grip) and verify that **COLUMN SPACING** displays at the cursor prompt. Enter **2400**, as shown on the right in Figure 11–32. Press <Enter>.

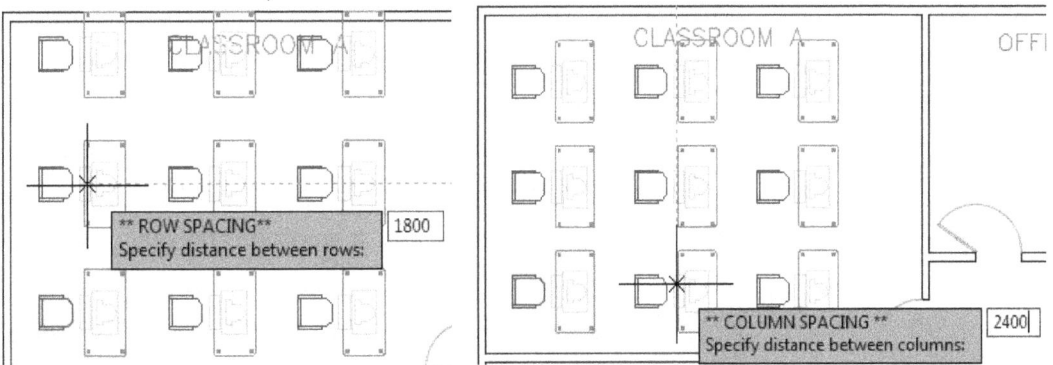

Figure 11–32

7. Press <Enter> to exit the command.

8. Save and close the file.

Practice 11i

Polar Array

Practice Objective

- Make copies of an object around a center point.

Estimated time for completion: 5 minutes

In this practice, you will use **Polar Array** to make copies of the nut around the flange, as shown in Figure 11–33.

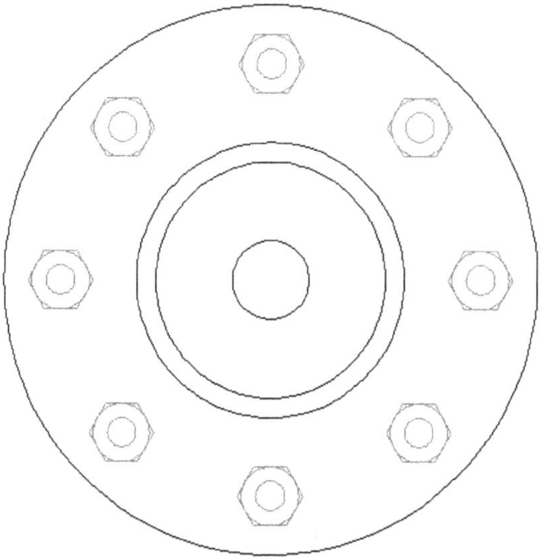

Figure 11–33

1. Open **Flange-M.dwg** from your practice files folder.

2. Select the **Center** object snap option and verify that **Object Snap** is active in the Status Bar.

3. In the *Home* tab>Modify panel, expand the Array drop-down list and click ⬚⬚⬚ (Polar Array).

4. At the *Select objects:* prompt, select the nut. Press <Enter> to finish selecting objects.

5. At the *Specify center point of array:* prompt, select the center of any circle.

6. Note that the *Array Creation* contextual tab displays in the ribbon. In the Items panel, for *Items* enter **8** and press <Enter>. Note that the *Between* angle value changes to accommodate the specified number of items, as shown in Figure 11–34.

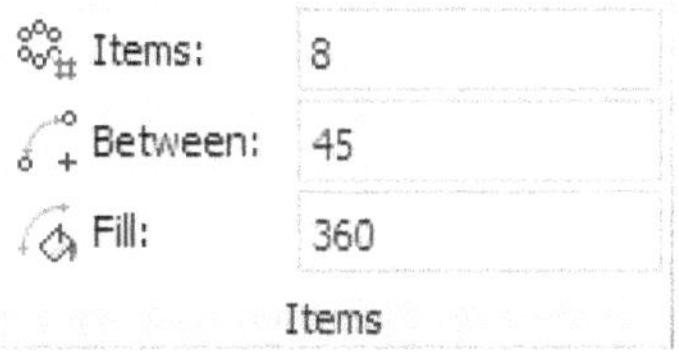

Items:	8
Between:	45
Fill:	360
	Items

Figure 11–34

7. In the preview of the array, note that the nuts are rotated. In the *Array Creation* contextual tab>Properties panel, click

   (Rotate Items) to clear it. Note that the nut is correctly arrayed around the flange.

8. Press <Enter> to complete the command.

9. Save and close the file.

Practice 11j | # Path Array

Practice Objective

- Make copies of an object along a selected path.

Estimated time for completion: 5 minutes

In this practice, you will use a **Path Array** to make copies of a deck chair around the edge of a pool, as shown in Figure 11–35.

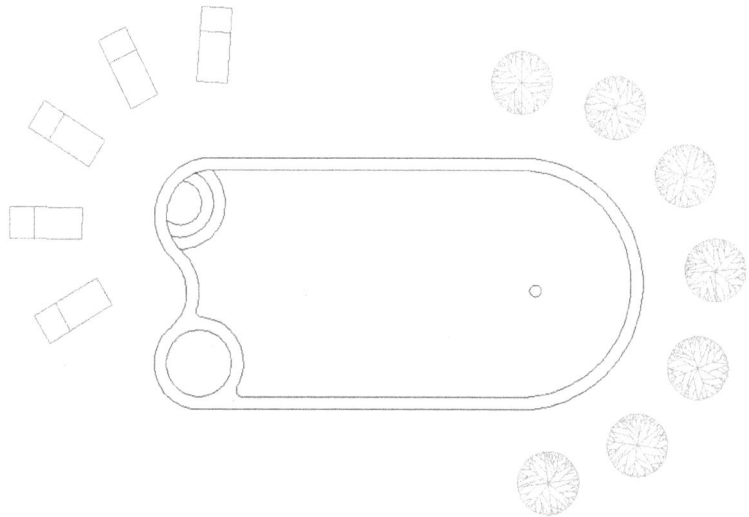

Figure 11–35

1. Open **Deckchair-M.dwg** from your practice files folder.

2. In the *Home* tab>Modify panel, expand the Array drop-down list and click (Path Array).

3. At the *Select objects:* prompt, select the tree to the right of the pool. Press <Enter> to finish selecting objects.

4. At the *Select path curve:* prompt, select the magenta arc that starts at the tree.

5. Select the arrow grip (located on the second tree) and enter **2400**, as shown in Figure 11–36. Press <Enter>.

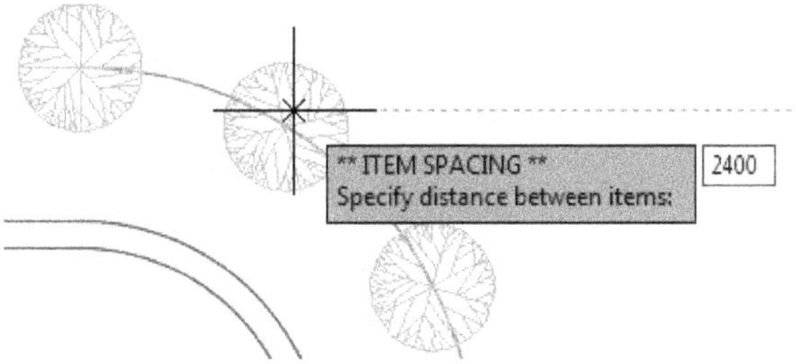

Figure 11–36

6. Press <Enter> again to exit the command.

7. Start the **Path Array** command again.

Select both rectangle and a line that makes up the chair.

8. At the *Select objects:* prompt, select the chair to the left of the pool. Press <Enter> to finish selecting objects.

9. At the *Select path curve:* prompt, select the magenta arc that starts at the chair.

10. In the *Array Creation* contextual tab, in the Properties panel, expand the Measure drop-down list and click (Divide). The chairs are now evenly spaced along the path.

11. In the *Array Creation* contextual tab, in the Items panel, for *Items* enter **5** and press <Enter>.

12. Press <Enter> to end the command.

13. Toggle off the layer **Path** to hide the paths that were used to create the arrays.

14. Save and close the file.

Chapter Review Questions

1. When you start the **Trim** command, what do you select first?

   a. The trimming distance.

   b. The objects to trim.

   c. The cutting edge(s).

   d. The base point.

2. What method do you use for selecting objects to **Stretch**?

   a. Any selection method.

   b. Window selection.

   c. Crossing selection.

   d. Pick individual objects.

3. Which of the following objects cannot be stretched? (Select all that apply.)

   a. Circles

   b. Rectangles

   c. Blocks

   d. Polygons

4. Which **Chamfer** option creates beveled edges at all of the vertices of a selected polyline?

   a. Angle

   b. Multiple

   c. Method

   d. Polyline

5. What do you need to set before you apply a fillet in your drawing?

   a. Distance

   b. Radius

   c. Angle

   d. Thickness

6. You can fillet two parallel lines to add an arc tangent to both lines.

   a. True

   b. False

7. Which command would you use to array a number of trees around an irregularly-shaped pond?

   a. **Polar Array**

   b. **Path Array**

   c. **Spline Array**

   d. **Rectangular Array**

8. Which of the following commands creates parallel objects of the selected objects?

   a. **Fillet**

   b. **Mirror**

   c. **Offset**

   d. **Extend**

Command Summary

Button	Command	Location
	Break	• **Ribbon:** *Home* tab>expanded Modify panel • **Command Prompt:** break
	Break at Point	• **Ribbon:** *Home* tab>expanded Modify panel • **Command Prompt:** break
	Chamfer	• **Ribbon:** *Home* tab>Modify panel> expand Trim and select Chamfer • **Command Prompt:** chamfer or CHA
	Extend	• **Ribbon:** *Home* tab>Modify panel • **Command Prompt:** extend or EX
	Fillet	• **Ribbon:** *Home* tab>Modify panel • **Command Prompt:** fillet or F
	Offset	• **Ribbon:** *Home* tab>Modify panel • **Command Prompt:** offset or O
	Path Array	• **Ribbon:** *Home* tab>Modify panel (*expanded Array drop-down list*) • **Command Prompt:** arraypath
	Polar Array	• **Ribbon:** *Home* tab>Modify panel (*expanded Array drop-down list*) • **Command Prompt:** arraypolar
	Rectangular Array	• **Ribbon:** *Home* tab>Modify panel (*expanded Array drop-down list*) • **Command Prompt:** arrayrect
	Stretch	• **Ribbon:** *Home* tab>Modify panel • **Command Prompt:** stretch or S
	Trim	• **Ribbon:** *Home* tab>Modify panel • **Command Prompt:** trim or TR

Inserting Blocks

In this chapter you learn about blocks and dynamic blocks, and how to insert them using the Insert command, Tool Palettes, and DesignCenter.

Learning Objectives in this Chapter

- Convert a group of objects into a single block.
- Add blocks to a drawing and modify dynamic blocks.
- Insert blocks using various tools.

12.1 What are Blocks?

A group of objects can be converted into a single symbol or block. Blocks can be anything from furniture (as shown in Figure 12–1) to schematic symbols, to entire drawings, such as a roof detail. Different types of drawings use different blocks. For example, architects need blocks, such as doors, windows, and roof sections. Mechanical designers would have a stock of nuts, bolts, and reusable parts.

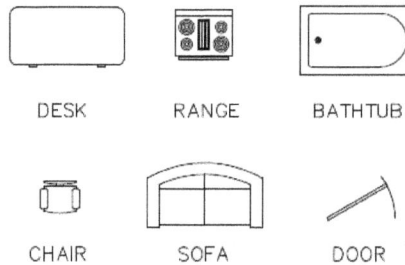

DESK   RANGE   BATHTUB

CHAIR   SOFA   DOOR

Figure 12–1

The benefits of using blocks in the AutoCAD software:

* Ease of manipulating the blocks in a drawing, since they are unified objects. Some blocks, called *dynamic blocks*, are designed so that you can adjust their size or other features after inserting them.

* Consistency of standard details or parts.

* Reduced file size, since each instance of the block in a drawing refers to a single block definition.

'Creating blocks' has been discussed in the AutoCAD/AutoCAD LT Fundamentals - Part 2 and in the Beyond the Basics student guides.

You can insert blocks into your drawings in several ways, including the **Insert** command, Tool Palettes, DesignCenter, and Autodesk Seek.

Hint: Blocks and Layers

When you insert a block, the insertion point is always placed on the current layer. The way the block was created determines whether the block objects use the properties of the current layer, or have a layer or layers that are already associated with objects in the block. Block objects created on layer **0** use the properties of the current layer. Block objects created on other layers use the properties of those layers, no matter which layer is current when the block is inserted. Ask your CAD Manager how blocks are handled in the drawings in which you work.

While there is no absolute standard for how blocks are created, you are most likely to use multilayer compound blocks. For example, you might create a detail that includes hatching, text and the objects, as shown in Figure 12–2. These blocks should be inserted on layer **0**.

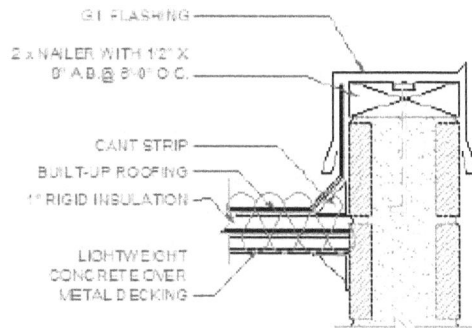

Figure 12–2

Simple blocks, such as a symbol or screw (as shown in Figure 12–3), are more likely to be created on layer **0** and inserted on the required layer.

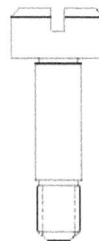

Figure 12–3

12.2 Working with Dynamic Blocks

Dynamic blocks are special kinds of blocks that can be changed dynamically. Once they are in your drawing, they can be manipulated in a variety of ways, including lengthening a side, flipping the direction, aligning to other objects, rotating, or selecting from a list of options, as shown in Figure 12–4. Dynamic blocks are powerful tools and in many cases, several standard blocks can be replaced by one dynamic block.

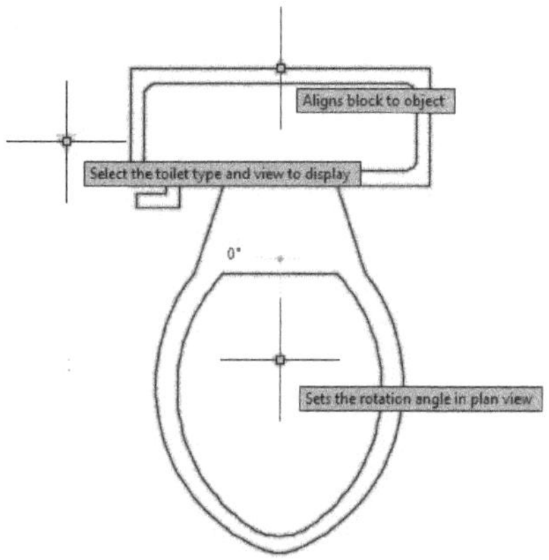

Figure 12–4

Manipulating Dynamic Blocks

When you select a dynamic block, special grips display the types of modifications that are available. Hover the cursor over one of the grips to display its tooltip. Click on the required grip to change the block, as shown in Figure 12–5.

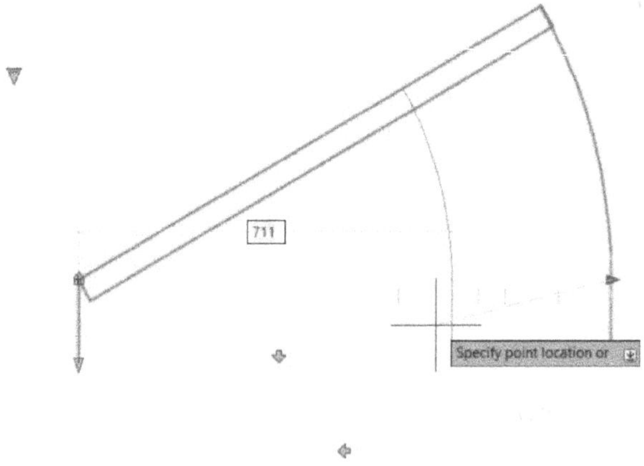

Figure 12–5

- The modification features in dynamic blocks can differ from one block to another. For example, one block might only have the Lengthen/Shorten grip, while another might have the Flip, List, and Rotate grips.

Dynamic Block Grips

The available block grips are described as follows.

	Lengthen/ Shorten	Enables you to scale, stretch, or array a block. The action depends on how the block was defined.
	List	Opens a list of options from which to select, such as size, number of items, view displayed, etc.
	Insert/Move	Indicates the insertion point of the block and other points that might have been assigned in the block. It can move the entire block or just one entity in the block.
	Flip	Flips the entire block in the direction of the arrow.
	Align	Aligns the entire block at the angle of an object when you move the block near that object.
	Rotate	Enables you to rotate the block or specific objects in the block. The objects that rotate are preset in the block definition.

- Blocks that are not dynamic only have an Insert/Move grip, which you can use to drag the block to a new location.

- After you have finished modifying the dynamic block, press <Esc> to clear it and its grips from modification.

12.3 Inserting Blocks

Blocks can be placed in a drawing using the **Insert** command where you can either use the Insert dialog box or Insert drop-down list, as shown in Figure 12–6. You are prompted to select the block name, insertion point, scale, and rotation. It also enables you to insert other drawings into the current drawing.

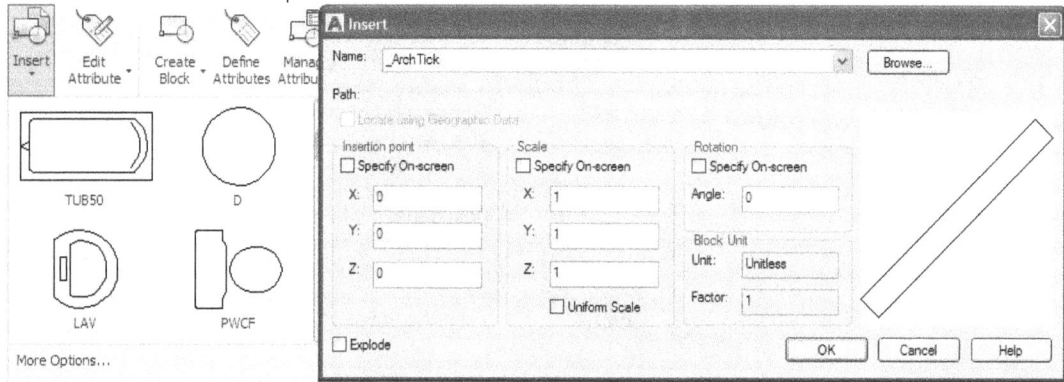

Figure 12–6

How To: Insert a Block from the Insert Dialog Box

1. In the *Home* tab>Block panel or *Insert* tab>Block panel, expand (Insert Block) and select **More Options...** to open the Insert dialog box.
2. In the Insert dialog box, expand the Name: drop-down list and select a block. The blocks must be available in the drawing.
3. Specify the *Insertion point*, *Scale*, and *Rotation*. You can set these in the dialog box or on-screen.
4. Click **OK**.

How To: Insert a Block from the Drop-down List

1. In the *Home* tab>Block panel or *Insert* tab>Block panel, expand (Insert Block) and select a block.
2. In the drawing, either click to place the block at the required location or select the **Basepoint**, **Scale**, **X**, **Y**, **Z**, or **Rotate** options and set their values.

- Since you do not usually know the precise X,Y coordinates of the *Insertion point*, you can specify them in the drawing rather than by entering them in the dialog box.

- You can insert any AutoCAD drawing as a block by clicking **Browse** in the Insert dialog box. The file becomes a block in the current drawing and is then listed with the other blocks in the Name: drop-down list in the dialog box and the Insert drop-down list in the ribbon.

- If you select the **Explode** option in the Insert dialog box, the block is converted into its component parts when it is inserted into the drawing. If you use this option, the block is hidden while you specify its insertion point, scale, and rotation on-screen (you can also explode a block after it has been inserted using the **Explode** command).

- The *Block Unit* area in the Insert dialog box displays the units (inches, millimeters, etc.) in which the block was drawn. If inserted into a drawing that uses different units, the block is scaled automatically.

- Blocks are normally created at the appropriate size for the drawing and the insertion scale should generally be set to **1**.

Hint: Blocks and Object Snaps

You can snap to Object Snap points (**Endpoint**, **Midpoint**, etc.) on the objects in a block, as shown in Figure 12–7. Additionally, the **Insertion** Object Snap snaps to the insertion base point of a block.

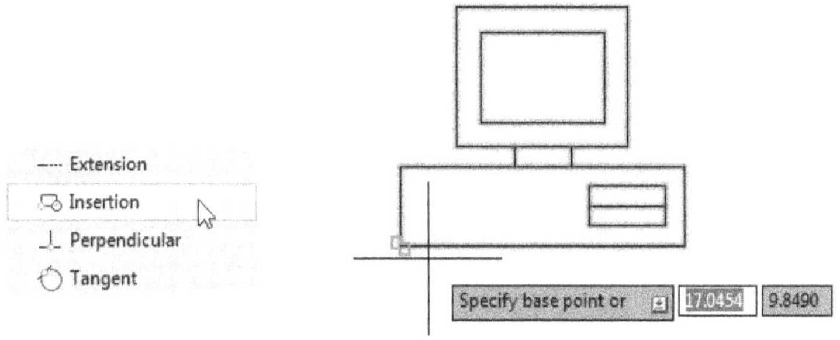

Figure 12–7

12.4 Inserting Blocks using the Tool Palettes

The AutoCAD software comes with many blocks, which are stored in the Tool Palettes window (*View* tab>Palettes panel> (Tool Palettes)). After you locate the required block in one of the Tool Palette tabs, you can drag and drop it from the palette into the drawing.

- The AutoCAD software comes with example blocks that are located on several tabs of the palette, as shown in Figure 12–8. You can also create custom palettes.

Press <Ctrl>+<3> to toggle the Tool Palettes open or closed.

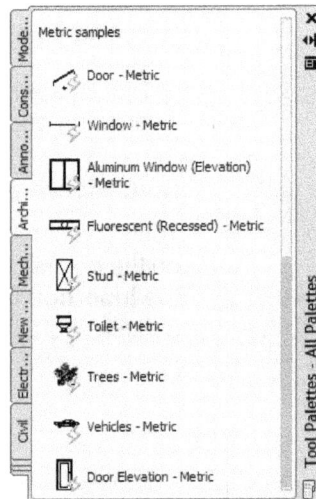

Figure 12–8

- In the Tool Palettes, dynamic blocks are indicated by a lightning bolt symbol.

- If there are more objects than can fit in the window, a scroll bar displays next to the title bar, enabling you to scroll through the list.

Insertion Options

The drag and drop method inserts the block without any options. The block is placed where you drop it. If you click on the block image in the palette instead, the block image gets attached to the cursor along with the *Specify insertion point:* prompt. You can either click to place the block at the required location or select one of the command options (<Down Arrow>), as shown in Figure 12–9.

Figure 12–9

- If you want to rotate the object before you insert it, select the **Rotate** option, enter the rotation angle, and select the point at which to insert the rotated block.

- The **Basepoint** option enables you to select a different base point on the object from the one that was created with the block.

- Most blocks are correctly scaled for the drawing in which you are inserting them. However, the **Scale** (uniform), **X**, **Y**, and **Z** options enable you to change the scale.

Controlling the Tool Palettes Window

It is useful to display the Tool Palettes as you are working. For efficient use of screen space, you can dock and hide the palette to one side of the drawing window with either the icon or text displayed. When you need to display the full palette, move the cursor over the icon (or text depending on your setting), as shown in Figure 12–10.

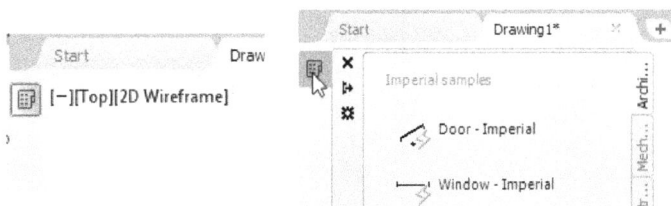

Figure 12–10

This process also applies to other palettes, such as Properties.

*Right-click on the title bar of an undocked palette, and select **Anchor Left** or **Anchor Right** to dock and auto-hide the palette. (**Allow Docking** must be selected first for anchoring to work.)*

How To: Dock and Hide a Palette

1. Open the Tool Palettes.
2. Place the cursor over the title bar of the palette and drag it to one side of the screen. It should dock. If it does not, right-click on the title bar, select **Allow Docking**, and try again.
3. Minimize the palette by clicking ▮◀ (Auto-hide). The palettes stack if more than one is docked.
4. Move the cursor over the title bar or icon to display the full-size palette.

- To save more space, right-click on the palette title bar and set the docked view to **Icons only**, as shown in Figure 12–11.

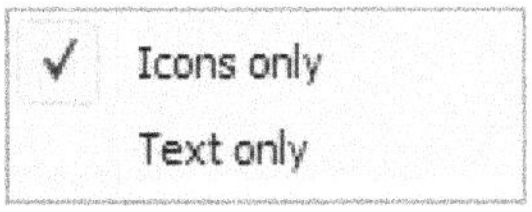

✓	Icons only
	Text only

Figure 12–11

12.5 Inserting Blocks using the DesignCenter

DesignCenter is available to manage your standards. It enables you to access named objects in any drawing to copy them into the current drawing and is also used for inserting blocks. You can have a library of drawings that include typical blocks grouped in a useful order, as shown in Figure 12–12. From DesignCenter, you can open the drawing and then drag and drop the blocks into your current drawing.

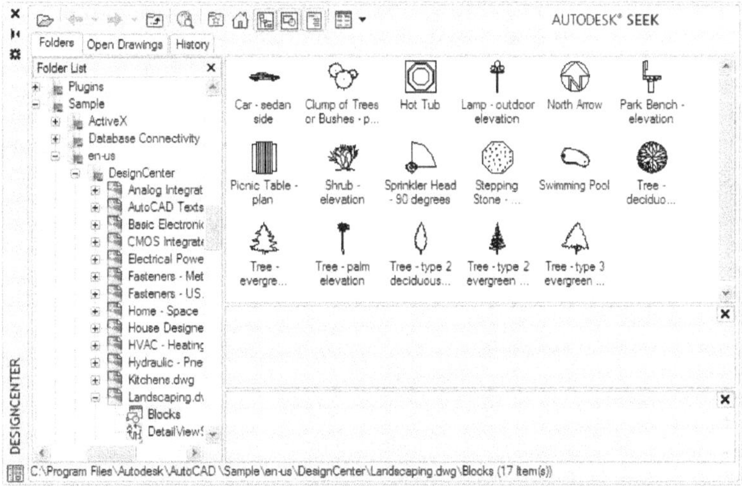

Figure 12–12

- In addition to blocks, you can copy other named objects using the DesignCenter, including layers, linetypes, layouts, reference files (xrefs), and text, table, or dimension styles. Open DesignCenter, locate the drawing containing the objects you want to use, and drag them into your current drawing.

- You can open the DesignCenter by clicking

  (DesignCenter) in the *View* tab>Palettes panel.

Press <Ctrl>+<2> to toggle DesignCenter open or closed. DesignCenter is a palette and can be docked and hidden in the same way as the Tool Palettes and Properties palette.

DesignCenter Content

Three tabs across the top of DesignCenter provide access to different parts of its content. These tabs are:

Folders	Enables you to use the *Folder List* to navigate to drawings on your computer or network drives.
Open Drawings	Provides access to drawing(s) that are open in the AutoCAD software. You can copy components from any of the open drawings into your current drawing window.
History	Lists several of the last drawings used in DesignCenter. Double-click on the filename to load the drawing in the *Folders* tab.

New in 2018

- Click **AUTODESK Seek** to launch the BIMobject® website. In the Welcome to BIMobject window, click **Browse BIM objects** to search for available content online, as shown in Figure 12–13. BIMobject is an online service that provides access to 2D drawings and 3D models, along with product information that has been made available directly by the product manufacturers and suppliers.

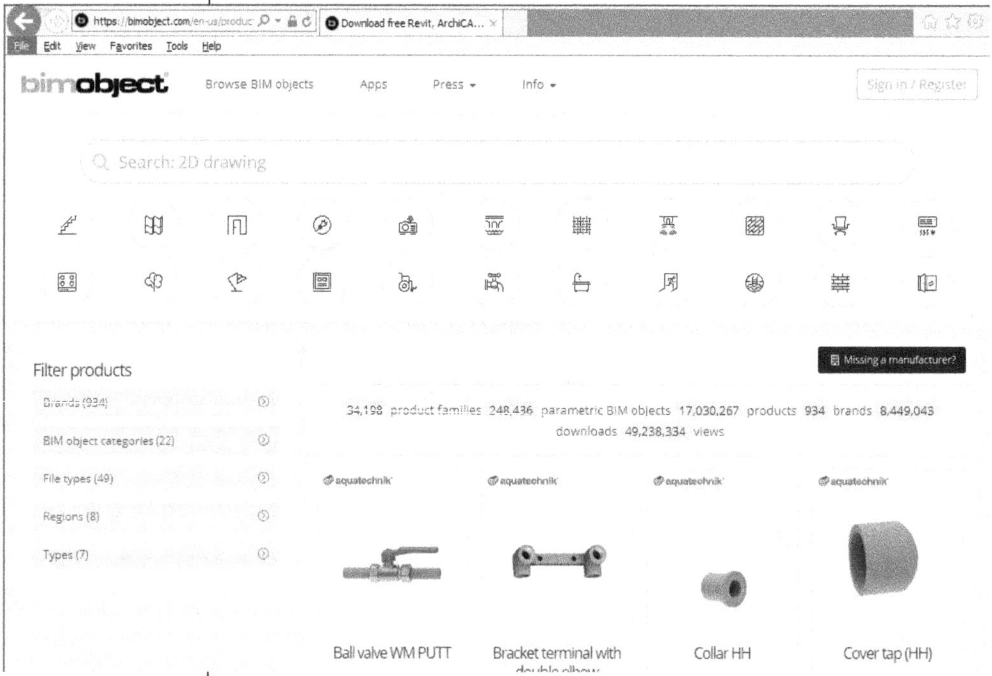

Figure 12–13

Navigation and Display Options

The DesignCenter palette contains tools for navigating to drawings and changing the display, as shown in Figure 12–14.

Figure 12–14

	Load: Opens the Load dialog box. When you select a drawing, it opens in DesignCenter without opening in the AutoCAD software.
	**Back/Forward:** Returns to the previous drawing selected. Click ▼ to expand the list of the available drawings.
	Up: Backs up one folder level each time the button is clicked. Use this if you have toggled off the tree view.
	Search: Opens the Search dialog box in which you can search for drawings, blocks, layers, etc., by name.
	Favorites: Similar to other Windows programs, you can specify favorite places from which to get drawings or web sites. Right-click in DesignCenter to add items to your favorites list.
	Home: Switches to the *DesignCenter* folder.
	**Tree View Toggle:** Toggles the left side of DesignCenter off and on. If it is off, only the level to which you have expanded displays.
	**Preview:** Displays a preview of the selected block.
	**Description:** Displays a description of the selected block if one is available.
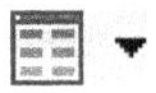	**Views:** Toggles through the various types of views. Use the **Large Icons** option to display a thumbnail image of the blocks.

- Set the drawings or folders that you need to access most often as **Favorites**. Right-click on the file or folder in DesignCenter and select **Add to Favorites**. Click (Favorites) in the toolbar for quick access.

Practice 12a | Working with Blocks

Practice Objective

Estimated time for completion: 25 minutes

* Add blocks and dynamic blocks using the **Insert** command, Tool Palettes, and DesignCenter.

In this practice, you will add blocks and dynamic blocks using the **Insert** command and the Tool Palette. You will also add landscaping blocks using the Design Center, as shown in Figure 12–15.

Figure 12–15

Task 1 - Insert blocks.

In this task you will insert blocks in a floor plan using the **Insert** command, as shown in Figure 12–16. The blocks in this drawing were created on their own layers. You will insert them all on layer **0**.

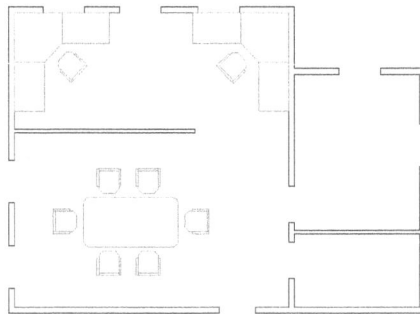

Figure 12–16

1. Open **Plan-AM.dwg** from your practice files folder.

2. In the *Insert* tab>Block panel, expand ⬚ (Insert) and select the block named **Desk Unit,** as shown in Figure 12–17.

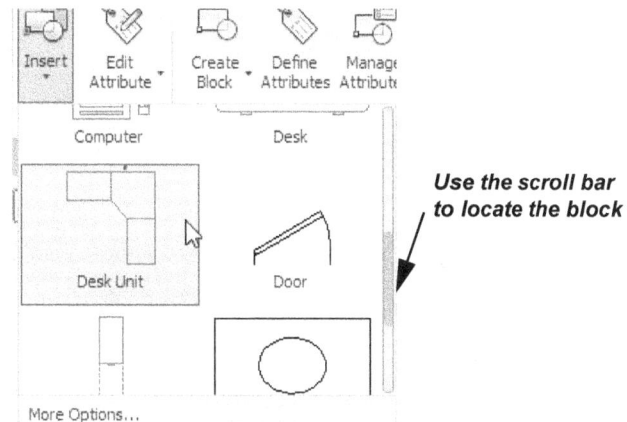

Use the scroll bar to locate the block

Figure 12–17

3. The desk is attached to the cursor. Type **R** and press <Enter> to select the **Rotate** option. Ensure that **0** is set for rotation angle, and press <Enter>.

4. Type **X** and press <Enter>. Ensure that **1** is set as the X scale factor, and press <Enter>.

5. Similarly, ensure that both for the Y and Z scale factors are set as **1**.

6. Place the desk in the top right corner of the office, as shown in Figure 12–16.

7. Insert another **Desk Unit** in the top left corner. Set the *Rotation Angle* to **90** degrees.

8. Insert **Chair** blocks facing each of the desks. Set the rotation angles to **45** and **-45**.

9. In the ribbon, expand **Insert** and select **More Options...** to open the Insert dialog box. Click **Browse** and select **Table-AM.dwg** (in your practice files folder) and click **Open**. Click **OK** in the Insert dialog box and place the table in the largest room.

10. Insert chairs around the table. You might want to insert one chair and then use other commands, such as **Copy** and **Mirror** to place the additional ones.

Task 2 - Work with dynamic blocks.

In this task you will add dynamic blocks from the Tool Palettes to the floor plan and then manipulate them, as shown in Figure 12–18.

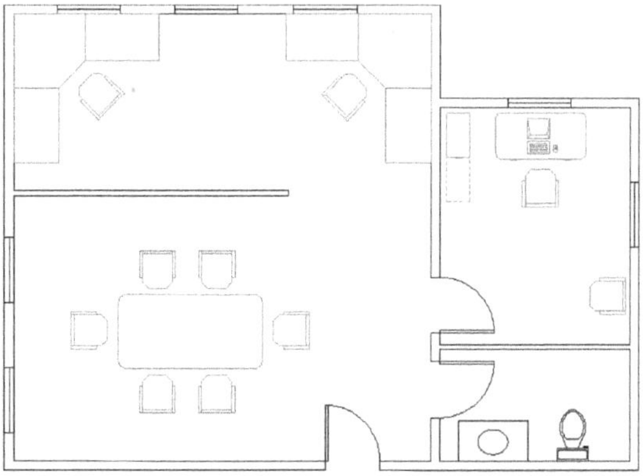

Figure 12–18

1. Zoom in on the opening along the bottom wall of the plan.

2. Ensure that ⬜ ▼ (Object Snap) is toggled on and **Endpoint** is selected.

3. Open Tool Palettes, if it is not already open. Note the types of blocks that are available in the different tabs.

4. In Tool Palettes, switch to the *Architectural* tab and insert a **Door-Metric** into the opening by dragging and dropping it from the Tool Palettes. Snap to the upper end point on the left wall. If the door snaps vertically, rotate it such that it aligns horizontally along the wall, as shown in Figure 12–19. The door does not fit in the opening.

Figure 12–19

View tab>Palettes panel, ⊞ (Tool Palettes).

You can display a tab by clicking on ▤ at the end of the tabs bar and selecting the required tab from the list.

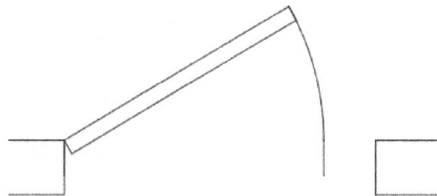

5. Select the inserted door to display the grips. Click
   ▷ (Lengthen) at the right end of the door and note the
   current length (750). Drag the cursor to the right to endpoint
   of the wall to make the length **900** (as shown in
   Figure 12–20), and click to place it at that location.

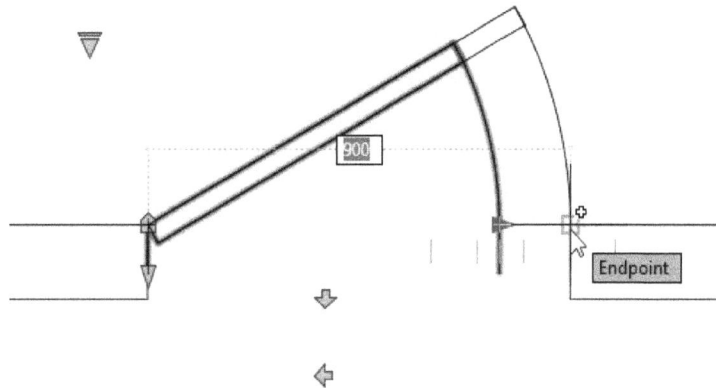

Figure 12–20

6. Click ▽ (List) and select **Open 90°**. The door swing
   changes to this angle. Press <Esc> to clear the door.

7. Pan to the smallest room, and then drag and drop a
   Toilet-Metric into it. The toilet displays as a front view.

8. Select the **Toilet** to display the grips. Click ▽ (List) and
   select **Elongated (Plan)**. A plan (top) view of the toilet
   displays.

Move the toilet from inside the room and then toward the inside wall.

9. Click ⬜ (Align) and move the cursor to place the toilet along
   the bottom wall. It aligns with the wall.

10. Use the **Insert** command to add a **Sink** along the wall on the
    left side of the toilet.

11. Move the sink and toilet to the layer **Plumbing**.

12. Add doors to the bathroom and the small office. (Place one
    door, rotate it, and adjust it with grips, as required. Then, copy
    it to create the other door and flip it using grips.)

13. Add windows using the **Window-Metric** dynamic block in the
    Tool Palettes. You can also use the **Insert** command to add
    computers and file cabinets to the offices.

Task 3 - Insert blocks using DesignCenter.

In this task you will insert landscaping blocks using DesignCenter, as shown in Figure 12–21.

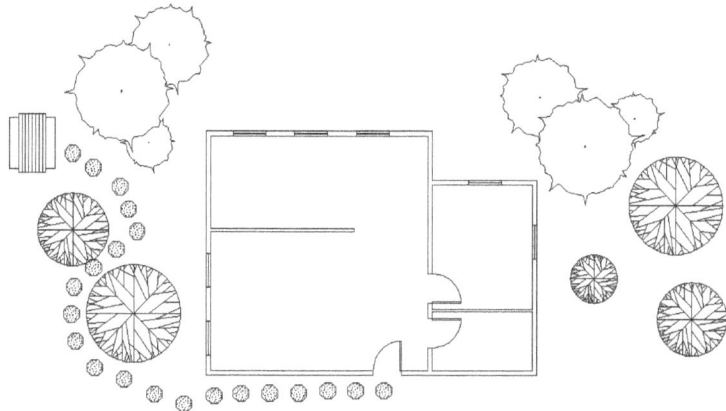

Figure 12–21

1. Toggle off the layers **Furniture** and **Plumbing**.

2. In the Layer Control, make the layer **Planting** as the current layer.

3. Zoom out so that there is room around the outside of the building.

4. Open DesignCenter.

5. In the *DesignCenter* folder supplied with the AutoCAD software (generally in *Sample>en-us* folder), find the file **Landscaping.dwg**. Expand it and select **Blocks** to open it.

6. Drag and drop several trees (in plan view) into the drawing. **Move**, **Rotate**, and **Scale** them as required.

7. Set the current layer to **Hardscape**.

8. Create a path of **Stepping Stone-Hexagonal** blocks around the trees.

9. Save and close the drawing.

The blocks in DesignCenter are created on layer 0. Therefore, you need to select the layer on which you want to place them.

You can open the DesignCenter in the View tab>Palettes panel, and click

(DesignCenter).

Chapter Review Questions

1. What are some advantages of using blocks? (Select all that apply.)

   a. Consistency of standard details and parts.

   b. Easier to select than separate objects.

   c. Can only be placed in the drawing where it was created.

   d. Reduced file size.

2. When inserting a block with the **Insert** command, which parameters must be specified?

   a. Insertion point, scale, and rotation angle.

   b. Angle, distance, and scale.

   c. Date and time.

   d. Insertion point, distance, and angle.

3. How can you insert another drawing into your current drawing file?

   a. Use the **Winsert** command.

   b. Use the **Make Block** command.

   c. Use the **Browse** button in the **Insert** command.

   d. You cannot insert a drawing into your current drawing file.

4. You can use Tool Palettes to insert blocks into the drawing by dragging and dropping.

   a. True

   b. False

5. What can you do using the DesignCenter?

   a. Return a layer to its previous state.

   b. Search for and drag and drop a block into your drawing.

   c. Create template files.

   d. Explode blocks into separate line segments.

6. Some dynamic blocks display the following modification grips:

   a. The grips are the same in every dynamic block.

   b. Explode, Move, and Align.

   c. Explode, List, and Scale.

   d. Flip, Rotate, and List.

Command Summary

Button	Command	Location
	DesignCenter	• **Ribbon:** *View* tab>Palettes panel • **Command Prompt:** adcenter (*on*), adcclose (*off*) or <Ctrl>+<2> (*toggle on/off*)
	Insert	• **Ribbon:** *Home* tab>Block panel or *Insert* tab>Block panel • **Command Prompt:** insert or I
	Tool Palettes	• **Ribbon:** *View* tab>Palettes panel • **Command Prompt:** toolpalettes (*open*), toolpalettesclose or <Ctrl>+<3> (*toggle on/off*)

Chapter

13

Projects: Creating More Complex Objects

This chapter contains practice projects that can be used to gain additional hands-on experience with the topics and commands covered so far in this student guide. These practices are intended to be self-guided and do not include step by step information.

Learning Objectives in this Chapter

- *Mechanical:* Create several machine parts that contain advanced features, such as chamfers, fillets, and offsets.
- *Architectural:* Create floor plans that contain advanced features, such as arrays, trims, fillets, and offsets.
- *Civil:* Create a parking lot that contains advanced features, such as trims, fillets, and offsets.

13.1 Mechanical Project 1: Plate

Estimated time for completion: 30 minutes

In this project you will construct a mechanical plate, as shown in Figure 13–1. Commands you can use include: **Line**, **Offset**, **Circle**, **Trim**, **Fillet**, and **Chamfer**.

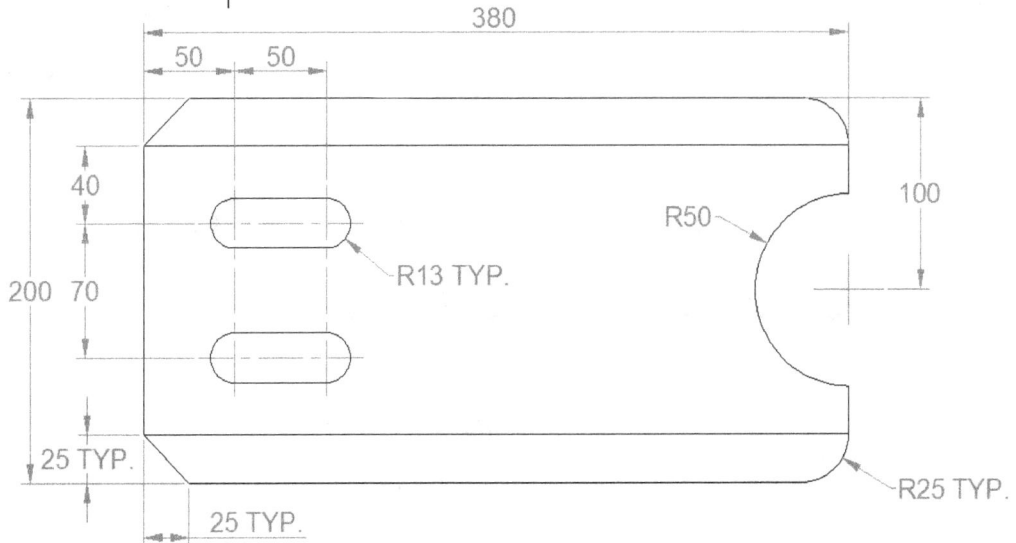

Figure 13–1

1. Start a new drawing called **Plate1.dwg** based on **Mech-Millimeters.dwt**, which is located in your practice files folder.

2. Draw the object shown in Figure 13–1. Commands you can use to construct the object include: **Line**, **Offset**, **Circle**, **Trim**, **Fillet**, and **Chamfer**.

   • Tip: To locate the slots, you can offset the lines from the side and top of the object to locate the center points of the **R13** arcs.

13.2 Mechanical Project 2: Gasket

Estimated time for completion: 20 minutes

In this project you will draw a gasket, as shown in Figure 13–2, using commands, such as **Circle**, **Array**, **Trim**, and **Fillet**.

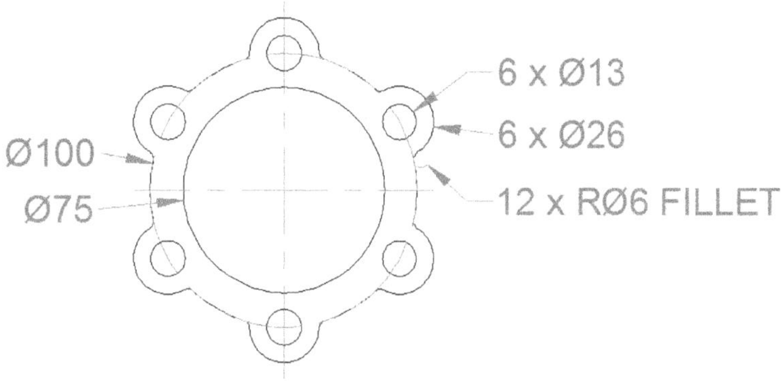

Figure 13–2

1. Start a new drawing called **Gasket.dwg** based on **Mech-Millimeters.dwt**, which is located in your practice files folder.

2. Draw the object shown in Figure 13–2. Commands you should use to construct the object include: **Circle**, **Polar Array**, **Trim**, and **Fillet**.

13.3 Mechanical Project 3: Plate

Estimated time for completion: 30 minutes

In this project you will draw a plate with slots and holes, as shown in Figure 13–3. Commands you can use to construct the object include: **Line**, **Offset**, **Circle**, **Mirror**, **Trim**, and **Array**.

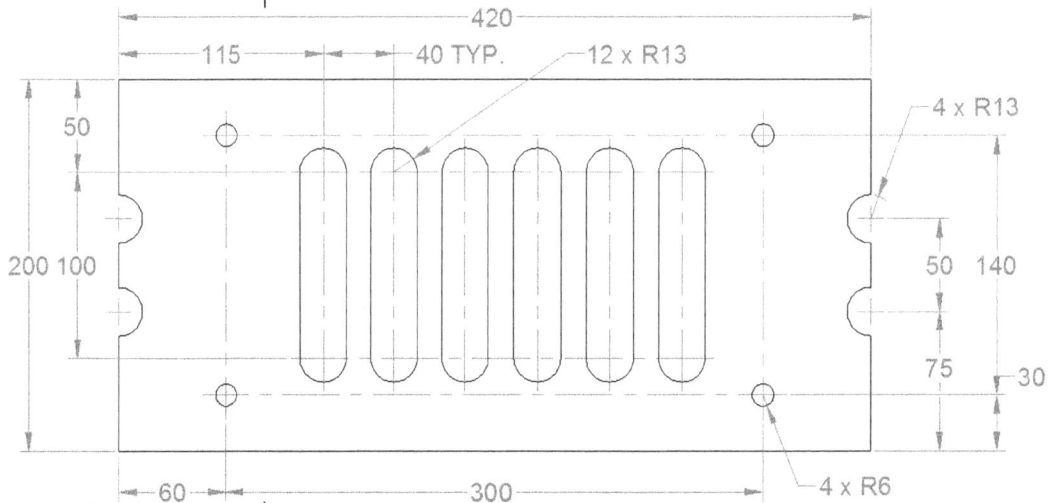

Figure 13–3

1. Start a new drawing called **Plate2.dwg** based on **Mech-Millimeters.dwt**, which is located in your practice files folder.

2. Draw the object shown in Figure 13–3. Commands you should use to construct the object include: **Line**, **Offset**, **Circle**, **Mirror**, **Trim**, and **Rectangular Array**.

   - Tip: To locate the circles or arcs for the holes and slots, you can offset the lines from the side and top of the object to locate the center points.

   - An alternative way of creating the top arc of the slots is to use the **Fillet** command and select the two vertical parallel lines.

13.4 Mechanical Project 4: Rocker Arm

Estimated time for completion: 25 minutes

In this project you will draw a rocker arm, as shown in Figure 13–4. Commands you can use include: **Circle**, **Line**, **Offset**, **Trim**, and **Polyline Edit**.

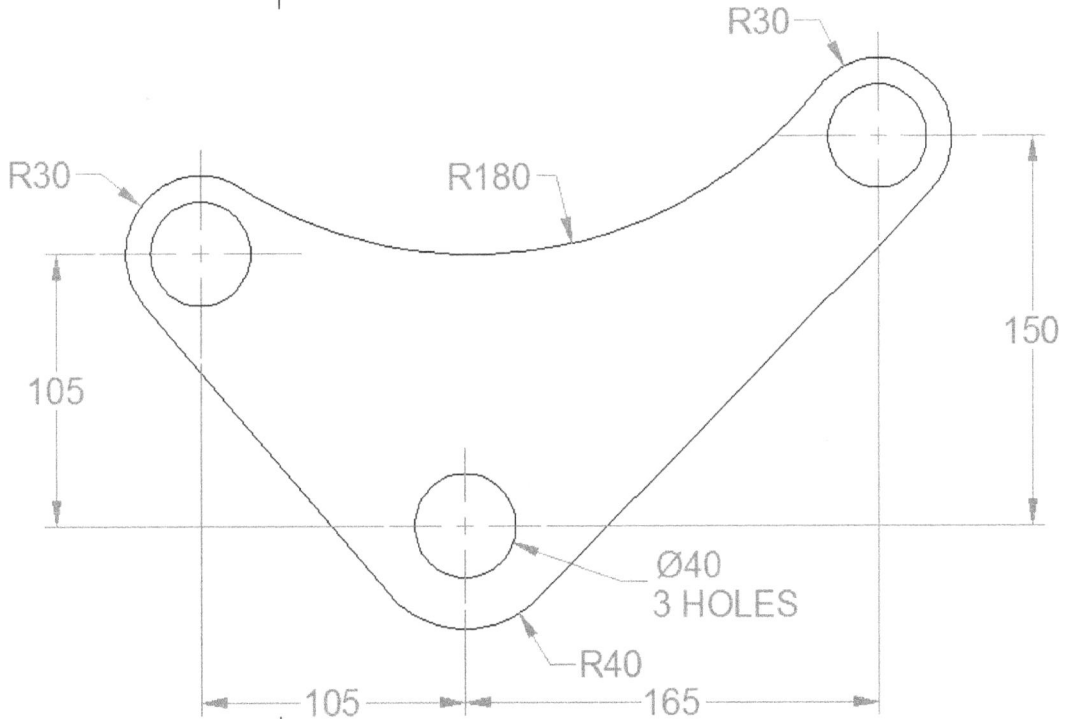

Figure 13–4

1. Start a new drawing called **Rocker.dwg** based on **Mech-Millimeters.dwt**, which is located in your practice files folder.

2. Draw the object shown in Figure 13–4. Commands you should use to construct the object include **Circle**, **Line**, **Offset**, **Trim**, and **Polyline Edit**.

- **Tip:** Start by drawing a circle of **R40** to create the arcs. Draw horizontal and vertical lines from the center of the circle. Offset the lines by the required distances to locate the centers of the **R30** circles, as shown in Figure 13–5.

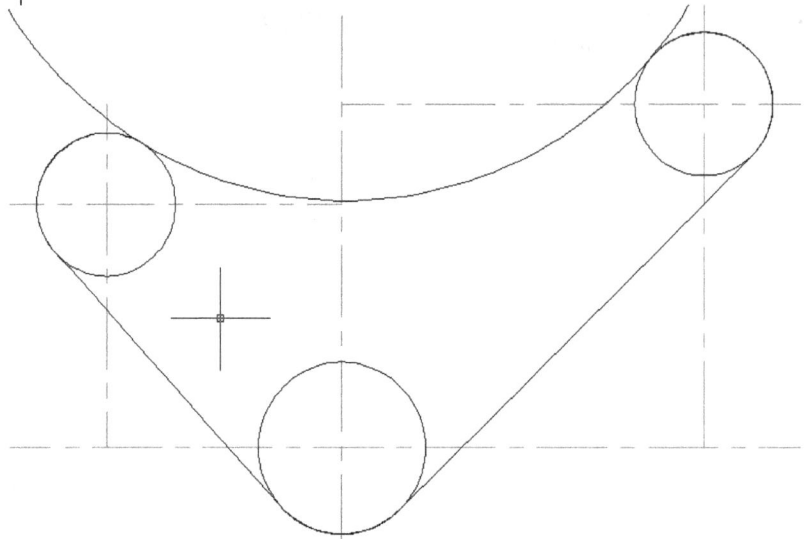

Figure 13–5

- For the **R180** arc, use a **Tan, Tan, Radius** circle. After trimming, join the outline of the object into a polyline.

13.5 Architectural Project 1: Floor Plan

Estimated time for completion: 50 minutes

In this project you will draw the office floor plan shown in Figure 13–6. Commands you can use include: **Polyline**, **Fillet**, **Offset**, and **Trim**. You will then insert dynamic blocks for the doors and windows from the Tool Palettes.

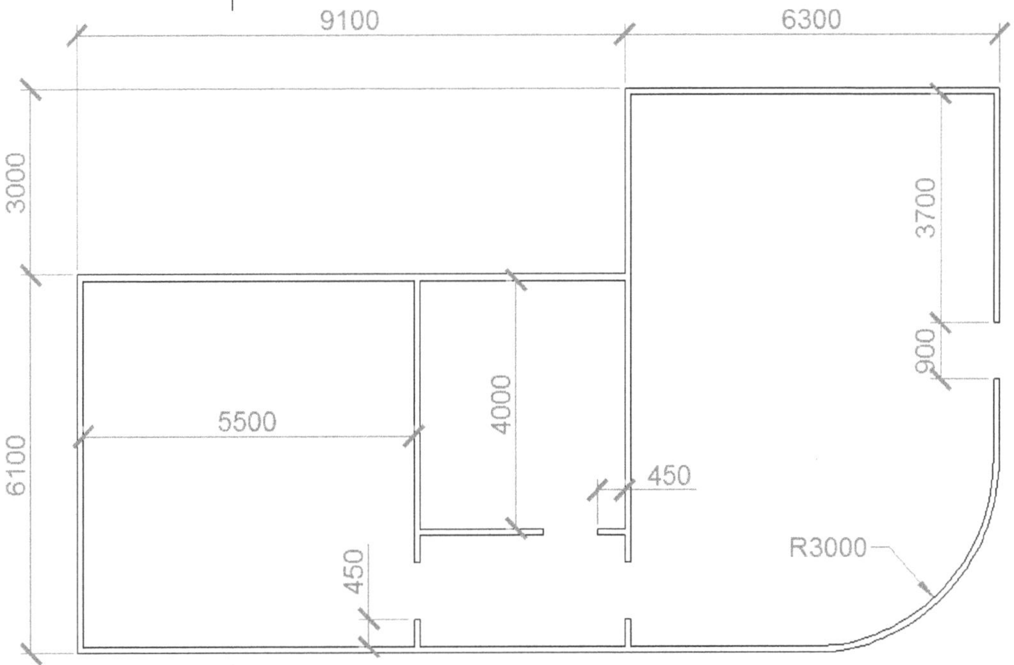

Figure 13–6

- All walls are **100mm** wide. All door gaps are **910mm** wide.

Task 1 - Draw the walls and door openings.

1. Start a new drawing based on **AEC-Millimeters.dwt**, which is located in your practice files folder.

2. Save the drawing as **Office3.dwg**.

3. Verify that the layer **Walls** is current and draw the walls.

   - Tip: To create the door gaps, offset the wall lines to create cutting edges at the required distances and then trim the doors.

4. Save the drawing.

Task 2 - Insert door and window blocks.

1. Open Tool Palettes and select the *Architectural* tab.

2. Add doors and windows from the palette to the drawing, as shown in Figure 13–7. Use the dynamic blocks in the Metric Tool Palette. Use grips to modify the locations and sizes of the doors and windows, and the swing of the doors.

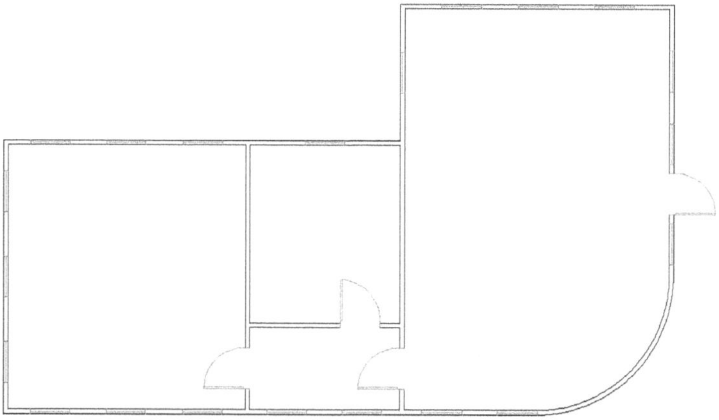

*Change the current layer to **Doors** as you place the doors and to layer **Windows** as you place the windows.*

Figure 13–7

- To locate the windows along the walls, use (Object Snap Tracking) and track from the outside corner of the wall. For example, along the bottom wall, the first window on the left side is placed **600mm** from the outside corner of the building.

- When you have positioned the first window along a wall, use **Rectangular Array** to evenly space the others. For example, to place windows along the bottom wall (as shown in Figure 13–7), use a **Rectangular Array** of **1** row and **7** columns (there are 7 windows) and a *Column offset* distance of **150mm**.

13.6 Architectural Project 2: Floor Plan

Estimated time for completion: 60+ minutes

In this project you will draw the office floor plan shown in Figure 13–8. Commands you can use include: **Line**, **Polyline**, **Polygon**, **Offset**, **Explode**, **Trim**, and **Array**. You will then insert blocks for the doors and windows.

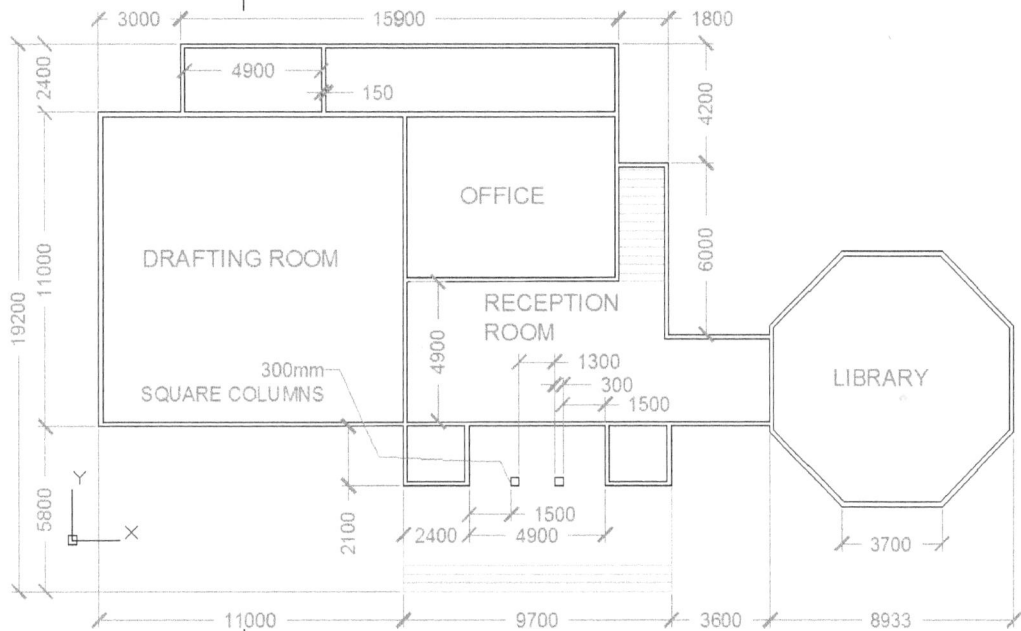

Figure 13–8

Task 1 - Draw walls and stairs.

---

1. Start a new drawing based on **AEC-Millimeters.dwt**, which is located in your practice files folder. Save it with the name **Wright Office.dwg**.

2. Draw the walls as shown in Figure 13–8 on the layer **Walls**. All walls are **150mm** thick. Clean up intersections by trimming.

3. To draw the Library, use the **Polygon** command with the **Edge** option.

4. Put the stairs on the layer **Misc**. The stairs are spaced **1'** apart.

Task 2 - Insert door and window blocks.

1. Create openings for the doors, as shown in Figure 13–9, by trimming. The opening should be **900mm wide** for *single doors* and **1800mm wide** for *double doors*.

2. Open the Tool Palettes and select the *Architectural* tab.

3. Add doors and windows from the palette to the drawing, as shown in Figure 13–9. Use grips to modify the locations, lengths and widths of the doors and windows, and the swing of the doors.

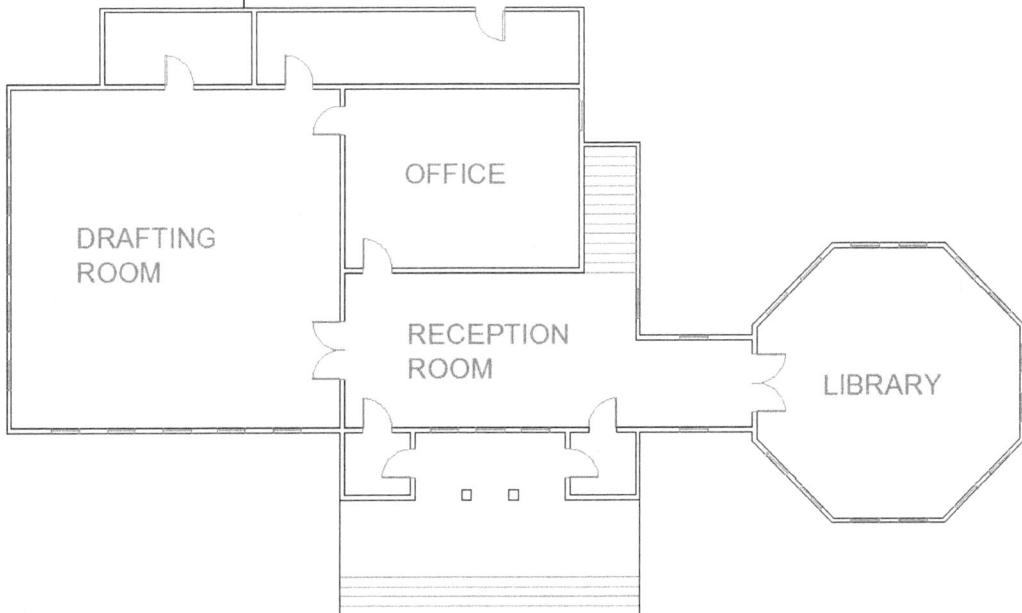

Figure 13–9

*Change the current layer to **Doors** as you place the doors and to **Windows** as you place the windows.*

• Use **Mirror** to create the double doors.

• To quickly add windows in the library, place two along one wall and then use a **Polar Array**. Erase the windows where the door is required.

13.7 Civil Project: Parking Lot

Estimated time for completion: 60+ minutes

In this project you will draw a building, sidewalk, driveway, and parking spaces, as shown in Figure 13–10. Use commands, such as **Trim**, **Extend**, **Fillet**, and **Offset** and use blocks to add trees and shrubs as required.

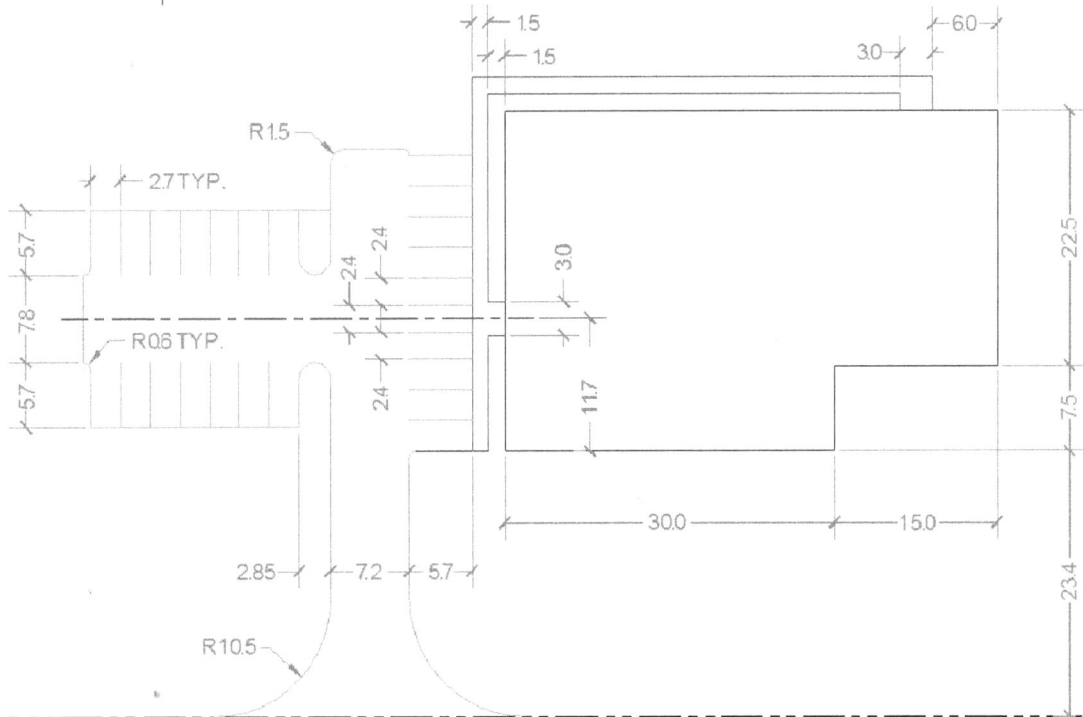

Figure 13–10

Task 1 - Draw the building, sidewalk, and parking spaces.

1. Start a new drawing using **Civil-Meters.dwt**, which is located in your practice files folder. Save it as **Parking1.dwg**.

2. Draw the objects shown in Figure 13–10. Place objects on the appropriate layers: the building on **Building**, the sidewalk on **Pavement Edge New**, the parking lot on **Parking**, and the property line on **PropertyLine**.

- Use the example shown in Figure 13–11 to help construct some of the fillets.

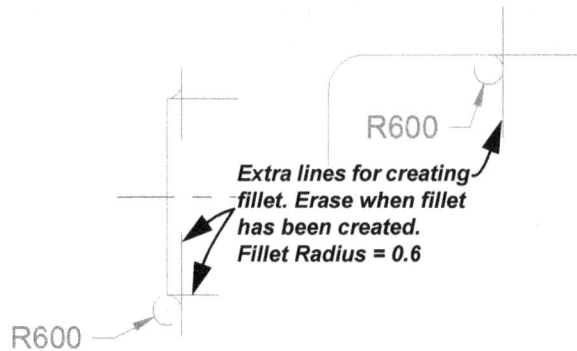

Figure 13–11

Task 2 - Insert landscape blocks.

1. Set the current layer to **Tree Line**.

2. Open DesignCenter and use the various tree blocks included with **Landscape.dwg** in the AutoCAD® *DesignCenter* folder, as shown in Figure 13–12.

Figure 13–12

3. Save and close the drawing.

Setting Up a Layout

In this chapter you learn about using layouts, how to switch between Paper Space and Model Space, how to create viewports in a layout, how to scale and manipulate viewports, and how to copy a layout.

Learning Objectives in this Chapter

- Modify objects in Model Space and Paper Space.
- Create new layouts by copying existing layouts or by using templates.
- Create rectangular and irregular shaped viewports in a layout.
- Create viewports from existing objects in a layout.
- Create single or multiple viewports in a layout.
- Modify viewports using grips and various commands.
- Learn the guidelines for setting up layouts.

14.1 Working in Layouts

When you first enter a layout, you are in a mode called Paper Space by default. You can identify this mode by the **Paper Space** icon displayed in the lower left corner of the screen and **Paper** displayed in the Status Bar, as shown in Figure 14–1.

- In Paper Space, you can add or edit the border and title block, add notes, and create or manipulate the viewports that display the model.

Paper Space icon

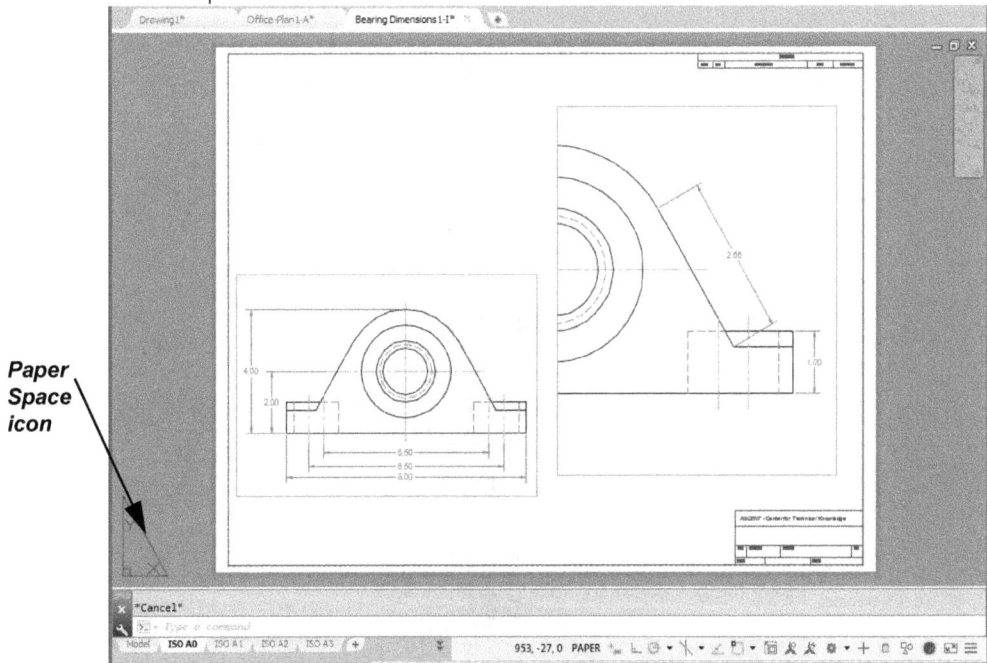

Figure 14–1

- Paper Space displays a graphic representation of the drawing sheet. A dashed boundary on the sheet represents the printable area (if a border is already inserted, it might hide the dashed boundary). The size of the layout reflects the actual sheet size specified in the layout settings. The model displays in one or more viewports in the layout.

- When working in layouts, you can use any of the AutoCAD commands.

- If several layout tabs are available, you can hover the cursor over a tab to display a thumbnail view of the layout, as shown in Figure 14–2. Select a tab to make it active.

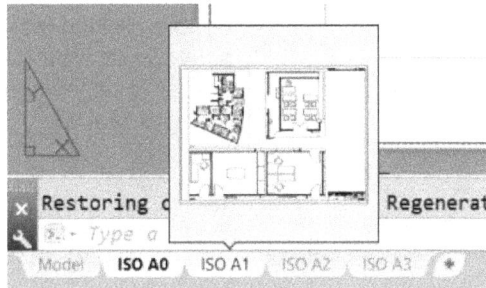

Figure 14–2

- If there are more layouts that cannot be accommodated in the Status Bar, a displays. When repositioning layout tabs, you can drag layouts into positions that are currently hidden by the overflow menu. As a layout is dragged to the edge of the displayed layout tab, either on the left or right (as shown in Figure 14–3), tabs automatically scroll to show hidden layouts. This enables you to drop a layout to any location even if it is hidden.

Figure 14–3

Switch Between Paper Space & Model Space

While making changes in a layout, you often switch between working on the sheet of paper and working on the model through the viewport to adjust the view.

Working Inside a Viewport (Model Space)

- When in a *Layout* tab, you can switch to Model Space by double-clicking inside a viewport. It makes that viewport the active work area. The active viewport displays with a thicker border (as shown in Figure 14–4), and the Status Bar displays **Model**.

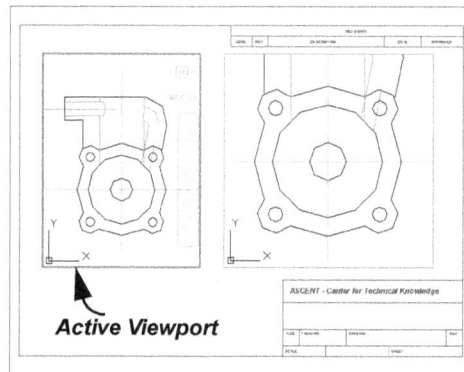

Active Viewport

Figure 14–4

- Only one viewport can be active at a time. The active viewport displays the crosshair cursor. In other viewports and in the paper area, the cursor is an arrow. To make a different viewport active, click inside its border.

- In the active viewport, you can **Zoom** or **Pan** to display any part of the model.

- Any change you make to the model's objects through a viewport, such as moving or deleting them, is reflected in the model, the drawing, and all other viewports.

Returning to Paper Space

Double-click on the paper area of the layout to change from Model Space back to Paper Space, as shown in Figure 14–5. This makes the paper the active work area again. The **Paper Space** icon displays in the drawing window and the Status Bar displays **Paper**. The viewport border returns to its default thickness.

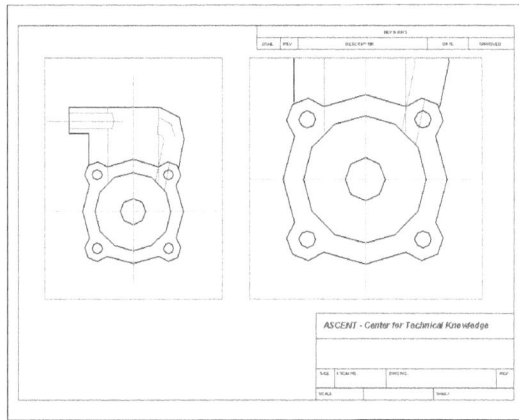

Figure 14–5

- If you double-click on the edge of the viewport, it opens the view in Model Space and fills the screen. This is called *maximizing* the viewport and makes it easier for you to modify

  the drawing. You can also click ⬚ (Maximize Viewport) in the Status Bar to maximize the viewport and then click

  ⬚ (Minimize Viewport) to return to Paper Space.

14.2 Creating Layouts

If you are working with large projects that contain many layouts, use the Sheet Sets Manager to coordinate the project.

When you are working with small projects, you need to have as many layouts in your drawing as the number of printed sheets required to describe the model. You can create new layouts from scratch (empty layouts), by copying existing layouts in your drawing, or create them from template files. You can then add viewports and other objects to the new layout.

How To: Copy and Rename a Layout

1. In the Status Bar, right-click on the layout tab that you want to copy and select **Move or Copy...**
2. In the Move or Copy dialog box, select the layout before which the copied layout is to be added. Alternatively, you can select the **(move to end)** option to add the copied layout as the last layout tab. Select the **Create a copy** option and click **OK**. The new layout is added before the selected layout or as the last layout, depending on the selected option, as shown in Figure 14–6.

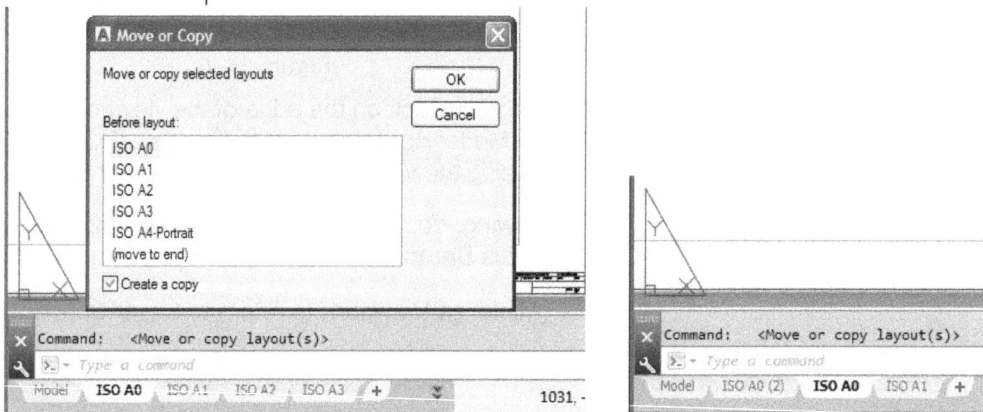

Figure 14–6

3. To rename the layout, double-click on the tab. It is highlighted in blue and you can type the new name, as shown in Figure 14–7. You can also right-click on the tab and select **Rename**.

Figure 14–7

- When you copy a layout, all of the related plotting information and any objects on the layout (such as titleblock, viewports, and notes) are copied as well.

Hint: Best Practice for Layouts

The best way to create a new layout is to copy an existing one that includes all of the settings that you want to use. It is recommended that you have standard layouts containing company title blocks and page setups available in template files, so the parameters do not have to be recreated every time you are ready to set up a sheet.

How To: Create a Layout from a Template

You can also copy layouts from template files or other drawings.

1. In the *Layout* tab>Layout panel, expand ▨ (New) and click **From Template**. You can also right-click on a layout tab and select **From Template...**
2. In the Select Template From File dialog box, locate the template file you want to use and click **Open**.
3. In the Insert Layout(s) dialog box, select the layout you want to use, as shown in Figure 14–8.

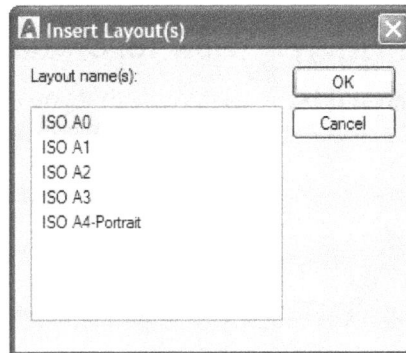

Figure 14–8

4. The new layout is added to the end of the row of tabs.

How To: Create a New Layout

Alternatively, use

▨ *(New Layout) in the Layout tab>Layout panel. This prompts you to enter a new name or accept the Layout 1 name.*

1. Click ➕ at the end of the *Layout* tabs to create a new layout. It creates a new layout with the name Layout 1 or the next available layout number.
2. Rename the layout (double-click or right-click and select **Rename**).

14.3 Creating Layout Viewports

You can create the required viewports in a layout using one of several viewport commands, or the Viewports dialog box. You can insert a single viewport, a standard configuration of multiple viewports, a polygonal viewport, or convert an object to a viewport. Each viewport in a layout can contain a different view of the model, displayed at any scale.

- Viewports should be placed on a layer that is used specifically for storing viewports. Toggling the layer off (or making it a non-plotting layer) hides the viewport border, but not the model objects inside the viewport.

- You can create multiple viewports in various shapes and sizes in a layout.

- You can create multiple viewports that overlap, but you should not place one completely inside another's boundaries.

Rectangular Viewports

How To: Create a New Rectangular Viewport

1. Verify that you are in a layout and in Paper Space.
2. Set the layer to which you want to add the viewports to be current.
3. In the *Layout* tab>Layout Viewports panel, expand the Viewports drop-down list and click ☐ (Rectangular).
4. Select the first corner of the viewport.
5. Select the opposite diagonal corner of the viewport.

- After starting the **Viewports, Rectangular** command, you can use the options at the Command Prompt to switch to the **Polygonal** or **Object** viewport creation by typing **P** for **Polygonal** or **O** for **Object**.

- Other options available at the start of the **Viewports, Rectangular** command are as follows:

ON/OFF	Toggle an existing viewport on or off.
Fit	Fits an entire rectangular viewport in the printable area of the layout sheet.
Shadeplot	Sets how viewports are plotted. Select from the **As Displayed**, **Wireframe**, **Hidden**, **Visual Styles**, and **Render Presets** options.

Lock	Locks or unlocks a viewport's view and scale.
Restore	Restores the settings of a saved viewport.
Layer	Removes any layer overrides in the selected viewport and resets them to the global layer properties
2/3/4	Creates multiple preconfigured viewports.

Polygonal Viewports

How To: Create a New Polygonal Viewport

1. Verify that you are in a layout and in Paper Space.
2. Set the layer to which you want to add the viewports to be current.
3. In the *Layout* tab>Layout Viewports panel, expand the

   Viewports drop-down list and click (Polygonal).
4. Select a start point for the viewport.
5. Select the next point(s).
6. If you want to create an arc segment, select the **Arc** option in the <Down Arrow> menu or press <A>, and follow the prompts to create the arc. To switch back to straight line segments, select the **Line** option or press <L>.
7. Complete the command, using the **Close** option or by pressing <Enter>.

Object Viewports

How To: Convert an Object to a Viewport

1. Verify that you are in a layout and in Paper Space.
2. Set the layer to which you want to add the viewports to be current.
3. In the *Layout* tab>Layout Viewports panel, expand the

   Viewports drop-down list and click (Object).
4. Select a closed object to convert to a viewport.

Named Viewports

How To: Create a Viewport using the Viewports Dialog Box

1. Verify that you are in a layout and in Paper Space.
2. Set the layer to which you want to add the viewports to be current.
3. In the *Layout* tab>Layout Viewports panel, click (Named). The Viewports dialog box opens with the *Named Viewports* tab selected.

4. Switch to the *New Viewports* tab, as shown in Figure 14–9.

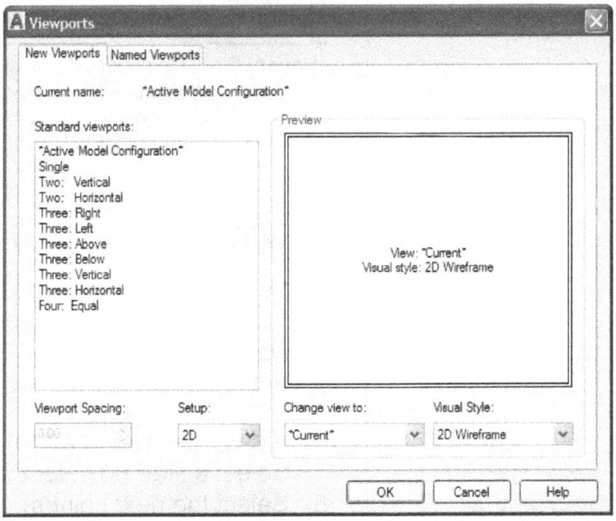

Figure 14–9

5. In the *Standard viewports* area, select the configuration you want to use. A preview of the arrangement displays in the *Preview* pane on the right, as shown in Figure 14–10.

*In the AutoCAD LT®
software, the Visual
Style drop-down list is
not available.*

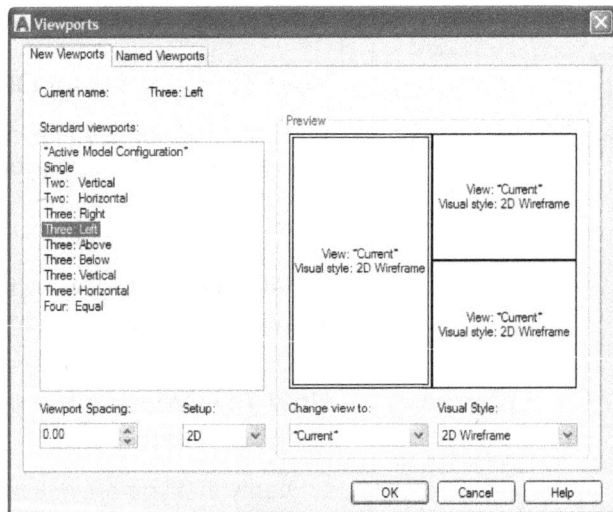

Figure 14–10

6. If you are creating multiple viewports, set the *Viewport Spacing*, which is the space or gap between viewports. The other options are primarily used in 3D drawings.
7. Click **OK**.
8. Select two corners to define the size and location of the viewport(s) in the layout.

Modifying Viewports with Grips

You can move or resize the viewports using grips, as shown in Figure 14–11. You must be in Paper Space to modify a viewport.

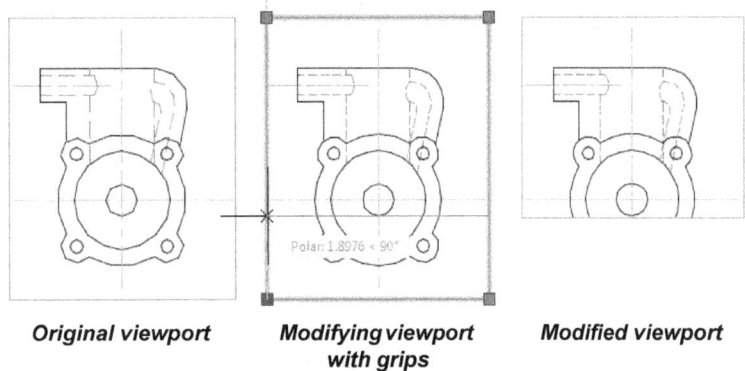

Original viewport   *Modifying viewport with grips*   *Modified viewport*

Figure 14–11

- You can also use the standard AutoCAD software editing tools, such as Copy, Move etc. to modify viewports.

- To remove a viewport, select the edge and erase the viewport. It is important that you select the viewport by its edge. The model objects are not affected when you erase or modify a viewport.

Scaling Viewports

You can scale the objects in a viewport to print at a specific scale factor relative to the paper. Select the edge of the viewport or make the viewport active to display the viewport tools in the Status Bar, as shown on the left in Figure 14–12. Expand

🔲 1:2 ▼ (Scale of the selected viewport) and select a scale, as shown on the right in Figure 14–12. The selected scale sets the size of the drawing relative to Paper Space and sets the Annotation Scale to match. This becomes critical when it is time to dimension and annotate the drawing.

Use the scroll bar in the list to display the required scale.

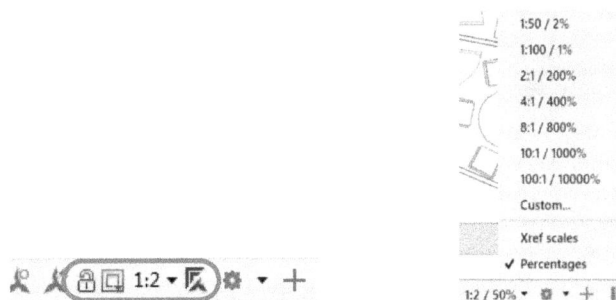

Figure 14–12

- It is useful to activate the viewport and zoom in on the part of the drawing you want to display before setting the scale.

- Once you have set the scale, you can pan in the viewport without changing the scale. However, using the **Zoom** command modifies the scale.

- If the scale you want to use is not in the list, you can add a custom scale factor (e.g., **1:200**) by selecting **Custom...** in the Scale of the selected viewport list. In the Edit Drawing Scales dialog box, click **Add**, type a name for the scale, and enter the values for the *Paper units* and *Drawing units*. Click **OK** to add the custom scale to the scale list.

Locking the Viewport

When the viewport is displaying the correct view and scale, you should lock the display so that it is not changed by accident. When you try to **Zoom** or **Pan** in a locked viewport, the entire layout zooms or pans instead.

- To lock a viewport, select it and click 🔒 (Lock/Unlock Viewport) in the Status Bar. To unlock a viewport, click 🔒 (Lock/Unlock Viewport).

- You can also use the shortcut menu to lock and unlock viewports. In Paper Space, select the viewport border, right-click, and select **Display Locked>Yes or No**, as shown in Figure 14–13.

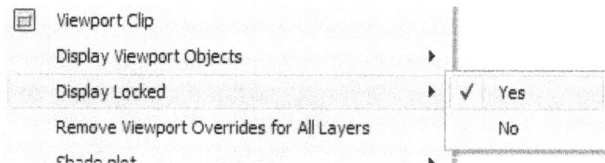

▣ Viewport Clip		
Display Viewport Objects	▶	
Display Locked	▶	√ Yes
Remove Viewport Overrides for All Layers		No
Shade plot	▶	

Figure 14–13

14.4 Guidelines for Layouts

Model Space geometry should be drawn at full scale in real-world units. Paper Space Layout objects (e.g., border, titleblock, title text, etc.) should be drawn at the actual size required for them to fit on the paper at a one-to-one scale.

Use the following guidelines to help when using layouts:

1. Create the drawing in Model Space at full scale in its real-world units.
2. Switch to a layout by selecting the *Layout* tab.
3. Insert a titleblock into the layout if it is not already there. The titleblock should be a block, rather than individual objects.
4. Create as many viewports in the layout as required to display the model.
5. Switch between Model Space and Paper Space to complete the rest of the steps.
6. Pan inside the viewport to center the required displayed area of the drawing. You must be in Model Space to be able to pan.
7. Set the scale factor for each viewport.
8. When the view is correct, lock the viewport so that the scale cannot be changed.
9. Annotate the drawing. General notes that are not linked to objects in the viewports, titleblocks, and titles are typically added in Paper Space. Add dimensions and some other annotations in Model Space.
10. When the drawing is finished, plot the layout in Paper Space mode at a 1:1 scale.

Practice 14a | Working With Layouts

Practice Objectives

- View Model Space and Paper Space in layouts.
- Create, update, modify, and delete viewports in a layout.

Estimated time for completion: 25 minutes

In this practice, you will note the differences between Model Space and Paper Space and switch between Model Space and Paper Space in a viewport in a layout. You will create, scale, and lock viewports in a layout. You will then create copies of the layout, rename the new layouts, and update them with different viewport information, such as the **Auditorium Wing** layout shown in Figure 14–14. You will also delete unused layouts.

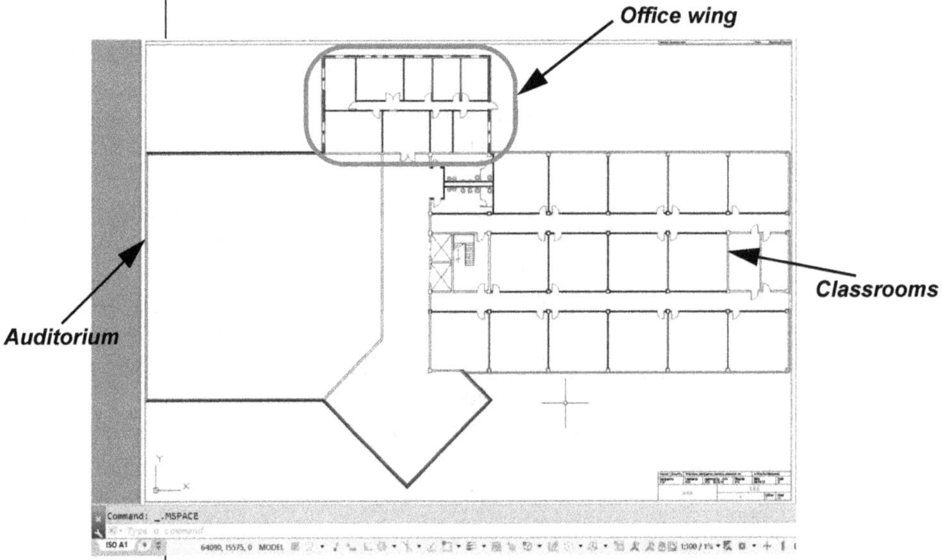

Figure 14–14

Task 1 - View Model Space and Paper Space in layouts.

In this task, you will note the differences between Model Space and Paper Space, and switch between Model Space and Paper Space in a viewport on a *Layout* tab.

1. Open **College Building-AM.dwg** from your practice files folder. Note that **Model** displays in the Status Bar, indicating that the *Model* tab is active and that you are in Model Space.

2. Zoom in on one of the single doors. Ensure that Endpoint

   ▢ ▾ (Object Snap) is toggled on and use the **Measure> Distance** command to measure its opening. Note that it displays as **914** which is the *real-world* distance in Model Space.

3. Select the *Sample* layout tab. You are now in Paper Space.

4. Zoom in on one of the open single doors and check the distance of the door (use Osnap). It displays the actual size of the door.

5. Toggle off ▢ ▾ (Object Snap) and check the distance again. It displays the approximate length of its printed size on the paper.

6. Toggle ▢ ▾ (Object Snap) back on.

7. Zoom out and measure the length of the border. It is drawn at the actual size required to fit on an A-sized sheet of paper.

8. Double-click inside the viewport (gray rectangle) to make it active.

9. **Zoom** and **Pan** so that only the Office Wing, near the top of the building displays, as shown in Figure 14–15.

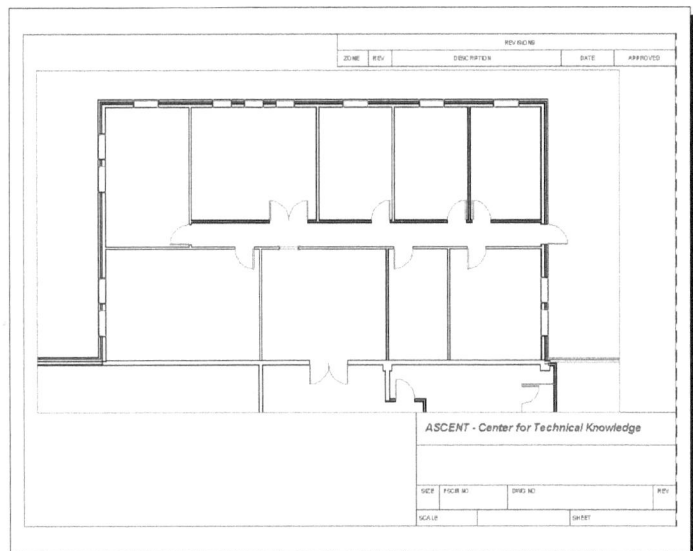

Figure 14–15

10. Save the drawing.

Task 2 - Work in a layout.

In this task, you will create, scale, and lock viewports in layout.

1. Switch to the **ISO A1** layout tab.

2. Make the layer **Viewports** current.

3. Delete the existing viewports in this *Layout* tab before beginning this step by selecting the gray rectangle and pressing <Delete>.

4. In the *Layout* tab>Layout Viewports panel, expand the

   Viewports drop-down list and click ⬚ (Rectangular). Create three viewports arranged inside the border, similar to that shown in Figure 14–16. The entire drawing displays in each viewport.

Press <Enter> after creating each viewport to quickly repeat the command.

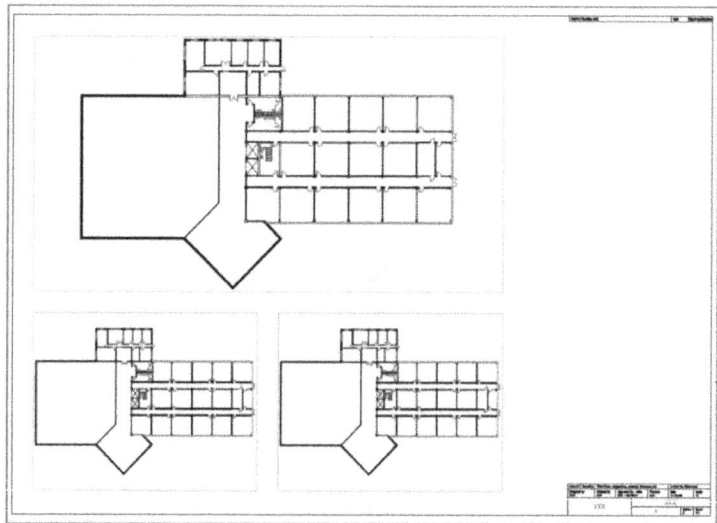

Figure 14–16

The active viewport has a thicker boundary edge.

5. Make the upper viewport active by double-clicking in it. **Zoom** and **Pan** until only the Classroom Wing (i.e., the right side rooms and staircase/elevator area) displays.

6. In the Status Bar, use the Viewport Scale Control list and select several different scales. Finish with a scale of **1:100**.

If you Pan and Zoom before locking the viewport, the scale changes.

7. Switch to Paper Space by double-clicking in an empty area outside any viewport. Select the edge of the bigger (top) viewport and use grips to adjust the viewport size, such that all the required area is inside the viewport.

8. When you are satisfied with the way the viewport looks, select its edge and in the Status Bar, click 🔒 (Lock/Unlock Viewport) to lock the viewport.

Zoom in on two other separate areas of the building for the lower two viewports.

9. Repeat the process with the other two viewports.

10. Zoom into the elevators and stairs for the lower left viewport and then zoom into the toilets for the lower right viewport. Set their scales to **1:50**, as shown in Figure 14–17. Use grips to adjust the sizes and then lock the viewports.

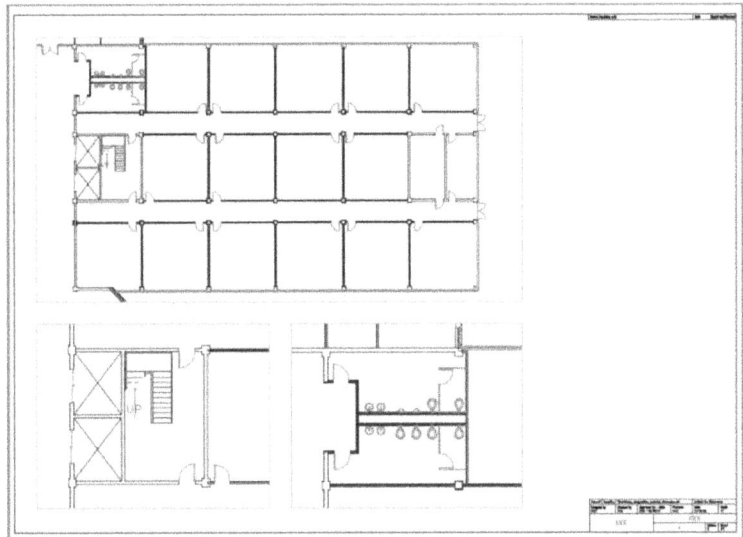

Figure 14–17

Task 3 - Copy and modify layouts.

In this task, you will create copies of the layout, rename the new layouts, update them with different viewport information, and delete unused layouts.

1. Make a copy of the **ISO A1** layout by right-clicking on its tab name in the Status Bar and selecting **Move or Copy...** In the dialog box, select **(move to end)** and **Create a copy**. Click **OK** to add a copy of the tab, named D-Sized (2) to the end of the row. Repeat the process to create one more layout.

2. Double-click on **ISO A1** tab name and type the name **Classroom Wing** to change it. Rename the other two layouts based on the **ISO A1** layout as **Office Wing** and **Auditorium Wing**, as shown in Figure 14–18.

Figure 14–18

3. Select each of the new layouts and note that they contain the same information.

4. Open the **Office Wing** layout and delete the bottom two viewports.

5. Unlock the large viewport and change it so that it displays the **Office Wing** (top area of model) at a **1:50** scale. Re-lock the viewport.

6. Open the **Auditorium Wing** layout and delete the bottom two viewports.

7. Unlock the large viewport and change the display so that it displays the **Auditorium** and **Entrance** at a **1:100** scale. You might need to modify the size of the viewport so that the entire area displays. Re-lock the viewport.

8. Delete the **Sample** layout by right-clicking on the layout, selecting **Delete**, and then clicking **OK** in the confirmation dialog box.

9. Save the drawing.

Chapter Review Questions

1. Once you have scaled a viewport, how do you prevent the scale from being changed?

   a. Explode the viewport.

   b. Lock the viewport.

   c. Freeze all layers in the drawing.

   d. Lock the layer that the viewport is on.

2. When you copy a layout, which of the following is true of the new layout?

   a. Everything in the new layout matches the original layout.

   b. The new layout is always added at the end of all of the other layouts.

   c. The new layout is always empty and you need to setup the new layout.

   d. Only the title block is copied over from the original layout into the copied layout.

3. How can you modify the viewports? (Select all that apply.)

   a. Using grips.

   b. Using the Insert Layout dialog box.

   c. Using the standard AutoCAD editing commands, such as **Copy**, **Move** etc.

   d. You cannot modify the viewports once they are created.

4. Which of the following is true with respect to viewports in a layout?

   a. You cannot create multiple overlapping viewports.

   b. You can create multiple viewports only if they are of the same shape and size.

   c. You can create multiple viewports in various shapes and sizes.

   d. You can create only one viewport per layout.

Command Summary

Button	Command	Location
	Lock/Unlock Viewport	• **Status Bar**
	Maximize Viewport	• **Status Bar**
	Minimize Viewport	• **Status Bar**
MODEL	Model Space	• **Status Bar**
PAPER	Paper Space	• **Status Bar**
	Viewports, Object	• **Ribbon:** *Layout* tab>Layout Viewports panel, expanded Viewports, Rectangular
	Viewports, Polygonal	• **Ribbon:** *Layout* tab>Layout Viewports panel, expanded Viewports, Rectangular
	Viewports, Rectangular	• **Ribbon:** *Layout* tab>Layout Viewports panel • **Command Prompt:** -vports or mview
1:2 ▾	Viewport Scale	• **Status Bar**

Printing Your Drawing

In this chapter, you learn about printing in the AutoCAD® software, how to select what to print or plot, how to select a plotter, and how to preview a printed drawing.

Learning Objectives in this Chapter

- Print a drawing from Model Space as a check plot or finished drawing.
- Print a drawing from Paper Space using viewports.
- Preview and plot layouts.
- Set options for printing and plotting.

15.1 Printing Concepts

As you work on a drawing, it sometimes needs to be printed. For example, you can print a check plot while the drawing is in progress, and when the drawing is finished, you can print a full set of working drawings with dimensioning, text, and titleblocks, as shown in Figure 15–1. Depending on the size of your project, you can do all of these things from one or several drawing files.

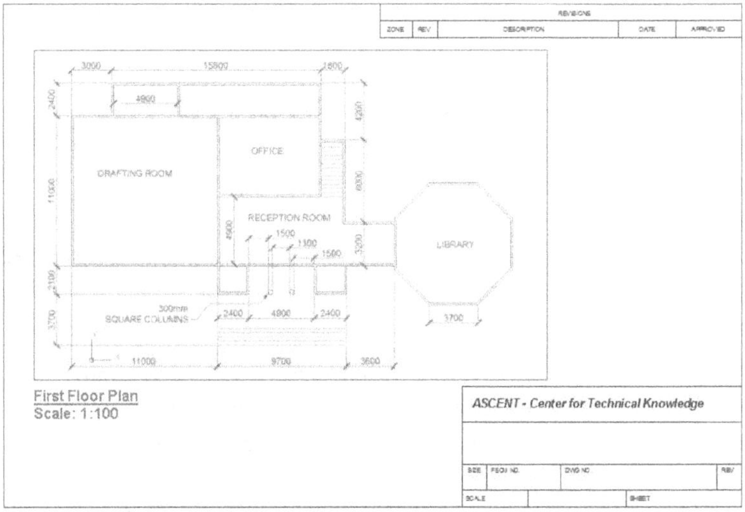

Figure 15–1

There are two methods of printing in the AutoCAD software:

* From *Model Space*.

* From *Paper Space Layouts*.

Hint: Printing vs. Plotting

Both of these terms are used to describe the process of getting an AutoCAD drawing onto a piece of paper. Most of what you do now is technically printing, but many people refer to large format printing as plotting because of the old plotters that were used before laser technology. Printing and plotting mean essentially the same thing today.

Model Space Printing

*When you print from Model Space, you set a scale in the **Plot** command. DO NOT scale the objects in the drawing.*

Everything you have done so far has been in AutoCAD *Model Space*. In Model Space, you draw the model full-size in its real-world units. You can print directly from Model Space for a quick *check plot* of all or part of the drawing, as shown in Figure 15–2.

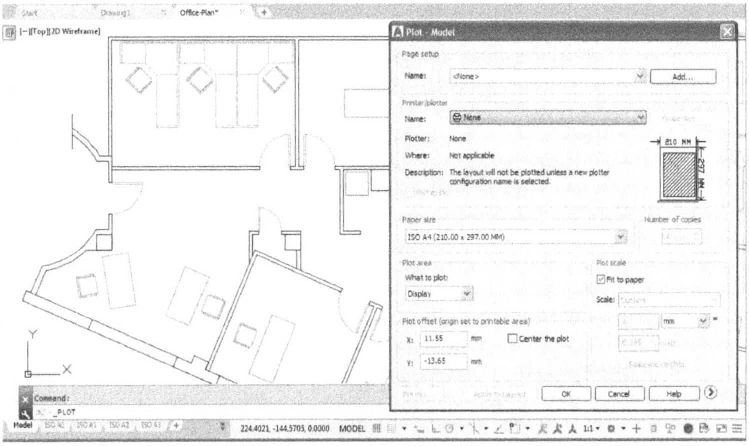

Figure 15–2

- You can set the scale in the **Plot** command to print the model at a precise scale factor, such as 1:50.

- If you need a border, titleblock, dimensions or other annotations to be printed at a specific size, these non-representational objects need to be scaled up to the scale of the drawing. This ensures that when the drawing is shrunk down to fit on the sheet of paper during the **Plot** command, their sizes are printed correctly.

- With Model Space printing you cannot easily print multiple views of the same drawing at different scales.

Paper Space Layout Printing

The primary way to print in the AutoCAD software is to use Paper Space Layouts. Think of the layout as a sheet of paper on which you can place snapshots of your model in *viewports*. These snapshots can be any size and at any scale, as shown in Figure 15–3. You can arrange, enlarge or crop them, as required.

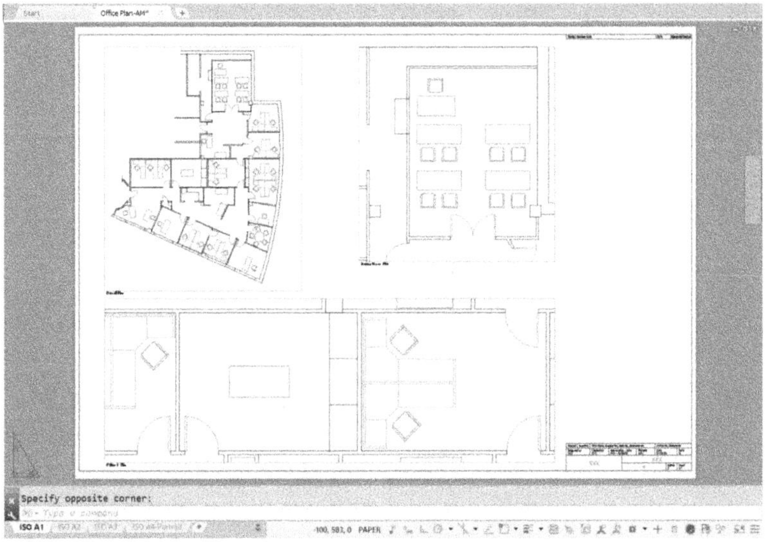

Figure 15–3

Using this method of printing separates the tasks of drawing into two stages:

1. In Model Space, all of the elements are drawn full scale (i.e., at their actual real-world size).
2. In Paper Space Layouts, all of the elements are drawn at the appropriate size for the sheet of paper and you add viewports to display the model.

- The border, titleblock, general notes, schedules, and titles are placed on the layout. They should be drawn at the actual size at which you want them to print on the sheet of paper. Most dimensions and text can be added through the viewport on the model. Their size is controlled by the scale of the viewport and the associated annotation scale.

Only one model can be displayed per drawing, but you can have multiple layouts. Each layout can have a different sheet size, scales, and plotter and these settings are stored in the layout.

15.2 Printing Layouts

When creating layouts in a drawing, each layout represents one sheet, as shown in Figure 15–4. By creating the layout, you define what should be printed. The layout is based on a paper size that is determined by the printer. If the layout is set up correctly, you can plot it without reviewing any additional information in the Plot dialog box.

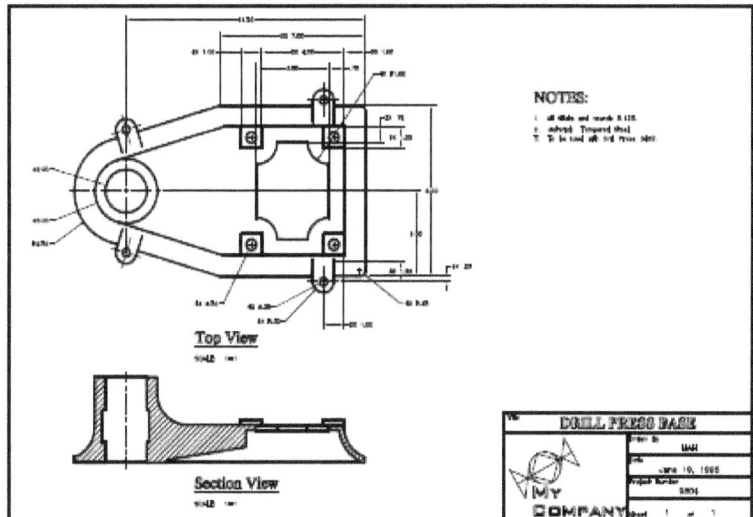

Figure 15–4

How To: Plot a Layout

1. Select the layout that you want to plot.

2. In the *Output* tab>Plot panel, click 🖶 (Plot).

3. If everything is set up as required, in the Plot dialog box, click **OK**.

You can also start the **Plot** *command in the Status Bar by clicking*

🖶 *(Plot), or in the Application Menu by selecting* **Print**.

- If the drawing has multiple layouts, a Batch Plot notification dialog box opens where you can either use the **Try Batch Plot (Publish)** or select **Continue** to plot a single sheet, as shown in Figure 15–5.

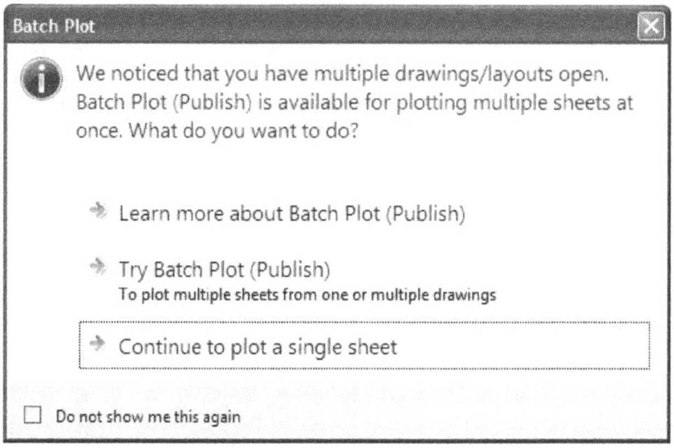

Figure 15–5

- If you are plotting to a DWF plotter or creating a PDF file (which creates a file rather than a paper plot), you are prompted for a name and location for the file in the Browse for Plot File or a Save PDF File As dialog boxes respectively.

- When the plot is finished, a balloon notification displays in the Status Bar, as shown in Figure 15–6. You can click on the link in the balloon to display details about the plot job.

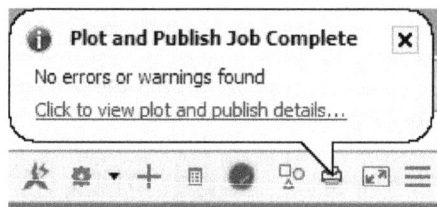

Figure 15–6

Previewing the Plot

Previewing your plot can be helpful to ensure that you are plotting the correct objects before wasting paper and ink.

- You can access the preview in the *Output* tab>Plot panel by clicking [icon] (Preview), or in the Application Menu by selecting **Print>Plot Preview**.

- You can also click **Preview** in the Plot dialog box. This is useful when you are making changes in the dialog box and want to display the results before printing.

- In Preview mode, viewing tools, such as Pan and various Zoom options display instead of the ribbon. You can also right-click and select an option, as shown in Figure 15–7.

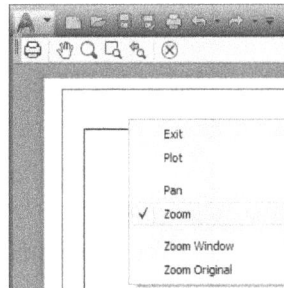

Figure 15–7

15.3 Print and Plot Settings

While most of the options are typically set in a layout, you can adjust some additional options when plotting. For example, you might want to make a half-sized plot or just plot part of a layout or model so that you can check the design, as shown in Figure 15–8. You can make changes in the Plot dialog box without impacting the layout.

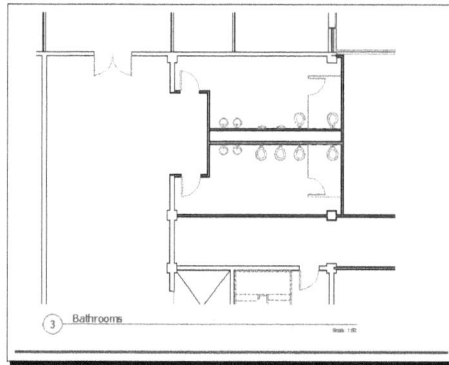

Figure 15–8

You can modify the plot settings in the Plot dialog box, as shown in Figure 15–9.

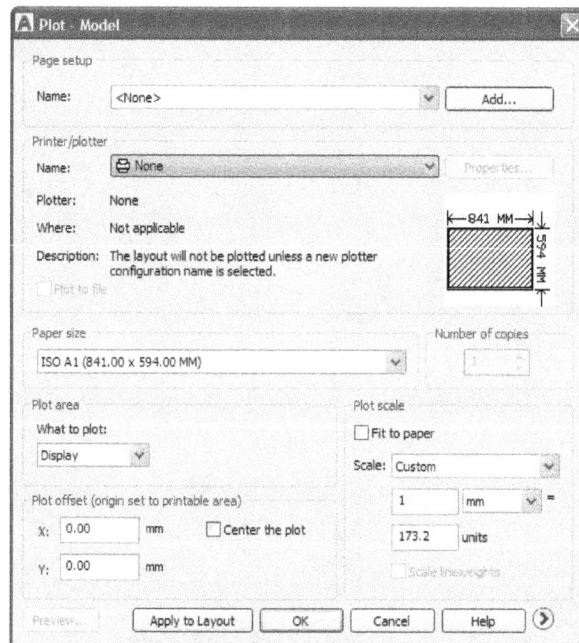

Figure 15–9

Printer/Plotter

- You need to select the plotter first because it determines the paper size.

- Depending on the type of plotter specified, the *Number of copies* area might be available, to set the number of copies to print, as shown in Figure 15–10. It is grayed out when you are using a DWF plotter and some options of PDF version because it plots to a file, rather than directly to paper.

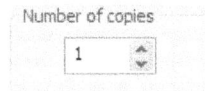

Figure 15–10

What to Plot

The *Plot area* controls the part of the drawing that is plotted.

- The **Display** or **Window** options, as shown in Figure 15–11, can be used to plot part of a layout or model. While the **Display** option plots the objects that display on the screen, the **Window** option enables you to create a window around the area that you want to plot.

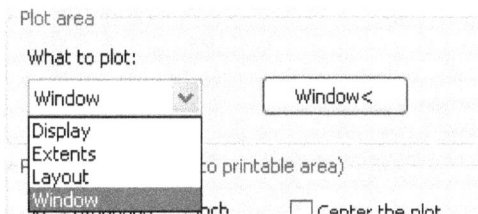

Figure 15–11

- The **Extents** option plots a view that includes every object in the drawing. It includes any objects that might be outside your main drawing. Note that with this option, the objects in the plot might be very small depending on how far apart they are in the drawing.

- The **Limits** option is only available in Model Space and plots an area that is defined by the limits that have been set in the drawing.

Setting the Plot Scale

- While you typically print layouts at a 1:1 scale, you can print half-sized plots by selecting a *Scale* of **1:2**.

- The **Fit to paper** option, as shown in Figure 15–12, can be used when printing a check plot to a letter-sized plotter. Note that the drawing is not to scale when this option is selected.

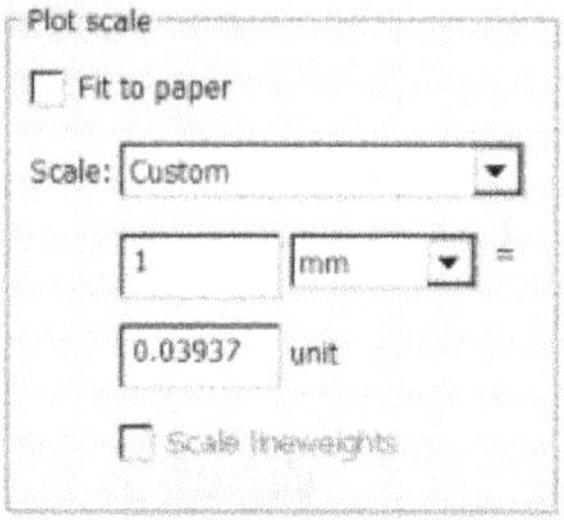

Figure 15–12

- The **Scale lineweights** option scales the lineweights in proportion to the plot scale. If not selected (the default), the lineweights plot at the line width size.

Plot Offset

- By default, the lower left corner of the plot area starts printing at the lower left corner of the page margin. You can move the plot area to the left or up from the lower left margin by specifying an X- or Y-offset, as shown in Figure 15–13.

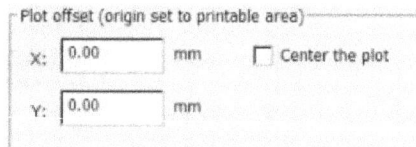

*The **Center the plot** option is not available when the Plot area is set to **Layout** because the layout fills the printable area completely.*

Figure 15–13

- The **Center the plot** option automatically calculates X- and Y-offsets so that the plot is centered on the paper.

More Options

If the dialog box displays in the compressed form, click ⊘ (More Options) in the lower right corner to display more options. Some of the options are shown in Figure 15–14.

Most of the options relate to advanced features.

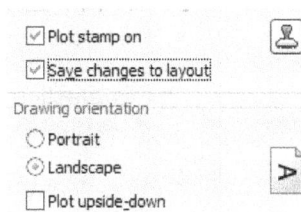

Figure 15–14

Plot stamp on	Adds a plot stamp with standard information, such as drawing name, date and time, etc. The (Plot Stamp Settings) icon becomes available when the **Plot Stamp On** is selected.
Save changes to layout	Automatically saves any changes you make to the plot settings with the layout, which become the new defaults when you plot the layout.

- **Apply to Layout** is similar to the **Save changes to layout** option, except that it only saves changes to the layout when you click the button, rather than automatically, all the time.

- You can also select the *Drawing orientation* options such as printing with **Portrait** or **Landscape** orientation.

Practice 15a

Printing Layouts and Check Plots

Estimated time for completion: 10 minutes

Practice Objectives

- Plot a layout to a file.
- Print a check plot from Model Space.

In this practice, you will plot a layout to a file and create a check plot, as shown in Figure 15–15.

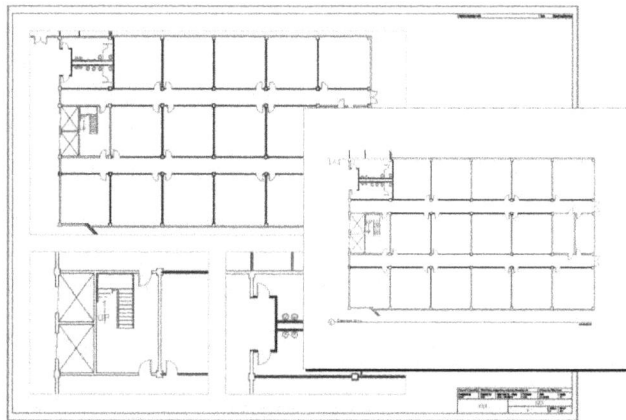

Figure 15–15

Task 1 - Print layouts.

In this task you will plot a layout to a file, as shown in Figure 15–16.

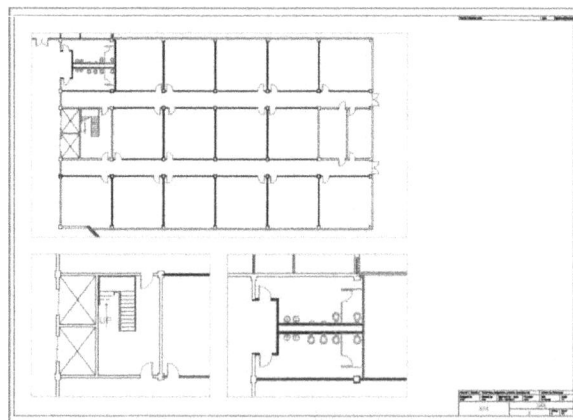

Figure 15–16

1. Open **College Building1-AM.dwg** from your practice files folder.

2. Switch to the **Classroom Wing** layout tab and verify that you are in Paper Space.

3. In the *Output* tab>Plot panel, click ⌱ (Plot). If the Batch Plot confirmation dialog box opens, click **Continue to plot a single sheet**.

4. In the Plot dialog box, note that *Printer/plotter*, *Paper size*, and other options are all set according to the page setup for this layout. The layout is set to use the **DWF6 ePlot.pc3** plotter, which automatically plots to a file.

5. Click **Preview**. The viewing tools indicate that you are in **Zoom Realtime** mode. Zoom in a little, right-click, and select **Pan**.

6. After experimenting with panning and zooming, right-click and select **Zoom Original**. Right-click again and select **Exit** to return to the Plot dialog box.

7. Click **OK** to create the plot file. Accept the default filename and save it in your practice folder.

8. In the Status Bar, a balloon message displays when the plot is complete. Select **Click to view plot and publish details...** to display the plot details. Click **Close**.

Task 2 - Print check plots.

In this task you will create a check plot, as shown in Figure 15–17.

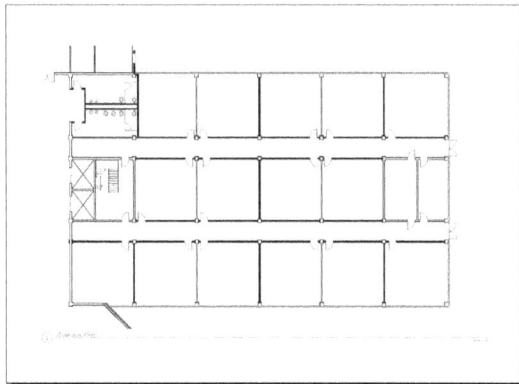

Figure 15–17

1. Start the **Plot** command again. If the Batch Plot confirmation dialog box opens, click **Continue to plot a single sheet**.

2. Set the *Paper size* to **ISOA4 (210 x 297 MM)** and click **Preview**. Only a small portion of the entire plot displays. Right-click and select **Exit**.

3. In the *Plot area*, expand the What to plot drop-down list and select **Window**, draw a window around the Elevators and Stairs viewport, and preview again. The selected viewport displays as it fits on an ISO A4 sheet of paper at a 1:50 scale. Exit the preview.

4. Click **Window<**, draw a window around the Classroom Wing viewport at the top of the layout, and preview the plot. A portion of the viewport displays. Exit the preview.

5. Set the *Plot Scale* to **Fit to paper** and the *Plot Offset* to **Center the plot**. Preview again. The whole viewport displays but is not to scale. Exit the preview.

6. Click **OK** to plot the drawing and name the file **Check Plot.dwf**.

7. Ensure that you are in the **Classroom Wing** layout tab. In the *Layout* tab>Plot panel, click **Preview**. The preview indicates that the entire layout is going to be plotted as was intended. The changes you just made to the **Plot** command did not change the layout information.

8. Exit the preview. Save and close the drawing.

Chapter Review Questions

1. With Model Space printing, it is very easy to print multiple views of the same drawing at different scales.

   a. True

   b. False

2. What does the dashed boundary on a layout represent?

   a. The printable area.

   b. The active viewport.

   c. The default viewport.

   d. The model space.

3. To plot a layout, what scale should you typically use in the *Plot Scale* area in the Plot dialog box?

   a. 1:1

   b. Custom

   c. Any standard scale

   d. Scale to fit

4. What is determined when you select the plotter first in the Plot-Model dialog box?

   a. Plot area

   b. Paper size

   c. Plot Scale

   d. Plot offset

5. Which of the following can you do using the preview of a plot?

   a. Modify objects in the drawing.

   b. Zoom or pan around the drawing.

   c. Only preview a portion of the entire drawing.

   d. Delete viewports from a layout.

6. In the Plot dialog box, which *What to plot* option do you set in the *Plot* area to plot the objects that are currently displayed in the drawing window?

   a. **Extents**

   b. **Window**

   c. **Layout**

   d. **Display**

Command Summary

Button	Command	Location
	Plot	• **Quick Access Toolbar** • **Ribbon:** *Output* tab>Plot panel • **Application Menu:** Print • **Command Prompt:** print, plot, or <Ctrl>+<P>
	Plot Preview	• **Ribbon:** *Output* tab>Plot panel • **Application Menu:** Print>Plot Preview • **Command Prompt:** preview

Projects: Preparing to Print

This chapter contains practice projects that can be used to gain additional hands-on experience with the topics and commands covered so far in this student guide. These practices are intended to be self-guided and do not include step by step information.

Learning Objective in this Chapter

- *All*: Create viewports and adjust viewport views by zooming in and out.

16.1 Mechanical Project

Estimated time for completion: 20 minutes

In this project you will set up a drawing in a layout. You will create and scale viewports and then adjust the view in each viewport, as shown in Figure 16–1.

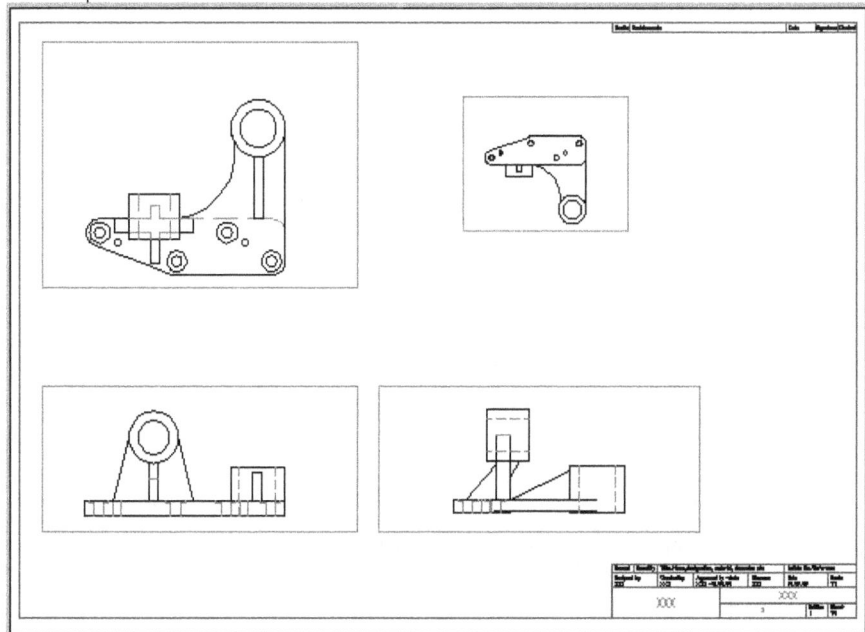

Figure 16–1

1. Open **Leverbracket-M.dwg** from your practice files folder.

2. Switch to the **ISO A2** layout.

3. Erase the existing viewport and create four new viewports, as shown in Figure 16–1.

4. Zoom and pan in each viewport to display the correct view. Scale the Front, Top, and Side views to **1:2**.

5. Scale the Bottom view to **1:4**.

6. Align the views precisely using ✎ (Object Snap Tracking) to track from a second point in another view.

7. Save the drawing.

8. Preview and then plot to a file.

16.2 Architectural Project

Estimated time for completion: 20 minutes

In this project you will set up a drawing in a layout and create and scale viewports. You will zoom and pan to adjust the view in each viewport, and use **Plot** to plot the drawing to a file, as shown in Figure 16–2.

Figure 16–2

1. Open **New Office-AM.dwg** from your practice files folder.

2. Switch to the **ISO A1** layout.

3. Erase the existing viewport and create three new viewports, as shown in Figure 16–2. Scale the large viewport on the left side to **1:100** to display the entire floor plan. Scale the other two viewports to **1:20** and pan to display the details of the classroom and cubicles (the viewports are labeled).

4. Preview and then plot to a file.

Text

In this chapter you learn how to set up and use Annotation Scales and to create, edit, and format Multiline text.

Learning Objectives in this Chapter

- Create, edit, import and format paragraphs of text.
- Check and correct the spelling of the text in a drawing.
- Control the scale and display of text, dimensions, hatches, and multileaders.
- Modify text styles, existing Multiline text, and multilinear objects.
- Format the paragraph style and change the line spacing in a paragraph.
- Select and modify individual leaders in a multileader object.
- Combine, align and evenly space leader lines.
- Add and remove leader lines to a multileader object.
- Add leaders with text or balloons to point at objects in the drawing.
- Create a unified table object that includes title, column headers, and multiple rows and columns.
- Populate table cells with text, blocks, and fields and add calculations in a table.
- Add and remove columns, merge and unmerge cells, and modify cell properties in a table.

17.1 Working with Annotations

When you set up layouts with viewports at various scales, the parts of the model display at different sizes. However, the final printed sheet should have text and dimensions that are all of the same size when they are plotted, as shown in Figure 17–1. The *Annotation Scale* feature enables you to add text and dimensions to a drawing with views at many different scales. These annotation objects are scaled to suit and do not display in viewports with other annotation scales.

Annotation objects include: text, dimensions, hatches, and multileaders.

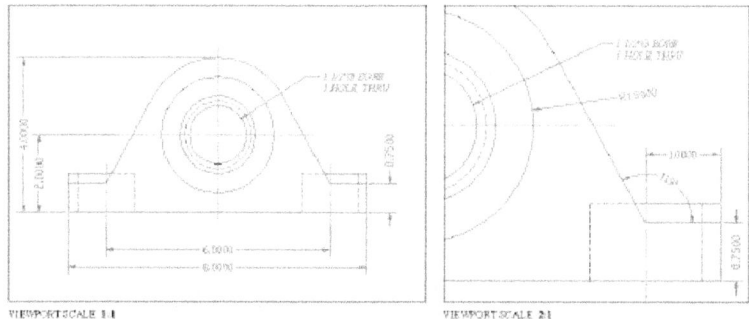

Figure 17–1

• When you create each viewport, set [icon] 1:2 ▼ (Viewport Scale) in the Status Bar, as shown in Figure 17–2. The Annotation Scale is automatically matched to the viewport scale.

Figure 17–2

• To add annotation objects, double-click inside the viewport to make it active and select the annotation tool. It is automatically scaled to match the viewport/annotation scale.

Click [icon] (Lock/Viewport) to lock the viewport so that the scale and location are not changed by mistake.

• To understand the differences between annotations placed in Model Space and Paper Space, open the Properties palette and note the two parameters: **Paper text height** and **Model text height**. For example, in the room shown in Figure 17–3, the text **Service Area** is placed in a viewport at a scale of *1:50*, while the text for the title and scale is placed in Paper Space at a scale of 1:1. Note that the two text objects look the same size.

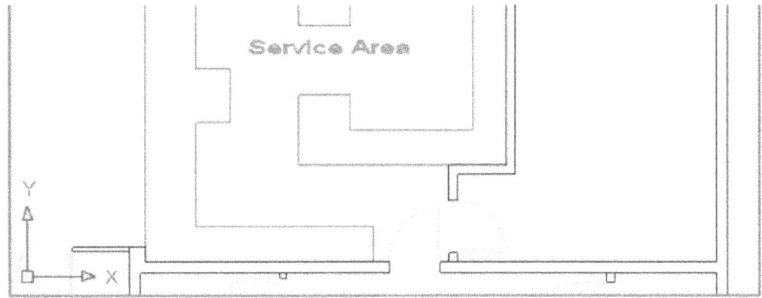

Figure 17–3

- If you select the text in Paper Space and then note the values of the parameters in the Properties palette, the **Paper text height** and **Model text height** are the same, as shown on the left in Figure 17–4. If you select the text inside the viewport and then note the values of the parameters in the Properties palette, the **Paper text height** and the **Model text height** are different, as shown on the right in Figure 17–4. The AutoCAD® software automatically scales the text inside the viewport so that it is 6mm.

Text	▲
Contents	Service Area
Style	⚠ Title
Annotative	Yes
Annotative scale	1:1
Justify	Top left
Direction	By style
Paper text height	6
Model text height	6
Match orientation to layout	No

Text	▲
Contents	Service Area
Style	⚠ Title
Annotative	Yes
Annotative scale	1:50
Justify	Top left
Direction	By style
Paper text height	6
Model text height	300
Match orientation to layout	No

Figure 17–4

Working with Annotative Styles

Many annotation objects are created using styles. The annotation styles (Text Styles, Dimension Styles, and Multileader Styles) can be made annotative. You should select a style that is designed to work with the Annotation Scale so that objects are correctly placed in each viewport.

- ⚘ (Annotation) displays next to annotative style names in the Text Style, Dimension Style, and Multileader Style Controls, as shown in Figure 17–5.

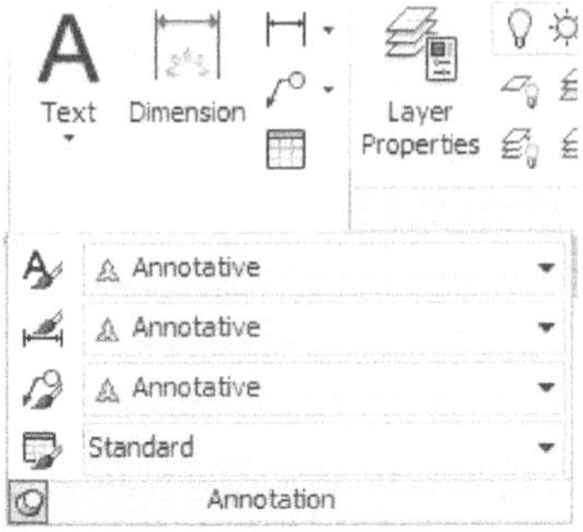

Figure 17–5

- When you have objects in your drawing that are annotative,

  ⚘ (Annotation) displays when you hover the cursor over them, as shown in Figure 17–6.

NEW ACCOUNTS

Figure 17–6

- You must change the Viewport Scale in the Status Bar for the annotative objects to change scale.

- You can annotate objects in Model Space by setting the

  ⚘ 1:1 ▾ (Annotation Scale) in the Status Bar, as shown in Figure 17–7. It is linked to the Viewport Scale and the annotation displays in viewports that have the same annotation scale.

Figure 17–7

- When you use annotation styles, the *Model text height* in the Properties palette is read-only.

17.2 Adding Text in a Drawing

Many drawings include notes about the objects and about the project, as shown in Figure 17–8. This might be a set of general notes in the titleblock or notes specific to a particular view.

Multiline Text

Text should be placed on its own layer.

You can use the **Multiline Text** command to create, edit, and format paragraphs of text.

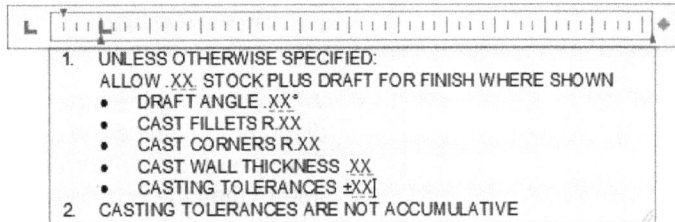

1. UNLESS OTHERWISE SPECIFIED:
    ALLOW .XX. STOCK PLUS DRAFT FOR FINISH WHERE SHOWN
    • DRAFT ANGLE .XX°
    • CAST FILLETS R.XX
    • CAST CORNERS R.XX
    • CAST WALL THICKNESS .XX
    • CASTING TOLERANCES ±XX
2. CASTING TOLERANCES ARE NOT ACCUMULATIVE

Figure 17–8

*   Any text created in the Text Editor becomes one object, no matter how many lines it contains. Because you type it in a Text Editor, the text automatically wraps at the end of the line.

*   Set the layer and the text style before you start the **Multiline Text** command. The text style sets the default font and height of the text.

How To: Add Multiline Text

If you are creating an annotative object, you might be prompted to set the annotation scale.

1. In the *Annotate* tab>Text panel or in the *Home* tab>

    Annotation panel, click A (Multiline Text).

    *   An example text string (abc) displays near the cursor as shown in Figure 17–9. This preview indicates the current text height and font.

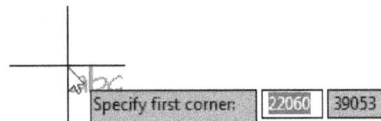

Specify first corner: 22060 39053

Figure 17–9

2. Select two points in the drawing to define a boundary box for the text. The Text Editor opens, as shown in Figure 17–10.

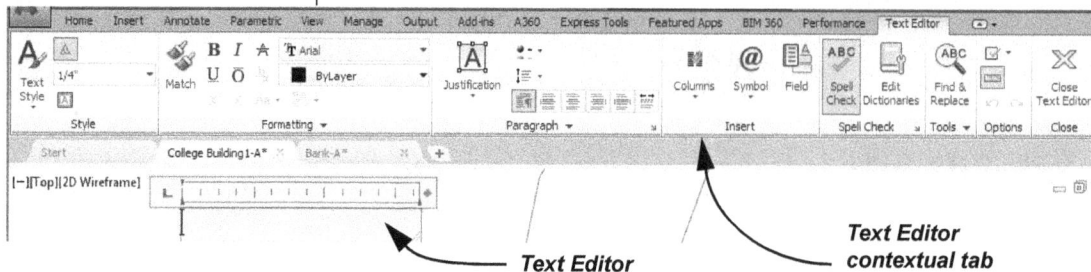

Figure 17–10

- When creating the boundary box for the text, an arrow displays indicating the direction in which the text is going to flow, based on the current vertical justification. The boundary determines the position of the text and its width (i.e., the length of a line before words wrap to the next line), but does not limit the number of lines you can type.

3. Type the text in the Text Editor and apply formatting options from the contextual tab.

4. Click ✕ (Close Text Editor) or click in the drawing window to finish creating the text. The text is inserted in the drawing as one object.

- The background of the text editor is transparent. This enables any drawing objects that are covered by the text box to be displayed.

How To: Set the Text Height

1. In the *Annotate* tab>Text panel or in the *Home* tab> Annotation panel, click A (Multiline Text).
2. Select the first point of the boundary box.
3. Select **Height** from the Command Line or shortcut menu (<Down Arrow>), as shown in Figure 17–11.

*The text height specified with the **Height** option becomes the default text height for that text style. If you change the text height in the Text Editor, it is not saved.*

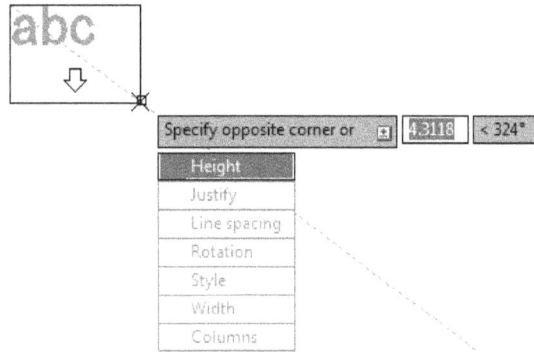

Figure 17–11

4. Enter the text height and press <Enter>.
5. Select the other point of the boundary box.

- Text can be placed in Paper Space or Model Space. In most cases, and especially if you are using an annotative text style, you should specify the height of the text to be the final plotted size.

Copying and Importing Text

You can copy text from a word processing software or other text editor and paste it directly into the Text Editor, as shown in Figure 17–12. You can also import text files that are saved in the ASCII or RTF format.

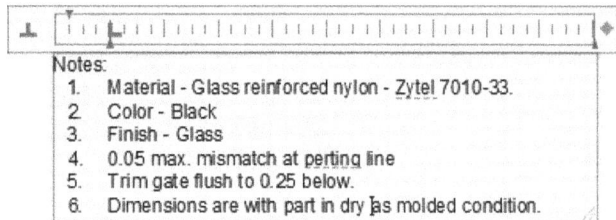

Notes:
1. Material - Glass reinforced nylon - Zytel 7010-33.
2. Color - Black
3. Finish - Glass
4. 0.05 max. mismatch at perting line
5. Trim gate flush to 0.25 below.
6. Dimensions are with part in dry as molded condition.

Figure 17–12

How To: Copy and Paste Text into the Text Editor

1. In a document file, copy the text to the Windows Clipboard.
2. In the AutoCAD software, in the *Annotate* tab>Text panel or in the *Home* tab>Annotation panel, click A (Multiline Text).
3. Select points for the boundary box.
4. In the Text Editor, right-click and select **Paste**. The text you copied is pasted into the Text Editor.

If you are creating an annotative object, you might be prompted to set the annotation scale.

- If you use **Paste Special**, you can set the copied text to be pasted without character or paragraph formatting, as shown in Figure 17–13.

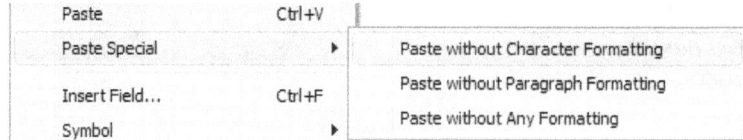

When you copy and paste text created with Microsoft Word, it keeps the formatting from the document, including numbering or bullets and specific headings.

Paste	Ctrl+V	
Paste Special	▶	Paste without Character Formatting
		Paste without Paragraph Formatting
Insert Field...	Ctrl+F	Paste without Any Formatting
Symbol	▶	

Figure 17–13

How To: Import Text

1. In the *Annotate* tab>Text panel or in the *Home* tab> Annotation panel, click **A** (Multiline Text).
2. Select points for the boundary box.
3. In the *Text Editor* contextual tab>expanded Tools panel, click **Import Text**. You can also right-click in the Text Editor and select **Import Text**.
4. In the Select File dialog box, select the file that you want to use and click **Open** to import the text.

- Imported text does not include formatting.

Hint: Text Symbols

You can add symbols to your text. In the *Text Editor* contextual tab>Insert panel, expand **@** (Symbol) and select a symbol in the list. You can select **Other...** at the end of the list to open the Character Map dialog box to access specialty symbols in different fonts.

In the *Text Editor* contextual tab>Insert panel, click ⬚ (Field) to add text objects that gather their information from objects or system variables, such as the date or drawing name in the AutoCAD software.

Spell Checking

The spellings are checked by default when you are in the Text Editor. It can be toggled on and off in the *Text Editor* contextual tab>Spell Check panel, as shown in Figure 17–14.

Figure 17–14

- Any misspellings are underlined with a dashed red line, but only in the Text Editor. Right-click on the word to display a list of suggestions, as shown in Figure 17–15. You can also add words to the dictionary or ignore the misspelled words.

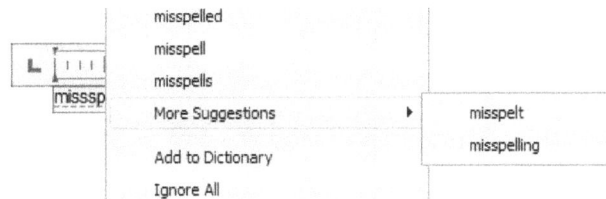

Figure 17–15

- Click ⌄ in the Spell Check panel title to open the Check Spelling Settings dialog box.

Practice 17a | Adding Text in a Drawing

Practice Objectives

- Add text to a cover sheet with different text styles and sizes.
- Import text into the Text Editor.

Estimated time for completion: 10 minutes

In this practice, you will use the **Multiline Text** command to place text on a cover sheet using two different text styles and sizes, as shown in Figure 17–16. You will also import text into the Text Editor.

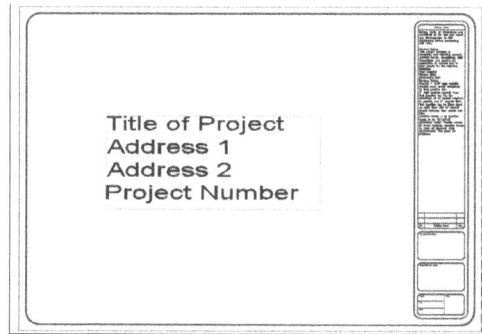

Title of Project
Address 1
Address 2
Project Number

Figure 17–16

Task 1 - Add General Notes to the Cover Sheet.

1. Open **Cover Sheet-AM.dwg** from your practice files folder.

2. Ensure that you are in the **Cover Sheet** layout tab.

The text style can also be set in the Annotate tab>Text panel.

3. Set the current layer to **Notes**. In the *Home* tab>expanded Annotation panel, set the current text style to **Standard**, as shown in Figure 17–17.

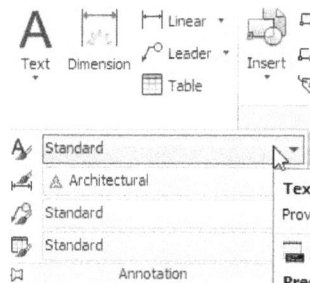

Figure 17–17

4. Zoom in on the top right corner of the layout, where it says General Notes.

*The **Multiline Text** command can also be accessed in the Annotate tab>Text panel.*

5. In the *Home* tab>Annotation panel, click A (Text), which is the **Multiline Text** command. The alphabet is attached to the cursor indicating the height of the text.

6. If ▼ (Object Snap) is on, toggle it off to avoid snapping to the lines in the titleblock.

7. In the *General Notes* area of the titleblock, select near the upper left corner under the General Notes line as the first point of the boundary box. Right-click, select **Height**, enter **3**, and press <Enter>. Select the second point diagonally on the right side in the *General Notes* area, as shown in Figure 17–18. The Text Editor displays and the *Text Editor* contextual tab opens.

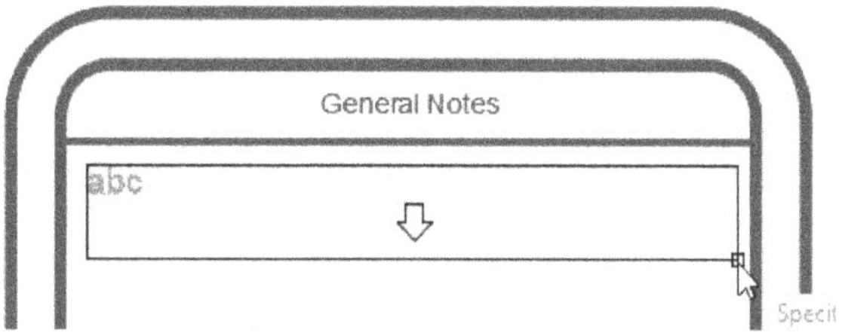

Figure 17–18

8. Type the text shown in Figure 17–19 and remain in the Text Editor.

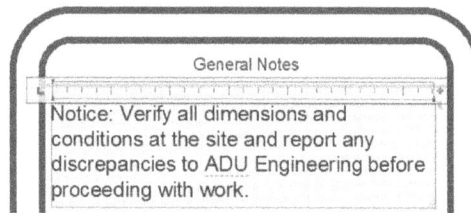

Figure 17–19

*For the words to be underlined, in the Text Editor tab, in the Spell Check panel, **Spell Check** must be toggled on.*

9. Note that **ADU** is underlined in red because the word is not recognized by the spell checker. Highlight it, right-click, and select **Add to Dictionary**.

10. Ensure that the cursor is at the end of the text, and press <Enter> twice to create a new line and a space.

11. Right-click in the Text Editor and select **Import Text**.

12. In the Select File dialog box, select the **General Notes-M.txt** file from your practice files folder and click **Open**. The text from the file is added.

Your word wrap might be different because the size of your text boundary box might be different.

13. Select a point anywhere on the screen, outside of the Text Editor, to close it. The text displays as shown in Figure 17–20.

General Notes

Notice: Verify all dimensions and conditions at the site and report any discrepancies to ADU Engineering before proceeding with work.

General Notes:
This project consists of furnishing and installing conduit, junction boxes, receptacles, data connectors, and cabling for connection to devices and to riser panels for the following buildings:
West Hospital
Cancer Clinic
Ambulatory Care
Nursing School
Conduit - 20mm rigid metallic conduit from device receptacle to first junction box. 50mm rigid metallic conduit from first junction box for the remainder of all conduit required.
In general, run 50mm conduit from first junction box to Riser panel on each floor with 50mm conduit shunts between riser panels and MAU.

Figure 17–20

Task 2 - Add Project Information to the Cover Sheet.

1. Zoom out to display the entire cover sheet.

2. In the *Annotate* tab>Text panel, select the **Title** text style.

   Then, click A (Multiline Text).

The text style can also be set in the Home tab> expanded Annotation panel.

3. For the first corner, select the top left corner of the green rectangle at the center of the layout. (Use **Object Snap**.) Right-click, select **Height**, enter **25**, and press <Enter>. Then, select the bottom right corner of the green rectangle.

4. Type the text shown in Figure 17–21.

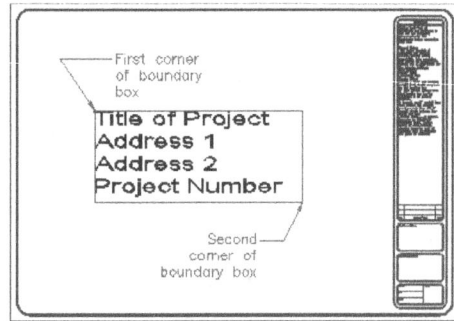

First corner of boundary box

Title of Project
Address 1
Address 2
Project Number

Second corner of boundary box

Figure 17–21

5. In the *Text Editor* contextual tab, click ✕ (Close Text Editor) to close the Text Editor.

6. Save and close the drawing.

17.3 Modifying Multiline Text

You can manipulate Multiline text with grips and adjust its various settings in the Properties palette. However, changing the text's layer, and copying, moving, and rotating the text can be achieved by using standard AutoCAD commands and processes.

Editing Multiline Text

*You can also right-click on the selected text and select **Mtext Edit**.*

You can edit the already existing multiline text in the Text Editor.

How To: Edit Multiline Text

1. Double-click on a text object to open the Text Editor. The *Text Editor* contextual tab also opens.
2. Edit the text, as shown in Figure 17–22.

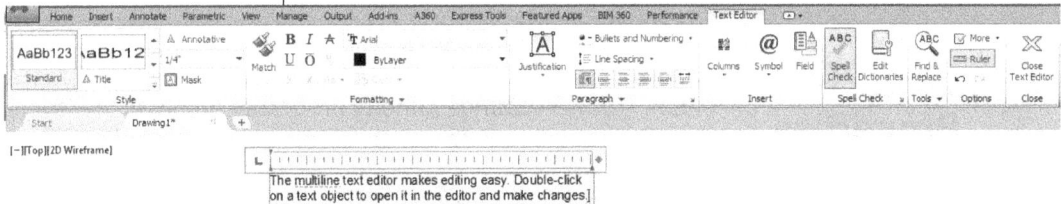

Figure 17–22

3. In the *Text Editor* contextual tab, click ✕ (Close Text Editor) or click in the drawing window to finish editing the text.

- If you press <Esc> to close the Text Editor, you are prompted to save your text changes.

Changing Text Width and Length

After you have placed Multiline text in your drawing, you can control the text boundary box width and length using grips or the Text Editor.

- Select some Multiline text without any commands running. Grips display at the location point and at the column width and height, as shown in Figure 17–23. Click on a grip to select it (it turns red), and then move the cursor and select another point to stretch the column width or height to a different size. To clear the grips, press <Esc>.

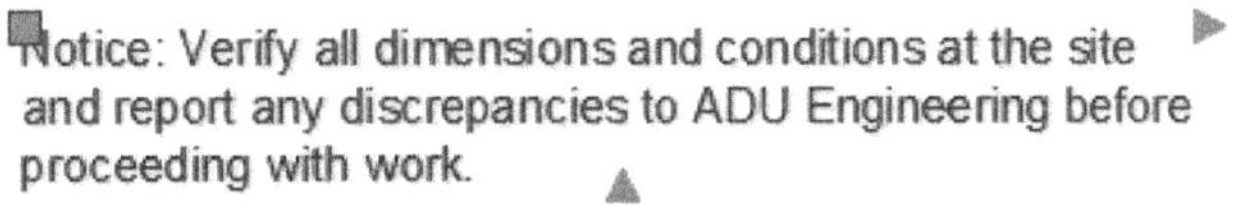

Notice: Verify all dimensions and conditions at the site and report any discrepancies to ADU Engineering before proceeding with work.

Figure 17–23

- The location grip (square grip box) moves the entire Multiline text. It also designates the justification of the object.

- You can modify the text width and length in the Text Editor by hovering the cursor over the edges or the corner of the Text Editor and then dragging the double-arrows. You can also use the horizontal diamond on the right end of the ruler to modify the text box *Width*, as shown in Figure 17–24.

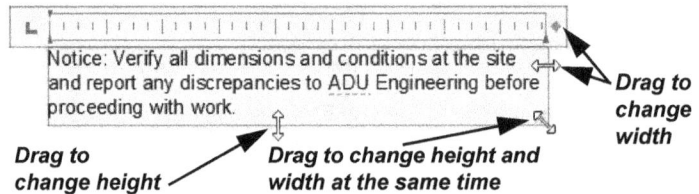

Notice: Verify all dimensions and conditions at the site and report any discrepancies to ADU Engineering before proceeding with work.

Drag to change width

Drag to change height

Drag to change height and width at the same time

Figure 17–24

Changing Text Properties

The Properties palette is useful for changing multiple instances of text. You can change general properties (such as the layer) or specific properties (such as style, height, or justification).

- You can also add a Text Frame around multi-line text, as shown in Figure 17–25.

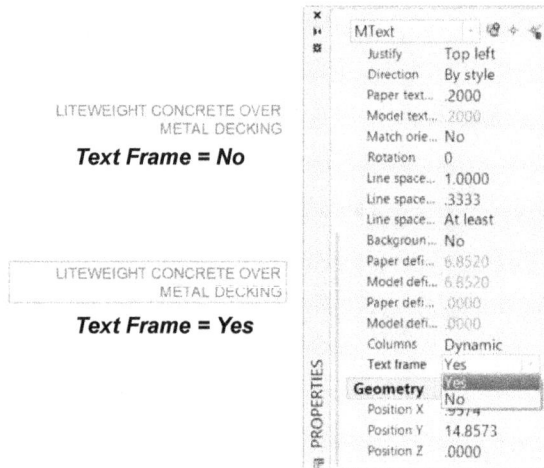

LITEWEIGHT CONCRETE OVER METAL DECKING

Text Frame = No

LITEWEIGHT CONCRETE OVER METAL DECKING

Text Frame = Yes

Figure 17–25

How To: Add a Text Frame

1. Select the multi-line text.
2. Right-click and select **Properties**.
3. In the Properties palette, change the *Text Frame* field to **Yes**.

'Background Mask' is discussed in the next section.

Hint: Frame Offset Value

The Text Frame is offset from the text by the value specified in the Background mask, Border offset factor, as shown in Figure 17–26.

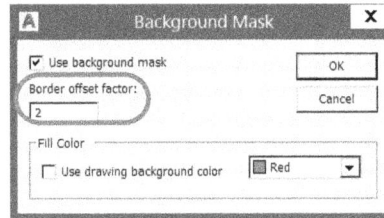

Figure 17–26

Spell Checking

While you are in the Text Editor you can have spell checking on and fix spelling errors on the fly. You can also check the spelling in an entire drawing or part of a drawing.

How To: Check the Spelling in a Drawing

You can also click

⌖ *(Select Objects) to specify which objects to check.*

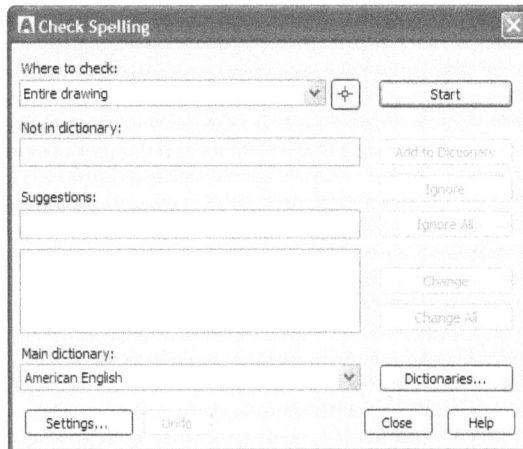

1. In the Annotate tab>Text panel, click ABC ✓ (Check Spelling).
2. In the Check Spelling dialog box (shown in Figure 17–27), expand the Where to check drop-down list and select **Entire drawing**, **Current space/layout**, or **Selected objects**.

Figure 17–27

3. Click **Start**.

4. The AutoCAD software zooms to the text being checked and highlights any misspelled words. As with other spell checkers, you can:

   - Click **Change** or **Change All** to change the word to the selected suggestion.
   - Click **Ignore** or **Ignore All** to maintain the spellings.
   - Click **Add to Dictionary** to add a word to your custom dictionary.
   - Click **Undo** if you modify a spelling error by mistake.

5. When the spelling check is complete, a message box opens. Click **OK** and then **Close** in the Check Spelling dialog box.

- Click **Dictionaries...** to specify the Main and Custom dictionaries, and add words to your custom dictionary.

- Click **Settings...** to specify the types of items you want to check and how you want the checker to deal with specific variations of words.

Practice 17b

Modifying Multiline Text

Practice Objectives

*   Modify Multiline text objects.
*   Check the spelling in the drawing.

Estimated time for completion: 10 minutes

In this practice, you will modify text using grips, the Text Editor, and the Properties palette to clean up a redlined detail, as shown in Figure 17–28. You will also check the spelling in the drawing file.

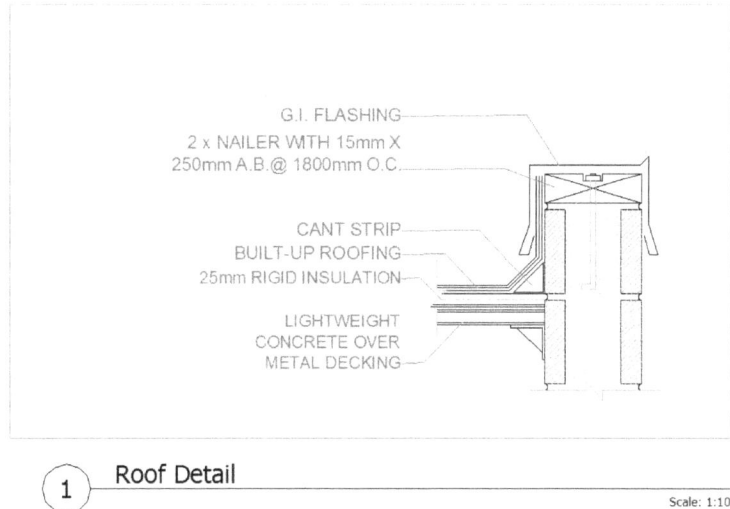

Figure 17–28

Task 1 - Edit multiline text in a drawing.

1. Open **Detail Sheet-AM.dwg** from your practice files folder.

2. Ensure that you are in the **Detail Sheet** layout.

3. Zoom in on the Roof Detail in the upper left corner of the layout.

4. Double-click inside the viewport to make it active.

The red markings and text are for reference purposes.

5. Click once on the text that ends in **O.C.** Select the top left grip and select a point farther to the left to make the text fit in two lines. Press <Esc> to clear the grips, as shown in Figure 17–28.

6. Double-click on the same piece of text. In the Text Editor, change *200mm* to **250mm**, as shown in Figure 17–29. Verify that the complete text is still in two lines, and use the left double-arrows to adjust the width as required. Press <ESC> and then click **Yes** to save the text changes or simply click outside to close the text editor.

Figure 17–29

7. Select the two pieces of text for the lower two leaders (starting with 25mm and Liteweight), right-click and select **Properties**.

8. In the Properties palette, in the *Text* area, the *Paper text height* is **2**. Click on it, change it to **3** (as shown in Figure 17–30), and press <Enter>.

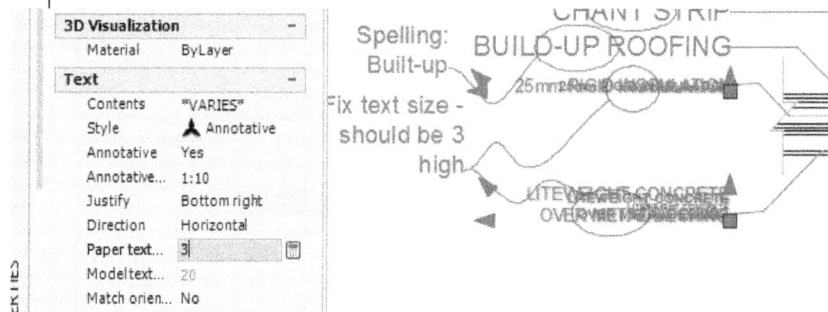

Figure 17–30

9. Close the Properties palette. Note that the selected text has become larger. Press <Esc> to clear the text.

10. Select the text **25mm RIGID INSSULATION**. Use grips to stretch the text to the left so that it fits on one line. Press <Esc> to clear the text.

Task 2 - Check the spelling.

---

1. Remain in the Roof Detail viewport.

2. In the *Annotate* tab>Text panel, click ^{ABC}✓ (Check Spelling).

3. In the Check Spelling dialog box, in the Where to check drop-down list, select **Current space/layout**. Click **Start**.

4. Work through each of the spelling errors, correcting them as required and ignoring proper names. Note that the word **NAILER** is highlighted although it is spelled correctly. It is a technical term that is not found in the standard dictionary. Click **Ignore**.

5. Next, *INSSULATION* is highlighted. Correct it by clicking **Change** to use the spelling in the *Suggestions* area as shown in Figure 17–31.

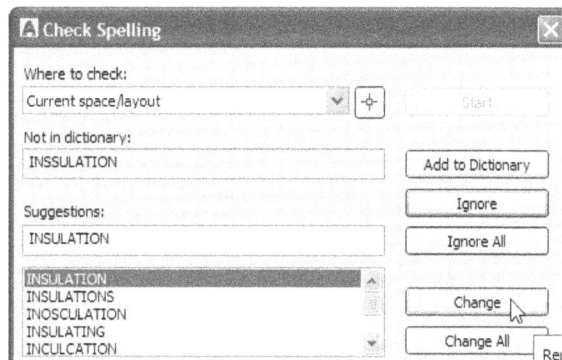

Figure 17–31

6. Similarly, the word **liteweight** should be corrected.

7. In the message box, click **OK** to finish checking the spelling.

8. Click **Close** to close the Check Spelling dialog box.

9. Two of the misspelled words are not modified by the Spell Checker because they are actual words. You need to modify these directly.

10. Double-click on the text *CHANT* and in the Text Editor, correct the spelling to **CANT** and then save the change.

11. Similarly, change the text *BUILD-UP* to **BUILT-UP**.

12. Toggle the layer **redline** off.

13. Double-click outside the viewport to return to Paper Space.

14. Save the drawing.

17.4 Formatting Multiline Text

Multiline text offers formatting features similar to those found in word processing software. For example, you can bold, underline, or strikeout specific text, use bullets or numbered lists, and create columns of information, as shown in Figure 17–32.

Construction Notice:
1. Remove *existing steps and walks*; provide new access ramp from sidewalk up to grade of existing garden walk. Provide handrail.
2. Remove *existing porch*; replace with porch at finished floor elevation. Provide new steps and wheelchair lift.

Figure 17–32

*   Some options affect the entire Multiline text object, some modify specific paragraphs in the text, and some only change selected text.

Formatting the Multiline Text Object

Changing the *Text Style* and *Justification* affects the entire Multiline text object. If you need to change these features, do so before you make any other modifications to the formatting.

Changing the Text Style

You can change the *Text Style* of the overall text object once you are in the Text Editor.

*   Changing the style overrides any other formatting you have done. A warning box opens if you select a different style, as shown in Figure 17–33.

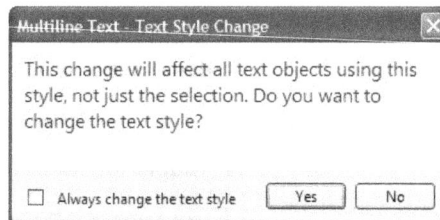

Multiline Text - Text Style Change

This change will affect all text objects using this style, not just the selection. Do you want to change the text style?

☐ Always change the text style   [Yes]   [No]

Figure 17–33

*   If you are not using an annotative text style, you can click

    ⚐ (Annotative) in the *Text Editor* contextual tab to make that instance of the text annotative without changing the text style.

Changing the Justification

The *Justification* sets the overall justification for the entire text object. In this case, the width and height of the boundary box are considered. For example, if you set the *Justification* to **Middle Center**, the text is centered in the middle of the boundary box, as shown in Figure 17–34. To change the Multiline text object, use the Justification tools located in the *Text Editor* contextual tab>Paragraph panel in the ribbon.

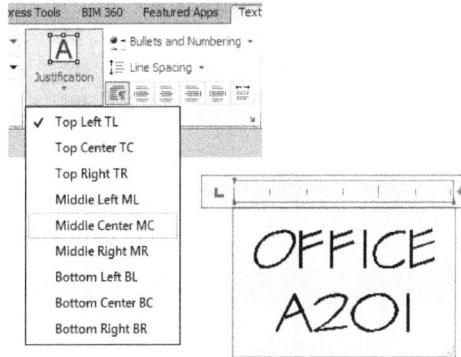

Figure 17–34

- (Background Mask) in the Style panel places a masking element behind the text so that other objects do not show through. You can use the drawing background color or a specific color, as shown in Figure 17–35.

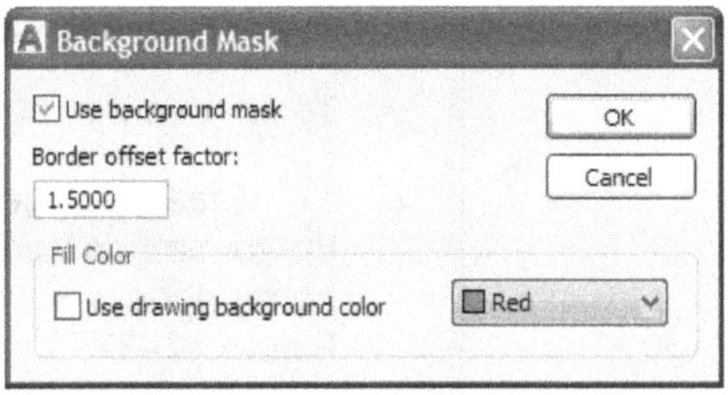

Setting a background mask applies it to the entire Multiline text object.

Figure 17–35

Formatting Selected Text

In hand drafting, most text was placed on a drawing using all uppercase letters. However, as computers have taken over much of the text work, many people are using the sentence case format.

The Formatting panel in the *Text Editor* contextual tab enables you to change the font of individual text that you have selected, as well as bold, italicize, underline, overline, strikethrough, and change the case of the text, as shown in Figure 17–36.

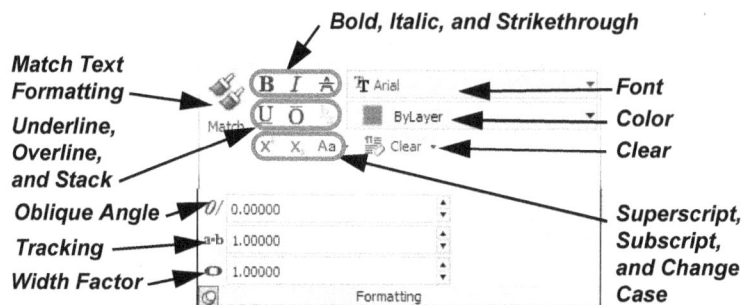

Figure 17–36

- Buttons are grayed out if the text is not selected or if the font does not support an option, such as **Bold** or *Italic*.

- In many cases, setting the color impacts the printed weight of the text, because colors are often used to control plotted line width.

- Three other text modification tools in the expanded area in the Formatting panel enable you to modify the text angle or spacing: **Oblique Angle**, **Tracking**, and **Width Factor**.

- You can use **Match Text Formatting** to copy the formatting from one set of text to another while using the Text Editor. You can also use this option to modify dimensions and tables.

- To remove the formatting from an mtext object, expand (Clear) and select the required option, You can remove the formatting from selected characters, from selected paragraphs, or from all of the text in a text object, as shown in Figure 17–37.

Figure 17–37

Fractions in Multiline Text

When you first enter a fraction in the Text Editor, it is automatically displayed as stacked, as shown in Figure 17–38.

Click ⚡ to display the **Stack** options.

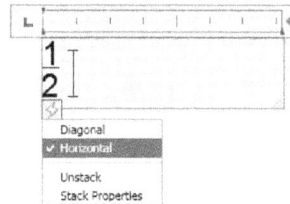

Figure 17–38

Select a fraction in the Text Editor, click ⚡ to use the basic **Stack** options or double-click on it to open the Stack Properties dialog box where you can modify the more advanced settings, as shown in Figure 17–39.

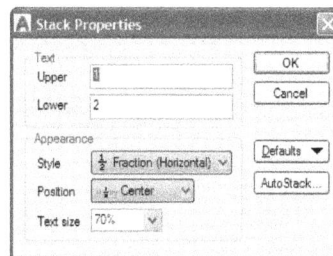

Figure 17–39

Formatting Paragraph Text

Paragraph settings also affect the next paragraph typed.

You can modify entire paragraphs of text including changing paragraph level justifications, line spacing, indents, bullets, and numbering, as shown in Figure 17–40.

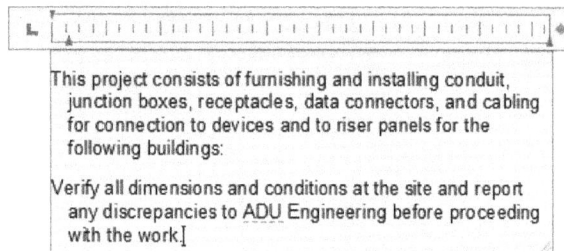

This project consists of furnishing and installing conduit, junction boxes, receptacles, data connectors, and cabling for connection to devices and to riser panels for the following buildings:

Verify all dimensions and conditions at the site and report any discrepancies to ADU Engineering before proceeding with the work.

Figure 17–40

- The paragraph formatting tools are located in the *Text Editor* contextual tab>Paragraph panel, as shown in Figure 17–41.

Bullets and Numbering
Line Spacing
Justification
Paragraph

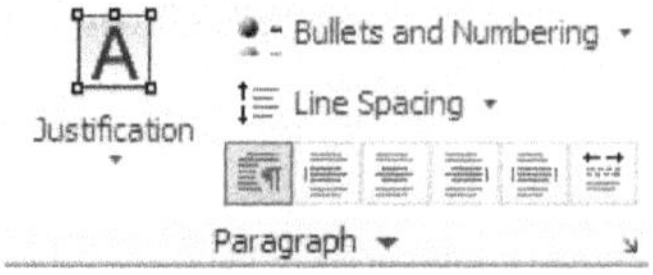

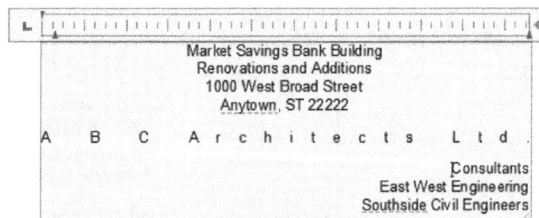

Figure 17–41

- A paragraph is any text that is typed before you press <Enter> to create a new line.
- To modify paragraphs, you can either select the entire paragraph or place the cursor somewhere in the paragraph.

Justifications

You can set justifications for individual paragraphs in a Multiline text object, as shown in Figure 17–42. The options are as follows:

- (Default)
- (Left)
- (Center)
- (Right)
- (Justify (Fit))
- (Distribute)

Market Savings Bank Building
Renovations and Additions
1000 West Broad Street
Anytown, ST 22222
A B C Architects Ltd.
Consultants
East West Engineering
Southside Civil Engineers

Figure 17–42

- **Justify (Fit)** spreads out the text so that the sentences are left- and right-justified. **Distribute** justifies to the left and right sides and spreads out whole words and individual letters across the space.

Line Spacing

You can set the line spacing using the supplied multiples of the text height, as shown in Figure 17–43, or select **More...** to create custom line spacing in the Paragraph dialog box. **Clear Line Spacing** returns the distance to the default setting.

Figure 17–43

Bullets and Numbers

You can add bullets, numbers, or letters to text as you are typing, or add them to paragraphs that are already in the text object.

Select the type of list from the **Bullets and Numbering** list in the *Text Editor* contextual tab, as shown in Figure 17–44.

To create a sub-list of a list, press <Tab> at the beginning of the line. Press <Shift>+<Tab> to back up.

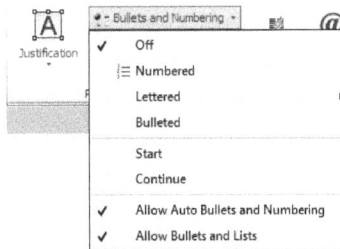

Figure 17–44

- The list can be in upper or lowercase letters, numbers, or bullets. Each time you press <Enter>, a new paragraph is created and numbered appropriately.

- You can **Restart** or **Continue** a numbered list and modify the default methods of using lists in the menu.

- Modify the indent and tab settings to set the locations of the numbers and text.

- Bullets and numbering are automatically applied to the text as you type if the line begins with a symbol or number followed by a space or <Tab>.

Setting Indents and Tabs

You can set the indents and tabs by using the ruler at the top of the Text Editor.

* Select the text that you want to indent and slide the markers to locate the indent. The top marker controls the first line of a paragraph and the bottom marker controls subsequent lines in the paragraph, as shown in Figure 17–45.

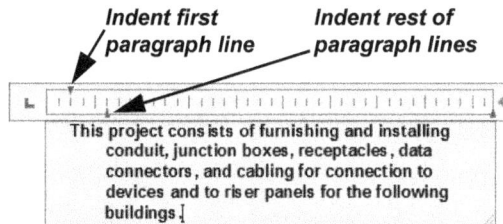

Figure 17–45

* The heavy **L** in the ruler marks preset tab stops, as shown in Figure 17–46. To add a manual tab, click on the ruler at the required location. You can drag the tab marker along the ruler to move it, or drag it off the ruler to delete it.

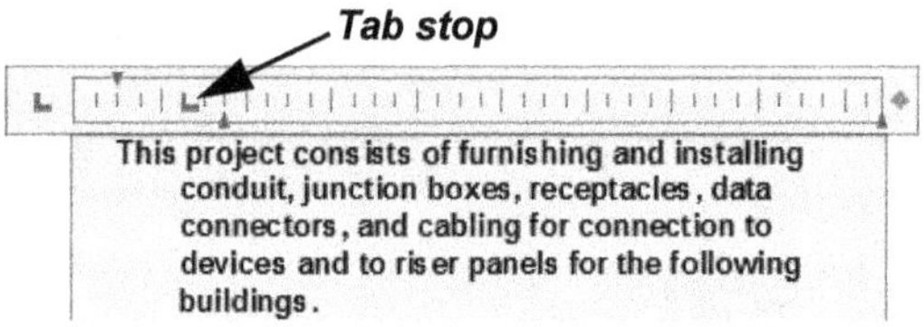

Figure 17–46

* There are tabs for ⌊L⌋ (Left), ⌊⊥⌋ (Center), ⌊⌐⌋ (Right), and ⌊⊥⌋ (Decimal). Click the tab box on the left side of the ruler to switch between the different types of tabs.

* You can also modify the tab settings in the Paragraph dialog box.

Creating Paragraph Formats

To modify the Paragraph settings, click ⁿ in the Paragraph panel title. You can set the paragraph format options at any time using the Paragraph dialog box, as shown in Figure 17–47.

- You can only set the *Paragraph Spacing* in the Paragraph dialog box. It controls the distance before or after any paragraph.

If you do not select items in the dialog box, they do not affect the selected paragraph.

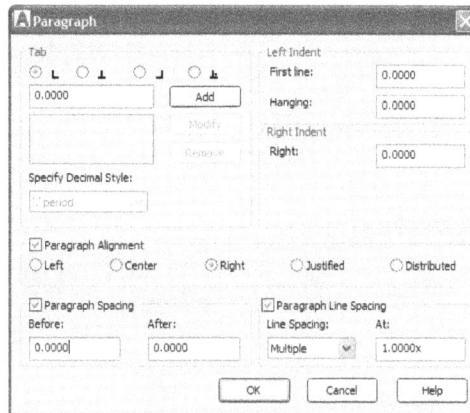

Figure 17–47

Creating Columns

You can place the text in a column format, as shown in Figure 17–48, using the column options in the Text Editor. There are two methods of column creation: **Dynamic** and **Static**.

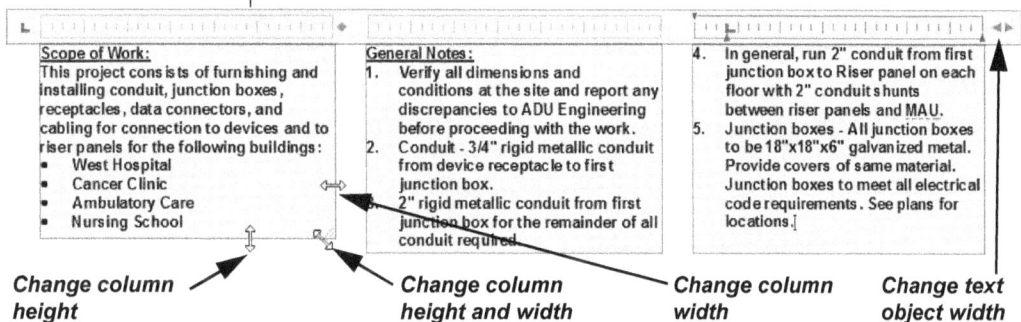

Figure 17–48

Column settings affect the entire Multiline text object.

- By default, all of the Multiline text is set up to display dynamic columns with a manual height. This can be adjusted with grips or by dragging the edges of the first column to adjust the height and width separately, or both at the same time, as shown in Figure 17–48.

Static Columns

With **Static Columns**, you can specify the number of columns in the list, as shown in Figure 17–49. The columns are evenly divided in the text box.

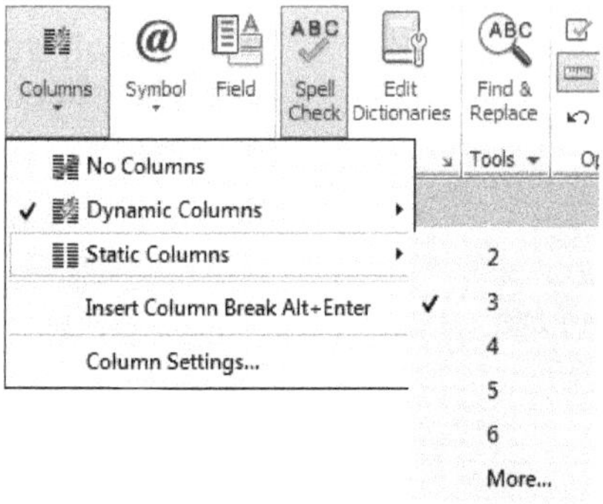

Figure 17–49

- If you need more than six columns, select **More…** or **Column Settings…** In the Column Settings dialog box, you can set the number of Static Columns, their height and width, and the gutter width.

Dynamic Columns

With **Dynamic Columns**, you can specify an automatic or manual height, as shown in Figure 17–50. The number of columns varies depending on the amount of text.

Figure 17–50

You can also set the height and width of columns in the Column Settings dialog box and modify them with grips.

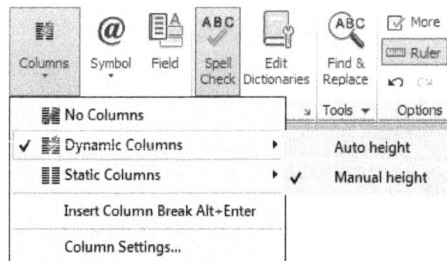

- After you start typing column information in the Mtext boundary, you can select **Insert Column Break** or type <Alt>+<Enter> to add a break before the end of the column. This enables you to control the flow of text in the Mtext object.

- When you have columns in your drawing, you can control the spacing with grips, depending on the type of columns and their settings.

Practice 17c

Formatting Multiline Text in a Drawing

Practice Objectives

Estimated time for completion: 10 minutes

- Change the formatting options of text objects.
- Add text and create columns.

In this practice, you will use formatting options in the Text Editor to set the style, modify individual objects, add numbering and indents, and set the justification of the text, as shown in Figure 17–51. If you have time, you can also add text and create columns.

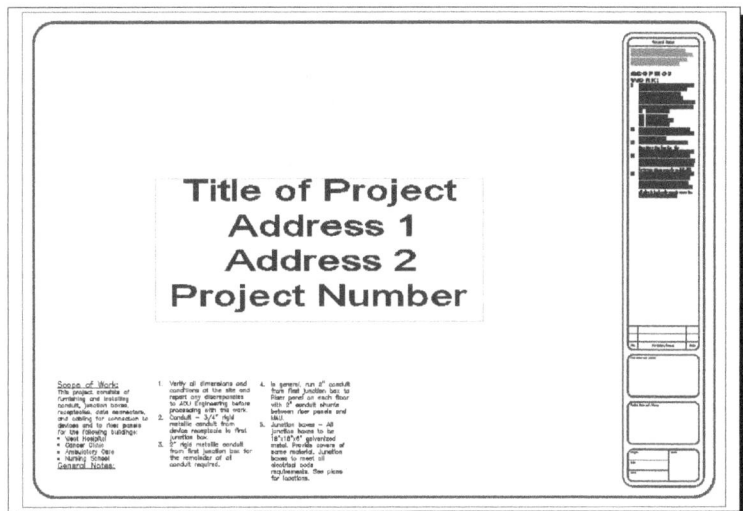

Figure 17–51

Task 1 - Format multiline text in a drawing.

1. Open **Cover Sheet2-AM.dwg** from your practice files folder.

2. Zoom in on the *General Notes* area in the upper right corner of the titleblock.

3. Double-click on the text below the General Notes to open it in the Text Editor.

4. In the *Text Editor* contextual tab>Style panel, click ⬇ and select the style **Hand**. In the alert box, click **Yes**. The entire text object updates to the new style.

5. Highlight the first sentence (four lines), which starts with **Notice**. In the *Text Editor* contextual tab>Formatting panel, click $\underline{U}$ to make the sentence underlined and in the Color list, select **Red**, as shown in Figure 17–52.

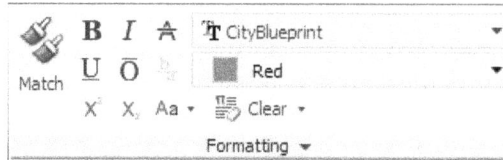

Figure 17–52

6. In the next paragraph of the text, highlight the text **General Notes** and change it to read **Scope of Work**. Change its *Font* to **Arial**, *Text Height* to **5** and make all of the words **Uppercase,** as shown in Figure 17–53.

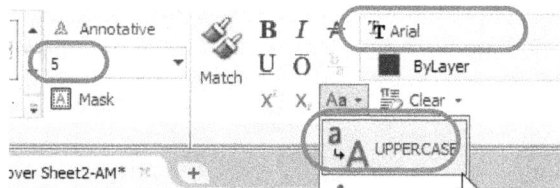

Figure 17–53

7. Select all of the text below SCOPE OF WORK. In the *Text Editor* contextual tab>Paragraph panel, expand **Bullets and Numbering** and select **Numbered** to apply autonumbering. Each paragraph becomes numbered.

8. Items 2-5 in the list should be sub-items under the first note. Select the insertion point in front of the text *West Hospital* and press <Tab>. The line becomes a sub-item. Repeat for the next three lines.

9. To adjust the indent for the sub-items, highlight those four lines. In the ruler, drag the first line indent marker to the **9mm mark**, as shown in Figure 17–54.

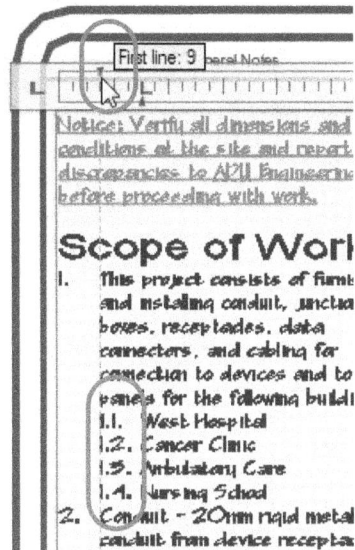

Figure 17–54

10. Click ✖ (Close Text Editor) to close the Text Editor.

11. Zoom out to display the entire layout.

12. Double-click anywhere on the four lines of Title text in the center of the cover sheet.

13. In the *Text Editor* contextual tab>Paragraph panel, change the *Justification* to **Middle Center MC**, as shown in Figure 17–55.

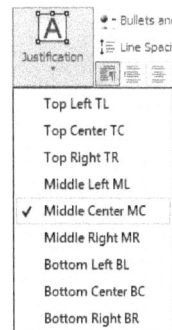

Figure 17–55

14. Exit the Text Editor.

15. Save the drawing.

Task 2 - (Optional) Create columns.

In this task, you will import a text file, apply formatting, and divide the text into columns, as shown in Figure 17–56.

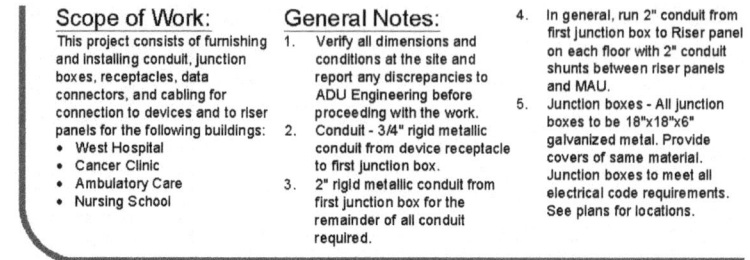

Scope of Work:

This project consists of furnishing and installing conduit, junction boxes, receptacles, data connectors, and cabling for connection to devices and to riser panels for the following buildings:

- West Hospital
- Cancer Clinic
- Ambulatory Care
- Nursing School

General Notes:

1. Verify all dimensions and conditions at the site and report any discrepancies to ADU Engineering before proceeding with the work.
2. Conduit - 3/4" rigid metallic conduit from device receptacle to first junction box.
3. 2" rigid metallic conduit from first junction box for the remainder of all conduit required.
4. In general, run 2" conduit from first junction box to Riser panel on each floor with 2" conduit shunts between riser panels and MAU.
5. Junction boxes - All junction boxes to be 18"x18"x6" galvanized metal. Provide covers of same material. Junction boxes to meet all electrical code requirements. See plans for locations.

Figure 17–56

1. In the lower left corner of the cover sheet, create a new Multiline Text object. Set the current text style to **Standard** with a *Height* of **5**.

2. From the practice files folder, import the text file **Scope of Work.txt**. (This is similar to the text you placed under General Notes.)

3. Modify the formatting so that the items are bulleted and numbered (as shown in Figure 17–56), and the titles are larger and underlined.

4. In the *Text Editor* contextual tab>Insert panel, expand

   (Columns) and select **Static Columns>2**. The text is divided into two columns.

5. Click (Columns) and select **Column Settings**. The Column Settings dialog box opens.

6. In the *Width* area, set the *Column* to **75** and *Gutter* to **13**, as shown in Figure 17–57.

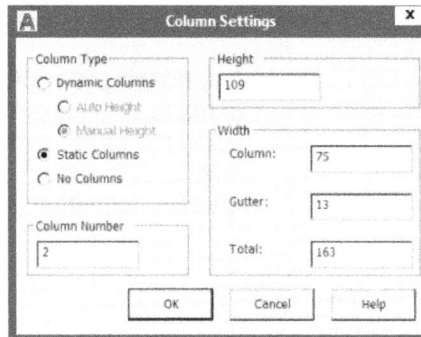

Figure 17–57

7. Click **OK** to close the Column Settings dialog box. The columns adjust to match the new values.

8. Close the Text Editor. The text is still not completely on the sheet.

The right pointing arrow increases the width. Drag and drop the bottom arrow to create columns and modify the column height.

9. Open the Text Editor again, expand 📊 (Columns), and select **Dynamic Columns>Manual height**. Close the Text Editor.

10. Use grips (i.e, the right pointing arrow and bottom arrow) to modify the columns so that the headings are on separate lines and the notes do not run over from column to column, as shown in Figure 17–58.

Scope of Work:
This project consists of furnishing and installing conduit, junction boxes, receptacles, data connectors, and cabling for connection to devices and to riser panels for the following buildings:
• West Hospital
• Cancer Clinic
• Ambulatory Care
• Nursing School

General Notes:
1. Verify all dimensions and conditions at the site and report any discrepancies to ADU Engineering before proceeding with the work.
2. Conduit - 20mm rigid metallic conduit from device receptacle to first junction box.
3. 50mm rigid metallic conduit from first junction box for the remainder of all conduit required.

4. In general, run 50mm conduit from first junction box to Riser panel on each floor with 50mm conduit shunts between riser panels and MAU.
5. Junction boxes - All junction boxes to be 450mm x 450mm x 150mm galvanized metal. Provide covers of same material. Junction boxes to meet all electrical code requirements. See plans for locations.

Figure 17–58

11. Save and close the drawing.

17.5 Adding Notes with Leaders to Your Drawing

In a drawing, you often need to use an arrow to point to objects in the drawing and add either text or keynotes. This can be done using the **Multileader** command. Multileaders consist of straight lines or splines can contain multiple leaders. You can use Multiline text or blocks for content, as shown in Figure 17–59.

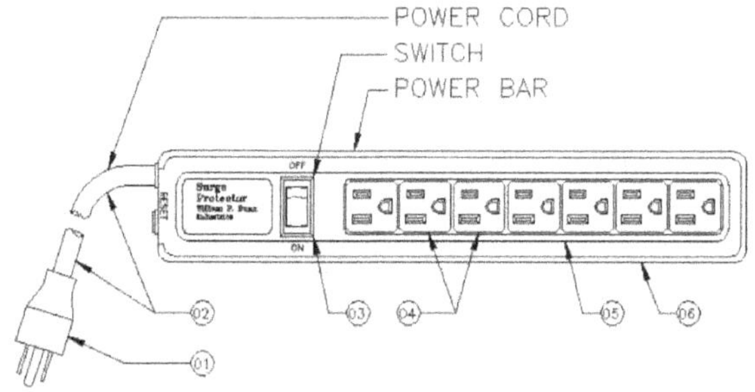

The style of a multileader determines whether it uses text for the note or a block, such as a circle.

Figure 17–59

- As with other text and dimension objects, multileaders use a style and can be annotative.

How To: Add a Text Note

1. Select a Multileader style that uses text. Both the Standard and Annotative styles provided with the AutoCAD templates are designed this way.
2. In the *Annotate* tab>Leaders panel or in the *Home* tab>Annotation panel, click ⌐○ (Multileader)
3. Select a point for the leader arrowhead location.
4. Select a point for the leader landing. By default, a horizontal tag is attached to the end.
5. Type the text. To specify the text width so that it word-wraps, you can use the Text Width arrows in the Text Formatting ruler.

6. Click ✕ (Close Text Editor) in the *Text Editor* contextual tab or click away from the text in the drawing. The multileader displays as shown in Figure 17–60.

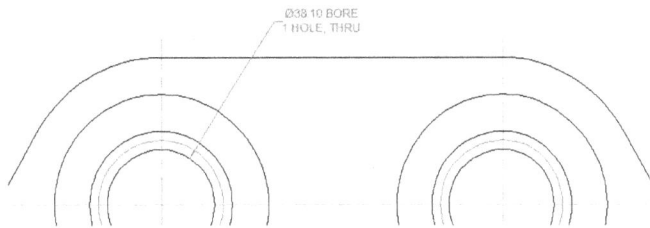

Ø38.10 BORE
1 HOLE, THRU

Figure 17–60

- The *Text Editor* contextual tab displays when you place multiline text using the **Multileader** command.

- You can change the order in which you place the leader using the **Leader Landing first** or **Content first** options, as shown in Figure 17–61. If you change the method of placing the leader, it becomes the default and is used the next time you start the command.

*You can use **Options** to modify the appearance of the leader, but creating Multileader Styles is recommended.*

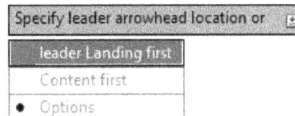

Specify leader arrowhead location or
leader Landing first
Content first
• Options

Figure 17–61

Drawing Keynotes

You can draw Multileaders with numbers in a block that are related to a list of keynotes located elsewhere in the drawing, as shown in Figure 17–62. You need to use a multileader style that uses blocks.

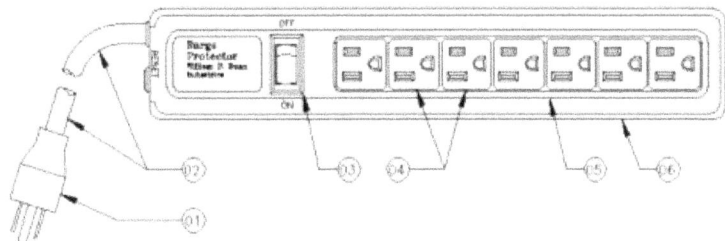

Figure 17–62

Modifying Multileaders

The leader and text (or block) of a multileader are one object. Multileaders can be modified using grips and text editing tools.

Grip Editing

You can use grips to modify the landing length (as shown in Figure 17–63), leader length and angle, and to move the multileader.

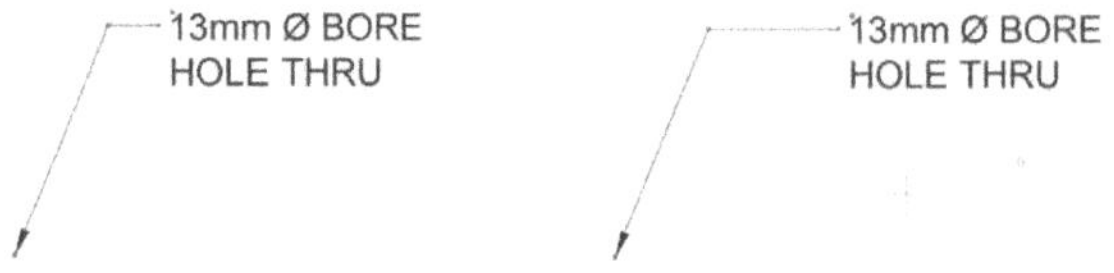

Figure 17–63

- The square grip at the end of the leader line changes the location at which the leader line is pointing.

- The square grip at the top left of the text moves the multileader.

- The arrow grip on the landing changes its length.

- If you hover over the square multi-functional grips on the leader line as shown in Figure 17–64, additional options display, such as **Add Vertex** and **Add/Remove Leader**.

Figure 17–64

- If you are working with text leaders that have a specific text length, you can modify the text boundary using grips, as shown in Figure 17–65.

Figure 17–65

- If the text does not have a specified boundary, you can create one by clicking on the text again and modifying the boundary box using the Text Width ruler, as shown in Figure 17–66.

13mm Ø BORE
HOLE THRU

13mm Ø BORE
HOLE THRU

Figure 17–66

Adding and Removing Leaders

You can add or remove leader lines to create a single leader object, which points to multiple locations in the drawing, as shown in Figure 17–67.

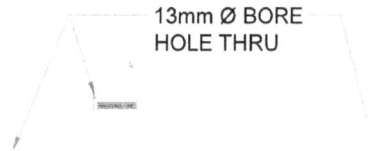

13mm Ø BORE
HOLE THRU

Figure 17–67

How To: Add Leaders

1. In the *Annotate* tab>Leaders panel, click ⚲ (Add Leader).
2. Select an existing Multileader.
3. Select the location at which you want to add the new leader.
4. Continue adding leaders as required.
5. Press <Enter> to complete the command.

How To: Remove Leaders

1. In the *Annotate* tab>Leaders panel, click ⚲ (Remove Leader).
2. Select an existing Multileader.
3. Select the leaders that you want to remove.
4. Press <Enter> to complete the command.

Select Individual Leaders to Edit

You can select individual leaders and modify them. For example, in Figure 17–68, several leaders were modified to distinguish new plants from existing plants of the same type.

DWARF BURNING BUSH

VIBURNUM WENTWORTH

PLANTING LEGEND	
⟵	NEW PLANTING
⟵ - -	EXISTING PLANTING

Figure 17–68

How To: Select and Edit Individual Leaders

1. Select an existing Multileader.
2. Hold <Ctrl> and click to select one or more leaders in a Multileader. The leaders display with red grips.
3. Once selected, right-click and select Properties. Use the Properties palette to change the properties of the selected leaders, such as their color, leader, or arrowhead size, as shown in Figure 17–69.

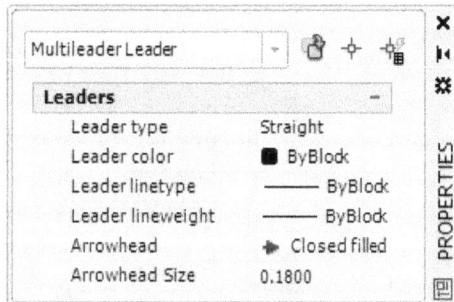

Multileader Leader	
Leaders	–
Leader type	Straight
Leader color	■ ByBlock
Leader linetype	—— ByBlock
Leader lineweight	—— ByBlock
Arrowhead	➤ Closed filled
Arrowhead Size	0.1800

Figure 17–69

Aligning Multileaders

You can use the **Multileader Align** command to arrange multileaders so that they are evenly spaced and aligned, as shown in How To:Figure 17–70.

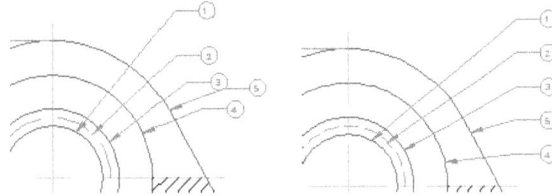

Figure 17–70

How To: Align Multileaders

1. In the *Annotate* tab>Leaders panel, click (Align, Multileader).
2. Select the multileaders that you want to align and press <Enter>.
3. You can change the current mode of aligning by pressing <Down Arrow>, selecting **Options**, and selecting an option.
4. Select the multileader or points to which you want to align.

The last option used becomes the default when you use the command again.

Distribute	Select two points. The multileaders are evenly spaced between them.
Make leader segments Parallel	Select a multileader to which to make the other leader segments parallel. The content remains in place and the leaders' angles are made parallel to the selected leader.
Specify Spacing	Select to type a distance for the spacing and then select a multileader to which to align and direction for alignment.
Use current spacing	Select to use the current spacing settings. The content is aligned and the spacing between the multileaders does not change.

Collecting Multileaders

You can collect several multileaders together using one leader, as shown in Figure 17–71. This only works with multileaders that have block content, not those with text content. This enables you to combine multiple blocks into a string. The blocks can be displayed vertically, horizontally, or wrapped to fit into a selected space.

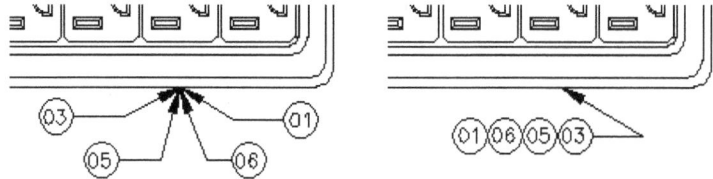

Figure 17–71

How To: Collect Multileader Blocks

1. In the *Annotate* tab>Leaders panel, click (Collect).
2. Select the leaders that you want to group together and press <Enter>
3. Select a location for the newly collected leaders.

- The default layout is **Horizontal**, but you can change it to **Vertical** using the shortcut menu. If there is a long line of bubbles, select the **Wrap** option and specify the wrap distance.

Practice 17d | Adding Notes to Your Drawing

Practice Objectives

- Add text and block-based multileaders to a drawing.
- Add leaders to multileaders, align and modify multileaders.

Estimated time for completion: 10 minutes

In this practice, you will add text and block-based multileaders. You will add leaders to multileaders and then align and modify leaders with grips as required, as shown in Figure 17–72.

- The multileader style **Keynotes** was created for this drawing.

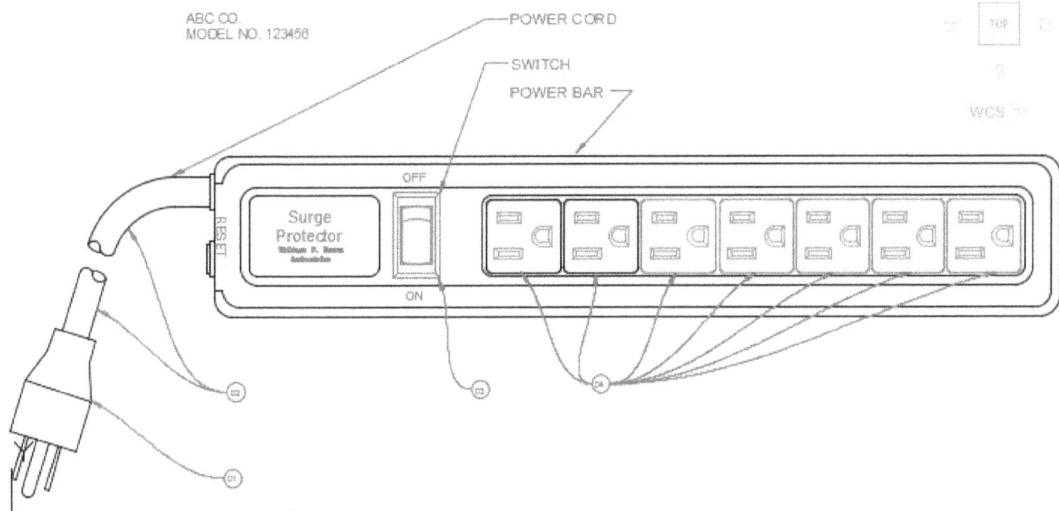

Figure 17–72

Task 1 - Draw multileaders.

1. Open **Power Protector-M.dwg** from your practice files folder.

2. Switch to the **ISO A3** layout and activate the viewport. You might have to use **Zoom Extents** to display the drawing in the viewport.

3. Set the *current layer* to **Text**.

4. If required, in the *Annotate* tab>Leaders panel, in the *Multileader style* list, click **Annotative**.

5. In the *Annotate* tab>Leaders panel, click ✏ (Multileader).

---

6. Add multileaders as shown in Figure 17–73, to label the **POWER CORD**, **SWITCH,** and **POWER BAR**. Place the multileaders so they are not aligned.

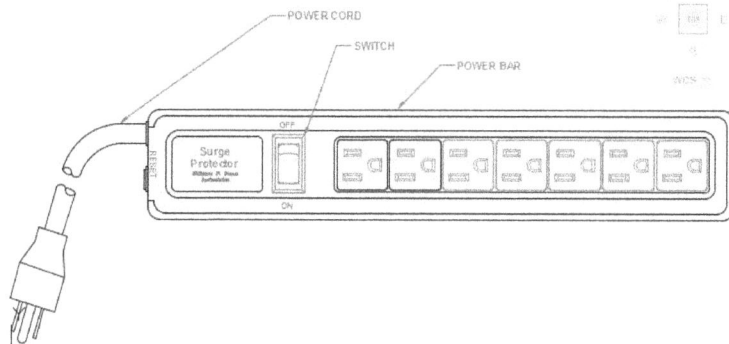

Figure 17–73

7. Set the current *Multileader style* to **Keynotes**.

8. Start the **Multileader** command. Add several multileaders and with each multileader, in the Edit Attributes dialog box, enter tag numbers to label the components as **01**, **02**, **03**, and **04**, as shown in Figure 17–74.

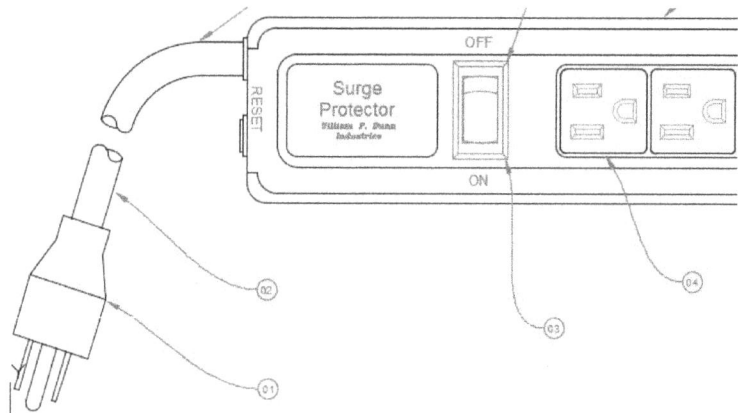

Figure 17–74

Task 2 - Modify multileaders.

1. Select the multileader with the label **02** and then in the *Annotate* tab>Leaders panel, click ⌖ (Add Leader). A leader is attached to the cursor. Add a leader to the other half of the power cord (as shown in Figure 17–75) and press <Enter>.

2. Similarly, add leaders to the multileader labeled **04** to point to each of the remaining sockets, as shown in Figure 17–75.

3. In the *Annotate* tab>Leaders panel, click ✍ (Align, Multileader).

4. Select the multileaders **POWER BAR**, **POWER CORD**, and **SWITCH** and then press <Enter>. Align the multileaders to **SWITCH** by selecting it. To set the direction, move the cursor perpendicularly above the **SWITCH** multileader. Click to place the multileaders.

5. Modify the exact locations of the leaders and text as required using grips.

Task 3 - Add text.

1. Set the current *Text style* to **Annotative** (*Annotate* tab>Text panel).

2. Start the **Multiline Text** command.

3. Using Quick Properties, change the *Paper text height* to **3.5** and then add a note above and to the left of the power bar, as shown in Figure 17–75. Use the grips to place the note in two lines.

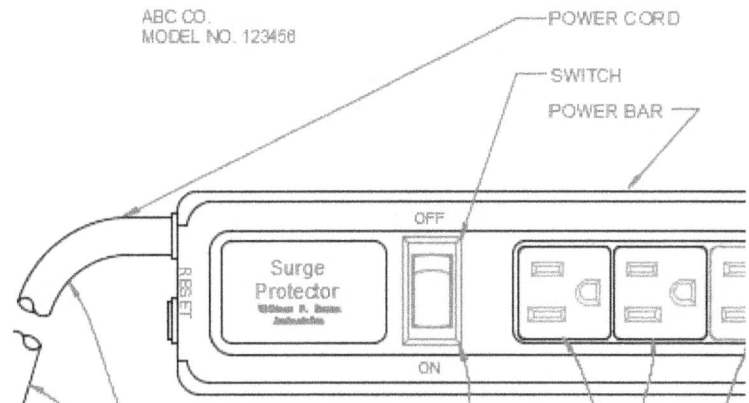

Figure 17–75

4. Save the drawing.

17.6 Creating Tables

The **Table** command creates a unified table typically containing title and column headers with any number of rows/columns of data, as shown in Figure 17–76.

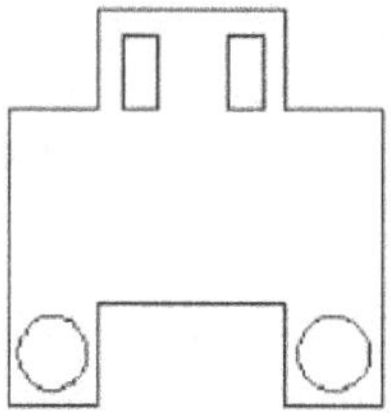

DESCRIPTION OF HOLES		
SIZE	DESCRIPTION	QTY
A	Ø9 THRU	2
B	5X9 RECT	2

Figure 17–76

- You can create table styles that define custom standard properties. When you insert a table object, you add the values for each of the cells.

- You can also create tables to which you can add custom information by linking external Excel spreadsheet files, or by extracting AutoCAD object data and creating a table from the information.

- Tables can include calculations.

How To: Create an Empty Table

The **Table** command is used to create tables from scratch, and from links and data extractions.

1. In the *Annotate* tab>Tables panel or in the *Home* tab>Annotation panel, click ⊞ (Table).
2. The Insert Table dialog box opens, as shown in Figure 17–77. In the Table style drop-down list, select the table style.

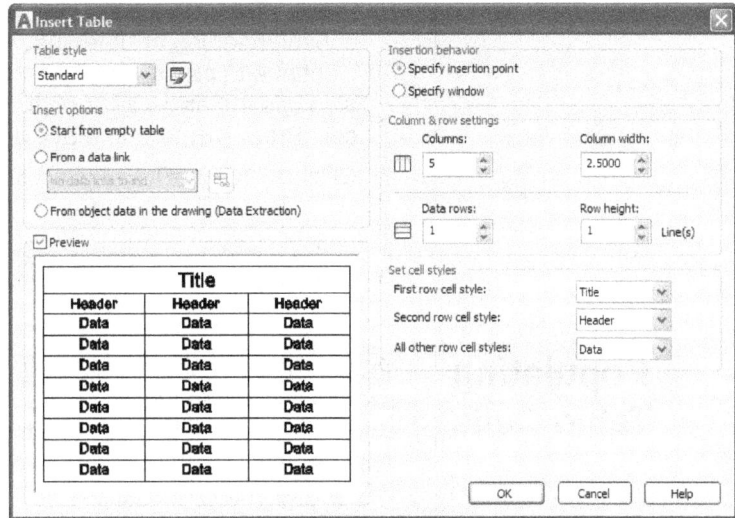

Figure 17–77

3. In the *Insert options* area, select **Start from empty table**.
4. In the *Insertion behavior* and *Column & row settings* areas, select the required options.

- If you select the **Specify insertion point** option, you can set the number of columns and rows and their sizes.

- If you select the **Specify window** option, you can set either the number of columns or the column width, and the number of rows or the row height (where the information not specified is automatically calculated by the size of the window).

5. In the *Set cell styles* area, select the required styles.
6. Click **OK** to place the table in the drawing.
7. Select a point in the drawing window to place the table or select two points to draw a window, depending on the option that you selected in the *Insertion behavior* area.
8. The *Text Editor* contextual tab opens and the title bar of the table is highlighted, as shown in Figure 17–78. Type the title.

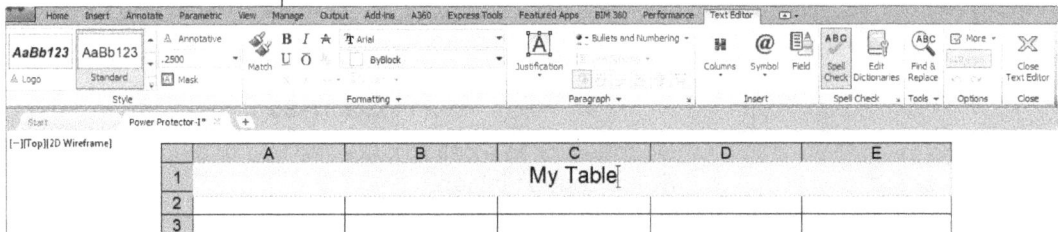

Figure 17–78

9. Press <Tab>. The first column and row highlight. Type the column heading or other information.

10. Continue to press <Tab> to move through the cells. You can also use the arrow keys on the keyboard to move from cell to cell. Press <Enter> to move down a row.

11. Click ✕ (Close Text Editor) to end the command.

- In the Insert Table dialog box, click 📝 (Launch the Table Style dialog) in the *Table style* area to create a table style.

Populating Table Cells

Table cells can contain plain text, blocks, and fields. The example shown in Figure 17–79 has blocks in the *Room #* column, fields that are linked to the area of polyline objects in the *Area* column, and the total area of the building using a formula next to the *Total Area* cell.

Occupancy Table			
Room #	Department	Area	Use
101	Marketing	40677979	Office
102	Marketing	41691504	Office
103	Sales	40677979	Office
104	Engineering	244150791	Drafting Room
105	Engineering	41749658	Office
106	Engineering	42024316	Office
107	Engineering	41749658	Office
	Total Area:	492721885	

Figure 17–79

- Click once in a cell to open the *Table Cell* contextual tab. It contains a variety of tools for adding and modifying cells. The current cell is highlighted with a gold edge, as shown in Figure 17–80.

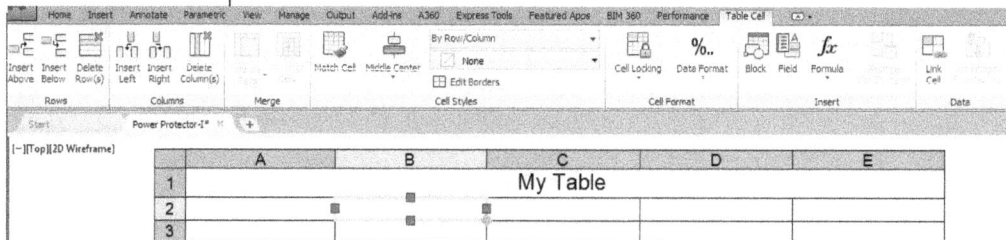

Figure 17–80

- Double-click in a cell to place the text and open the *Text Editor* contextual tab.

Inserting Blocks, Fields, and Formulas

Table cells can include text, blocks, fields, and formulas. Tools for inserting them are located in the *Table Cell* contextual tab> Insert panel and in the shortcut menus.

Insert Block: Opens the Insert a Block in a Table Cell dialog box. Select the name of the block or browse for a file. Then set the properties and cell alignment. The **AutoFit** option scales the size of the block to fit the cell size.

Insert Field: Adds a field selected in the Field dialog box into the cell. Hyperlinks are added using fields.

Insert Formula: Select **Sum**, **Average**, **Count**, **Cell**, or **Equation** to add a formula to the cell.

- To remove cell content, select the cell(s) and press <Delete>. You can also right-click and select **Delete All Contents**. This only deletes the selected cell(s).

- Tables are typically created in Paper Space. However, you sometimes need to access information in Model Space, such as the area of a hatch or polyline. When you are working with Object fields in a text object or table, you can select an object in a viewport even if the table is in Paper Space.

Calculations in Tables

You can make calculations directly in an AutoCAD table and the basic mathematical calculations are available, such as addition, subtraction, multiplication, division, and exponents, as well as **Sum** (as shown in Figure 17–81), **Average**, and **Count**. You can combine arithmetic functions, including parentheses, to create formulas.

	A	B	C	D
1		Replacement Costs		
2	Item #	Cost	Count	Total
3	AZ–408	255.45	12	3065.40
4	DG–411	18.29	22	402.38
5	DA–862	35.30	8	282.40
6			Grand Total:	=Sum(D3:D5)

Figure 17–81

- When the table is in edit mode, it displays letters for the columns and numbers for the rows. As in a standard spreadsheet, you specify a cell by its location, such as D3 (Column D, Row 3). When you finish editing, the table displays without this information.

- Cells used for calculations must only contain numeric information. The numeric information can be text or fields that have a numeric value (i.e., the area of a hatch or polyline).

Types of Calculations

The available types of calculations are described as follows.

Sum	Adds up numbers in the selected table cells.
Average	Computes the average of the numbers in the selected table cells. It adds up all of the numbers and divides the sum by the number of cells selected.
Count	Adds the number of selected cells, not the information in the cells. The cells must contain numerical information.
Cell	Repeats the information from a selected cell in the current cell. The selected cell can be in another table. The selected cell must have numerical information; otherwise, #### displays in the field.
Equation	Computes the entered equation. You can add (+), subtract (-), multiply (*), divide (/), and set exponents (^). You can also group items together in parentheses, such as =(B3 / B7) * 2. The calculation in parentheses is computed first. For example, =B3*B7.

How To: Add Calculations to a Table

1. Create a table containing the numeric information that you want to calculate.
2. Click once in the cell in which you want the calculated value to be placed.
3. In the *Table Cell* contextual tab>Insert panel, expand

   fx (Formula) and select the type of formula that you want to calculate, as shown on the left in Figure 17–82. Alternatively, right-click and select **Insert>Formula** and select the type of formula, as shown on the right in Figure 17–82.

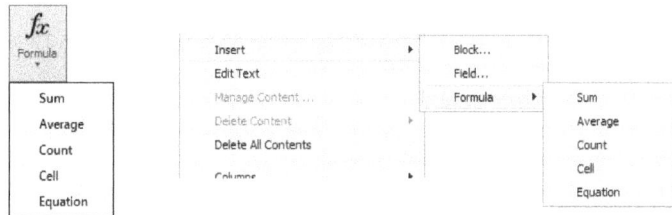

Figure 17–82

- **For Sum, Average, and Count:** Select two points for the corners of the table cell range. Click in the cells to be calculated when you select the points.

- **For Cell:** Click in another cell to place its value in the current cell. This can be a cell in another table.

- **For Equation:** Enter an equation using the cell coordinates, such as = B4 * C4.

- You can modify the equations created by any of the formulas. For example, you might select a cell range and want to add a cell or group of cells that are not in that range. In such a case, separate the new cell or range of cells by a comma, as follows.

=SUM (B3:E3)	Original formula
=SUM (B3:E3,C4)	Adding an additional cell
=SUM (B3:E3,C4:E4)	Adding a range of cells

- The calculated value in the cell is a formula field. It displays with a shaded background. You can edit the field to display the formula or change the formatting by double-clicking on the text.

Practice 17e | Creating Tables

Practice Objective

Estimated time for completion: 15 minutes

- Create a table and add a formula.

In this practice, you will create a table that includes text, blocks, fields, and a hyperlink using the **Table** command. You will also add a formula summing up the values in one column using the **Formula** command.

1. Open **Occupancy-AM.dwg** from your practice files folder.

2. Switch to the **Occupancy** layout.

3. Make the layer **0** current, and freeze all of the layers except **0**, **A-Area**, **A-Room-Symb**, and **Viewports**.

4. In the *Annotate* tab>Tables panel, start the **Table** command.

5. In the Insert Table dialog box, verify that the **Standard** table style and the **Specify insertion point** option are selected.

6. In the *Column & row settings* area, set the *Columns* to **4**, set the *Column width* to **100**, and set the *Data rows* to **8**. Click **OK** and place the table in the drawing below the Floor Plan viewport.

7. Double-click inside the top row and type **Occupancy Table** for the title, as shown in Figure 17–83. Type the remaining titles for each of the column headings shown, using <Tab> to move to the next column.

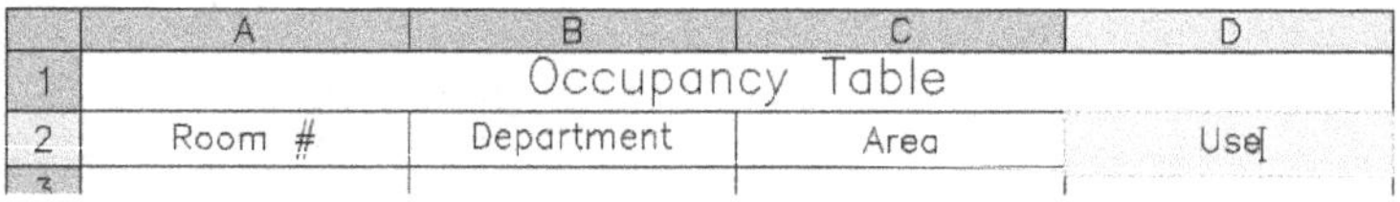

	A	B	C	D
1	Occupancy Table			
2	Room #	Department	Area	Use

Figure 17–83

Click once on a cell (until the individual cell is highlighted) to open the Table Cell contextual tab. The tools required are located in the Insert panel.

You might have to press <Esc> twice to select the next cell.

8. For the cells in each column, add the following information, as shown in Figure 17–84 (**Hint:** Use the Auto-Fill cells grip for similar content.)

Room #	Use ⬚ (Block) to insert the block name **Room Number**. Set the *Overall cell alignment* to **Middle Center**. Toggle on **Auto-Fit**. Change the attribute to be the correct room number.
Department	Type the text shown in Figure 17–84 for the departments.
Area	Use ⬚ (Field) to insert a field in each cell in the column (for the 7 rooms). In the Field dialog box, set the *Field category* to **Objects** and the *Field names* to **Object**. In the *Object type* area, click ⬚ (Select object) and then select the magenta polyline around the corresponding room in the floor plan. In the *Property* area, select the **Area** property. Set the *Format* to **Architectural** and the *Precision* to **0.0**.
Use	Type the text shown in Figure 17–83 into each cell in the column.

9. In the bottom cell of the *Area* column, add a formula using **Sum** (select the cell, right-click, and select **Insert>Formula> Sum**). Using a window, select the room areas in that column as the range and then press <Enter>. The calculated sum displays in the last Area column, as shown in Figure 17–84.

Occupancy Table			
Room #	Department	Area	Use
101	Marketing	40677979	Office
102	Marketing	41691504	Office
103	Sales	40677979	Office
104	Engineering	244150791	Drafting Room
105	Engineering	41749658	Office
106	Engineering	42024316	Office
107	Engineering	41749658	Office
	Total Area:	492721885	

Figure 17–84

10. Select the cell with the sum, right-click, and select **Insert> Edit Field**. Set the *Precision* to **0.0**.

11. Thaw all of the layers that you had previously frozen.

12. Save the drawing.

17.7 Modifying Tables

You can modify tables and table data in a variety of ways. Modifications can be made to individual cells, rows, columns, or to the entire table.

Modifying Cells, Rows, and Columns

When you select multiple cells, rows, or columns you can add and remove rows and columns, merge and unmerge cells, and modify cell properties. You can also modify an individual cell using grips.

- To select more than one cell, hold <Shift> or click and drag across the cells that you want to select.

- To select an entire row or column, select the corresponding letter or number that displays (gold) when a cell is selected with grips.

- You can also **Cut**, **Copy**, and **Paste** cell contents using the shortcut menu.

Cell Grips

The square grips around a cell change its height and width. If you modify the grips of a selected cell, it impacts all of the rows or columns in which it is located. The diamond shaped grip is used to click and drag to automatically fill the selected cells with the contents of the current cell. First select, and then right-click on the diamond grip to change the options, as shown in Figure 17–85.

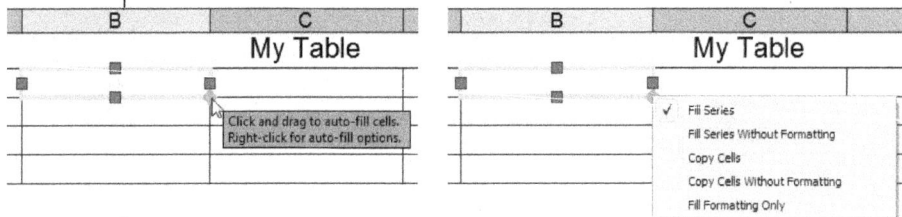

Figure 17–85

Modification Tools

With a cell selected, use the various tools available in the *Table Cell* contextual tab (as shown in Figure 17–86) to modify the tables.

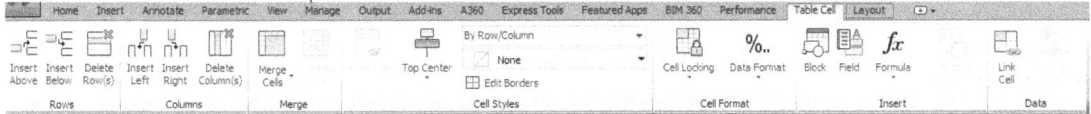

Figure 17–86

Adding and Removing Rows and Columns

	Insert Above: Inserts a row above the selected cell or row.
	Insert Below: Inserts a row below the selected cell or row.
	Delete Row(s): Deletes the selected row(s).
	Insert Left: Inserts a column to the left of the selected cell or column.
	Insert Right: Inserts a column to the right of the selected cell or column.
	Delete Column(s): Deletes the selected column(s).

Merging and Unmerging Cells

	Merge Cells: Merges selected cells depending on the selected option (**All**, **By Row**, or **By Column**). Multiple cells must be selected for this to be available.
	Unmerge Cells: Returns merged cells to an unmerged state. Merged cells must be selected for this option to be available.

Modifying Cell Properties

	**Match Cell:** Applies the properties of a selected cell to other cells, similar to the **Match Properties** command.
	Alignment: Applies the alignment selected from a list to the objects in the cell. You can align multiple cells at the same time. The current cell alignment icon might be displayed.
	Cell Styles: Changes the style of the cell to the one selected from the list. 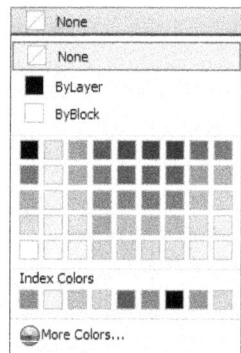
	Background Fill: Changes the background color of the cell to the color selected from the list.
	Cell Locking: Sets cells to be **Unlocked**, **Content Locked**, **Format Locked**, or **Content and Format Locked**.
%₀..	**Data Format:** Sets the data format of items in a cell. It is set to **General** by default. However, you can change the numerical data to **Angle**, **Currency**, **Data**, **Decimal Number**, **General**, **Percentage**, **Point**, **Text**, and **Whole Number**. If you need to customize the data format, right-click in the cell and select **Custom Table Cell Format** to open the Table Cell Format dialog box.
	Manage Cell Contents: Controls the location and flow of objects if there is more than one type of content in a cell, such as a block and text. This opens the Manage Cell Content dialog box.

⊞ **Edit Borders:** Opens the Cell Border Properties dialog box, in which you can specify lineweights, linetypes, color, and border types for individual cells, rows, or columns. Toggle on **Lineweight** in the Status Bar, expanded Customization list to display the lineweights.

Modifying the Entire Table

When you select the entire table (click the edge of the table), as shown in Figure 17–87, you can use grips to modify its overall size, the width of columns, the height of rows, and to break the table into columns. You can also modify some of these options in the Properties palette or through the shortcut menu.

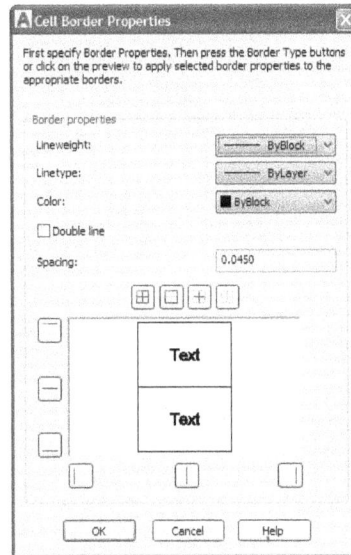

Figure 17–87

- Table-specific shortcut options include **Table Style**, **Size Columns Equally**, **Size Rows Equally**, **Remove All Property Overrides**, **Export**, and **Table Indicator Color**.

- **Table Indicator Color** is the color of the row numbers and column letters that display when the table is selected.

Table Grips

Tables can be extensively modified with grips, as shown in Figure 17–88. You can use them to adjust the width, height, and columns to fit the available space as required.

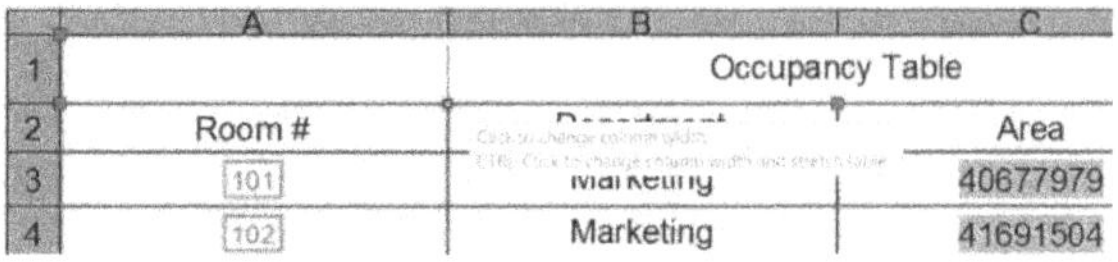

Figure 17–88

■	**Column Width:** Controls the column width. Click the grip to change the width without changing the overall table width. The adjacent columns resize accordingly. Hold <Ctrl> to modify the overall width of the table. The upper left square grip moves the entire table.
▼	**Table Height:** Uniformly stretches the table height. The height of each row changes, including the title and headers. Rows are not added.
►	**Table Width:** Uniformly stretches the table width. The width of each column changes. Columns are not added.
◄	**Table Height and Width:** Uniformly stretches both table height and width.
▼	**Table Breaking:** Activates table breaking, enabling you to control where the table is broken when it is in columns.

Breaking a Table

When a table is too long to fit on a sheet, you can break it and change its overall height. Click the grip ▼ (Table breaking) and drag it upwards until it reaches the required location in the table, as shown in Figure 17–89. The rest of the table is placed next to it in as many columns as required to contain all of the rows.

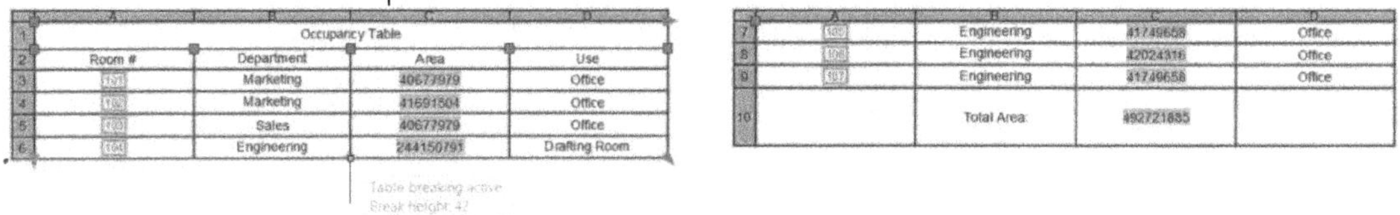

Figure 17–89

Practice 17f

Modifying Tables

Practice Objective

- Modify the table using various modification tools.

Estimated time for completion: 10 minutes

In this practice, you will use grips to modify the width and height of rows and columns, add and merge rows to create a new header, insert rows, copy and paste information, use Auto-fill to add information to cells, and break the table into columns. The completed table is shown in Figure 17–90.

Figure 17–90

1. Open **Occupancy1-AM.dwg** from your practice files folder.

2. Zoom into the *Table* area of the drawing.

3. Select the table to display the grips. Hold <Ctrl>, click and drag the square grip of the *Area* column to the right to increase the *Area* column width while also stretching the table, as shown in Figure 17–91. Click again to accept the stretch.

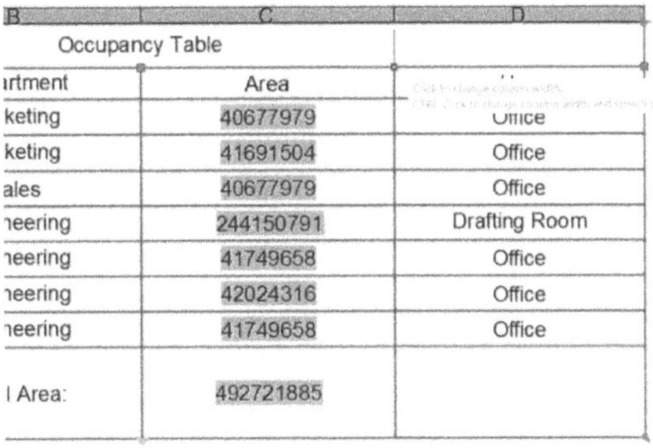

Figure 17–91

4. Click on the last row and use the bottom grip to make it the same height as the other rows.

5. Select the Row 2 of the table. In the *Table Cell* contextual tab>Rows panel, click ⌐C (Insert Above) to place a row above Row 2. Fill in the first cell of the new row with the text **First Floor**.

6. Select the newly created Row 2. Right-click and select **Merge>By Row**.

7. With the row still selected, in the *Table Cell* contextual tab>Cell Styles panel, expand the Table Cell Styles list, and set the *style* to **Title**, as shown in Figure 17–92.

Occupancy Table			
First Floor			
Room #	Department	Area	Use
101	Marketing	40677979	Office
102	Marketing	41691504	Office
103	Sales	40677979	Office
104	Engineering	244150791	Drafting Room
105	Engineering	41749658	Office
106	Engineering	42024316	Office
107	Engineering	41749658	Office
	Total Area:	492721885	

Figure 17–92

8. Select the bottom row. In the *Table Cell* contextual tab>Rows panel, click ⌐C (Insert Below) eleven times (the last number displays row 22).

9. Select one of the cells containing a room number block. Right-click and select **Copy** to copy the cell to the clipboard.

10. Leave three open rows after the *Total Area* row and paste the block into the cell in the *Room #* column (Row 15).

11. Select the copied cell and click on the Auto-fill grip (cyan diamond) of the cell. Drag it to the Room # cell of Row 21, as shown in Figure 17–93. Click to copy the block to the next six cells below.

Figure 17–93

12. Double-click on the first new block to open the Edit Block in a Table Cell dialog box. Click **OK**. In the Enter Attributes dialog box, change the *Room Number* to **201** and click **OK**.

13. Modify the rest of the room numbers.

14. Repeat the Copy and Auto-fill process for the *Department* and *Use* columns. Do not fill in the *Area* column at this time.

15. Select the entire table (use window selection) and break it under the *Total Area* row. Select ▼ (Table breaking) and then drag it near the right side of the existing table. Move the cursor down until all eleven rows display and click to break the table, as shown in Figure 17–94.

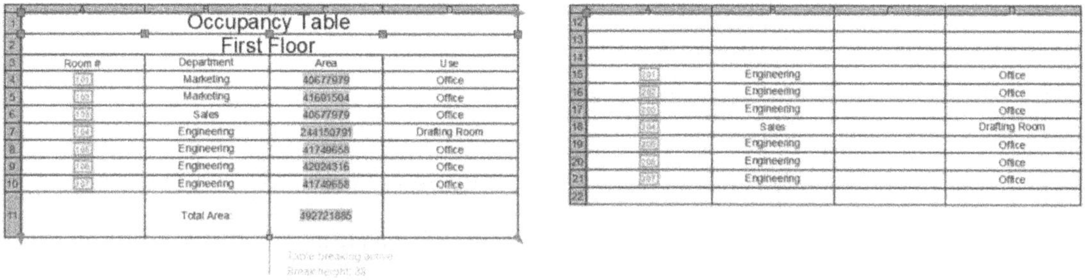

Figure 17–94

16. You can add and merge rows to specify an additional Title and Headers for the Second Floor, as shown in Figure 17–95. Set the Cell Styles, as required.

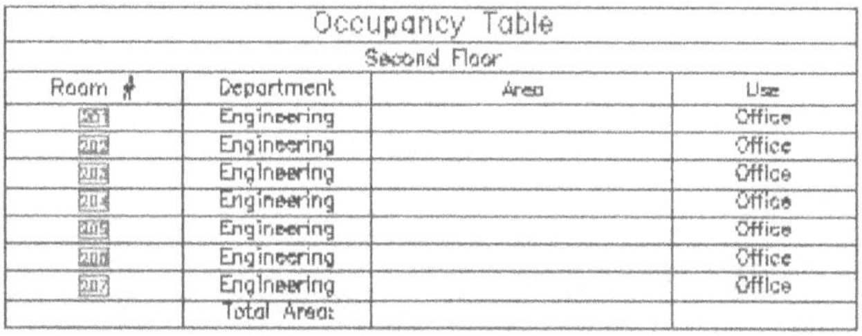

Figure 17–95

17. Save the drawing.

Chapter Review Questions

1. To understand the differences between annotations placed in Model Space and Paper Space, open the Properties palette and note the following two parameters:

   a. **Paper text height** and **Annotation scale**.

   b. **Model text height** and **Annotation scale**.

   c. **Paper text height** and **Model text height**.

   d. **Annotative** and **Annotation scale**.

2. When creating Multiline text, you pick two points. What do those points determine?

   a. The text height.

   b. The text location and width of the lines.

   c. The rotation angle of the text.

   d. The thickness of the text.

3. Using the **Import Text** tool located in the *Text Editor* contextual tab>expanded Tools panel, the text that is imported does not include formatting.

   a. True

   b. False

4. What happens when you double-click on a text object?

   a. It opens the Properties palette.

   b. It opens the text for editing.

   c. It explodes the text.

   d. It updates the text to the current text style.

5. How do you add a text frame around a multiline text?

   a. By drawing a rectangle separately and adding it to the multiline text properties.

   b. Selecting **Outline** in the *Text Editor* contextual tab.

   c. Setting the *Text Frame* to **Yes** in the Properties palette.

   d. You cannot add a text frame to the multiline text.

6. When editing text, how do you change the justification of the multiline text object (left, right, centered, etc.)?

   a. Edit the Text Style.

   b. Click the ruler above the editing frame.

   c. You cannot change the justification after the text is created.

   d. Tools in the *Text Editor* contextual tab>Paragraph panel in the ribbon.

7. Which of the following statements is true regarding multileaders?

   a. The leader and text (or block) of a multileader are separate objects.

   b. The square grip at the end of the leader line moves the multileader.

   c. The square grip at the top left of the text moves the multileader.

   d. The arrow grip on the landing of the leader line changes the location to which the leader line is pointing.

8. To collect several multileaders together into one leader, the multileaders should have:

   a. Block content only.

   b. Text content only.

   c. String content only.

   d. Both block and text content.

9. What object types can be contained in a table? (Select all that apply.)

   a. Text

   b. Blocks

   c. Fields

   d. Lines

10. When a table is selected, what does the square grip do?

   a. Breaks the link between the table and the Excel spreadsheet.

   b. Resizes the column width in the table.

   c. Uniformly stretches the table width.

   d. Uniformly stretches the table height.

Command Summary

Button	Command	Location
	Annotation	• **Ribbon:** *Text Editor* contextual tab
1:1 ▾	Annotation Scale	• **Status Bar:** (*in Model Space*)
	Columns	• **Ribbon:** *Text Editor* contextual tab
	Field	• **Ribbon:** *Text Editor* contextual tab
	Justify: Center	• **Ribbon:** *Text Editor* contextual tab
	Justify: Default	• **Ribbon:** *Text Editor* contextual tab
	Justify: Distribute	• **Ribbon:** *Text Editor* contextual tab
	Justify: Fit	• **Ribbon:** *Text Editor* contextual tab
	Justify: Left	• **Ribbon:** *Text Editor* contextual tab
	Justify: Right	• **Ribbon:** *Text Editor* contextual tab
A	Mtext Edit	• **Shortcut Menu:** (*on selected text*) Mtext Edit • **Double-click:** (*on text*) • **Command Prompt:** mtedit
	Multileader	• **Ribbon:** *Home* tab>Annotation panel or *Annotate* tab>Leaders panel • **Command Prompt:** mleader
	Multileader: Add Leader	• **Ribbon:** *Home* tab>Annotation panel or *Annotate* tab>Leaders panel
	Multileader: Align	• **Ribbon:** *Home* tab>Annotation panel or *Annotate* tab>Leaders panel • **Command Prompt:** mleaderalign
	Multileader: Collect	• **Ribbon:** *Home* tab>Annotation panel or *Annotate* tab>Leaders panel • **Command Prompt:** mleadercollect
	Multileader: Remove Leader	• **Ribbon:** *Home* tab>Annotation panel or *Annotate* tab>Leaders panel

	Multiline Text	• **Ribbon:** *Home* tab>Annotation panel or *Annotate* tab>Text panel • **Command Prompt:** mtext or T
A		
ABC	Spell Check	• **Ribbon:** *Annotate* tab>Text panel • **Command Prompt:** spell
@	Symbol	• **Ribbon:** *Text Editor* contextual tab
	Table	• **Ribbon:** *Home* tab>Annotation panel or *Annotate* tab>Tables panel • **Command Prompt:** table
	Table: Alignment	• **Ribbon:** *Table Cell* contextual tab>Cell Styles panel
	Table: Cell Locking	• **Ribbon:** *Table Cell* contextual tab>Cell Format panel
	Table Column: Delete Column(s)	• **Ribbon:** *Table Cell* contextual tab>Columns panel
	Table Column: Insert Left	• **Ribbon:** *Table Cell* contextual tab>Columns panel
	Table Column: Insert Right	• **Ribbon:** *Table Cell* contextual tab>Columns panel
%..	Table: Data Format	• **Ribbon:** *Table Cell* contextual tab>Cell Format panel
	Table: Edit Borders	• **Ribbon:** *Table Cell* contextual tab>Cell Styles panel
	Table Row: Delete Row(s)	• **Ribbon:** *Table Cell* contextual tab>Rows panel
	Table Row: Insert Above	• **Ribbon:** *Table Cell* contextual tab>Rows panel
	Table Row: Insert Below	• **Ribbon:** *Table Cell* contextual tab>Rows panel
	Table: Insert Block	• **Ribbon:** *Table Cell* contextual tab>Insert panel
	Table: Insert Field	• **Ribbon:** *Table Cell* contextual tab>Insert panel
fx	Table: Insert Formula	• **Ribbon:** *Table Cell* contextual tab>Insert panel
	Table: Manage Cell Content	• **Ribbon:** *Table Cell* contextual tab>Insert panel
	Table: Match Cell	• **Ribbon:** *Table Cell* contextual tab>Cell Styles panel
	Table: Merge Cells	• **Ribbon:** *Table Cell* contextual tab>Merge panel
	Table: Unmerge Cells	• **Ribbon:** *Table Cell* contextual tab>Merge panel

Hatching

In this chapter you learn how to hatch areas of your drawing and to edit applied hatching.

Learning Objectives in this Chapter

- Create patterns of lines or shapes to fill specific areas of a drawing.
- Drag and drop hatch patterns onto objects in the drawing.
- Set and modify hatch, hatch pattern properties, and hatch options.
- Modify a hatch pattern, scale, angle, and boundaries.

18.1 Hatching

Hatching is a pattern of lines or shapes that is used to distinguish certain areas of a drawing from other areas. For example, hatching might be used to indicate which rooms on a floor plan are occupied by a specific department, as shown in Figure 18–1. In mechanical design, hatching is typically used to indicate section views. The AutoCAD® software contains many predefined hatch patterns.

*There are two ways to apply hatching: Tool Palettes and the **Hatch** command.*
Many patterns for specific applications can be purchased from commercial third-party developers.

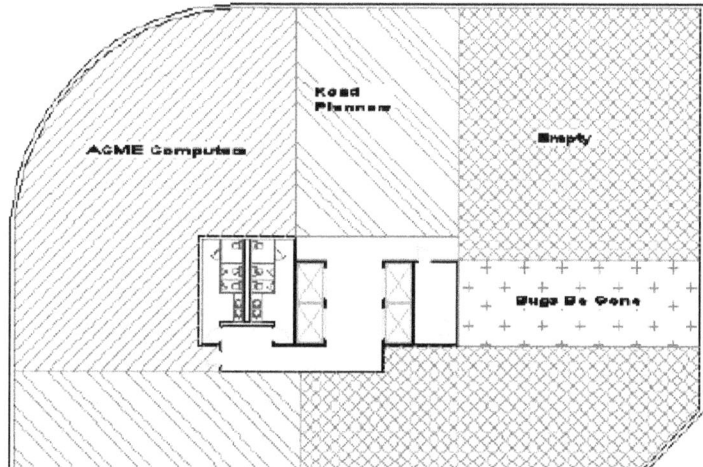

Figure 18–1

- Hatching should be placed on a separate hatch layer so that it can be easily toggled off or frozen.

- Hatching can be annotative, so you should apply it after a viewport has been prepared and scaled.

Applying a Hatch: Tool Palettes

Tool Palettes (*Hatches and Fills* tab) contains several hatch patterns that can be used for hatching a closed area in a drawing.

- Click on a pattern. It is attached to the cursor, as shown in Figure 18–2. Move the cursor inside the closed area that you want to hatch. A preview of the hatch in the area displays. Click to hatch the area.

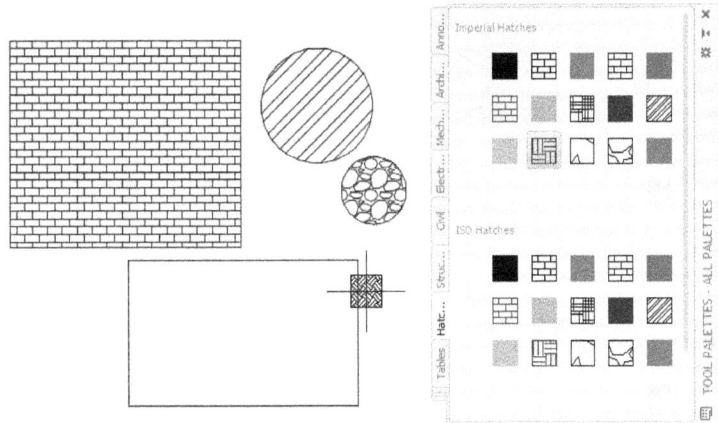

Figure 18–2

- The area for hatching should be completely bounded, with no gaps.

- Closed objects and text inside the bounded area (known as *islands*) are not normally hatched.

*In the Tool Palettes, if the tab is hidden, click on the area just below the bottom tab and select **Hatches and Fills**.*

- The default *Hatches and Fills* tab in Tool Palettes comes with hatches that are scaled for Imperial and ISO (Metric) drawings, and several gradient hatches, as shown in Figure 18–2.

- By default, the hatch patterns provided are not annotative. You can change that after the hatch has been applied to the object by opening its Properties palette, and changing *Annotative* to **Yes**, as shown in Figure 18–3.

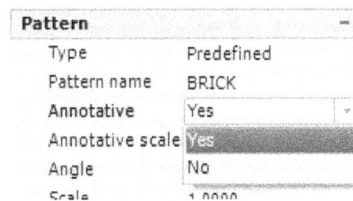

Figure 18–3

Applying a Hatch: Hatch Command

The **Hatch** command provides more control and options than hatching using Tool Palettes. Using this command, you can select from many different patterns and adjust the scale or angle of the hatch as you apply it, as shown in Figure 18–4.

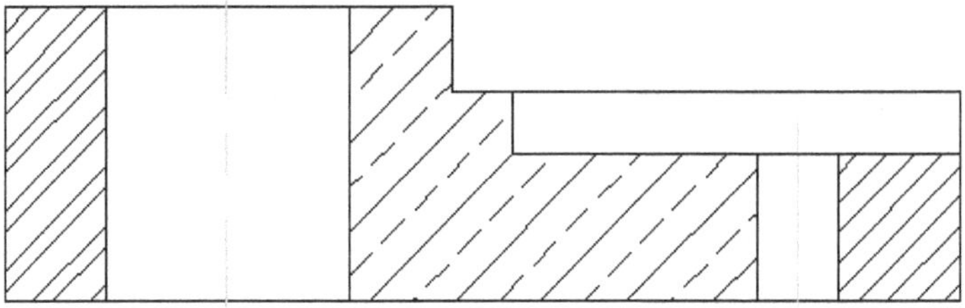

Figure 18–4

How To: Hatch Objects

1. In the *Home* tab>Draw panel, click ▨ ⁻ (Hatch).
2. In the *Hatch Creation* contextual tab, set the *Pattern*, *Scale*, *Angle*, and *Transparency*, as shown in Figure 18–5.

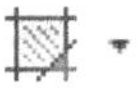

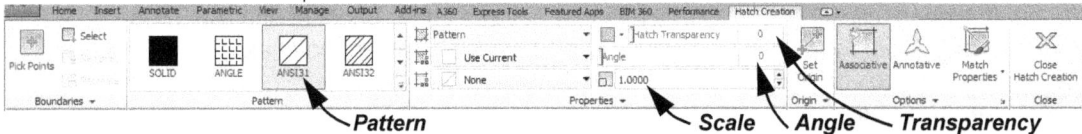

Figure 18–5

3. Click ⊞ (Pick Points) and hover the cursor inside the bounded area to preview the hatch. Click to add the hatch or modify the settings until the correct results display in the preview.

   - You can also click ▨ (Select Boundary Objects) and select a closed object or group of objects that form a closed boundary.
   - If the hatch cannot be created due to invalid hatch boundaries, an alert box opens, as shown in Figure 18–6.

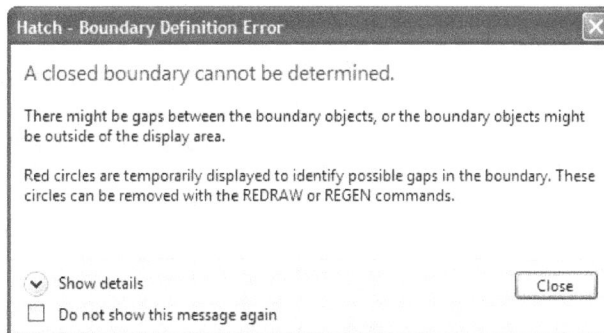

Figure 18–6

4. Press <Enter> or click ✕ (Close Hatch Creation) to end the command.

• Click ▨ (Remove Boundaries) to select objects in the drawing to remove them from the selection.

Hatch Pattern and Properties

If your ribbon is reduced in size due to the size of the interface, you might

need to expand ▨ (Hatch Pattern) in the Pattern panel first.

In the *Hatch Creation* contextual tab, you can set the *Pattern*, *Scale*, *Angle*, and *Transparency* of the hatch.

Pattern Panel

In the Pattern panel, select a pattern from the list. You can expand the list by clicking ▾, as shown in Figure 18–7.

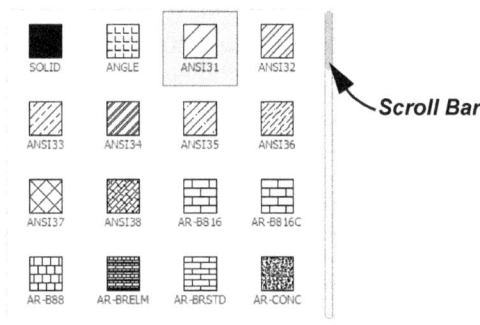

Figure 18–7

Properties Panel

In the Properties panel, you can set the *Hatch Type*, *Hatch Color*, *Background Color*, *Hatch Transparency*, *Hatch Angle*, *Hatch Pattern Scale*, and *Hatch Layer Override*. These enable you to customize how the hatch displays in the drawing.

Hatch Type

The type of hatch can be **Solid**, **Gradient**, **Pattern**, or **User defined**, as shown in Figure 18–8. Select the hatch type, and then select a pattern in the Pattern list.

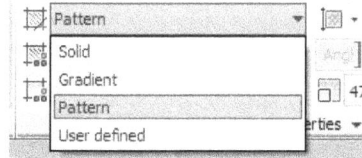

Figure 18–8

- User-defined patterns are parallel lines with a spacing and angle that you specify. You can create a cross-hatch by

  expanding the Properties panel and clicking ⊞ (Double).

- To create a solid fill, set the *Hatch Type* to **Solid** and the *Hatch Color* to **ByLayer** or a color.

- To create a gradient fill, set the *Hatch Type* to **Gradient** and set the colors for *Gradient Color 1* and *Gradient Color 2*.

Hatch Color

Use this option to set the color of the hatch. You can select a specific color, use the current color, or set the color to **ByLayer**, where the color of the hatch is controlled by the color of the layer.

Background Color

Use this option to add a background color to the hatch. For example, if you have two hatches of the same pattern, you can set a different background color for each one.

Hatch Transparency

Use this option to control the level of transparency for the hatch. This is useful for displaying objects below the hatch, such as furniture, walls, or annotations. You can use the slider or enter the value, as shown in Figure 18–9. You can also expand

▨ ▾ (Transparency Values) and set the transparency to **ByLayer Transparency** or **ByBlock Transparency**.

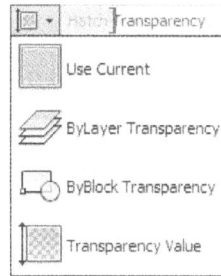

Figure 18–9

Hatch Angle

The *Hatch Angle* sets the rotation angle of the hatch pattern. An angle of **0** creates the pattern at its original angle. Increase the value to get an angled pattern, as shown in Figure 18–10.

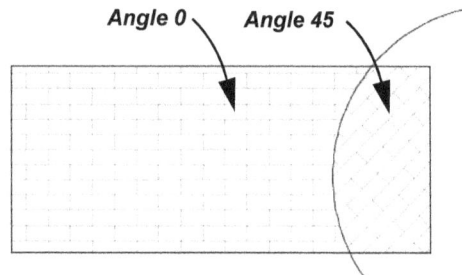

Figure 18–10

Hatch Pattern Scale

The *Hatch Pattern Scale* controls the space between the lines in the pattern (which are normally based on the drawing's plot scale factor). Enter the scale required to correctly display the hatch pattern so that its lines and spaces display clearly.

- If you are working in a viewport and using Annotative scaling, you should expand the Properties panel and click

  (Relative to Paper Space). It calculates the scale based on the viewport scale. **Annotative** maintains the hatch scale relative to Paper Space if the viewport scale is changed.

Hatch Layer Override

You can set the layer on which the hatch is placed, overriding the current layer.

- You can use the **HPLAYER** system variable to set the layer on which the hatch is placed, overriding the current layer.

- If the layer you want to use does not exist in the drawing, type the new layer name. The next time you start the **Hatch** command, the layer is created and the hatch is placed on it.

Hatch Origin

The hatch origin determines how the hatch fits into the selected area. If you are using a pattern (such as brick hatching), the hatch origin enables you to start and end the pattern appropriately inside the boundary.

- Click ⊞ (Set Origin), select the point at which the pattern is going to start, and then select an internal point to set the boundary. You can use the preset options to set the origin to the **Bottom Left**, **Bottom Right**, **Top Left**, **Top Right**, or **Center**, as shown in Figure 18–11.

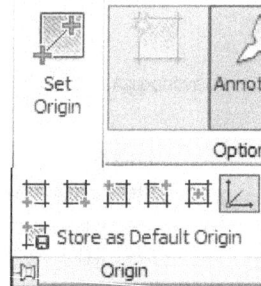

Figure 18–11

- You can select **Use Current Origin** to return to the default origin point.

- You can select **Store as Default Origin** to save the current location as the default origin.

Hatch Options

You can set the hatch to be **Annotative**, so that it uses the annotative scale of the viewport in which it displays, as shown in Figure 18–12.

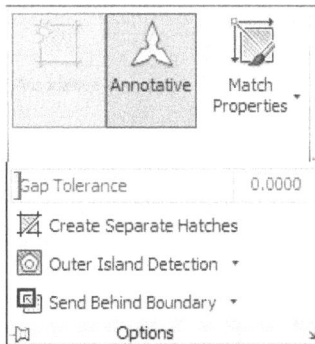

Figure 18–12

- Hatches are typically set to **Associative** (the default if **Annotative** is selected). This means that the hatch is associated with the boundary. If the boundary is changed (i.e., moved, stretched, etc.), the hatch pattern area changes to fill the new boundary.

- Click ⬚ (Create Separate Hatches) if you want each boundary selected during one command to be created as individual hatches. Otherwise, they are all one hatch object no matter how many boundaries you select.

- ⬚ (Send Behind Boundary) controls whether the hatch is behind or in front of overlapping objects. You can specify the relationship for any overlapping objects or just the boundary.

- Click ⬚ (Match Properties) to select an existing hatch object in the drawing and use it to hatch other areas.

- ⬚ (Island Detection) sets whether or not the areas in overlapping or complex objects are hatched. Expand the drop-down list and select the required type of detection, as shown in Figure 18–13.

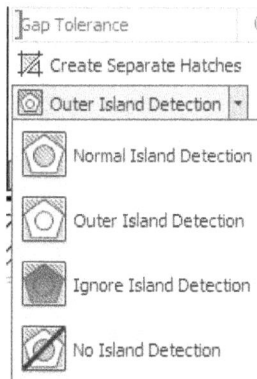

Figure 18–13

- **Gap Tolerance** sets the largest gap permitted in the boundary of an area to be hatched. If set to **0** (the default), no gaps are permitted.

Hint: Finding the Area of a Hatch

The *Area* of a hatch displays in the Properties palette, as shown in Figure 18–14. It can be used as a quick way to find the area of an object with holes.

Figure 18–14

If more than one hatch is selected, it provides the cumulative area. For example, you might want to know the area of several rooms in a building. Hatch the rooms, select the hatches, and note the *Cumulative Area* in the Properties palette, as shown in Figure 18–15.

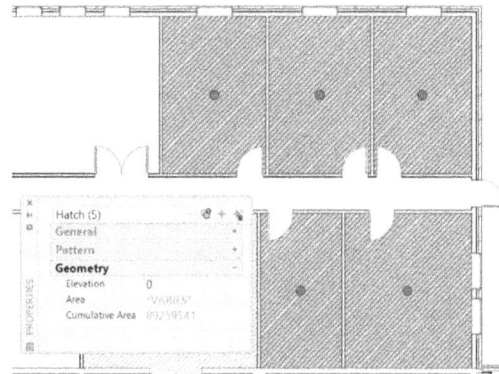

Figure 18–15

18.2 Editing Hatches

Instead of erasing and reapplying hatching to change the pattern or scale, you can adjust the hatch using:

- The *Hatch Editor* contextual tab in the ribbon.

- The **Edit Hatch** command.

- Grips.

You can change the hatch pattern, scale, or angle, and add or remove areas from the existing hatch boundary.

When you modify the boundaries of associative hatches, the hatch automatically updates, as shown in Figure 18–16.

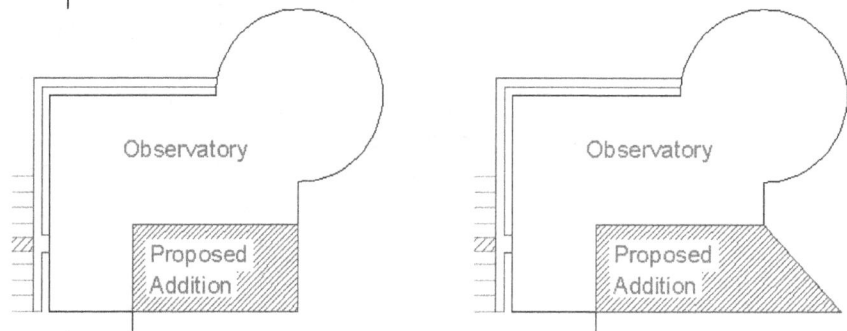

Figure 18–16

Hatch Editor Tab

To edit an existing hatch, select a hatch by clicking on it to display the *Hatch Editor* contextual tab.

How To: Edit a Hatch Using the *Hatch Editor* Tab

1. Select the hatch to be modified.
2. In the *Hatch Editor* contextual tab, change the properties as required.
   - The options in this contextual tab are the same as those available for placing the hatch.

3. If required, modify the boundaries using ⊞ (Recreate Boundary) or ⊠ (Display Boundary Objects).

▨	**Recreate Boundary:** Creates a new object around the hatch area, and associates the hatch with the new object separate from the original boundary.
▨	**Display Boundary Objects:** Displays the selected objects and their boundary with grips. Modifying the grips changes both the boundary and the hatch if the hatch is associative. If the hatch is not associative, different grips display and you can modify the hatch separately from the original boundary.

4. Press <Enter> to apply the changes.

Edit Hatch Command

To open the Hatch Edit dialog box (shown in Figure 18–17), in the *Home* tab>expanded Modify panel, click ▨ (Edit Hatch). The dialog box contains tools that are similar to the Hatch Editor.

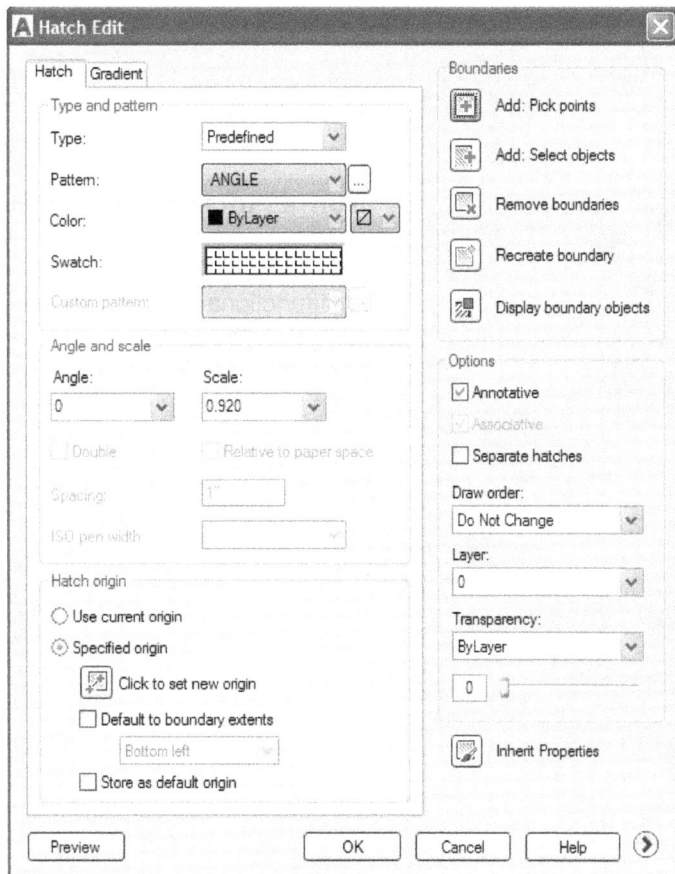

Figure 18–17

Grip Editing Hatch Boundaries

When associative hatches are selected, a single grip displays at the centroid of the hatch, as shown on the left in Figure 18–18. However, non-associative hatch boundaries display grips at each of their corners and at the midpoint of the edges, as shown on the right in Figure 18–18.

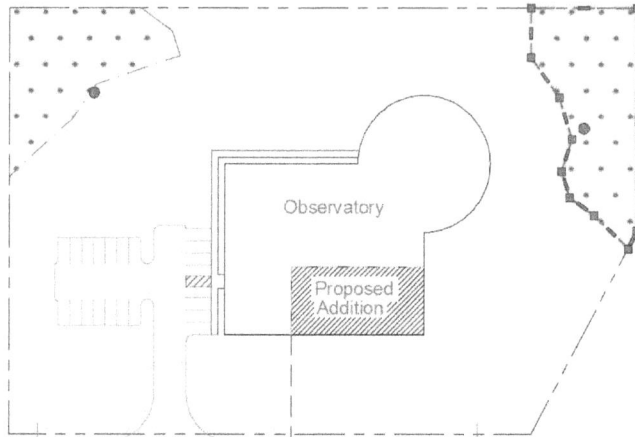

Figure 18–18

Non-associative Hatch Boundaries

Add Vertex: To add a vertex to the boundary, hover over a multifunctional edge grip at the required location and select **Add Vertex** in the dynamic list, as shown in Figure 18–19. Drag and place the new vertex point.

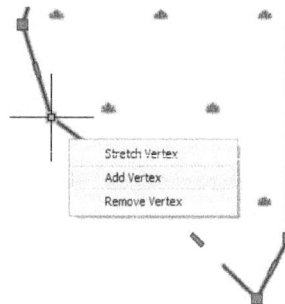

Figure 18–19

Convert to Arc: To change an edge to an arc, hover over the multifunctional edge grip and select the **Convert to Arc** option, as shown in Figure 18–20. Drag and place the midpoint of the arc.

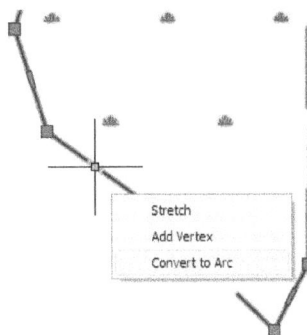

Figure 18–20

Arc Grip Options: When you hover over a multifunctional arc grip, the options enable you to stretch it, add a vertex, or convert the arc to a line.

Remove Vertex: To delete a vertex, hover over the multifunctional vertex grip, and select the **Remove Vertex** option.

Associative Hatch Boundaries

When you are editing associative hatches, you can use one multifunctional grip to access several options (**Stretch**, **Origin Point**, **Hatch Angle**, and **Hatch Scale**) using the dynamic list, as shown in Figure 18–21.

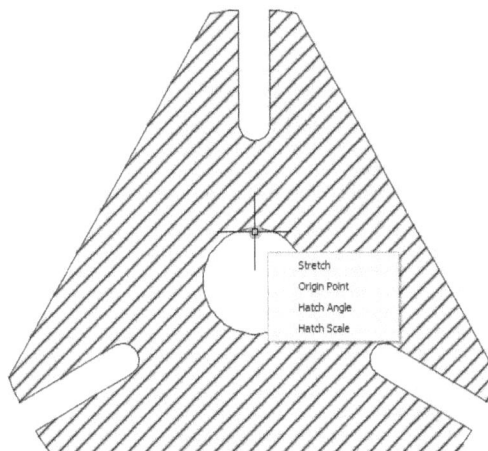

Figure 18–21

Hover the cursor over the grip and select one of the following options:

Stretch	Moves the entire hatch and makes it non-associative. This is the default when you select the grip.
Origin Point	Enables you to select a new point for the origin of the hatch.
Hatch Angle	Enables you to specify an angle at the Command Line or select a point to define the angle.
Hatch Scale	Enables you to specify a scale at the Command Line or select a point to define the scale.

Practice 18a

Hatching Using the Tool Palettes

Practice Objective

- Add hatching to a floor plan.

Estimated time for completion: 5 minutes

In this practice, you will add hatches to a floor plan using the Tool Palettes, as shown in Figure 18–22.

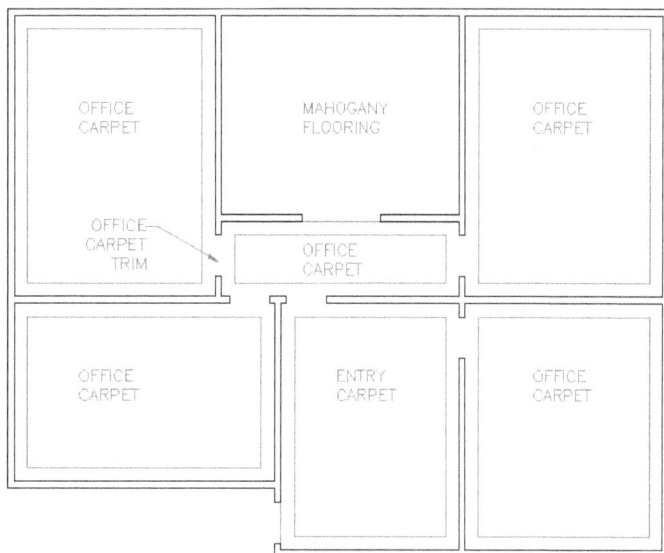

Figure 18–22

1. Open **Law Office-AM.dwg** from your practice files folder.

2. Toggle off the layer **A-Door**. Toggle on the layer **A-Flor**, and make it active.

3. Open Tool Palettes (*View* tab>Palettes panel) if it is not already open.

*Click on the area just below the bottom tab and select **Hatches and Fills**.*

4. In Tool Palettes, in the *Hatches and Fills* tab, click on any of the solid colors. Click inside one of the *Office Carpet* areas to fill it with the solid hatch color.

5. Similarly, use the same solid color to fill all of the Office Carpet areas.

6. Use different solid colors for the Office Carpet Trim, Entry Carpet, and Mahogany Flooring.

7. Use the Properties palette to find the areas of the Office Carpet Trim and the Mahogany Flooring. Select the hatch, and open the Properties palette. The Area displays in the Geometry section, as shown for Mahogany Flooring in Figure 18–23.

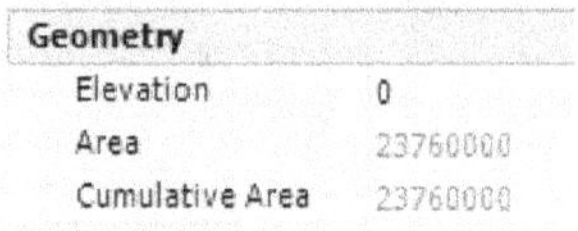

Geometry	
Elevation	0
Area	23760000
Cumulative Area	23760000

Figure 18–23

8. Save and close the drawing.

Practice 18b

Estimated time for completion: 5 minutes

Hatching (Mechanical)

Practice Objectives

- Apply hatching to a section and modify it.
- Create a hatch with an annotative scale.

In this practice, you will apply hatching to a section and then modify it using the *Hatch Creation* contextual tab. You will also create a hatch with an annotative scale, as shown in Figure 18–24.

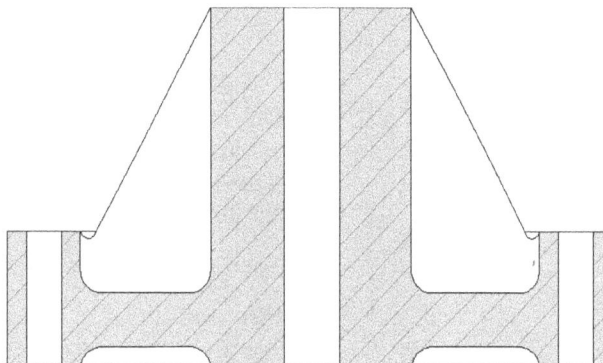

Figure 18–24

Task 1 - Apply a hatch.

1. Open **Wheel-Section-M.dwg** from your practice files folder.

2. Set the current layer to **Hatching**.

3. In the *Home* tab>Draw panel, click ⬚ ▾ (Hatch).

4. In the *Hatch Creation* contextual tab>Properties panel, verify the following:
   - *Hatch Type* is set to **Pattern**.
   - *Scale* is set to **1**.
   - *Angle* is set to **0**.

5. In the Pattern panel, verify that *Hatch Pattern* is set to **ANSI31**.

6. In the Options panel, select **Annotative**. In the expanded Options panel, verify that ⬚ (Create Separate Hatches) is NOT selected.

7. In the Boundaries panel, click ⊞ (Pick Points). Select points inside the areas of the section view that display hatching. as shown in Figure 18–25.

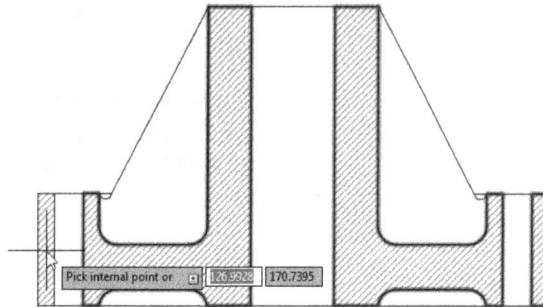

Figure 18–25

8. The hatch pattern lines are very close together. Change the *Scale* to **2**. Press <Enter> to apply the hatching. The hatch updates in the drawing.

9. Press <Esc> to exit the hatching selection.

10. Hover the cursor over the hatching and note that it is a single object.

Task 2 - Edit a hatch pattern.

---

1. Select the hatching. The *Hatch Editor* contextual tab opens.

2. Set the *Scale* to **4** and click ✕ (Close Hatch Editor).

3. Use the **Move** command to move each of the two vertical lines near the center of the part, **13** units closer to the center. The hatch pattern automatically adjusts, as shown in Figure 18–26.

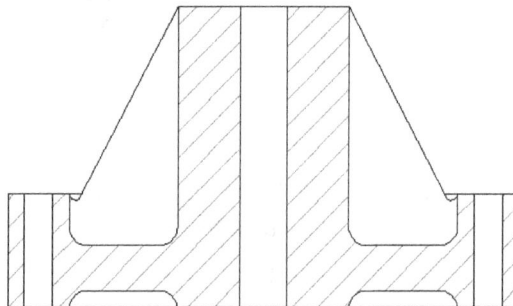

Figure 18–26

4. Save the drawing.

Task 3 - Change the background color, origin, and transparency of the hatch.

1. While not in a command, select the hatch object. The grip and the *Hatch Editor* contextual tab display.

2. Change the *Background Color* to **Cyan,** as shown in Figure 18–27.

3. Set the *Hatch Angle* value to **15,** as shown in Figure 18–27.

4. Set the *Hatch Transparency* value to **6,** as shown in Figure 18–27.

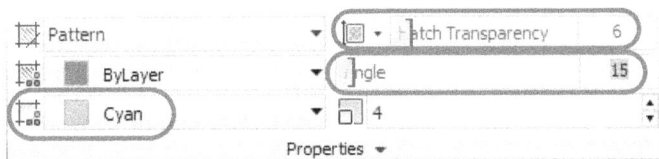

Figure 18–27

5. Click ✕ (Close Hatch Editor).

Task 4 - Hatch with the Annotative Scale (optional).

1. Switch to the **ISO A3** layout. It contains two viewports that have been set to different scales. If **Annotative** was selected in the *Hatch Creation* contextual tab, hatching is not displayed in either viewport because the hatch in Model Space was set to 1:1.

2. Make the bottom the viewport active.

3. Start the **Hatch** command.

4. Use the **ANSI31** pattern and set the *Scale* to **1.**

5. In the expanded Properties panel, select **Relative to Paper Space**. In the Options panel, verify that **Annotative** is selected.

6. Select the points for hatching the appropriate areas and accept the hatch. No hatch displays in the top viewport.

7. With the bottom viewport still active, in the Status Bar, note that the scale is **1:2**.

8. Click in the top viewport to make it active. In the Status Bar, note that the scale is **1:4**.

9. Activate the bottom viewport. Select the hatch, right-click and then select **Properties**.

10. With the hatch still selected, in the Properties palette, in the *Pattern* area, click the button to the right of *Annotative scale*, as shown in Figure 18–28.

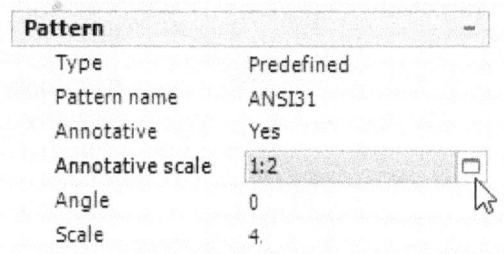

Figure 18–28

11. In the Annotation Object Scale dialog box, click **Add**.

12. In the Add Scales to Object dialog box, select the **1:4** scale from the list.

13. Click **OK** in both the dialog boxes. The hatch displays in the top viewport automatically, as shown in Figure 18–29.

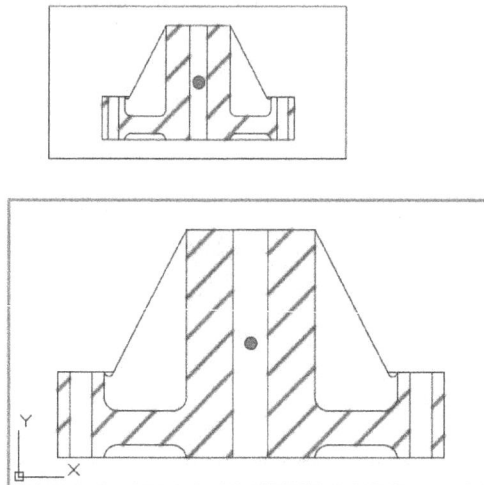

Figure 18–29

14. Press <Esc> to clear the hatch selection.

15. Save and close the drawing.

Practice 18c

Hatching (Architectural)

Practice Objective

Estimated time for completion: 5 minutes

- Apply hatching to a floor plan.

In this practice, you will apply hatching to a floor plan using the **Hatch** command, as shown in Figure 18–30.

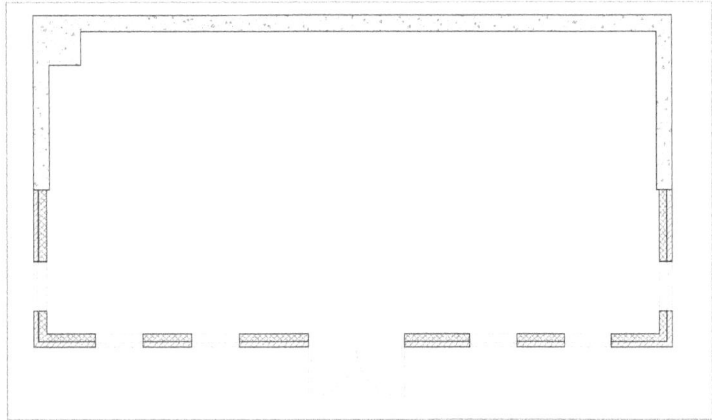

Figure 18–30

1. Open **Basement-AM.dwg** from your practice files folder.

2. Set the layer to **Hatching**.

3. Switch to the **ISO A1** layout tab. This layout has two viewports at different scales.

4. Double-click in the larger viewport to make it active.

5. Start the **Hatch** command. Set the *Hatch type* to **Pattern** and the *Pattern* to **AR-CONC** (used to show poured concrete). Set the *Scale* to **40** and leave the *Angle* at **0**.

6. Click ⊞ (Pick Points). At the *Pick internal point:* prompt, select a point inside the back wall.

7. Click ✕ (Close Hatch Creation) to close the *Hatch Creation* contextual tab.

8. Start the **Hatch** command again. Set the *Hatch Pattern* to **ANSI37** (a crosshatch that symbolizes a concrete block). Set the *Scale* to **40**. In the expanded Properties panel, select **Relative to Paper Space**. In the Options panel, select **Annotative**. Use ⊞ (Pick Points) to select internal points on the inside portions of the other walls, as shown in Figure 18–31. Zoom in as required to accurately select the areas to hatch. Ensure that the *Scale* is still at **40**. If it is not, reset it to **40**.

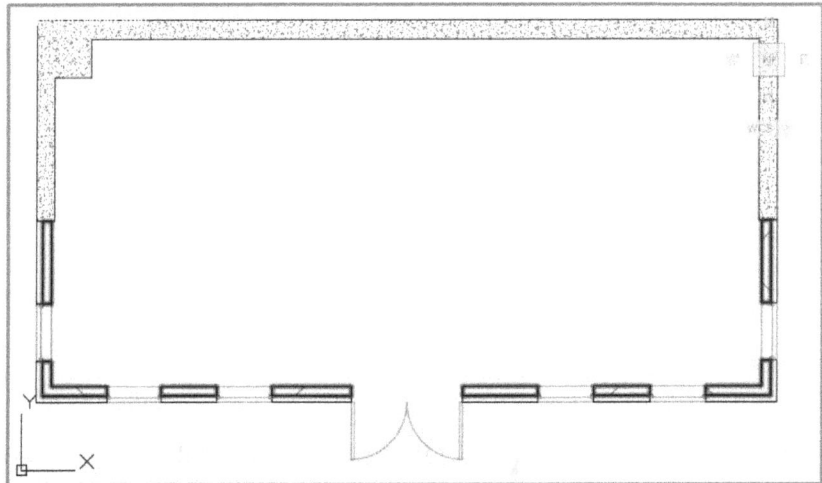

Figure 18–31

9. Press <Enter> to apply the hatch. If the hatch does not display correctly (i.e., as a cross hatch), you might have to select it and reset the *Scale* to **40** in the *Hatch Editor* contextual tab. You might also need to click on **Relative to Paper Space** again and reset the scale to **40** until you get the correct crosshatch pattern. Press <Esc> to clear the hatch selection.

If the hatch displays at the wrong scale, select the hatch and reset the Scale to 40 in the Hatch Editor contextual tab.

10. Hatch the outside portions of the walls, as shown in Figure 18–30, using the *Hatch pattern* **ANSI31** (a hatch that symbolizes brick). Use a *Scale* of **40**, and select **Relative to Paper Space** and **Annotative**.

11. Click ✕ (Close Hatch Creation) to close the *Hatch Creation* contextual tab.

12. Zoom out to display both viewports. The first hatch pattern that you applied displays in both viewports, while the other two hatch patterns only display in the larger viewport. This is because they are annotative and only display in a viewport matching the scale 1:20.

13. Hover the cursor over the **ANSI37** hatch. (Annotative) displays next to the cursor, indicating that it is annotative. Hover the cursor over the **AR-CONC** hatch. An icon is not displayed because it is not annotative.

14. Save and close the drawing.

Chapter Review Questions

1. In the *Hatch Creation* contextual tab, which tool do you use to specify an area of the drawing that you want to hatch?

   a. **Inherit Properties**

   b. **Island Detection**

   c. **Remove Islands**

   d. **Pick Points**

2. To hatch an area in a drawing, it must be...

   a. On the layer named **Hatch**.

   b. A closed area.

   c. A single polyline.

   d. Set to **Annotative**.

3. Increasing the *Hatch Angle* value creates an angled hatch pattern.

   a. True

   b. False

4. How do you find the area of a Hatch?

   a. Use the **Measure** command.

   b. Use the **Area** command.

   c. Select the hatch to display its area in the Properties palette.

   d. Use the **Distance** command.

5. What happens when an associative hatch is selected?

   a. Grips display at each of the boundary corners.

   b. Grips display at the midpoints of the boundary edges.

   c. Grips display at the centroid of the hatch and the midpoints of the boundary edges.

   d. A single grip displays at the centroid of the hatch.

6. Which option do you use to create new vertices on non-associative hatch boundaries?

   a. Remove vertex

   b. Convert to arc

   c. Add vertex

   d. New vertex

Command Summary

Button	Command	Location
	Edit Hatch	• **Ribbon:** *Home* tab>expanded Modify panel • **Select:** (*a hatch object*) • **Shortcut Menu:** (*on a hatch object*) Hatch Edit... • **Command Prompt:** hatchedit
	Hatch	• **Ribbon:** *Home* tab>Draw panel • **Command Prompt:** hatch or H

Adding Dimensions

In this chapter you learn how to place linear, aligned, radial, and angular dimensions. You learn to add continuous and baseline dimensions. You also learn to edit dimensions, select a dimension style, and to place leaders.

Learning Objectives in this Chapter

- Create dimensions using various commands.
- Add linear, aligned, angular, and radial dimensions to a drawing.
- Edit dimensions grips, text, and placement location of existing dimensions.
- Annotate a drawing to include additional text.

19.1 Dimensioning Concepts

The AutoCAD® dimensioning commands create dimensions based on points that you specify or by selecting the object for dimensioning. The AutoCAD software automatically draws the dimension with the appropriate extension lines, arrowheads, dimension lines, and text, as shown in Figure 19–1.

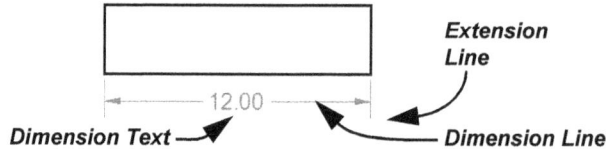

Figure 19–1

- Dimensions recalculate automatically when the objects that they refer to are modified. For example, when you stretch a wall 600mm to the right, the associated dimensions update.

As you prepare to dimension, you should:

- Set up a viewport in a layout that displays the part of the model that you want to dimension. You should set the Viewport Scale before you start dimensioning.

- Select the layer for dimensioning.

- Select a Dimension Style to be used for dimensioning.

- Use the *Annotate* tab>Dimensions panel, as shown in Figure 19–2, to access the dimensioning commands and set up the layer and dimension style.

Lock the viewport to make it easier to zoom around the drawing without changing the scale by mistake.

Dimension styles can be annotative.

Some dimensioning commands can also be accessed in the Home tab>Annotation panel.

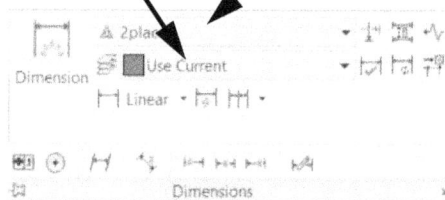

Figure 19–2

General Dimensioning

Dimensions can be added using a general dimension command or using commands specific to the type of dimension being added. The general dimension command automatically determines the type of dimension required based on the object or point selected.

- You can use a single **Dimension** command to add various dimensions, such as linear (horizontal, vertical), aligned, angular, radial etc. After placing a required dimension, the **Dimension** command remains active, enabling you to add other dimensions as required, without re-launching the command.

How To: Add Dimensions

Instead of selecting an object for dimension, you can use object snaps to snap to points to be dimensioned.

1. In the *Annotate* tab>Dimensions panel, click ⬚ (Dimension) or in the *Home* tab>Annotation panel, click ⬚ (Dimension).
2. Hover the cursor on the object that you want to dimension. Depending on the object that touches the cursor, a preview of a relevant dimension displays, as shown in Figure 19–3.

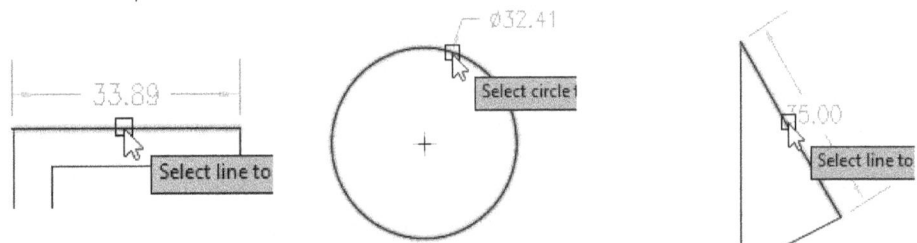

Figure 19–3

3. If the preview dimension is the correct one, click to save the dimension.
4. Drag the cursor to the location where you want the dimension to be located. Click to place the dimension or select an option from the Command Line (or use the <Down Arrow> menu).
5. Dimension another object in the drawing or press <Esc> to exit the command.

19.2 Adding Linear Dimensions

Linear dimensions measure a distance from one point to another, as shown in Figure 19–4.

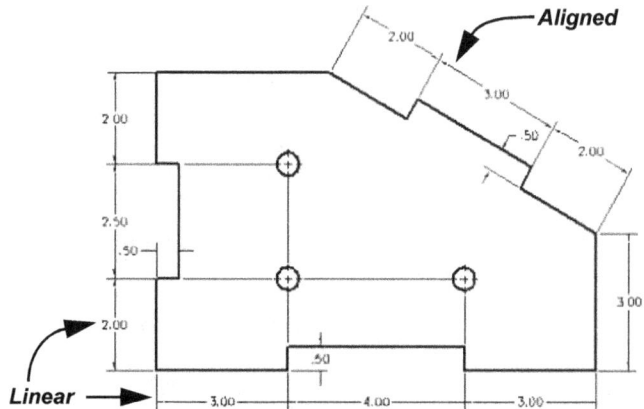

Figure 19–4

Individual Linear Dimensions

Linear dimensions can be horizontal or vertical, as shown in Figure 19–4. Aligned dimensions are also linear dimensions, however, they measure the linear distance parallel to the selected line or the selected points. The dimension line is placed parallel to the line between the points, as shown in Figure 19–4.

- The AutoCAD software determines the linear orientation (horizontal, vertical, or aligned) based on the selected object or where you select the point for the dimension line location.

How To: Add Linear and Aligned Dimensions

1. In the *Annotate* tab>Dimensions panel or the *Home* tab> Annotation panel, click [icon] (Dimension).
2. Select a line in the drawing.
3. Select a point to place the dimension line.

or

1. In the *Annotate* tab>Dimensions panel or the *Home* tab> Annotation panel, click [icon] (Dimension).
2. Select a point for the first extension line origin.
3. Select a point for the second extension line origin.
4. Select a point to place the dimension line.

Use Object Snaps to select the exact points for the extension line origins.

Hint: Oblique Extension Lines

If you want the extension lines of a linear dimension to be at an angle, you can click ⊢⊣ (Oblique) in the *Annotate* tab> expanded Dimensions panel, to angle the lines.

Adding a Break in a Linear or Aligned Dimension

In some cases, you need to have a dimension with a break because the length of the dimension is too long to display on a sheet, as shown in Figure 19–5.

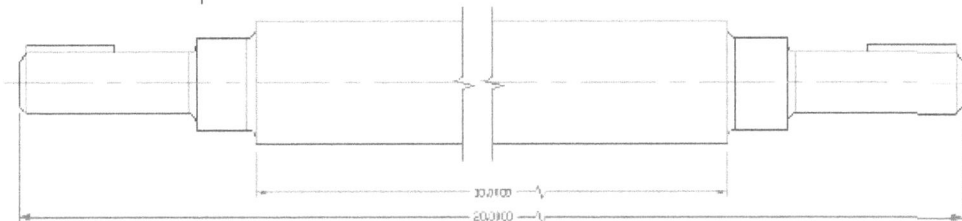

Figure 19–5

How To: Create a Jogged Linear Dimension

1. In the *Annotate* tab>Dimensions panel, click ⁺⋀ (Dimjogline).
2. Select the dimension to which you want to add the jog.
3. Specify the jog location along the dimension or press <Enter> to accept the default location.

- To remove a jog line, use the command's **Remove** option.

Multiple Linear Dimensions

After you have placed a linear, aligned, or angular dimension, you can use that dimension as the beginning of a series of related dimensions by clicking ⊢⊢⊢ (Continue) or ⊢⊣ (Baseline), as shown in Figure 19–6.

These commands can be used with Linear, Aligned, or Angular dimensions.

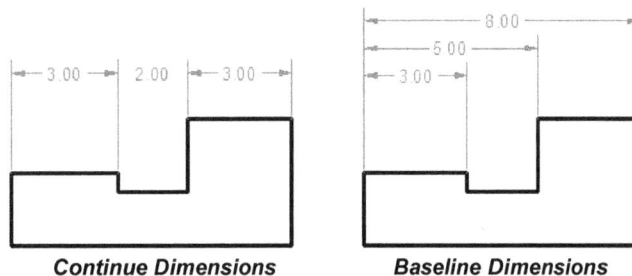

Continue Dimensions   **Baseline Dimensions**

Figure 19–6

Continue dimensions use the last extension line placed as the first extension line for the next dimension. The dimension line remains at the same distance from the object.

Baseline dimensions use the first extension line as the base for all other dimensions. As you select additional extension line points, the new dimension is placed over the previous one. The distance between the dimension lines is set by the dimension style.

How To: Add Continue and Baseline Dimensions

1. Place a linear or aligned dimension.
2. In the *Annotate* tab>Dimensions panel, click ⊓⊓⊓ (Continue) or ⊢→ (Baseline).
3. Select a point for the second extension line origin. The first extension line origin is automatically assumed to be from the last dimension you placed.
4. Continue selecting points for additional extension line origins.
5. Press <Enter> twice to finish the command.

- By default, the AutoCAD software uses the last dimension placed as the starting dimension. Use the **Select** option to select a different dimension to be referenced.

Quick Dimensioning

In some cases, you can place all of your dimensions along one edge of an object using one command, regardless of whether it is **Linear**, **Aligned**, **Baseline**, or **Continue**. As shown in Figure 19–7, the outside lines of the walls were selected using the **Quick Dimension** command and dimensioned at the same time.

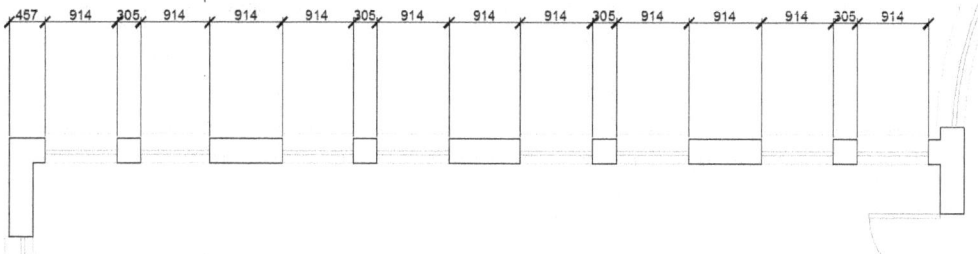

Figure 19–7

How To: Add Quick Dimensions

Quick Dimension does not enable you to place a type of dimension that is not appropriate for the selection. For example, if you select a line, you cannot place a Radius or Diameter dimension on that line.

1. In the *Annotate* tab>Dimensions panel, click ⊞ (Quick Dimension).
2. Select the objects that you want to dimension. When you have finished selecting objects, press <Enter>.
3. Specify the dimension line position.

- By default, the AutoCAD software creates continuous dimensions if you select linear objects or more than one object.

- You can switch between a number of other types of dimensions, including **Staggered**, **Baseline**, and **Ordinate**, in the Command Prompt, shortcut menu, or dynamic input drop-down list.

- Baseline and Ordinate dimensions start from a common point. You can set that point using the **datumPoint** option.

- There is also an **Edit** option that enables you to add or remove points. However, it is easier to do this using other commands.

Practice 19a | Adding Linear Dimensions (Architectural)

Practice Objective

Estimated time for completion: 10 minutes

- Add dimensions using various dimensioning techniques.

In this practice, you will start to add dimensions using the general **Dimension** command. You will then dimension different portions of the architectural drawing using **Quick**, **Baseline**, and **Continue** dimensions, as shown in Figure 19–8.

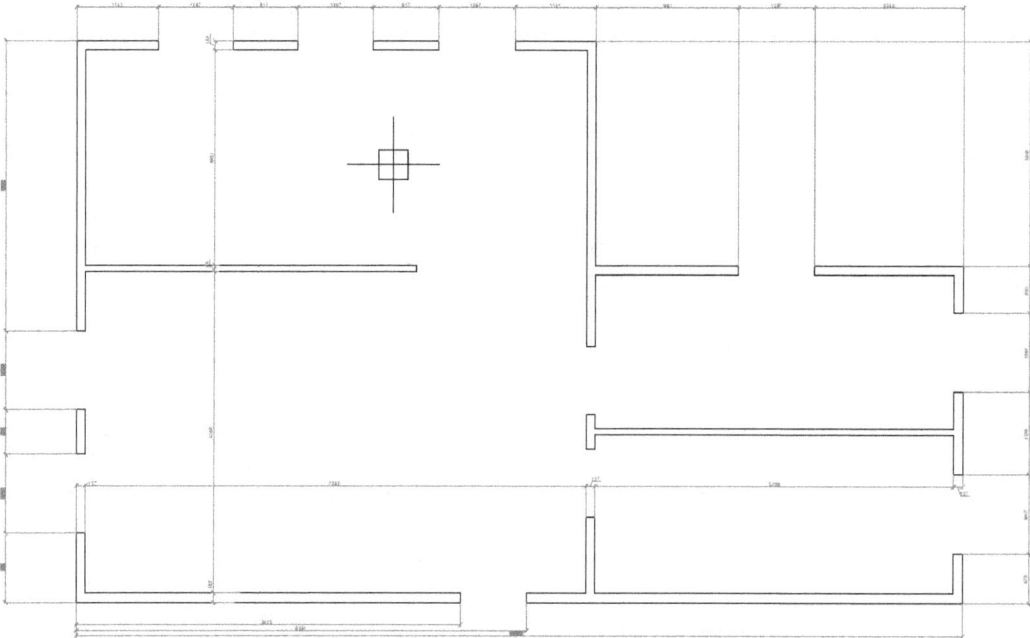

Figure 19–8

1. Open **Dimensioned Plan-AM.dwg** from your practice files folder.

2. Switch to the **ISO A1** layout. Make the existing viewport active and zoom extents.

3. In the Status Bar, set the *Viewport Scale* to **1:30** and lock the viewport.

4. Freeze the layers **Doors** and **Windows** to make it easier to select only the walls to be dimensioned.

5. In the *Annotate* tab>Dimensions panel, select the layer **Dimensions** in the drop-down list, as shown in Figure 19–9, to make it the active dimensioning layer. Also, set the current *Dimension Style* to **Architectural-MM**, as shown in Figure 19–9. This is an annotative style.

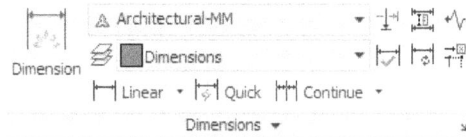

Figure 19–9

6. Verify that **Object Snap** is toggled off.

7. While still active in the viewport, in the *Annotate* tab> Dimensions panel, click ⊡ (Dimension). Hover the cursor on the top left wall (outer line), as shown in Figure 19–10.

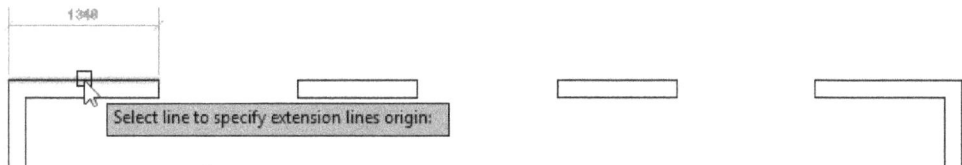

Figure 19–10

8. Select the object, drag the cursor up and click to place the dimension outside the building.

9. In the Status Bar, toggle on **Object Snap** and verify that **Endpoint** object snap is selected.

10. Start the **Continue** command. Note that the cursor is attached with the last dimension you placed. Select the left endpoint of the second wall, as shown in Figure 19–11.

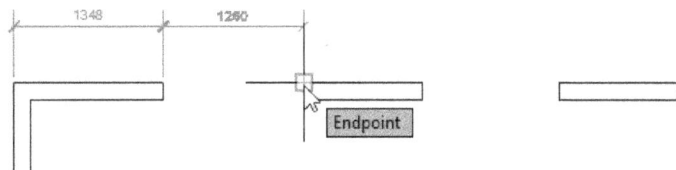

Figure 19–11

The order of selection of points determines the start point of the baseline.

11. Select the rest of the dimension points along the same wall. Press <Enter> twice to complete the command.

12. Start the **Dimension** command. Select the two endpoints (first left and then right) of the bottom left wall. Place the dimension along the bottom side of the building.

13. Start the **Baseline** command and note that the cursor dimension is attached to the left extension line of the dimension.

14. Select the right endpoint of the left side bottom wall to place the dimension.

15. Select the left endpoint of the right side bottom wall to place the third dimension. Press <Enter> twice to complete the command.

16. Start the **Quick Dimension** command.

17. Add dimensions to the left side of the building by selecting three outside wall objects, pressing <Enter>, and then clicking to place the dimensions.

18. Add dimensions to the right exterior of the building, and the interior.

19. Save and close the drawing.

Practice 19b

Adding Linear Dimensions (Mechanical)

Practice Objective

Estimated time for completion: 5 minutes

- Add linear dimensions to a mechanical drawing.

In this practice, you will add Linear and Aligned dimensions to a mechanical drawing.

Task 1 - Add Linear dimensions.

1. Open **Bearing Dimensions-M.dwg** from the practice files folder.

2. Switch to the **ISO A2** layout. Create two viewports (*Layout* tab>Layout Viewports panel>**Rectangular**). If a single viewport already exists, resize it to be used as one and make room for the second viewport. Verify that both viewports are in the layer **Viewports**. In both the viewports, leave empty space as shown in Figure 19–12 for adding the dimensions.

3. Zoom to display the views similar to those shown in Figure 19–12. Set the *scales* to **1:1** (left viewport) and **2:1** (right viewport). Lock the viewports.

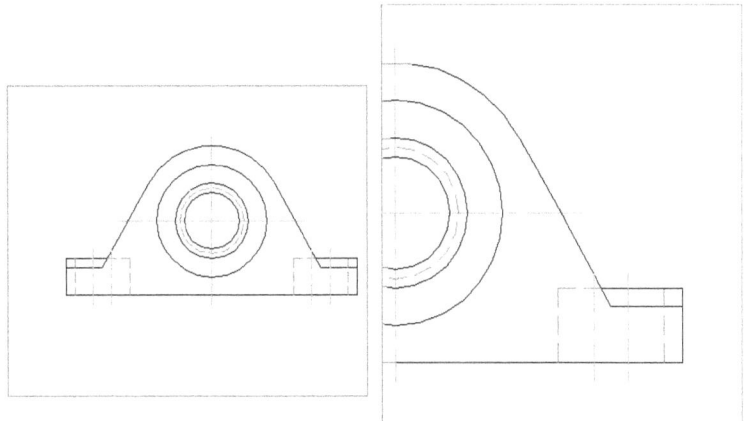

Figure 19–12

4. Make the **1:1** viewport active.

5. Change the active dimension layer to **Dimensions** (*Annotate* tab>Dimensions panel, layer **Dimensions**), as shown in Figure 19–13.

6. Set the active *Dimension Style* to **2places**. This is an annotative style, as shown in Figure 19–13.

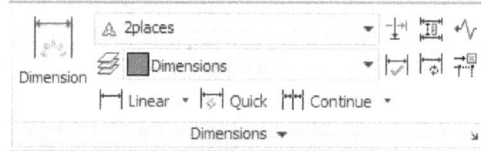

Figure 19–13

7. Start the **Dimension** command. Select the bottom left endpoint and then select the left endpoint of the green horizontal center line. Drag the cursor left and down until a vertical dimension displays, as shown on the right in Figure 19–14. Click to place the vertical dimension.

When you drag the cursor left, an aligned dimension might display. Drag the cursor downwards to force the display of a vertical dimension instead.

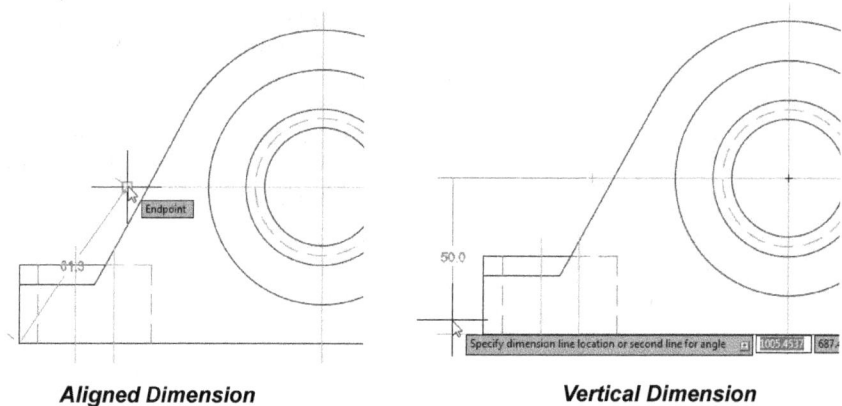

Aligned Dimension   **Vertical Dimension**

Figure 19–14

8. Still in the **Dimension** command, add the remaining vertical and horizontal dimensions shown in Figure 19–15. After placing all of the dimensions, exit the command.

*Start the **Dimension** command once, select the relevant endpoints and place the dimension for each vertical and horizontal dimension using the same command. You do not have to exit or relaunch the **Dimension** command after placing each dimension.*

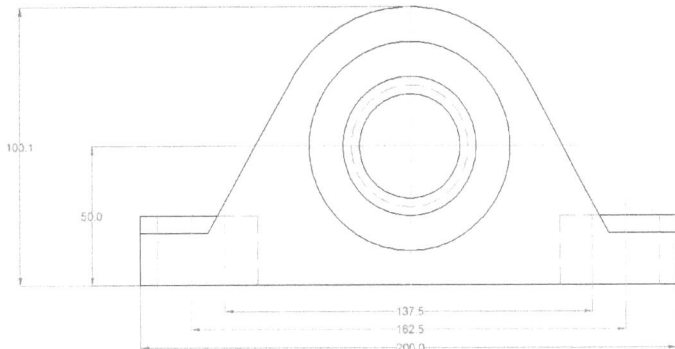

Figure 19–15

9. If required, unlock the viewport and pan to fit the dimensions into the available space. Be careful not to change the scale while the viewport is unlocked. Lock the viewport, if required, when you are finished.

Task 2 - Add aligned dimensions.

1. Make the **2:1** viewport active.

2. Start the **Dimension** command and add the vertical dimension shown in Figure 19–16.

3. Still in the **Dimension** command, select the two endpoints of the aligned line on the right side and add the aligned dimension as shown in Figure 19–16. Exit the command.

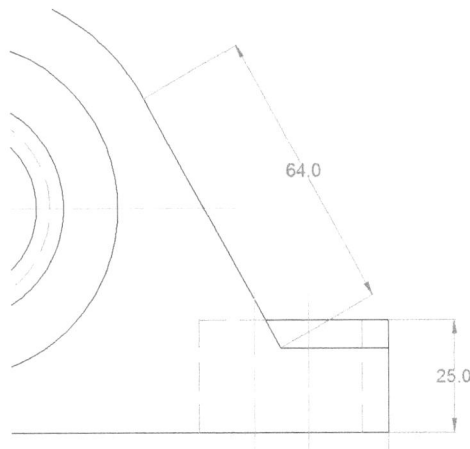

Figure 19–16

4. Save and close the drawing.

19.3 Adding Radial and Angular Dimensions

Other types of dimensions include Radius, Diameter, and Angular dimensions. Radius/Diameter dimensions for arcs and circles are placed with a leader from the object. You can also create a Jogged Radial dimension for arcs whose center point would be outside the drawing and for dimensioning the length around the curve of an arc. Angular dimensions measure the angle of an arc or the angle between two objects.

Radius and Diameter Dimensions

Radius is typically used on arcs, while **Diameter** is normally used on full circles, as shown in Figure 19–17. You can also add a radius dimension for a circle.

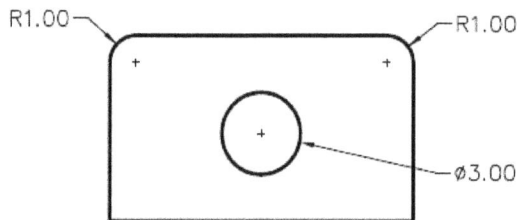

Figure 19–17

How To: Add Radius or Diameter Dimensions

1. In the *Annotate* tab>Dimensions panel, click ⬚ (Dimension). You can also use ◌ (Radius) or ◌ (Diameter) individually.
2. Select a point on the rim of an arc or circle. (You do not need to use Object Snaps for this.)
3. Select a location along the arc or circle for the dimension line text.

• When you are dimensioning a radius, you can place the dimension beyond the arc. The AutoCAD software creates an additional arc extension line as required.

• **Quick Dimension** creates a radial dimension by default if you select an arc or circular object. However, you can select **Diameter** in the options.

Associative Center Marks and Centerlines

There are two new tools which indicate the center of a arc or circle regardless of the objects' perspective. Both tools are on the *Annotate* tab>Centerlines panel.

- The 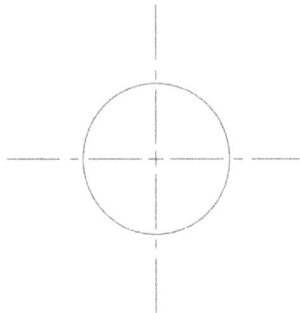 Center Mark tool adds an associate center mark at the center of selected circles, arcs, or polygonal arcs, as shown in Figure 19–18.

- The 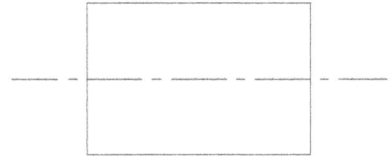 Centerline tool creates centerline geometry that is associated with selected lines and polylines, as shown in Figure 19–19.

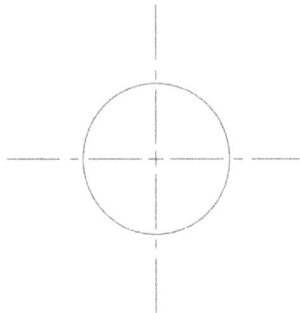

Figure 19–18	**Figure 19–19**

- If the associated objects move, the centerlines and center marks also update.

When a center mark or centerline is selected, grips display that enable you to control the extension line lengths, as shown in Figure 19–20. The appearance of center marks and centerlines is controlled by multiple system variables. Figure 19–20 and the table below lists the controlling variables and describes their effects.

CENTEREXE	• Sets the length of the extension line overshoots for centerlines and center marks.
CENTERMARKEXE	• Determines whether extension lines are created for center marks.
CENTERLAYER	• Sets the layer on which the centerlines and center marks are created.
CENTERLTYPE	• Sets the linetype used by centerlines and center marks.
CENTERLTSCALE	• Sets the linetype scale used by centerlines and center marks.
CENTERCROSSSIZE	• Sets the size of the central cross for center marks.
CENTERCROSSGAP	• Sets the extension line gap between the central cross and the extension lines in center marks.

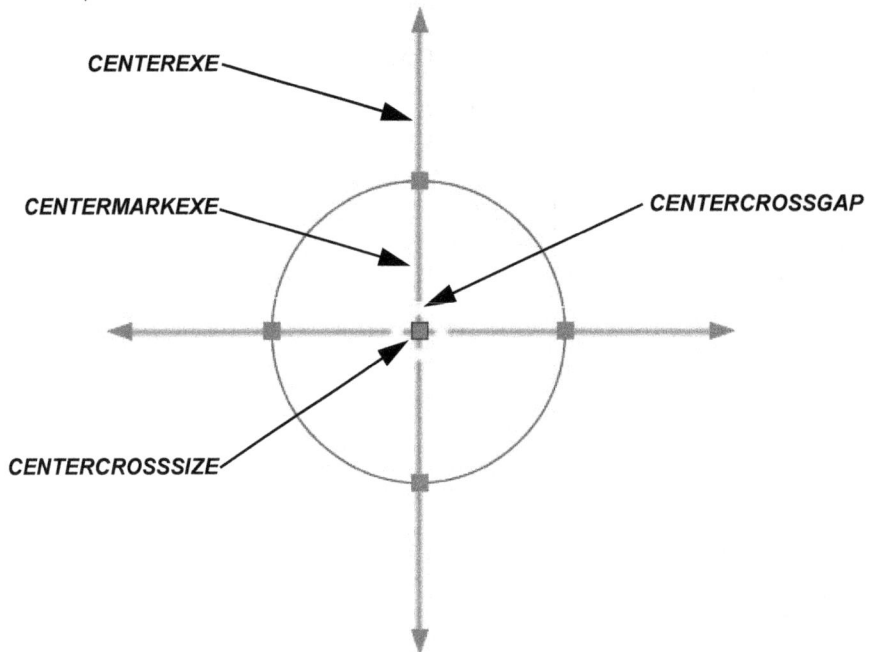

Figure 19–20

- The system variables must be set prior to creating the center mark or centerline for the variable to take effect.

- The Properties palette can be used to modify select attributes, as shown in Figure 19–21.

- A multi-functional grip menu offers additional controls, as shown in Figure 19–22.

Figure 19–21

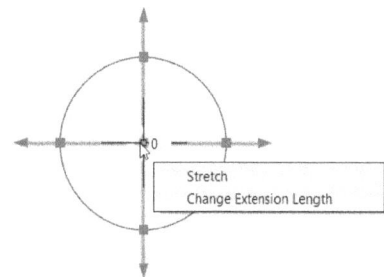

Figure 19–22

Jogged Radial Dimension

If the center mark of the circle or arc you are dimensioning does not display in the view, you can use the **Jogged** command to create an override for the center, as shown in Figure 19–23.

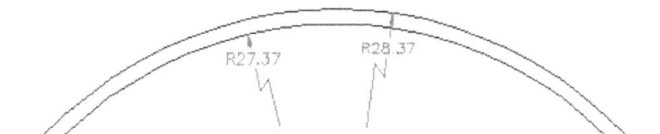

Figure 19–23

How To: Create a Jogged Radial Dimension

You can also find the ***Jogged*** *option (<Down Arrow>) in the* ***Dimension*** *command.*

1. In the *Annotate* tab>Dimensions panel, click 〽️ (Jogged).
2. Select the arc or circle that you want to dimension.
3. Specify a point for the center location override.
4. Specify the dimension line location. This also sets the location of the text.
5. Specify the jog location.

Arc Length Dimension

The arc length describes the distance from one end point of an arc to the other end point along the curve of the arc, as shown in Figure 19–24. This command can be used to dimension individual arcs or arcs that are parts of polylines.

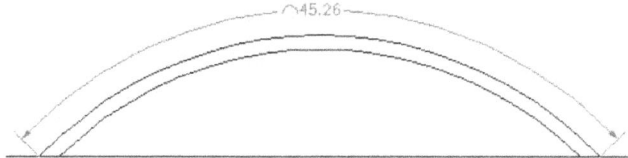

Figure 19–24

How To: Dimension the Arc Length

1. In the *Annotate* tab>Dimensions panel, click (Dimension).
2. Hover the cursor over the arc that you want to dimension.
3. Press <Down Arrow> and select **arc Length** from the list.
4. Specify the dimension location.

Angular Dimensions

You can add angular dimensions to lines, circles, and arcs and from a vertex, as shown in Figure 19–25.

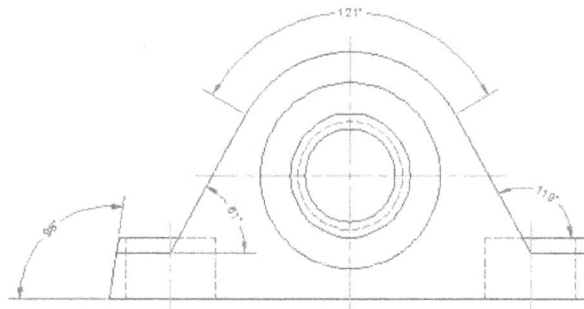

Figure 19–25

- When you are placing the Angular dimension, you can place it at any of the four quadrants of the angle.

How To: Add Angular Dimensions

1. In the *Annotate* tab>Dimensions panel, click ⬚ (Dimension).
2. Select a line, arc, or circle.
3. If you select a **line**, you are prompted to place a linear dimension. As you hover the cursor over another line, the preview changes to an angle dimension, as shown in Figure 19–26. Select the second line and specify the location of the dimension line.

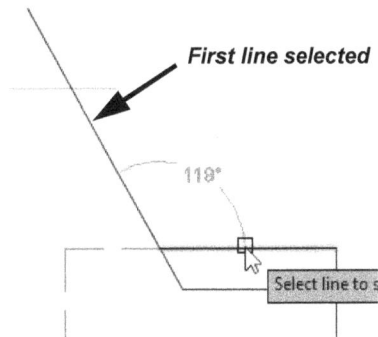

First line selected

119°

Select line to s

Figure 19–26

4. If you hover over an **arc**, by default you can place a radial dimension. Press <Down Arrow> and select **Angular**. Then, click the arc to select it. Click again to set the location of the dimension line.
5. If you hover over a **circle**, by default you can place a diameter dimension. Press <Down Arrow> and select **Angular**. Then click the circle to select it. Click to specify the first side of the angle. Click again to set the second side of the angle. Click one more time to set the location of the dimension line.

- You can also dimension an angle from a vertex. Before selecting an object, press <Enter> and use Object Snaps to select an angle vertex. Specify the first and second angle end points and place the dimension line.

Practice 19c | Adding Radial and Angular Dimensions (Architectural)

Practice Objective

- Add dimensions including radial and angular to a drawing.

Estimated time for completion: 5 minutes

In this practice, you will add Angular, Radial, Diameter, Aligned, and Arc Length dimensions, as shown in Figure 19–27.

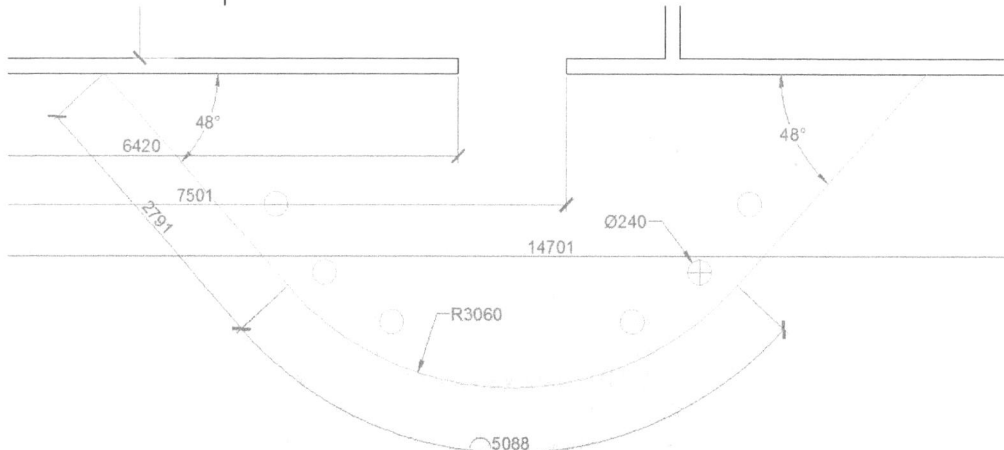

Figure 19–27

1. Open **Dimensioned Plan1-AM.dwg** from your practice files folder.

2. In the Layer Control, thaw the layer **Misc** to display the entrance portico.

3. Modify the viewport to display the entire entrance portico. If the viewport is locked, unlock it and pan the view until it fits. Zooming in and out of the view changes the viewport scale. Verify that the *Viewport Scale* is set at **1:30**. Re-lock the viewport when you are finished. You can also change the size of the viewport if it is too small.

4. Activate the viewport. Verify that the layer **Dimensions** is active.

5. In the *Annotate* tab>Dimensions panel, verify that the dimension layer is set to **Use Current**.

6. In the *Annotate* tab>Dimensions panel, click ⬚ (Dimension).

7. Hover the cursor over one of the six circled columns. If the cursor does not display the diameter dimension (while hovering over the circle), toggle off **Object Snap** in the Status Bar. Select the circle to accept the diameter dimension and click again to place it at the required location.

8. Still in the **Dimension** command, hover the cursor over the arc of the portico. It displays the radial dimension.

9. Press <Down Arrow> and select **arc Length**, as shown in Figure 19–28.

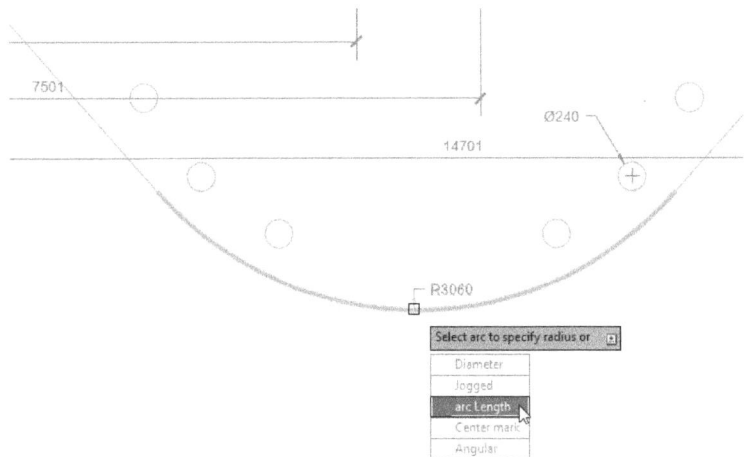

Figure 19–28

10. Select the arc and click again to place the dimension outside the arc, as shown in Figure 19–27.

11. Still in the **Dimension** command, hover the cursor over the arc of the portico again. Press <Down Arrow> and select **Radius**. Select the arc and click again to place the radius dimension on the inside of the portico arc.

12. Toggle on **Object Snap** in the Status Bar.

13. Still in the **Dimension** command, select the two endpoints of the angled line that joins the portico arc with the building wall. Add Aligned dimension to both the angled lines. (Use the end of the arc length dimension line to keep the connected dimensions in line.)

14. Still in the **Dimension** command, select one of the angled line again. Hover the cursor over the wall line that touches the selected angled line to display the angled dimension, as shown in Figure 19–29.

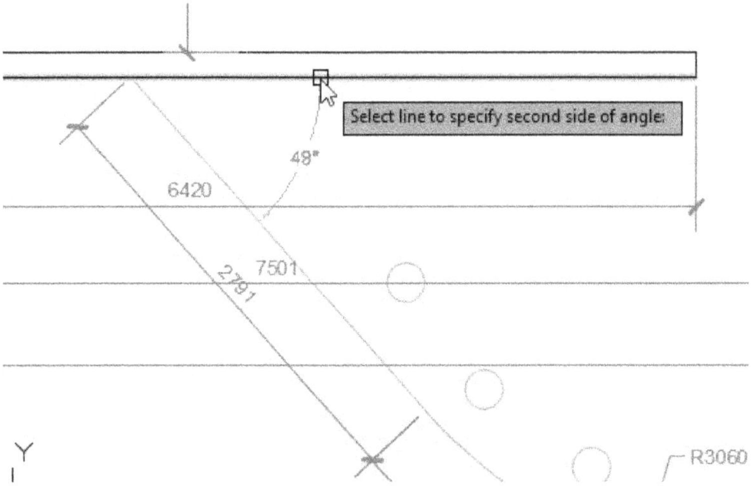

Figure 19–29

15. Select the line to accept the angled dimension and click again to place it, as shown in Figure 19–27.

16. Add **Angular** dimensions on the other side as well.

17. Exit the **Dimension** command.

18. Save and close the drawing.

Practice 19d

Adding Radial and Angular Dimensions (Mechanical)

Practice Objective

- Add a center mark, radius, diameter, and angular dimensions to a drawing.

Estimated time for completion: 5 minutes

In this practice, you will add a center mark, radius, diameter, and angular dimensions to a mechanical drawing, as shown in Figure 19–30.

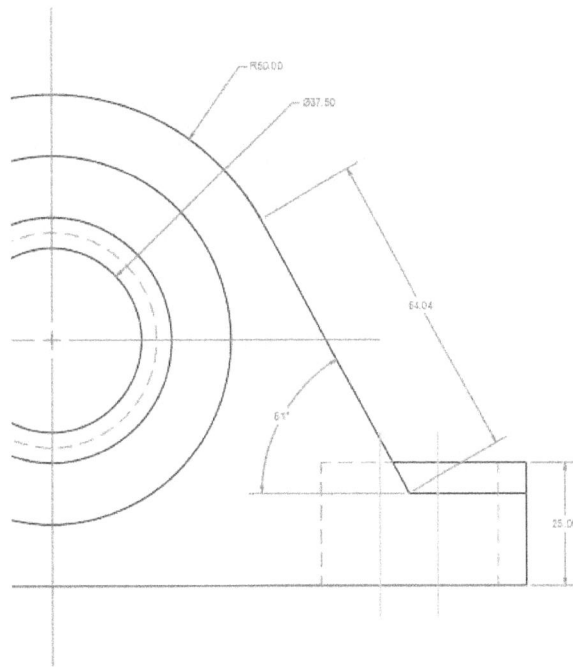

Figure 19–30

1. Open **Bearing Dimensions1-M.dwg** from your practice files folder.

2. Activate the **2:1** (right side) viewport.

3. In the *Annotate* tab>Dimensions panel, set the dimension layer to **Dimensions**.

4. In the *Annotate* tab>Centerlines panel, click ⊕ (Center Mark). Select the innermost circle to add a center mark with extension lines to it. Note that the extension lines are just touching the dashed circle. Press <Esc> to exit the command.

5. In the Command Line, type **CENTEREXE**. Enter **50** for the value and then press <Enter>.

6. In the Command Line, type **CENTERRESET**.

7. Select the center mark and press <Enter>. The center mark extension lines extend beyond the outermost circle, as shown in Figure 19–30.

8. Using the **Dimension** command, add a **Radius** dimension to the arc at the top of the bearing.

9. Add a **Diameter** dimension to the innermost circle.

10. Add an **Angular** dimension to the inner angle of the sloped line, as shown in Figure 19–30. (Select the horizontal line first and then hover on the sloped line.)

11. Save and close the drawing.

19.4 Editing Dimensions

If the dimensions are interfering with other parts in a drawing, as shown in Figure 19–31, you can edit and modify them using grips and special tools in the shortcut menu. You can also edit the dimension text. Additional tools available to clean up dimensions include: aligning dimensions and breaking extension lines.

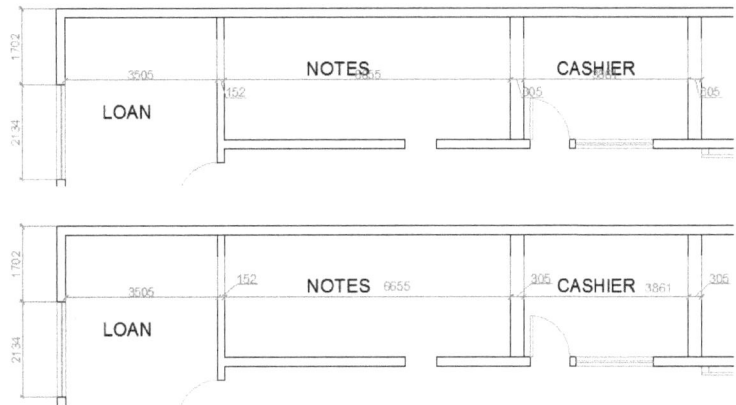

Figure 19–31

- The AutoCAD dimensions are associative. Therefore, when you change a dimensioned object, the dimensions update to reflect the change. If you move an object, the dimensions move as well. If you change the size of an object, the dimensions display the change.

- To change the dimension style of an existing dimension, select it and then set the appropriate dimension style in the Dimension Style drop-down list, in the *Annotate* tab> Dimensions panel.

Dimension Shortcut Menu

You can select a dimension or multiple dimensions, and then right-click to access additional options in the shortcut menu, as shown in Figure 19–32.

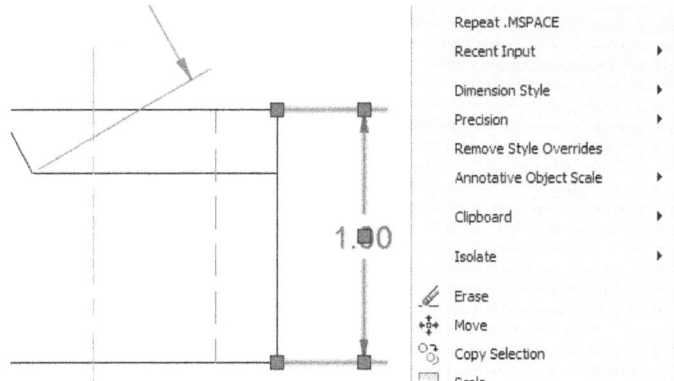

Figure 19–32

- You can change the Dimension Style of selected dimensions using the **Dimension Style** option. The dimension style controls the basic features of a dimension, such as the text location and number of decimal places.

- You can change the precision of selected dimensions using the **Precision** option. Precision helps you to display dimensions to a specific number of decimal places.

Editing Dimensions Using Grips

Grips can be used to relocate dimension elements. Without starting a command, select the following to display its grips at various parts of the dimension, as shown in Figure 19–33.

- Where extension lines touch the dimensioned object

- Where the extension line and dimension line meet

- On the dimension text

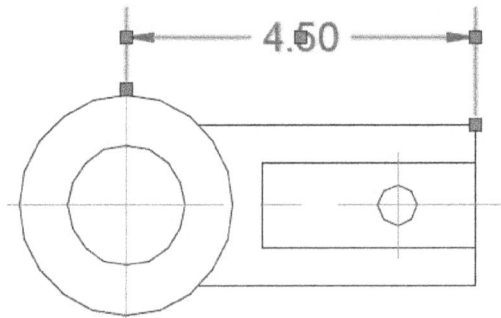

Figure 19–33

Once the dimension grips display, you can edit the dimension as follows:

- Select the grip at the dimension line and move it to change the distance from the object.

- Select the grip on the text and move it to change the location of the text (and sometimes the dimension line).

- Select the grip at the extension line origin to change the length of the dimension. (This option might disconnect the associativity to the object it is dimensioning.)

- Press <Esc> to clear the grips.

Dimension Grips Shortcut Options

Additional options are available for editing dimensions using the multifunctional grips. Hover the cursor over a grip, and select an option in the dynamic input list. Depending on the specific grip you hover over, a different list of options displays, as shown in Figure 19–34.

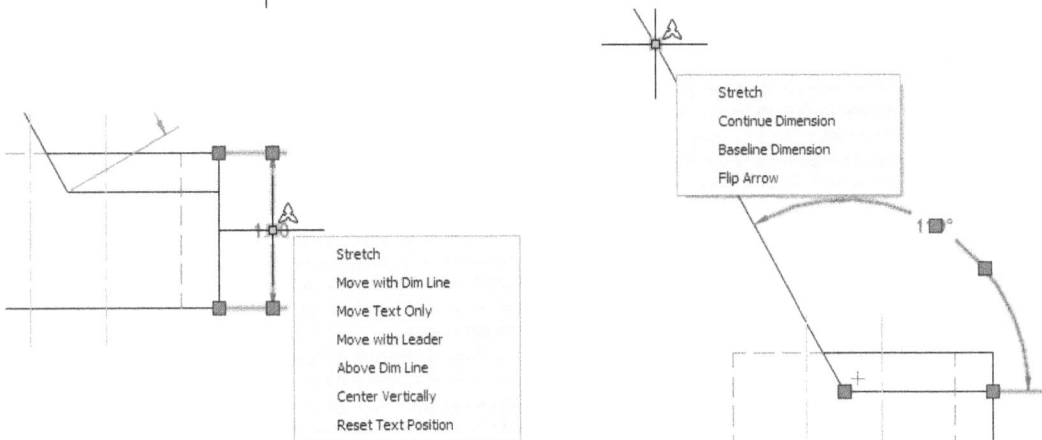

Figure 19–34

- Use the various text options, such as **Move Text Only** and **Above Dim Line** to move the text to a different position.

- **Reset Text Position** returns the moved text to its original location.

- You can use an existing dimension as the beginning of a series of related dimensions in either **Continue** or **Baseline**.

- Use **Flip Arrow** if the arrowheads on a dimension were pushed out and you want them to be inside the extension lines or on the opposite side.

- You can also access these options by selecting a grip (making it hot), and then using <Ctrl> to cycle through the options, or right-clicking and selecting one in the shortcut menu, as shown in Figure 19–35.

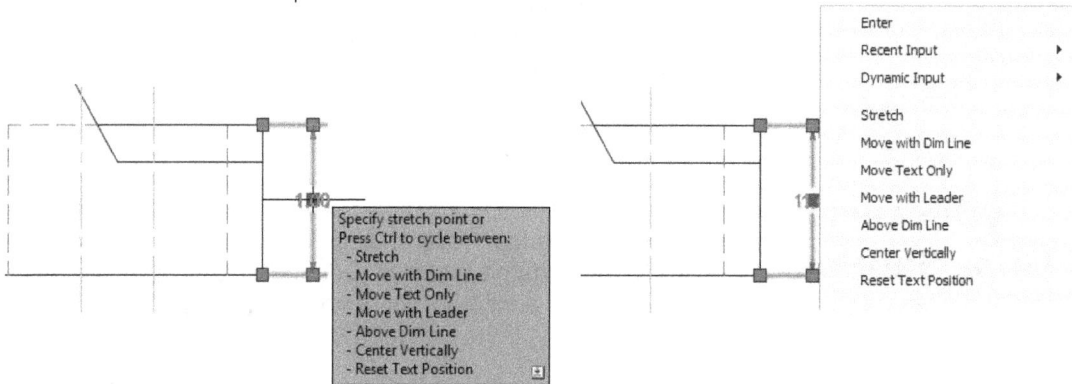

Figure 19–35

Editing the Dimension Text

Dimensions are associated with the objects they reference. However, sometimes you might need to add text to a dimension (such as +/- in renovation work), as shown in Figure 19–36.

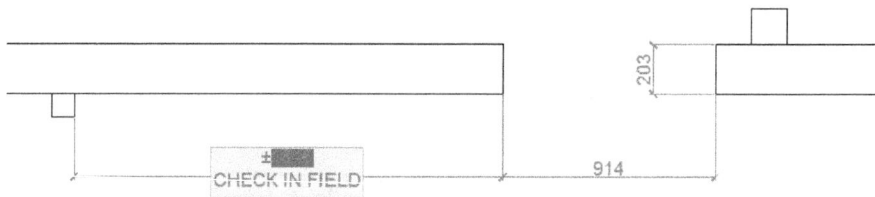

Figure 19–36

- To change the dimension text, double-click on the dimension text or type **ddedit**. The default dimension text or value is inserted as a special field in the Text Editor. You can add text before or after the field, or delete the field to completely replace the default text When editing dimension text, a width sizing control displays above the text. This enables you to adjust the text width for text wrapping, as shown in Figure 19–37.

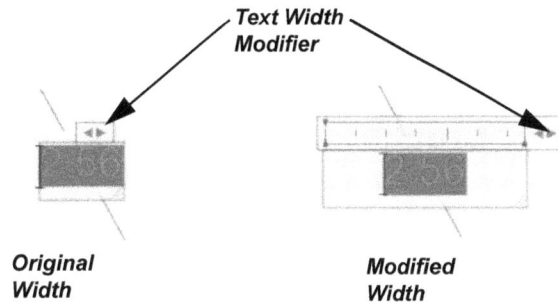

Text Width Modifier

Original Width   *Modified Width*

Figure 19–37

- If you remove the text associated with the dimension by mistake and want to get it back, type <> in the Text Editor.

Adjusting Dimension Spacing

When you create stacked angular or linear dimensions of any type, they might be too close together or unevenly spaced, as shown in Figure 19–38. Instead of moving each dimension, you can modify the space between sets of dimensions using the **Adjust Space** command.

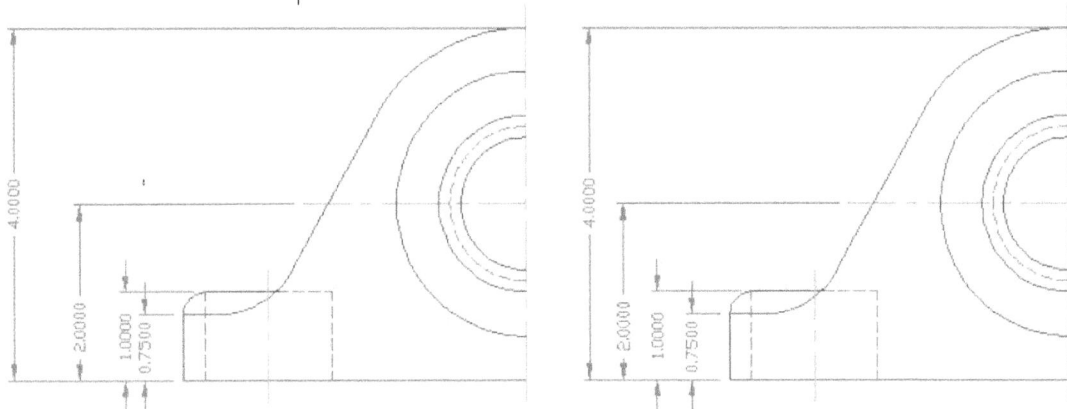

Figure 19–38

How To: Modify the Space Between Dimensions

1. In the *Annotate* tab>Dimensions panel, click ⊞ (Adjust Space).
2. Select the base dimension (the one closest to the object) of the group you want to modify.
3. Select the rest of the dimensions in the group.
4. Enter the distance that you want to have between dimensions or press <Enter> to accept the automatic distance.

Dimension Breaks

When there are many dimensions in a drawing, the various extension lines and dimension lines can start to overlap. In that case, you can create dimension breaks without changing the associativity of the dimension object, as shown in Figure 19–39.

- When the object is stretched, the dimensions change and the breaks remain in place. This makes revising a drawing easier, as you no longer need to re-dimension a modified part.

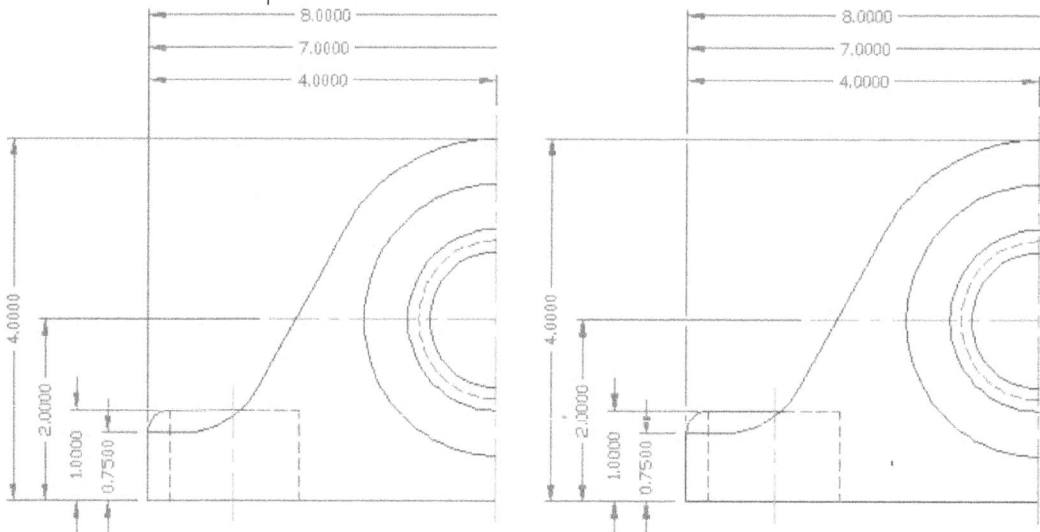

Figure 19–39

How To: Break One Dimension

1. In the *Annotate* tab>Dimensions panel, click ⊥ (Dimension Break).
2. Select a dimension to break.
3. Select an object to break the dimension or select one of the options.
4. Continue to select other objects to break their dimensions as required.
5. Press <Enter> to complete the command.

- The **Multiple** option enables you to select more than one dimension to break. The selected dimensions are broken where they overlap other dimensions.

- To remove breaks from a dimension, start the **Break** command, select the dimension, and select the **Remove** option.

Practice 19e | Editing Dimensions (Architectural)

Practice Objective

- Modify dimensions, edit dimension text, and break dimensions in a drawing.

Estimated time for completion: 10 minutes

In this practice, you will modify dimensions using grips, edit the dimension text, and break dimensions using the **Dim, Break** command, as shown in Figure 19–40.

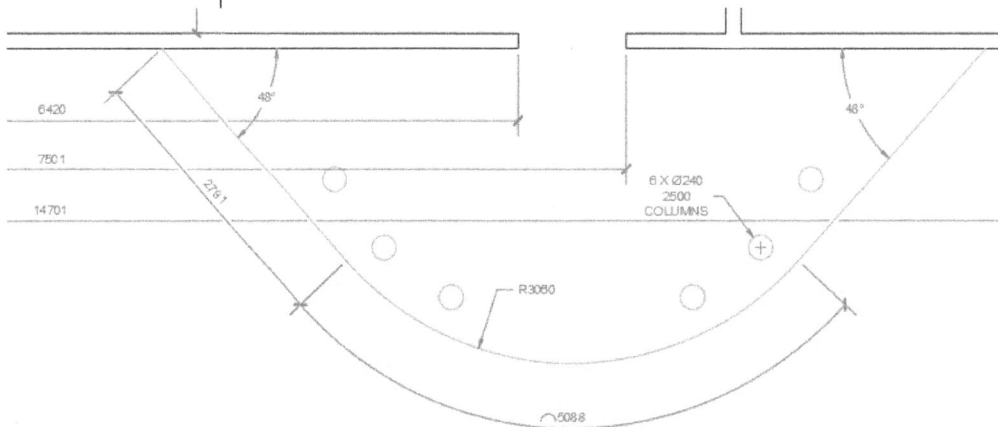

Figure 19–40

1. Open **Dimensioned Plan2-AM.dwg** from your practice files folder.

2. Make the viewport active and verify that it is locked, so that you can zoom and pan as required to modify the dimensions.

3. Focusing on the portico area, use grips to move the three horizontal dimension text to the left hand side, outside of the portico area.

4. In the *Annotate* tab>Dimensions panel, click ⊤⊢ (Break) and press <Down Arrow> to open the options menu. Select **Multiple**.

5. Select the three horizontal dimensions and press <Enter>.

6. Select the green portico line. Note that the three horizontal dimension lines break where they are passing through the portico arc object.

7. Select the aligned dimension line on the left side to create a break.

8. Press <Enter> to exit the command.

*You can also use the **ddedit** command.*

9. Double-click on the diameter Ø240 dimension for the column and type **6 X Ø240 2500 COLUMNS**, as shown on the left in Figure 19–41.

10. Use to change the width for text wrapping, as shown on the right in Figure 19–41.

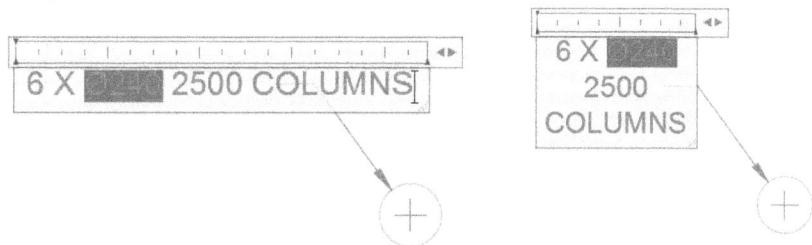

Figure 19–41

11. Exit the command.

12. Save and close the drawing.

Practice 19f | Editing Dimensions (Mechanical)

Practice Objective

* Modify the text and move dimensions.

Estimated time for completion: 5 minutes

In this practice, you will modify the text of several dimensions and move the dimensions as required using grips, as shown in Figure 19–42.

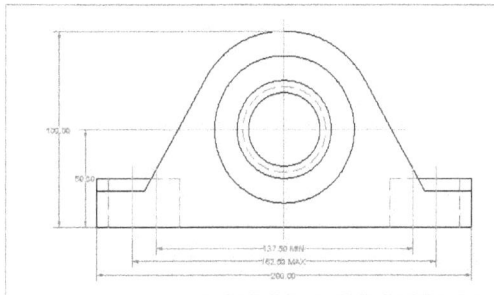

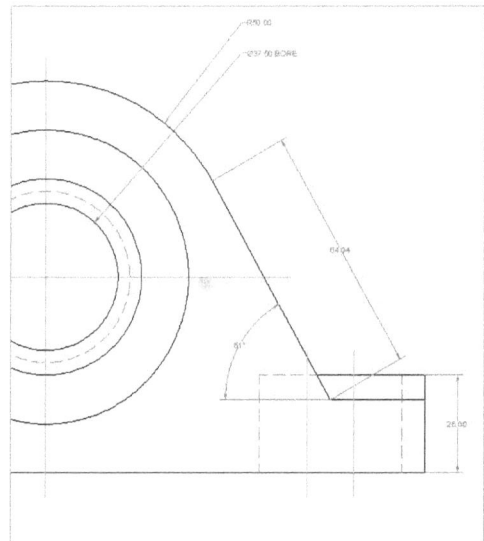

Figure 19–42

1. Open **Bearing Dimensions2-M.dwg** from your practice files folder.

2. Activate the **2:1** viewport (right side) and modify the text of the diameter dimension (of the innermost circle) so that it reads **Ø37.50 BORE**. Then change the width for text wrapping to display it in single line.

3. Activate the **1:1** viewport, modify the text of the two horizontal dimensions, as shown in Figure 19–43.

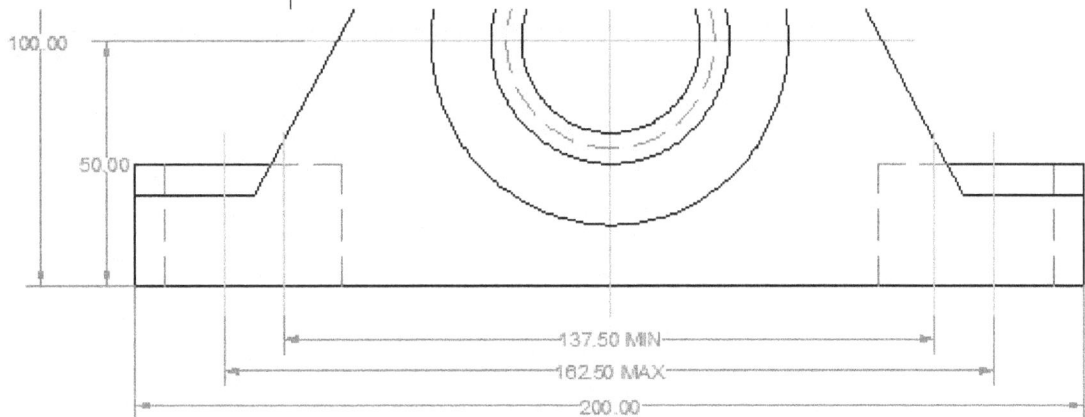

Figure 19–43

4. Use grips to move any of the other dimensions as required to a location where they are easier to read. You can also use the **Adjust Space** command to even out the bottom dimensions as required.

5. Save and close the drawing.

Chapter Review Questions

1. Which command would you use to display the length of a diagonal line so that the dimension line is parallel to the diagonal line (Aligned dimension)?

   a. **Dimension**

   b. **Quick Dimension**

   c. **Baseline Dimension**

   d. **Adjust Space**

2. Dimensions recalculate automatically when the objects they refer to are modified.

   a. True

   b. False

3. The **Center Mark** tool adds an associative center mark at the center of which objects? (Select all that apply.)

   a. Lines

   b. Polylines

   c. Circles

   d. Polygonal arcs

4. Which command would you use to create an arc length dimension from one end point of an arc to the other end point along the curve of the arc?

   a. **Dimension**

   b. **Quick Dimension**

   c. **Baseline Dimension**

   d. **Ordinate Dimension**

5. How would you move a dimension so that the dimension line is farther away from the object?

   a. Use the **Move** command.

   b. Use the **Baseline Dimension** command.

   c. Use grips to stretch the dimension.

   d. Use the **Dimension Update** command.

6. Which command do you use to clean up overlapping dimension lines?

   a. **Adjust Space**

   b. **Dimension Cleanup**

   c. **Dimension Break**

   d. **Jogged**

Command Summary

Button	Command	Location
	Centerline	• **Ribbon:** *Annotate* tab>Centerlines panel
		• **Command Prompt:** centerline
	Center Mark	• **Ribbon:** *Annotate* tab>Centerlines panel
		• **Command Prompt:** centermark
	Dimension	• **Ribbon:** *Annotate* tab>Dimensions panel or *Home* tab>Annotation panel
		• **Command Prompt:** dim
	Dimension: Adjust Space	• **Ribbon:** *Annotate* tab>Dimensions panel
		• **Command Prompt:** dimspace
	Dimension: Aligned	• **Ribbon:** *Home* tab>Annotation panel or *Annotate* tab>Dimensions panel
		• **Command Prompt:** dimaligned
	Dimension: Angular	• **Ribbon:** *Home* tab>Annotation panel or *Annotate* tab>Dimensions panel
		• **Command Prompt:** dimangular
	Dimension: Arc Length	• **Ribbon:** *Home* tab>Annotation panel or *Annotate* tab>Dimensions panel
		• **Command Prompt:** dimarc
	Dimension: Baseline	• **Ribbon:** *Annotate* tab>Dimensions panel
		• **Command Prompt:** dimbaseline
	Dimension: Break	• **Ribbon:** *Annotate* tab>Dimensions panel
		• **Command Prompt:** dimbreak
	Dimension: Continue	• **Ribbon:** *Annotate* tab>Dimensions panel
		• **Command Prompt:** dimcontinue
	Dimension: Diameter	• **Ribbon:** *Home* tab>Annotation panel or *Annotate* tab>Dimensions panel
		• **Command Prompt:** dimdiameter
	Dimension, Dimjogline	• **Ribbon:** *Home* tab>Annotation panel or *Annotate* tab>Dimensions panel
		• **Command Prompt:** dimjogline
N/A	**Dimension: Edit Text**	• **Command Prompt:** ddedit
	Dimension: Jogged (Radial)	• **Ribbon:** *Home* tab>Annotation panel or *Annotate* tab>Dimensions panel
		• **Command Prompt:** dimjogged
	Dimension: Linear	• **Ribbon:** *Home* tab>Annotation panel or *Annotate* tab>Dimensions panel
		• **Command Prompt:** dimlinear
	Dimension: Radius	• **Ribbon:** *Home* tab>Annotation panel or *Annotate* tab>Dimensions panel
		• **Command Prompt:** dimradius

	Oblique	• **Ribbon:** *Annotate* tab>expanded Dimensions panel
	Quick Dimension	• **Ribbon:** *Annotate* tab>Dimensions panel • **Command Prompt:** qdim

Projects: Annotating Your Drawing

This chapter contains practice projects that can be used to gain additional hands-on experience with the topics and commands covered so far in this student guide. These practices are intended to be self-guided and do not include step by step information.

Learning Objectives in this Chapter

- *Architectural:* Add features such as text, annotative text, hatching, dimensions, layout styles and viewports to an existing floor plan.
- *Mechanical:* Add features such as text, hatching, and dimensions to an existing mechanical part.
- *Civil:* Add features such as text, hatching, and dimensions to an existing parking layout.

20.1 Mechanical Project

Estimated time for completion: 20 minutes

In this project you will add dimensions, hatching, and text to an existing drawing, as shown in Figure 20–1.

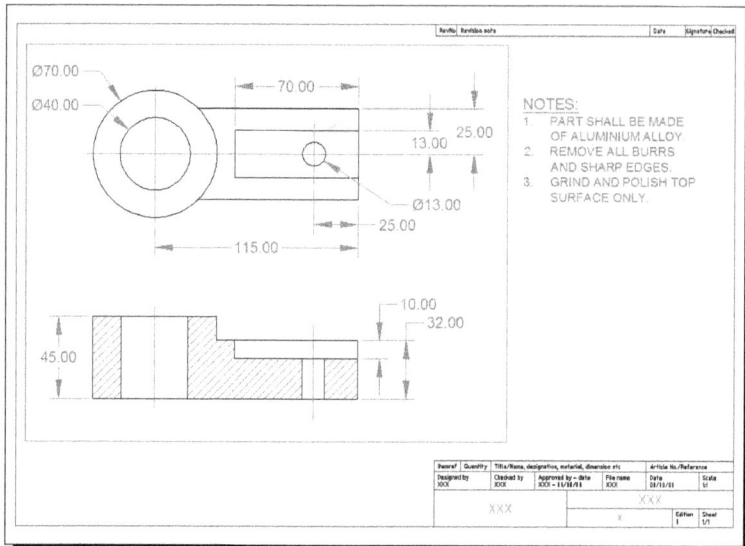

Figure 20–1

1. Open **Annotate-M.dwg** from your practice files folder.

2. Switch to the **ISO A3** layout and activate the viewport.

3. **Zoom Extents** to display the entire drawing in the viewport. Set the *Viewport Scale* to **1:1** and pan to fit it on the sheet. Lock the viewport.

4. Make the layer **Hatching** current and hatch the lower view, as shown in Figure 20–1. Use the **ANSI 31** pattern at a *Scale* of **1** and an *Angle* of **0**. Close the *Hatch Creation* contextual tab.

5. Make the layer **Dimensions** current and add dimensions to the drawing, as shown in Figure 20–1. Use Object Snaps to place the dimensions.

6. Switch to Paper Space.

7. Make the layer **Text** current. Use Multiline Text to create notes on the layout to the side of the drawing, as shown in Figure 20–1. Format the text **NOTES** so that it is larger than the other text and underlined.

8. Save and close the drawing.

20.2 Architectural Project 1

Estimated time for completion: 20 minutes

In this project you will add dimensions, text, and hatching to an existing drawing of a floor plan, as shown in Figure 20–2.

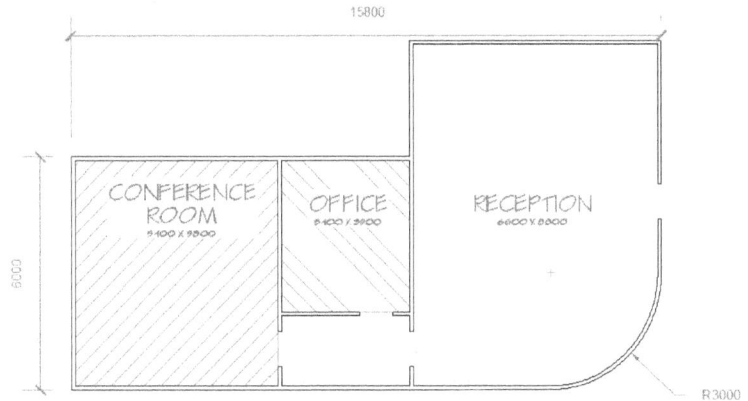

Figure 20–2

1. Open **Annotate-AM.dwg** from your practice files folder.

2. Switch to the **ISO A1** layout. Activate the viewport and set an appropriate Viewport Scale. Lock the viewport.

3. Make the layer **Text** current. Select a text style and add the text to label the rooms, as shown in Figure 20–2. Make the *Room Names* **8** high and the *Dimension Numbers* **3** high.

4. Toggle off the layers **Doors** and **Swing**. Make the layer **Hatching** current.

5. Draw lines across the doorways of the Office and Conference Room and hatch those rooms. Use the **ANSI31** pattern at an *Angle* of **0** for the Conference Room. Use the **ANSI34** pattern at an *Angle* of **90** for the Office. Set both hatches to **Annotative** and Relative to Paper Space.

6. Make the layer **Dimensions** current and add the dimensions.

7. Save and close the drawing.

20.3 Architectural Project 2

Estimated time for completion: 30 minutes

In this project you will set up layouts with an appropriate view and Viewport Scale. You will then use annotative text, hatch, and dimensions to label a floor plan with company names and hatch each area as shown in Figure 20–3. In a different layout you will then add dimensions. Remember to use the correct layers and styles as you add each annotation feature.

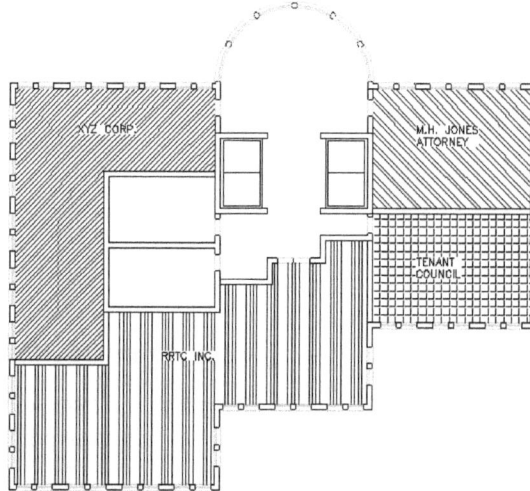

Figure 20–3

1. Open **Space-AM.dwg** from your practice files folder.

2. Switch to the **ISO A1** layout. Set up the viewport so that the entire building displays with enough space around it to dimension at an appropriate scale. Set the Viewport Scale. Lock the viewport.

3. Make a copy of the **ISO A1** layout. Rename one as **Tenant Plan** and the other as **Dimension Plan**.

4. In the **Tenant Plan** layout, add the text and hatching shown in Figure 20–3. (Toggle off the layer **Doors** and toggle on the layer **Headers** to have the hatching go up to the door openings.)

5. In the **Dimension Plan** layout, dimension the drawing. Add a few dimensions to identify the size of the rooms.

6. Save and close the drawing.

20.4 Civil Project

Estimated time for completion: 45 minutes

In this project you will add hatching, text, and dimensions to a parking layout, as shown in Figure 20–4.

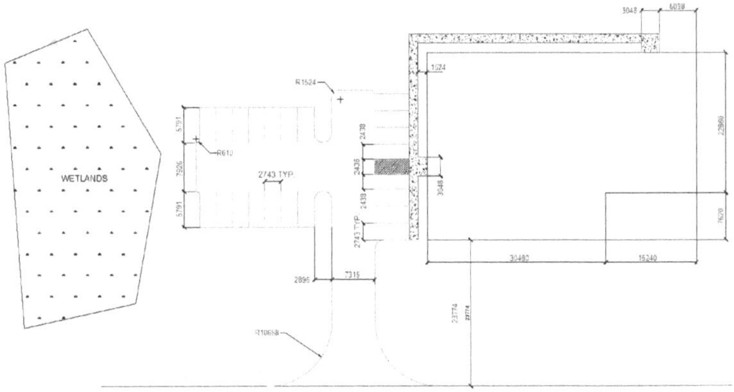

Figure 20–4

1. Open **Parking-CM.dwg** from your practice files folder.

2. Switch to the **ISO A1** layout and create an appropriately scaled view of the site with the Viewport Scale set. Lock the viewport.

3. Activate the viewport and make the layer **Pavement Edge New** current. Hatch the sidewalk with the **AR-CONC** pattern and the handicap parking space with the **ANSI31** pattern. Experiment with different scales to find the one with the best fit.

4. Make the layer **Wetlands** current. Draw an enclosed area (using the **Line** command) on the left side of the building on the layer **Wetlands**. Add the text **Wetlands** inside the enclosed area. Hatch the area with the **Swamp** pattern.

5. Dimension the building and parking lot. Make the layer **Dimensions** current. Move some of the dimensions around using grips. Use the **Edit Text** command to add **TYP.** below the appropriate dimensions.

6. Save and close the drawing.

Skills Assessment 1

To test your knowledge on the course material (Chapters 1 to 20), answer the questions that follow. Select the best answer for each question.

Part 1: General Knowledge

1. When you use the **Window** option in the **Zoom** command, everything in the window:

   a. Appears larger.

   b. Appears to shrink.

   c. Is erased.

   d. Is scaled up.

2. The **Move** and **Copy** commands both use a base point. What is a base point?

   a. The point from which you always move or copy.

   b. Always the absolute coordinate.

   c. The spacing between grid dots.

   d. A point that enables you to pick a group of objects.

3. Which phrase defines frozen layers?

   a. You see the layers and can manipulate objects on them.

   b. You see the layers but cannot manipulate objects on them.

   c. You do not see the layers but objects on them are still regenerated with the drawing.

   d. You do not see the layers and objects on them are not regenerated with the drawing.

4. A file designed to be the basis of new drawings is called a:

   a. Template

   b. Wizard

   c. Scratch File

   d. Setup File

5. In the **Trim** command, you must first pick:

   a. The objects to trim.

   b. The trimming distance.

   c. The base point.

   d. The cutting edge(s).

6. Any AutoCAD drawing can be inserted into the current drawing as a block.

   a. True

   b. False

7. The tool that controls whether you automatically snap to endpoints, midpoints, intersections, etc. is:

   a. Snap

   b. Grid

   c. Object Snap

   d. Ortho mode

8. The purpose of Polar Tracking is:

   a. To find a specific X,Y coordinate location.

   b. To copy an object in a circular pattern around a center point.

   c. To enable you to draw at angles, such as 30 or 45 degrees.

   d. To indicate the north direction.

9. To draw a series of continuous line segments that act as one unified object, you should use:

   a. Tracking

   b. A polyline

   c. Object Snaps

   d. A construction line

10. Which command creates parallel objects of the selected objects?

    a. **Extend**

    b. **Fillet**

    c. **Mirror**

    d. **Offset**

Complete either the Mechanical Drawing or Architectural Drawing sections. Answer the questions based on the provided drawings.

Part 2: Mechanical Drawing

Start a new drawing based on **Mech-Millimeters.dwt**. Draw the object shown in Figure A–1, starting with the center of the **Ø3** **circle** at **point 5,5**. Draw only the object, not the dimensions and then answer the following questions.

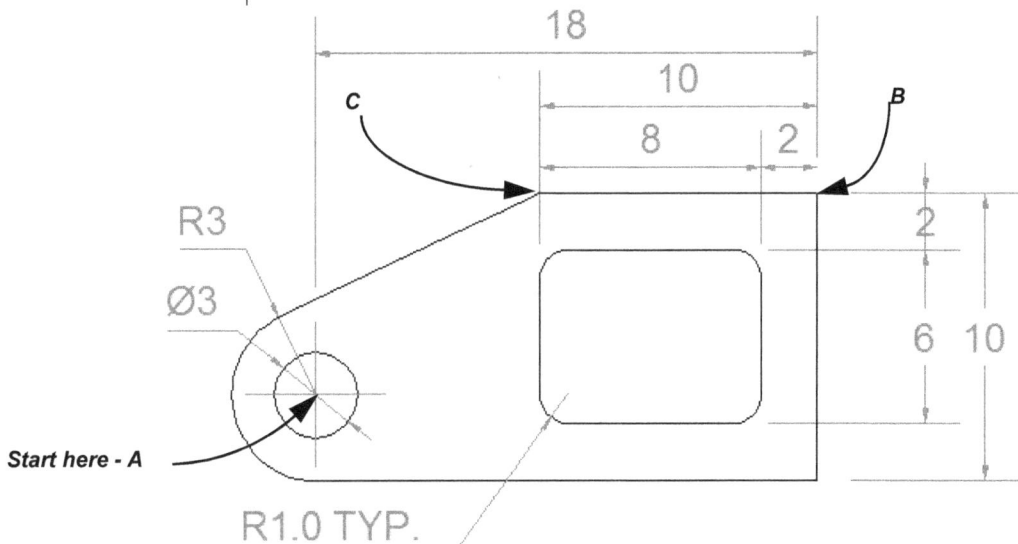

Figure A–1

1. What is the distance between the center of the circle at **A** and the corner at **B**?

    a. 19.8628

    b. 19.3132

    c. 17.1870

    d. 18.6794

2. The angle defined by the two intersecting lines at **C** is:
   (Hint: Use an angular dimension.)

   a. 152

   b. 153

   c. 155

   d. 160

3. What is the area of the outermost shape?
   (Hint: Make it into a polyline.)

   a. 179.4870

   b. 179.8045

   c. 180.6243

   d. 180.5940

4. What is the area of the outermost shape minus the inner shapes?

   a. 125.7012

   b. 126.7081

   c. 125.2768

   d. 126.2891

Part 3: Architectural Drawing

Start a new drawing based on **AEC-Millimeters.dwt**. Draw the floorplan shown in Figure A–2, starting with the lower left corner at point **900,900**. All walls are **100mm thick**. The doors are **900mm wide**, and are placed **150mm** from the nearest wall intersection. Draw only the walls, not the dimensions and then answer the following questions.

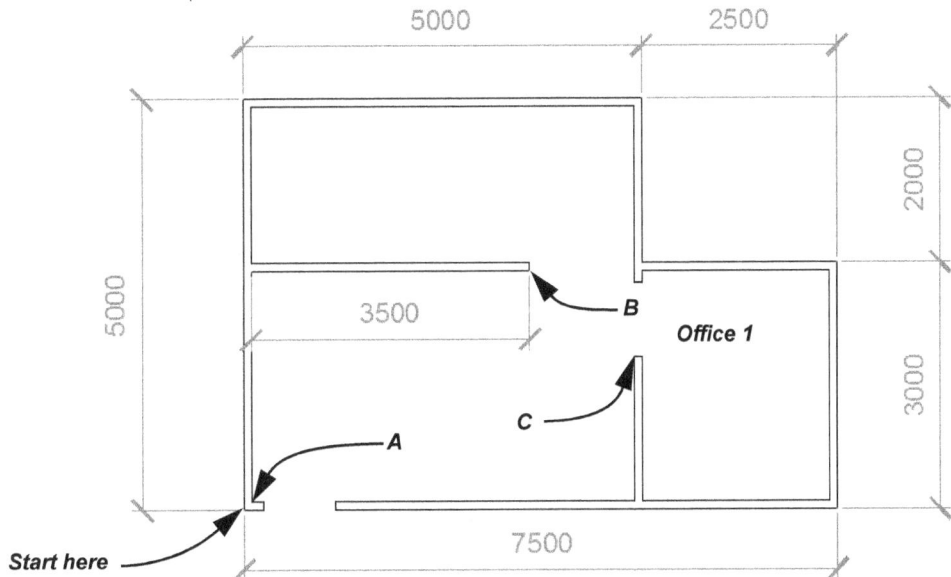

Figure A–2

1. What is the distance between the points labeled **A** and **B**?

    a. 4482

    b. 4400

    c. 4500

    d. 4562

2. What is the distance between the points labeled **B** and **C**?

    a. 1600

    b. 1700

    c. 1671

    d. 1641

3. What is the area of the room labeled **Office 1**?

   a. 7070000

   b. 6720000

   c. 6230000

   d. 7010000

4. What is the perimeter of the entire building around the outside? (Hint: Use the **Area** command.)

   a. 25000

   b. 30000

   c. 26000

   d. 35000

Index

---

www.ingramcontent.com/pod-product-compliance
Lightning Source LLC
Chambersburg PA
CBHW080118220326
41598CB00032B/4883

* 9 7 8 1 9 4 6 5 7 1 1 6 8 *